D0867021

Key Resources on Higher Education Governance, Management, and Leadership

Marvin W. Peterson
Editor

Lisa A. Mets
Assistant Editor

Key Resources on Higher Education Governance, Management, and Leadership

A Guide to the Literature

Jossey-Bass Publishers

San Francisco   •   London   •   1987

KEY RESOURCES ON HIGHER EDUCATION GOVERNANCE,
MANAGEMENT, AND LEADERSHIP
A Guide to the Literature
  by Marvin W. Peterson and Lisa A. Mets, Editors

Copyright © 1987 by: Jossey-Bass Inc., Publishers
                    433 California Street
                    San Francisco, California 94104
                             &
                    Jossey-Bass Limited
                    28 Banner Street
                    London EC1Y 8QE

Copyright under International, Pan American, and
Universal Copyright Conventions. All rights
reserved. No part of this book may be reproduced
in any form—except for brief quotation (not to
exceed 1,000 words) in a review or professional
work—without permission in writing from the publishers.

Library of Congress Cataloging-in-Publication Data

Key resources on higher education governance,
    management, and leadership.

  (The Jossey-Bass higher education series)
  Includes bibliographies and indexes.
     1. Universities and colleges—United States—
Administration. I. Peterson, Marvin W. II. Mets,
Lisa A. III. Series.
LB2341.K45 1987   378.73   87-45501
ISBN 1-55542-052-4

Manufactured in the United States of America

The paper in this book meets the guidelines for
permanence and durability of the Committee on
Production Guidelines for Book Longevity of the
Council on Library Resources.

JACKET DESIGN BY WILLI BAUM

FIRST EDITION

Code 8734

*The Jossey-Bass
Higher Education Series*

Contents

Preface   xiii

The Editors   xvii

Contributors   xix

1. An Evolutionary Perspective on Academic
    Governance, Management, and Leadership   1
    Marvin W. Peterson, Lisa A. Mets

        Part One: Governance

2. Organizational Concepts Underlying
    Governance and Administration   21
    Ellen Earle Chaffee

3. State Involvement in Higher Education   40
    Robert O. Berdahl

4. Federal Influences on Postsecondary Education   65
    John B. Lee

5. Governance and the Judiciary   93
    Barbara A. Lee

6. Institutional Governing Boards and Trustees   114
    Richard T. Ingram, Linda E. Henderson

ix

7. Administrative Structures and
    Decision-Making Processes   139
    Frank A. Schmidtlein

8. Institutional Planning, Strategy,
    and Policy Formulation   163
    Donald M. Norris, Nick L. Poulton

Part Two: Management

9. Financial Management and Resource Allocation   194
    Larry L. Leslie

10. Program Planning, Development,
    and Evaluation   218
    Robert J. Barak

11. Human Resource Development
    and Personnel Administration   238
    Ray T. Fortunato, Joseph A. Greenberg,
    Geneva Waddell

12. Decision Support Systems
    and Information Technology   263
    Bernard S. Sheehan

13. Policy Analysis and Institutional Research   282
    Cameron Fincher

14. Innovation, Planned Change,
    and Transformation Strategies   303
    Robert C. Nordvall

15. Improving Academic Quality and Effectiveness   322
    Kim S. Cameron

16. Managing Declining Enrollments and Revenues   347
    Raymond F. Zammuto

17. Equity and Affirmative Action   366
    Richard C. Richardson, Jr., Donald J. Vangsnes

Part Three: Leadership

18. Leadership and Administrative Style   390
    David D. Dill, Patricia K. Fullagar

19. Leadership Selection, Evaluation,
    and Development   412
    Charles F. Fisher

20. The College and University Presidency   441
    Joseph F. Kauffman

21. Academic and Administrative Officers   464
    *David G. Brown, Robert A. Scott,
    Linda C. Winner*

    Appendix A: Higher Education Journals,
    Periodicals, and Monograph Series   482

    Appendix B: Other Related Publications   486

    Appendix C: Higher Education Associations   490

    Name Index   495

    Subject Index   505

Preface

Higher education in the United States is unparalleled in the world in its breadth, diversity, and complexity. Our colleges and universities are significant socially and politically as well as educationally; they influence and are influenced by virtually every aspect of our social fabric. Yet these institutions are so loosely connected and highly differentiated that they are often described as unique, and they constitute a system that is quite unlike any other in American society.

Governing, managing, and leading these organizations have become the focus and concern of scholars and administrators alike over the past three decades. Governing board members, presidents, executive officers, deans, and department chairs have all expressed keen interest in learning more about their administrative functions and the broader patterns of governance, management, and leadership in their institutions. A growing array of faculty, higher education scholars, and graduate students also share this interest. A variety of publishing houses, journals, associations, and academic graduate and research centers have responded rapidly by contributing to an enormous increase in the quantity of literature available on these topics. Simultaneously, colleges and universities are faced with new resource constraints, shifting or declining clienteles, demands for new and different programs, increasingly complex governmental and political requirements, pervasive changes brought about by the information and telecommunications revolution, demands for quality improvement, new forms of educational competition and delivery modes, and other forces. These forces and changes are placing new strains on our governance, management, and leadership capacities and reinforcing the need for new information in the field.

This book is designed to capture and synthesize the vastly expanded body of literature on governance, management, and leadership in our colleges and universities, and to highlight how they are changing to meet modern demands. Other books on the literature in this area have either focused on governance, management, or leadership, or, even more narrowly, treated processes or problems within one of these three topics. This book offers a comprehensive, current overview of the literature on all three of the basic administrative functions. It is constructed as a guide to the best and most recent sources on these topics and is intended to serve practitioners and scholars alike.

The audience for this book includes administrators in higher education institutions, agencies, and associations. Faculty, graduate students, and research scholars interested in governance, management, and leadership will also find this book of value. Since the chapters are organized around conceptual topics, the book will be useful to individuals interested in any aspect and all levels of higher education administration.

Each chapter has been constructed by an individual who has played a major role in advancing our thinking in the area his or her chapter treats. Consequently, the chapters reflect contributors' knowledge of the literature, conceptual insights, and judgments about important emerging issues.

This book is organized into three major parts, reflecting the three broad functions named in the title: *governance, management,* and *leadership.* The chapters in each part focus on the primary processes and major issues relating to the broad function and combine to provide comprehensive coverage of that topic. Within each chapter, the authors present an overview of the chapter, discussion of the development of the area and its literature, major subtopics within the area the chapter treats, a final commentary on the state of the literature and future trends or issues, and an annotated bibliography of works organized under the subtopics that constitute the area the chapter covers. Because this book is intended as a resource, its table of contents is detailed enough to guide readers to general topics they wish to investigate. The index provides more specific topical references.

Works chosen for annotation in each chapter were selected by chapter authors because they were judged to be significant contributions that have served to advance the field and
to be useful, generally accepted, high-quality publications. Each
annotation describes the work's contents, summarizes its significance to the field, and offers the chapter author's judgment
of how it might be useful.

Chapter One provides an overview of governance, management, and leadership that distinguishes these three functions
and provides some historical perspective on their development
in practice and in the literature on higher education.

Part One, on governance, is concerned with the decision-
making processes that are designed to establish the overall direction and strategy of an institution of higher education. Chapter
Two examines the organizational theories of higher education
in which our views of governance are embedded. Chapters
Three, Four, and Five examine the state government, the federal
government, and the judicial system as major external, contextual structures that influence the institutional governance process. Chapter Six analyzes the role of institutional governing
boards as the groups ultimately responsible for most major institutional decisions as well as for designing or improving the
internal decision-making structure and process. Chapters Seven
and Eight focus on the internal processes and structures of institutional governance and on planning and policy formulation.

Management, the focus of Part Two, involves internal
processes and practices designed to accomplish the institution's
purposes. Thus, Chapter Nine describes the handling of financial resources; Chapter Ten, program development and evaluation; and Chapter Eleven, the management of the institution's
human resources. Chapters Twelve and Thirteen examine the
rapidly changing arenas of information technology, institutional
research, and policy analysis designed to make information more
supportive of rational management processes. In Chapters Fourteen, Fifteen, Sixteen, and Seventeen, we switch focus and examine four perennial problems in the management of most
organizations that are of critical concern to higher education
today: organizational change, quality control, resource conser-
vation, and equitable personnel practices.

Part Three addresses leadership as it pertains to the governance and management of our institutions. Chapters Eighteen and Nineteen provide overviews of theories of leadership and practices in leadership development that have been or may be useful in higher education. Chapters Twenty and Twenty-one focus on the roles of presidents and executive officers in colleges and universities.

Acknowledgments

We are deeply indebted to the twenty-eight authors who contributed to the chapters in this volume. The principal authors of these chapters are recognized experts in their areas who were challenged to provide brief overviews of complex topics, to select from a vast body of literature the works that are included here, and to provide succinct, informative annotations of those works. They carried out these tasks enthusiastically and extended their efforts to coordinate with authors of closely related chapters to ensure a well-integrated volume.

As in any extensive edited volume, many others assisted. It is not possible to credit all of those, but two very capable reviewers merit special thanks: Clifton F. Conrad and Aims C. McGuinness, Jr., took on the difficult task of critiquing this volume—no small task, given its breadth of chapter topics. Their comments were extremely helpful to the chapter authors and editors.

Our colleagues at the Center for the Study of Higher and Postsecondary Education were particularly helpful in conceptualizing and encouraging this volume. Shirley Goodman and Margaret Plawchan helped coordinate the project, typed numerous revisions of the manuscript, and provided that much needed commodity, good humor.

Ann Arbor, Michigan   Marvin W. Peterson
September 1987   Lisa A. Mets

The Editors

Marvin W. Peterson, principal editor, is professor of higher education and director of the Center for the Study of Higher and Postsecondary Education at the University of Michigan. He is also director of the research program on the organizational context for postsecondary teaching and learning of the National Center for Research to Improve Postsecondary Teaching and Learning. He received his B.S. degree in engineering science in 1960 from Trinity College (Hartford, Connecticut), his M.B.A. degree in 1962 from the Harvard Graduate School of Business Administration, and his Ph.D. degree in higher education in 1968 from the University of Michigan. From 1962 to 1966, Peterson served as an assistant dean at Harvard's Graduate School of Business Administration. Since 1968, he has been a faculty member in higher education, chair of the Division of Higher and Adult Continuing Education, and a faculty associate and study director at the Institute for Social Research at the University of Michigan prior to his current assignments.

Peterson is author or editor of *Institutional Research in Transition* (with M. Corcoran, 1985), *Improving Academic Management* (with P. Jedamus, 1980), *Black Students on White Campuses* (with R. Blackburn and Z. Gamson, 1978), and *Benefitting from Interinstitutional Research* (1976). He is associate editor of the sourcebook series *New Directions for Institutional Research.* He has served as the president of the Association for Institutional Research, the Association for the Study of Higher Education, and the Society for College and University Planning. He has received a variety of research grants, authored numerous articles, served on several national commissions and task forces, consulted with a wide array of higher educational institutions and agencies, and made many professional presentations on governance, management, and leadership topics.

Lisa A. Mets, assistant editor, is director of program review at Northwestern University, and is a candidate in the Ph.D. Program in Higher and Adult Continuing Education at the University of Michigan. She received her B.A. degree in French in 1976 from the University of Michigan, her M.A. degree in theoretical linguistics in 1978 from Indiana University, and her certificate in teaching English to speakers of other languages (TESOL) in 1979 from the University of Michigan. While at Indiana University, she was an associate instructor of Estonian. After completing her certificate in TESOL, she was a teaching fellow at the English Language Institute at the University of Michigan. From 1979 to 1984, she was a faculty member in English as a Second Language at Vincennes University (Indiana), and also served as department chair from 1981 to 1984. While completing doctoral course work, she was a research assistant in the Center for the Study of Higher and Postsecondary Education (1984 to 1987) and the National Center for Research to Improve Postsecondary Teaching and Learning (1986 to 1987).

Mets contributed to *Higher Education in South Carolina: An Agenda for the Future,* a report to the South Carolina Commission on Higher Education prepared by Augenblick, Van de Water & Associates (February 1986), and is coeditor of a forthcoming sourcebook in the series *New Directions for Institutional Research.* She has been on the program at the meetings of the Association for the Study of Higher Education and the Association for Institutional Research. She is currently involved in research on the impact of state-level initiatives to improve the quality of undergraduate education, faculty and their personal research agendas, and the organizational context for teaching and learning.

Contributors

Robert J. Barak is deputy executive secretary and director of Academic Affairs and Research, Iowa State Board of Regents.

Robert O. Berdahl is professor of higher education in the Department of Education Policy, Planning, and Administration and project director with the National Center for Postsecondary Governance and Finance at the University of Maryland.

David G. Brown is chancellor of the University of North Carolina at Asheville.

Kim S. Cameron is associate professor of higher education in the Center for the Study of Higher and Postsecondary Education and of organizational behavior and industrial relations in the Graduate School of Business Administration at the University of Michigan.

Ellen Earle Chaffee is associate commissioner for academic affairs, North Dakota State Board of Higher Education.

David D. Dill is associate professor of education and assistant to the chancellor at the University of North Carolina, Chapel Hill.

Cameron Fincher is Regents Professor and director of the Institute of Higher Education at the University of Georgia.

Charles F. Fisher is president of Leadership Development Associates in Washington, D.C., and former director of the Institute for College and University Administrators of the American Council on Education.

Ray T. Fortunato is president of Ray T. Fortunato Associates in State College, Pennsylvania, and assistant vice-president for personnel administration (emeritus) at Pennsylvania State University.

Patricia K. Fullagar is a Ph.D. candidate in the Department of Higher and Adult Education at the University of North Carolina, Chapel Hill.

Joseph A. Greenberg is professor of education in the School of Education and Human Development at George Washington University.

Linda E. Henderson is director of the Trustee Information Center, Association of Governing Boards of Universities and Colleges, Washington, D.C.

Richard T. Ingram is executive vice-president of the Association of Governing Boards of Universities and Colleges, Washington, D.C.

Joseph F. Kauffman is professor emeritus of educational administration in the Department of Educational Administration at the University of Wisconsin, Madison.

Barbara A. Lee is assistant professor in the Department of Industrial Relations and Human Resources, Institute of Management and Labor Relations, Rutgers–The State University of New Jersey.

John B. Lee is project director with the National Center for Postsecondary Governance and Finance at the University of Maryland.

Larry L. Leslie is professor of higher education and director of the Center for the Study of Higher Education at the University of Arizona.

Robert C. Nordvall is associate dean of Gettysburg College.

Donald M. Norris is vice-president of M & H Group, Inc., Herndon, Virginia.

Nick L. Poulton is senior associate with McManis Associates, Inc., Washington, D.C.

Richard C. Richardson, Jr., is professor of higher education at Arizona State University and associate director of the National Center for Postsecondary Governance and Finance at the University of Maryland.

Frank A. Schmidtlein is assistant professor of higher education in the Department of Education Policy, Planning, and Administration and associate director of research with the National Center for Postsecondary Governance and Finance at the University of Maryland.

Robert A. Scott is president of Ramapo College of New Jersey.

Bernard S. Sheehan is a member of the Faculty of Management at the University of Calgary, Canada.

Donald J. Vangsnes is a doctoral candidate in the Program in Higher Education at Arizona State University.

Geneva Waddell is staff development specialist and adjunct faculty member at Montgomery College, and president of G. W. Associates, Rockville, Maryland.

Linda C. Winner is director of special academic programs at the University of North Carolina, Asheville.

Raymond F. Zammuto is associate professor of organization management in the Graduate School of Business Administration at the University of Colorado, Denver.

Key Resources
on Higher Education
Governance, Management,
and Leadership

1

Marvin W. Peterson
Lisa A. Mets

An Evolutionary Perspective on Academic Governance, Management, and Leadership

> The heart of the matter is beyond all regulation [Whitehead, 1928, p. 638].

> This was also, except on rare occasions, the historic policy of the American college and university: drift, reluctant accommodation, belated recognition that while no one was looking, change had in fact taken place [Rudolph, 1962, p. 491].

> The real trouble with attempting to devise a strategy, let alone a plan for a university, is that basically we [faculty] are all anarchists—significant thought, art and action must have creativity. Creativity by definition defies prediction's plan [Brewster, 1965, p. 45].

The terms *governance, management,* and *leadership* imply a sense of purpose, direction, and control. Yet the preceding descriptive comments about colleges and universities by an esteemed philosopher and critic, a careful historian of higher education, and a recent and respected university president suggest a certain degree of folly in a resource book that attempts to describe governance, management, and leadership in organizations devoted to higher education. Indeed, such folly may exist, for colleges and universities are diverse and distinctive.

Note: Numbers in parentheses refer to works annotated in this volume.

1

Nonetheless, beginning with the founding of Harvard College 350 years ago, concern with governance, management, and leadership has been central to the development of our thinking about colleges and universities. To assure a college that was *pro modo Academiarum in Anglia* (''according to the manner of universities in England'') (Brubacher and Rudy, 1968, p. 3) and free of governmental control, the founders of Harvard placed its governance first in the hands of a board of overseers with a balanced membership of ministers and government officials. The legislature soon thereafter chartered Harvard as a separate corporation and delegated its governance to a second board consisting of the president, five fellows, and the treasurer. Like Harvard's, William and Mary's charter provided for an external governing board and a college corporation comprising those teaching in the college. However, the true governance prototype for the nation's first colleges and universities was established by the Connecticut legislature at Yale. Although the ten ministers who organized Yale arranged to hold full control of the university in their hands, the legislature recognized the president and trustees, the original organizers of the university, as a legal corporation and placed full control in a single board of external trustees. Virtually all other colonial colleges adopted the Yale College corporation model.

These simple models are a far cry from the complexity of the decentralized patterns of governance, differentiated styles of management, and diffused forms of leadership that comprise the various colleges of Harvard University, William and Mary, Yale, and our other colleges and universities today. Furthermore, none of these former or contemporary models adequately describes the patterns at many public or private, single or multicampus, specialized or multipurpose, two-year, four-year, or university institutions. Today the complexities of institutional type, the diverse array of students and learning styles, the variations in faculty behavior and patterns of teaching and scholarship, the many external and internal demands, the broad array of programs, and the variety of institutional roles, missions, structures, and processes further serve to confuse the organizational context. The challenge is how to govern, manage, and lead our colleges and universities, in spite of this complexity, to assure that they accomplish their educational goals and academic purposes.

This chapter will briefly discuss the nature of governance, management, and leadership in colleges and universities, describe the major contributors to the development of the literature in this area, and discuss the evolving content of that literature. The chapter is intended to provide background for the chapters that follow.

Conceptual Framework

Unlike teaching and learning, student services, and institutional advancement (other volumes in the Jossey-Bass annotated bibliography series), governance, management, and leadership do not delineate a clear institutional function or set of activities. Governance, management, and leadership can be discussed at state, system, or institutional levels. Furthermore, the terms *government, governance, management, administration,* and *leadership* often overlap in a confusing way.

In this book we have chosen to focus primarily on the institutional level. Actions at the state and federal levels, which involve their own governance, management, and leadership patterns, will be viewed as external influences on institutional patterns. Similarly, we recognize that the topics discussed in the various chapters may apply at the school, college, department, or other unit level in larger institutions. To allow for the greatest diversity of application, we have designed the chapters around theoretical views, processes, and problems related broadly to our three major concepts.

In order to minimize confusion, we will use the terms *governance, management,* and *leadership* to denote specific, though interrelated, functions that guide the behavior of individuals and groups or units in a college or university. By *governance* we refer to both the structure and the process of decision making. This is a broader definition of the term than the focus only on the process of decision making that was popularized in John Corson's book, *Governance of Colleges and Universities* (1960), which is used in most literature on governance in higher education. Our chapters on governance will deal with theories of organization and governance; with broad decision issues related to institutional mission, strategy, purposes, and policy; with major external actors or structures affecting such decision processes; and with major internal institutional governance structures (such as governing boards, senates, and unions) and decision-making and planning processes.

By *management* we refer to the structure and process for implementing or executing these broad decisions. Clearly, finances, programs, and human beings represent resources around which structures and processes for resource allocation, program development and evaluation, and human resource development are designed in most institutions. The rapidly changing technology of information suggests new structures and processes both for information systems design and maintenance and for research and policy analysis to inform decision making. The management of many institutions today involves modifying existing structures and processes or developing new ones to deal with problems of institutional change and innovation, quality and effectiveness, and decline and equity. Various chapters will cover these elements of management and sources of change.

By *leadership* we refer to the structures (positions, offices, and formal roles) and processes through which individuals seek to influence decisions. Typically we are interested in behavior that allows individuals to be influential beyond the degree suggested by their formally designated position and authority. In this volume we focus on conceptual views of leadership in higher education, processes of leadership development, and leadership roles of individuals in major administrative offices.

We have chosen not to use the term *government,* which John Millett (no. 145) defined in a way that includes all three of the areas we have just discussed. Neither have we used the term *administration,* which is variously defined as synonymous with governance, as the set of positions or individuals designated by administrative roles, or as the implementation activities associated with managing. In essence, we focus on the institutional guidance function of which governance, management, and leadership are three primary and interrelated subfunctions.

Development of the Literature

The published literature on governance, management, and leadership in higher education is largely a phenomenon of the last three decades. Although one can historically identify administrator/statesmen who wrote about higher education (for example, Thomas Jefferson, Charles Eliot, Abraham Flexner, and Robert M. Hutchins) and a few scholars who made significant contributions to the study of higher education before World War II (such as Floyd Reeves, John Dale Russell, Earl McGrath, and Hubert Beck), most research-based writing on governance, management, and leadership prior to the mid-1950s was embedded in institutional histories or in special studies and reports.

After 1960, however, the trickle of writing on these subjects became a deluge. In 1963, T. R. McConnell at the University of California, Berkeley, and Algo Henderson at the University of Michigan decried the paucity of research or conceptual knowledge about the organization and administration of higher education. In 1974, by contrast, M. W. Peterson's comprehensive review of research literature on "Organization and Administration in Higher Education" over the prior decade identified over 500 publications, of which 200 were research based. By 1985 one could easily find that many new publications every year.

Reasons for the deluge include the growth in size and complexity of colleges and universities; higher education's increasing importance as a social institution; increased government commitment of resources to and desire to control higher education; and the many societal problems that have been reflected in higher education. There is also a rapidly growing cadre of consumers of governance, management, and leadership literature among more professionally oriented administrators, a growing group of informed and concerned faculty, and an emerging group of graduate students and scholars who study higher education.

Contributors to the Literature

Several groups of scholars have contributed and continue to contribute significantly to the literature on governance, management, and leadership. Perhaps the most significant source of contributors has been the emerging group whose careers as faculty are devoted primarily to studying higher education and developing programs to train graduate students who will enter administrative and academic careers in higher education. Individuals such as W. H. Cowley at Stanford, Earl McGrath at Columbia, Algo Henderson at the University of Michigan, and T. R. McConnell at Berkeley were important contributors to the development of the field of higher education and to the early literature in this area. In 1957 their efforts attained more legitimacy and sparked the development of other programs and research groups when the Carnegie Foundation made grants to Berkeley, Columbia, and the University of Michigan to launch Centers for the Study of Higher Education. By 1970 an American Association for Higher Education (AAHE) survey identified 55 universities that offered doctoral programs with a concentration in higher education. Today that number exceeds 90, and there are around 400 full-time and 300 part-time faculty affiliated with such programs (Association for the Study of Higher Education, 1984). Because of the administrative career orientation of most graduates of these programs, a significant portion of the faculty and a number of their graduates have become regular contributors to the literature on governance, management, and leadership.

A second source of contributors to the literature is faculty from professions and disciplines outside of education (or higher education). Many higher education faculty migrated from other fields and brought their disciplinary perspectives with them. Burton Clark and J. Victor Baldridge from sociology, Kenneth Mortimer, Lyman Glenny, and Robert Berdahl from political science, Alexander Astin and T. R. McConnell from psychol-

ogy, and Algo Henderson from business and law are examples
of scholars from other disciplines who made contributions or
continue to contribute over a significant period. Other disciplinary and professional faculty remain in their own fields but
make occasional significant contributions to this one. They include David Riesman and Harold Orlans from sociology, Aaron
Wildavsky from public policy, David Breneman from economics,
Kim Cameron from organizational psychology, James March
from sociology and political science, Frederick Balderston and
David Whetten from business administration, and William
Kaplin from law. The significant contribution of this group
is the varying disciplinary perspectives they have brought to
the study of higher education governance, management, and
leadership.

Another major contributing source is the growing array of intra- and extrainstitutional research and development
units with a primary concern for governance, management, and
leadership issues. One group, the university-based research
group, often overlaps with the academic program and faculty
but provides a focus for ongoing research efforts. The Center
for the Study of Higher and Postsecondary Education at the
University of Michigan, the Center for the Study of Higher
Education at Pennsylvania State University, and the Higher
Education Research Institute at the University of California,
Los Angeles, are among the larger, continuing research units.
These units focus faculty research efforts, often draw on faculty
from throughout the university, and help to attract external
resources and grants. The federal government, through the Department of Education (DOE, formerly USOE), has also funded
a set of university-based research and development centers that
enhance research, development, and dissemination activities in
this area. Initially (1965–1973) the USOE funded the Center
for Research and Development in Higher Education at the
University of California, Berkeley, a sizable portion of whose
efforts were focused on governance, innovation, and change.
That center later moved to the National Center for Higher
Education Management Systems (NCHEMS) in Boulder, Colorado (1971–1985), where it focused extensive initial efforts on

the development of management information systems. It later concentrated on analytical approaches to management problems and finally turned to issues of institutional strategy, management of decline, and effectiveness. In 1985, the DOE research and development contract was awarded to a consortium of institutions that is centered at the University of Maryland and includes Arizona State University, Columbia University, and the University of Wisconsin, Madison. This center, known as the National Center for Postsecondary Governance and Finance, will focus on issues such as state and institutional governance, institutional planning and management problems, and leadership. Other DOE-funded research and development centers, such as the National Center for Research to Improve Postsecondary Teaching and Learning (NCRIPTAL) at the University of Michigan and the Center for Evaluation at UCLA, also devote part of their research efforts to governance- or management-related issues.

The government's support of the ERIC Clearinghouses on Higher Education at George Washington University, Community Colleges at UCLA, and Counseling and Personnel Services at the University of Michigan has both enhanced dissemination of literature in this field and stimulated publications such as the *ASHE-ERIC Higher Education Research Report* series, whose monographs often synthesize such literature. Research organizations such as these provide literature based on long-term, programmatic research efforts, conceptual and theoretical models, or informed syntheses on major governance, management, and leadership issues and are intended to stimulate related research and publication and to provide leadership in research dissemination.

Another major group of contributors to the literature on governance, management, and leadership is made up of institutional and administrative associations, which have grown considerably over the past three decades. Particularly during the 1970s, many such associations produced journals, monograph series, and even major book-length publications as they attempted to professionalize their field, provide opportunities for membership development, and inform their members about emerging governance, management, and leadership issues. The list of such publications and/or series is too extensive to include; however, they stimulate and provide an outlet for publication by many thoughtful scholar-administrators who may lack the time for more intensive research and scholarly writing. The major contribution of this group is to enhance the development of a practice-oriented literature.

In the 1970s, the Carnegie Commission on Higher Education and the Carnegie Council on Policy Studies made many significant contributions to the literature on higher education governance, management, and leadership. Produced under Clark Kerr's leadership, the over 125 books and reports in the Carnegie series include classic summaries, analyses, and recommendations on all aspects of higher education, many of which are cited in this volume. Earlier, in the 1960s, a Ford Foundation–funded program of research on university governance at the University of California, Berkeley, produced an extensive number of publications. Research and development projects funded by numerous other foundations have also made important contributions.

A final factor contributing to the growth of this area of literature has been the growing array of publication outlets or vehicles themselves. The role of institutional and administrative associations in sponsoring applied or practitioner-oriented journals and publication series has already been mentioned. Several associations have also begun sponsoring or publishing more scholarly journals related to this area. The Association for Institutional Research (AIR) journal *Research in Higher Education,* and the AIR and Jossey-Bass monograph series *New Directions for Institutional Research;* the AAHE Heldref publication *Change;* the ASHE *Review of Higher Education* and the *ASHE-ERIC Higher Education Research Report* series; and the American Council on Education's recent agreement with Macmillan to produce jointly sponsored books are all examples of association-publisher ventures that produce scholarly publications in this area. Finally, publishers themselves have more aggressively developed publication series directed toward this area; for example, Jossey-Bass Higher Education publications now include several new books on governance, management, or leadership each year, and their

sourcebook series are directly relevant to this volume (especially
the series on higher education, community colleges, and institutional research).

It is clear that an extensive literature related to the topic
of this volume has been created in the past three decades. An
active array of authors exists—scholars, researchers, and administrators who are eager to communicate. Organizations that
house such activity, such as graduate programs, research centers,
and associations, are in place. Institutional, foundation, and
governmental funding support for short- and long-term research,
development, and scholarly writing projects is available. Dissemination networks, publications, and publishers to distribute
the literature are now clearly identifiable. And, most significantly,
the number of consumers justifies the effort.

The Evolution of the Field

Three decades ago, the terms that describe this volume
were not well recognized. *Governance* was not a common term
until Corson focused our attention on it. *Management* was an
unacceptable term to colleagues in higher education in the 1950s
and '60s; it has only recently gained acceptance. *Leadership* was
acknowledged as a presidential function or attribute in the
historical literature on higher education but now is also accepted
as a more generic topic or process. Today the three terms seem
to connote a common or interrelated set of functions. The meaning and connotations of governance, management, and leadership, like their acceptance, have changed over this period.
Changing societal forces, the challenges and internal strains they
present to institutions, and our changing conception of colleges
and universities as organizations have caused changes in our
understanding of these terms. A brief overview of the past three
decades, divided into four eras, suggests how this understanding has evolved.

Growth, Expansion, and Optimism. During the 1950s
and 1960s, societal commitment to expanding higher education
was strong at all levels. Federal consensus extended from the
Truman Commission report, *Higher Education for American Democ-*

racy (President's Commission on Higher Education, 1947), and the Eisenhower-appointed Committee on Education Beyond High School, chaired by Devereaux C. Josephs, through the academic elite of the Kennedy cabinet to Johnson's "Great Society." At the state level, California's 1960 Master Plan, promising free education to all high school graduates, was considered the ideal model. During this era institutions struggled with rapidly growing enrollments, expanding campuses, and an increasingly complex array of curricular offerings and administrative structures and services. Two quite different organizational models or theories, both internally oriented and each assuming a well-focused purposive institution, competed for attention. Harold Stroup (1966), drawing on Max Weber (1947), portrayed our increasingly complex higher education institutions as rational bureaucracies. Paul Goodman (1964), Burton R. Clark (1963), and John D. Millett (1962) portrayed them, respectively, as communities of learners, communities of professionals, and groups of constituencies with a community of interest.

In large part because of the rapid growth, expansion, and pervasive sense of optimism about higher education's future, governance, though increasingly discussed in professional meetings and in the literature, was not a divisive issue. The notion of a rational decision process reflecting the growing administrative hierarchy was increasingly assumed, especially in larger institutions. In smaller institutions and within the academic administrative function of larger ones, however, the notion of community organization with decision by consensual processes was still accepted and reinforced by stronger faculty senates. A dual structure of governance was emerging. Because of the growth of administration, the issue of faculty representation in governance became the focus of a joint statement by the American Council on Education (ACE), the Association of Governing Boards (AGB), and the American Association of University Professors (AAUP), called the "Statement on Government of Colleges and Universities" (no. 149). This statement attempted to define the community of interest among faculty, administrators, and governing boards.

Leadership images during this era reflected the times and the two emerging governance models. On the one hand, presidents were viewed as "institution builders" who organized and guided the rapid, somewhat entrepreneurial growth of new or expanding institutions—a style consistent with the bureaucratic or rational model. On the other hand, presidents were still expected to be "educational leaders" who stressed participatory styles and provided a sense of community. These two somewhat conflicting perspectives are reflected in several discussions of the role of the president (Dodds, 1962; Stoke, 1959; Wriston, 1959).

Management during this era was mostly involved with expanding and creating more complex administrative structures (offices), processes, policies, and procedures in all areas—academic, financial, student services, and facilities. A major management need expressed by executive officers during this era was for data, analysis, and research about all aspects of their institutions (enrollments, students, finances, space and facilities, personnel, programs, and curricula) to provide better information both to justify the resource needs of their growing institutions and to better manage them. The growing concern for rationalizing management was highlighted in a national survey, *The Managerial Revolution in Higher Education* (Rourke and Brooks, 1966).

Disruption and Revolution. The late 1960s and early 1970s witnessed campus disruptions emanating both from within and from outside the institution. Student dissatisfaction with increasingly large and impersonal institutions reflected the residual problems of growth and of the increasingly professionalized faculty that had arisen during the 1950s and 1960s. Societal issues such as the United States' role in the Vietnam War and the growing civil rights movement found fertile ground among liberal faculty and alienated students on campuses. Faculties' sense of the infringement of these disruptions on their academic freedom and their own concerns about eroding autonomy in larger, more management-oriented institutions strengthened their identity as a special interest group. The emergence of systems of institutions (Perkins, 1972), the growth of state-level

coordination and governance in the 1960s to deal with the
pressures of expansion of higher education (Berdahl, 1971), and
the increasing role of the federal government reflected by the
expansive 1972 Higher Education Amendments all were becoming recognized as contributors to the complexity of the higher
education scene. It is not surprising that two new organizational
models began to dominate thinking about higher education at
this time—the open system model (Katz and Kahn, 1978) and
Baldridge's political model (no. 344). The first recognizes the
significant role of external actors and forces in shaping the governance and management of institutions, and the latter conceives
of institutions as made up of a collection of special interest groups
that do not necessarily accept a rational goal, a common shared
purpose, or a community of interest.

Governance, during this brief era, changed rapidly—
or, at least, views of it did. The open system perspective provided a rationale for linking institutions together into multicampus systems and raised governance issues regarding centralization and decentralization and regulation or autonomy, as Lee
and Bowen note (no. 147). It encouraged thinking about multipurpose institutions that were composed of units with differing
purposes, products, and resources, and it made people examine
issues of cooperation, coordination, and/or competition in governance. Similarly, a political decision-making process emphasized
conflict and negotiations rather than consensus or rational analysis. Issues of participation in governance became more critical
as students, faculty, administrators, state officials, boards, and
others all came to be viewed as potential partisan groups, even
in community governance forms such as academic or university
senates (Dill, 1971; Millett, no. 145). For others, collective bargaining became a new and rapidly growing structure for decision
making and shared authority as state laws were changed to permit public employee collective bargaining that included faculty as
well as nonacademic employment groups (see, for example,
Carnegie Council on Policy Studies in Higher Education, 1977).

Perhaps the greatest impact during this era was felt in
the area of leadership. Campus disruptions and the move to collective bargaining led to a large turnover in college presidents

and other executive officers. The institution builders and participatory leaders of the 1960s gave way to individuals with political and/or negotiating skills in many institutions. These skills were often combined with skills in working within and coordinating complex systems.

In addition to reflecting an increased complexity in administration, changes in institutional management reflected increased levels of coordination and negotiation. Improvement of the management of external relations (especially with the state government) and introduction of new staff and procedures to deal with collective bargaining and with disruptions (such as ombudsmen and grievance procedures) were probably the most notable changes in leadership patterns in this era.

Constraint and Consolidation. Student disruptions subsided, but the economic recession of the early and mid-1970s introduced a new challenge for higher education as financial resources became increasingly constrained. Enrollments continued to grow but at a reduced rate. Affirmative action, reflecting both the civil rights movement and the women's liberation movement, called for greater attention to and constraints on the selection and hiring process. By the late 1970s, inflation added more financial pressure. Throughout this decade, state agencies and other external government-related constituencies demanded greater accountability as they became increasingly sophisticated in gathering and analyzing data and in asking management questions. In short, institutions in the 1970s were challenged by state agencies, the public, and their own tight resources to ''do more with less.''

During this era two new and quite different models of organization were added to those popularized earlier. On the one hand, a management science view of colleges and universities as rational systems of tasks, information, and resource flows gained popularity. NCHEMS, drawing on their early efforts in information systems design, were joined by others in attempts to build simulations and models of university resource flows that could analyze and inform rational decision making (Lawrence and Service, 1977). Simultaneously, other scholars, who saw a much less rational or purposeful character in organizations composed of professionals, such as colleges and universities, focused on the academic study of organizational behavior and suggested that such organizations were "organized anarchies" (Cohen and March, no. 141), or "loosely coupled systems" (Weick, no. 8).

One model of governance popular during the 1970s saw the earlier separate collegial and political notions merely as differing ways of sharing authority (Mortimer and McConnell, 1978). Two new and quite different models of governance that reflected the two new organization models also emerged. One, the management science view of governance, emphasized rational problem solving and analytical techniques. It focused on long-range planning, management by objectives (MBO), and other rational approaches to structuring the management process and making decisions. The second model, that of "organized anarchy," emphasized the growing complexity and diffuseness of colleges and universities and viewed the governance and decision-making process as a "garbage can" in which decision makers chose solutions reflecting their personal perspectives and then matched these to problems. Because this mode of governance did not presume a particular structure, it was amenable to a decentralized structure and mode of organizing temporary or ad hoc decision groups around problems to be solved.

Similarly, leadership styles during this period moved in two directions. The corporate manager model emphasized a well-organized, analytically oriented or trained person who could implement long-range plans and rational management processes and attempt to improve the accountability, efficiency, and perhaps the effectiveness of the institution. This image contrasted with the model of the educational or political statesperson, who could lead a decentralized, anarchical institution (or system) by providing incentives, coordinating conflicting interests, and providing after-the-fact rationales as well as anticipatory leadership.

Management changes followed the other changes of the era. Resource allocation became a more quantitative, analytically sophisticated, automated process. Program review and evaluation practices became popular. A focus on human resource development for faculty and professional administrators as well as support staff began to emerge. Planning became a common process, if not a formally organized office. Administrative computing and analytical support staff became increasingly important. In spite of the "organized anarchy" theory popular in some quarters, the internal working of most institutions became more tightly organized. Thus the era that began by promising educational revolution ended with an emphasis on consolidation.

Reduction and Redirection. By the late 1970s, it became apparent that the emphasis on improved management—accountability, efficiency, and consolidation—would not be sufficient to meet the demands of the future. Despite an improved economy, financial constraints did not abate or even show signs of easing. The long-term realities of enrollment decline and substantial changes in the demographic characteristics and educational needs of potential learners became clearer to thoughtful educational leaders. The microcomputer and telecommunications revolution was now reaching radical proportions that directly affected the program priorities, educational practices and delivery systems, and administrative practices of institutions of higher education. As other educational organizations became active providers of postsecondary educational services to older students, higher education institutions had to become more competitive. Many outside higher education and some within began to ask questions about the appropriateness of its programs, its priorities, and even its quality.

This new perspective modified one earlier organizational model and suggested another. First, the emphasis on retrenchment, reduction, and reallocation (Mortimer and Tierney, no. 394) expanded the earlier "open system" view of colleges and universities. Instead of being seen merely as institutions that responded to or were affected by the environment, they began to be viewed in a more strategic or ecological perspective. Colleges and universities as strategic enterprises could revise purposes and priorities by selecting what to emphasize rather than merely continuing to share declining resources; they could change missions by emphasizing new clientele and program mixes; and they could change strategies to compete as well as to cooperate. In essence, the open system view began to stress proactive behavior to take advantage of or shape the institution's environment rather than merely react or adapt to it. An alternate model, the cultural model (Masland, 1985), also gained prominence. This model reflected the popular view of business organizations as cultures that was represented in *In Search of Excellence* (Peters and Waterman, 1982) and recaptured an earlier view of higher education that was used by Burton R. Clark in his study of "distinctive colleges" (no. 9) and Riesman, Gusfield, and Gamson in their study of a new institution in *Academic Values and Mass Education* (1970). The importance of examining institutional culture became apparent particularly in colleges and universities with stable, tenured, and often aging faculty and strong institutional self-image, patterns of beliefs and behaviors, and traditions.

Both models had clear implications for governance. The former implied an emphasis on strategic planning (that is, making major decisions about institutional mission, direction, and priorities in the context of an examination of environmental opportunities and constraints, internal capabilities and limitations, and the likelihood of attracting resources to make desired changes). The cultural model suggested that the governance process needed to be sensitive to the culture and climate of the institution but otherwise offered little prescription for the process's structure.

The models of leadership that emerged in the early 1980s were both old and new, simple and complex. The conditions of retrenchment and redirection suggested the need for leaders of broad perspective and skill in organizing strategic planning and guiding macro- and externally oriented (as opposed to internal and micro-) change efforts. The emphasis on culture called for individuals who were capable of infusing and/or changing values and providing visions of new institutional directions that faculty and staff could believe in. The need for a combination of strategic, cultural, and visionary skills presented a Herculean leadership task and harked back to the notions of college presidents as educational statesmen or Barnard's leadership analysis of *The Functions of the Executive* (1968). A recent study by Chaffee (1985) makes an attempt to examine the strategic and interpretative (cultural) styles of governance and leadership and stresses the combination of these two perspectives.

The management emphasis during the early 1980s continued earlier changes. Resource allocation continued to become more analytically sophisticated, with greater emphasis on reduction and reallocation. Program review placed greater emphasis on centrality and quality of programs and on procedures for discontinuance as well as new program development. There was greater concern for linking resource allocation and programming decisions to planning. Long-term concerns about human resources were reflected in concerns for human resource planning as well as selection, evaluation, and training. An era of continued constraint produced a shift from concern only with efficiency and effectiveness to more flexibility and willingness to examine purposes and direction.

Current and Future Development. This overview clearly demonstrates the interrelated character and evolution of the three areas of governance, management, and leadership. New perspectives on colleges and universities as organizations have emerged to help us better understand governance, management, and leadership dynamics. These three subfunctions of guidance in higher education institutions have all changed to meet the many challenges that such institutions have had to face.

As we move into the late 1980s, new challenges are emerging. An educational reform movement stressing the improvement of quality and educational outcomes surrounds us. Demographic changes promise even more extensive postsecondary educational demands. The information revolution continues unabated and promises to further reshape the structure, content, and delivery of higher education. Coming changes in American industry and employment economy are less clear, but the need for a more highly educated and reeducated work force is sure to grow. Strains between competition and coordination among postsecondary educational organizations promise to continue, as do debates about the degree of state regulation of higher educational institutions. Internally, an aging faculty with declining morale, constraints on resources, and outmoded facilities continue to be problems. Clearly governance, management, and leadership must continue to evolve to face these and other unforeseen challenges.

Conclusion

The view of governance, management, and leadership as interrelated subfunctions or processes that contribute to the guidance of colleges and universities has evolved in the last few decades. The evolution of this view has been accompanied by a growing market of producers, distributors, and consumers of its literature and by increased recognition of its importance. The current literature includes a comprehensive set of theoretical perspectives and substantive topics that describe the structure, the process, and other major issues related to each of these subfunctions, which will be covered in the chapters that follow. This literature includes theoretical and practice-oriented views; encompasses research-based, synthesized, and idea-oriented contributions; reflects disciplinary, interdisciplinary, and descriptive perspectives or styles; and incorporates administrative and scholarly contributors. In spite of its comprehensiveness, it has numerous inconsistencies and gaps. No doubt this field will continue to evolve. To paraphrase our introductory quotations, governance must always guard against "regulation" that destroys "the heart" of an institution; management must strive for that "reluctant accommodation" between "drift" and intransigence; and leadership must stimulate "creativity" among decision makers who are both "rationalists" and "anarchists."

References

Association for the Study of Higher Education. *Directory*. Washington, D.C.: Association for the Study of Higher Education, 1984.

Barnard, C. I. *The Functions of the Executive*. Cambridge, Mass.: Harvard University Press, 1968.

Berdahl, R. O. *Statewide Coordination of Higher Education*. Washington, D.C.: American Council on Education, 1971.

Brewster, K., Jr. "Future Strategy of the Private University." *Princeton Alumni Weekly*, 1965, pp. 45-46.

Brubacher, J. S., and Rudy, W. *Higher Education in Transition*. (2nd ed.) New York: Harper & Row, 1968.

Carnegie Council on Policy Studies in Higher Education, Garbarino, J. W., Feller, D. E., and Finkin, M. W. *Faculty Bargaining in Public Higher Education*. San Francisco: Jossey-Bass, 1977.

Chaffee, E. E. "The Concept of Strategy: From Business to Higher Education."

In J. C. Smart (ed.), *Higher Education: Handbook of Theory and Research.* Vol. 1. New York: Agathon, 1985.

Clark, B. R. "Faculty Culture." In T. F. Lunsford (ed.), *The Study of Campus Cultures.* Boulder, Colo.: Western Interstate Commission for Higher Education, 1963.

Corson, J. *Governance of Colleges and Universities.* New York: McGraw-Hill, 1960.

Dill, D. D. *Case Studies in University Governance.* Washington, D.C.: National Association of State Universities and Land-Grant Colleges, 1971.

Dodds, H. W. *The Academic President: Educator or Caretaker?* New York: McGraw-Hill, 1962.

Goodman, P. *Community of Scholars.* New York: Random House, 1964.

Katz, D., and Kahn, R. *The Social Psychology of Organizations.* (2nd ed.) New York: Wiley, 1978.

Lawrence, G. B., and Service, A. L. (eds.). *Quantitative Approaches to Higher Education Management: Potential, Limits, and Challenge.* AAHE-ERIC Higher Education Research Report no. 4. Washington, D.C.: American Association for Higher Education, 1977.

Masland, A. T. "Organizational Culture in the Study of Higher Education." *Review of Higher Education,* 1985, *8,* 157–168.

Millett, J. D. *The Academic Community.* New York: McGraw-Hill, 1962.

Mortimer, K. P., and McConnell, T. R. *Sharing Authority Effectively: Participation, Interaction, and Discretion.* San Francisco: Jossey-Bass, 1978.

Perkins, J. A. (ed.). *Higher Education: From Autonomy to Systems.* New York: International Council for Educational Development, 1972.

Peters, T. J., and Waterman, R. H., Jr. *In Search of Excellence.* New York: Harper & Row, 1982.

Peterson, M. W. "Organization and Administration in Higher Education: Sociological and Social-Psychological Perspectives." In F. Kerlinger (ed.), *Review of Research on Education.* Vol. 2. Itasca, Ill.: Peacock, 1974.

President's Commission on Higher Education. *Higher Education for American Democracy.* Washington, D.C.: U.S. Government Printing Office, 1947.

Riesman, D., Gusfield, J., and Gamson, Z. *Academic Values and Mass Education.* Garden City, N.Y.: Doubleday, 1970.

Rourke, F. E., and Brooks, G. E. *The Managerial Revolution in Higher Education.* Baltimore, Md.: Johns Hopkins University Press, 1966.

Rudolph, F. *The American College and University: A History.* New York: Vintage, 1962.

Stoke, H. W. *The American College President.* New York: Harper & Row, 1959.

Stroup, H. *Bureaucracy in Higher Education.* New York: Free Press, 1966.

Weber, M. *The Theory of Social and Economic Organization.* New York: Free Press, 1947.

Whitehead, A. N. "Universities and Their Functions." *Atlantic Monthly,* 1928, *141* (5), 638–644.

Wriston, H. M. *Academic Procession.* New York: Columbia University Press, 1959.

2

Ellen Earle Chaffee

Organizational Concepts Underlying Governance and Administration

Higher education executives and policymakers are in the business of leading organizations. Their colleges and universities are organizations, like and unlike other kinds of organizations, similar to and different from each other. The fundamental properties and dynamics that can explain those similarities and differences are the focus of organizational theory and research. Organizational studies are multidisciplinary, involving such academic fields as psychology, sociology, political science, anthropology, and history, as well as the professional fields of business management, public administration, and higher education administration.

Those who study organizations share with administrators and members of governing boards the search for behaviors that will make organizations more effective. Organizational theory and research provide the basic science that undergirds the practice of organizational leadership. They offer insights into the fundamental dynamics of the complex situations with which administrators and policymakers must deal.

Practical applications often are not immediately evident in basic sciences, and this is also the case with organizational studies. Applied works that are well grounded in research results have not yet appeared in significant number. However, the administrator or policymaker who turns to the literature on orga-

21

nizations for help with a given situation often finds insights that can be applied to practical ends. The more important an administrative problem is, the less likely it is to respond to "how-to" recipes and the more likely it is that understanding organizational studies will guide effective administrative action.

This chapter deals with the two levels of organizational analysis that are most critical for top executives and policy-makers—those of the organization as a whole and of organization-environment interactions. Other levels exist, such as individual and group action within organizational contexts, but this review includes only one such entry. David Dill's review of research on administrator behavior (no. 455) is included because it directly addresses issues that concern top executives.

This chapter provides a perspective on the way decision making works in organizations, what organizations need from their leaders, and what happens in organizations when resources become scarce or crises occur. It focuses on strategic matters, those which by definition arrive at the president's desk or the boardroom table. The pervasive theme is organizational change, recognizing both the refusal of organizations to stand still and the unremitting efforts of organizational leaders to change them for the better.

Development of the Literature

Organizational research and theory began to develop in the 1950s and grew through the 1960s, but only since 1970 have scholars begun to produce a coherent field of organizational studies. One of the most common tools in the field is the model, which allows researchers to communicate efficiently with one another and with those who seek practical benefit from organizational studies. A model is a metaphor or analogy. For example, a common model depicts organizations as biological entities, complete with processes of evolution and natural selection. Models cannot capture the full complexity of an organization, but they do provide useful lenses through which both theorists and working administrators can attempt to bring a particular situation into focus.

As organizational studies evolved, they followed the pattern of a model Boulding (1956) proposed to help understand any kind of system. The validity of Boulding's general systems theory is evident in the fact that it describes not only the evolution of the body of knowledge about organizations (Peterson, no. 137, and Pfeffer, 1982) but also the properties of organizations themselves (Chaffee, 1985).

Briefly, Boulding identified nine levels of systems that may be clustered into three groups, ranging from the simplest to the most complex: linear, adaptive, and interpretive. Linear systems are mechanical, having direct cause-effect relationships and definable parts that interact in stable, predictable ways. For example, colleges typically follow a linear model when they plan capital construction projects. Adaptive systems, by contrast, are biological. They respond to their environments, reproduce themselves, and can organize their awareness of the environment into a knowledge structure. When the number of eighteen-year-olds began to decline, colleges followed the adaptive model by increasing their recruiting efforts and courting adults as students. Interpretive systems, finally, are cultural. They are conscious of themselves and develop elaborate shared systems of meaning. A president typically follows the interpretive model in offering the annual "state of the university" address.

Each system level incorporates those that are less complex. Adaptive systems have machinelike properties, and interpretive systems exhibit both linear and adaptive characteristics. For example, the president's address has structure in its ideas and sequencing, and the president adapts the speech to the nature of the audience and often to audience responses during the speech. Human beings and organizations are interpretive systems. Understanding and working with them requires attention to their characteristics on all three levels.

The earliest literature on organizations typically viewed them as linear entities. Authors sought to identify key organizational parts and their interrelationships—organizational size, structure, control, design, and technology—as a way to make sense of unfamiliar territory. They dealt primarily with hierarchical organizations such as businesses, which lent themselves relatively well to linear analysis because of their structured management forms and clear technologies. They looked for answers to such issues as the best way to organize work groups or the optimum size for an organization with a certain kind of goal. The business management literature began to define key tasks of managers, such as planning, organizing, and controlling.

When they began attempting to refine the linear approach, authors encountered ever greater difficulty in making that model fit reality. In the language of quantitative researchers, the model did not explain much of the variance in organizational performance because of the impact of powerful, rapidly changing environments. In the late 1960s and throughout the 1970s, authors no longer treated organizations as tightly structured, monolithic agencies, but rather as systems that are open to their surroundings.

This new view corresponded to Boulding's biological, adaptive model. Authors suggested that organizations have life cycles. They defined the entities and forces that constituted an organization's environment, recommending that leaders monitor external events, shape them, and position their organizations effectively within them. Decline in organizational markets and resource scarcity came into focus and was often attributed to adaptive failures. Flexibility became recognized as a primary necessity to keep an organization from going the way of the dinosaur. Population ecologists took the metaphor further, suggesting that like a population of animals, a population of organizations inevitably contains weaker members that cannot survive the natural selection process. Political concepts such as power, interest groups, conflict, and coalition building arose as mechanisms for both intraorganizational responsiveness and organization-environment negotiations.

In the late 1970s and early 1980s, the literature turned toward understanding organizations not just as biological entities but as human ones. It focused on the distinctive human capacities for thought, language, communication, and culture building. This latest trend brought back an interest in people, both those who comprise the organization and those who deal with it. The change corresponds to Boulding's interpretive level.

Interpretive organizational literature dealt with perceptions, organizational stories and sagas, socialization into an organization, loyalty, and, most popularly, organizational cultures. It treated organizations as collections of people who agree to cooperate, more or less, to serve diverse purposes. It assumed that organizational success was due both to the effectiveness of that cooperation and to the perceptions of outsiders about the desirability of associating themselves with the organization as consumers, employees, board members, students, investors, or in other ways.

Recent exhortations for better leadership of organizations fit especially well with the interpretive model. People are looking for leaders who can, like Winston Churchill, put into words their thoughts and feelings, giving them a vision of what they can achieve. Organizational authors are becoming increasingly interested in understanding how leaders manage meaning through various forms of communication.

Framework for Organizing the Literature

The annotations in this chapter, like the development of the literature, follow Boulding's hierarchy of systems. Despite the chronological development of the field through linear, adaptive, and interpretive phases, authors continue to produce valuable works that fit each model.

The annotations move through the three models twice, first with works that focus attention on intraorganizational dynamics and then with works that deal with organization-environment relations. This structure permits an examination of materials that deal with all three levels of organizational complexity and both of the levels of analysis that concern chief executives and policymakers.

Organization Focus—Linear entries in this chapter deal with the structure of organizations, rational decision making, and responding to decline.

Organization Focus—Adaptive entries deal with loosely coupled organizational structure, political decision making,

power in higher education organizations, and organizational life cycles.

Organization Focus—Interpretive entries deal with interpretations of educational organizations, collegiate sagas, the
nature of administrative work, and organizational
socialization.

Organization/Environment Focus—Linear entries include coordination of interorganizational relations and strategy
in higher education organizations.

Organization/Environment Focus—Adaptive entries extend the
concepts of strategy and responding to decline and crisis
in higher education. One entry reviews the literature
on organization-environment relations, and another
discusses the importance of organizational flexibility.

Organization/Environment Focus—Interpretive entries include
two discussions of organizations as language-laden
cultures as well as extensions of strategy and leadership to the interpretive level.

Commentary on the Literature

Organizational literature has attracted researchers from
a wide variety of fields. It has grown relatively fast and has also
moved rapidly to highly sophisticated, complex models. However, several liabilities counterbalance these assets.

The study of organizations encompasses numerous and
diverse subtopics. At this point, few subtopics are well developed.
Each subtopic typically attracts a few interested authors, but
it could benefit from the scrutiny of many investigators with
different perspectives. Comprehensive organizational models
that integrate these subtopics and approximate complex organizational realities probably will not appear for a long time. The
field would benefit greatly from more works that synthesize existing knowledge by subtopics, by theories, and by types of
organizations.

In the short term, research and theory need to investigate
interpretive aspects of organizations more extensively and also
to examine how the three models interact. Just because the linear

model came first does not mean it is obsolete. Administrators facing the challenges likely to be presented to higher education in the 1980s and 1990s would benefit from understanding model interactions. Definition and differentiation of institutional missions is an increasingly important interpretive issue. Leaders need thoughtful assistance in deciding how to focus and communicate their mission (interpretive), how far to let the mission stray from its historical definition in order to respond to new environments (adaptive), and how to organize the institution in order to implement the mission (linear).

The organizational studies field is young and is still oriented toward basic science rather than practical applications. Therefore, many of its best works do not attract the attention of those who might benefit most from their insights. Most books for practitioners continue to present personal opinion, expert experience, or case histories, buttressed when convenient with theory and research. A few exceptions, books that are well-grounded in research and theory but written for policymakers, are beginning to appear and should be encouraged.

References

Boulding, K. E. "General Systems Theory—The Skeleton of Science." *Management Science,* 1956, *2,* 197–208.

Chaffee, E. E. "The Concept of Strategy: From Business to Higher Education." In J. C. Smart (ed.), *Higher Education: Handbook of Theory and Research.* Vol. 1. New York: Agathon, 1985.

Pfeffer, J. *Organizations and Organization Theory.* Boston: Pitman, 1982.

Organization Focus

Linear

1   Chaffee, Ellen Earle. "The Role of Rationality in University Budgeting." *Research in Higher Education*, 1983, *19* (4), 387–406.

This article is an empirical study of the Stanford University budgeting process, using an organizational level of analysis. The study decomposes bounded rationality theory into testable, observable stages and shows how a budget decision process can conform to its requirements. It reviews theoretical and empirical literature on the assumptions of rationality, showing that the Stanford process implemented its four criteria for resource allocation through a process that examined alternatives and consequences. The article concludes that the process was rational. It also discusses political and collegial decision models that may have been present. The study's qualitative data provide a description of the way one organization conformed to the principles of rational decision making. The example can guide budgeters, planners, and others in applying rational theory to actual organizational decision-making processes.

2   March, James G. "Bounded Rationality, Ambiguity, and the Engineering of Choice." *Bell Journal of Economics,* 1978, *9* (2), 587–608.

Although people generally take "rational" to mean "sensible," formal rational theories tend to be overly technical and stringent. March modifies formal rational theory to make it sensible, identifying the major block to rational behavior as people's limited ability to know what they will want in the future. The article gives a history of Simon's development of bounded rationality and describes many alternative forms of rationality. March suggests that organizations should not seek high levels of ambition, clarity of purpose, or rationality. Those engaged in goal-setting and planning activities will find the article philosophical and abstract, yet readable and provocative. It focuses attention on what individuals or organizations want, how they know or decide what they want, and whether they act accordingly. It expands understanding of sensible decision and action.

3   Mingle, James R., and Norris, Donald M. "Institutional Strategies for Responding to Decline." In James R. Mingle and Associates, *Challenges of Retrenchment: Strategies for Consolidating Programs, Cutting Costs, and Reallocating Resources.* San Francisco: Jossey-Bass, 1981. Pages 47–68.

For a description of this chapter, please see entry no. 411. The book as a whole is described in entry no. 410.

★4   Mintzberg, Henry. "The Professional Bureaucracy." In Henry Mintzberg, *The Structuring of Organizations.* Englewood Cliffs, N.J.: Prentice-Hall, 1979. Pages 347–379.

Mintzberg's book outlines several prototypes of organizational structure. This chapter deals with higher education organizations and others in which the activities of the professional staff are the core of the organization. Coordination depends on standardization of professionals' skills and knowledge (Meyer and Rowan, no. 11, expand this point). The chapter discusses the nature of professional activities, dual administrative structures for professionals and support staff, the nature of organizational strategy, and major problems in coordination and organizational change. It is a sobering account of the advantages and disadvantages of collegiate structures. Individuals who bring a business background to the role of top higher education administrator or board member will find here a valuable account of the way collegiate organizations differ from others and recommendations of ways to modify their expectations and actions to accommodate those differences.

★This symbol signifies classic works throughout this volume.

Adaptive

★5   Baldridge, J. Victor. "Organizational Characteristics
       of Colleges and Universities." In J. Victor Baldridge
       and Terrence Deal (eds.), *The Dynamics of Organizational
       Change in Education.* Berkeley, Calif.: McCutchan, 1983.
       Pages 38–59.

Baldridge provides a basic, layperson's review of organizational
decision-making theories as they apply to higher education. He
explains special characteristics of colleges and universities, suggesting that higher education organizations are organized anarchies. Baldridge reviews three major models of governance in
organized anarchies—bureaucratic, collegial, and political. He
suggests that all three are likely to be present and provides
specific illustrations for each. Baldridge focuses on the political
model, describes its stages, and points out the importance of
mediating and negotiating skills in academic leaders. The chapter is fundamental, clear, and focused on key points. Administrators can use it to help them assess actual events and recognize
the possibility that many forms of decision making coexist within
a single organization.

6   Cameron, Kim S., and Whetten, David A. "Models
       of the Organizational Life Cycle: Applications to Higher
       Education." *Review of Higher Education,* 1983, *6* (4),
       269–300.

This article provides a comprehensive review and synthesis of
the literature on group and organizational life cycles and discusses their implications for higher education institutions. It explains the concept of organizational life cycles, noting that some
authors do not accept the validity of the life cycle concept as
applied to organizations. The authors sum up six general stages
of various models of group life cycles and four general stages
from theories about organizational life cycles. They point out
that criteria for assessing organizational effectiveness necessarily
vary from one stage to another and that managing transition
periods is crucial. The article does not present detailed infor-

mation that managers can put directly into use, but it can help readers who deal with newly formed organizations to conceptualize their current and near-future developmental tasks.

7   Salancik, Gerald R., and Pfeffer, Jeffrey. "The Bases and Use of Power in Organizational Decision Making: The Case of a University." *Administrative Science Quarterly,* 1974, *19* (4), 453–473.

This empirical study is among the earliest examinations of higher education institutions by organizational theorists. Drawing on theories of subunit power, political decision making, and critical contingencies, the authors hypothesized and found that subunits got power by providing resources that were critical to the organization and used power to obtain critical and scarce resources for themselves. The study calls attention to power dynamics in higher education, shows how they are played out in one context, and illustrates why departments that are rich tend to get richer. These dynamics are increasingly relevant to many higher education administrators, especially those dealing with scarce resources. The study is fairly quantitative, but its basis in familiar higher education dynamics makes it easy to follow as well as instructive.

★8   Weick, Karl. "Educational Organizations as Loosely Coupled Systems." *Administrative Science Quarterly,* 1976, *21* (1), 1–19.

This classic article popularized the term *loosely coupled,* referring to the loosely linked subunits of some organizations. It describes educational organizations as federations of subunits that adapt to each other and to external events. Weick describes the mechanisms that couple subunits to one another, the factors that affect the strength of coupling among subunits, and the functions and dysfunctions that accompany a loosely coupled structure. In a discussion of research needs, Weick raises such practical issues as the nature of coupling when resources are scarce and the outcomes of attempted intervention in a loosely coupled organization. Readers who engage in organizational change will find insights on the feasibility of localized changes, the value of retaining some level of ambiguity and apparent disorder in an organization, and the importance of a shared vision of the future.

Interpretive

★9   Clark, Burton R. "The Organizational Saga in Higher Education." *Administrative Science Quarterly*, 1972, *17* (2), 178–184, and Clark, Burton R. *The Distinctive College: Antioch, Reed and Swarthmore.* Chicago: Aldine, 1970. 271 pages.

Clark's work on organizational sagas, reported in article and book form, is classic for both organizational theorists and higher education scholars. Clark reports his intensive study of three private liberal arts colleges and draws the conclusion that each benefits from a special resource—its saga. He defines *saga* as a narrative of heroic exploits and unique development that creates a community of believers. The article describes both the initiation stage and the fulfillment stage of sagas. It points out that the saga is a powerful means of developing unity among participants and therefore is a valuable organizational resource, fostering loyalty and pride. The book contains the story of each of the three colleges and a concluding chapter on the making of a saga. Both reports are readable, sensible, and well grounded in actual histories. The study provides powerful testimony to the practical value of one kind of interpretation.

10   Dill, David D. "The Nature of Administrative Behavior in Higher Education." *Educational Administration Quarterly*, 1984, *20* (3), 69–99.

Please see entry no. 455 for a full description of this article.

★11   Meyer, John W., and Rowan, Brian. "The Structure of Educational Organizations." In Marshall W. Meyer and Associates, *Environments and Organizations: Theoretical and Empirical Perspectives.* San Francisco: Jossey-Bass, 1978. Pages 78–109.

By definition, bureaucratic organizations seek to define and control all key elements of their operation. The authors explain the apparent paradox that educational organizations exhibit strong bureaucratic properties yet consistently leave instructional activities and outcomes uncontrolled. The fundamental function of educational bureaucracies is to certify that individuals and organizations are qualified. Because education operates under the "logic of confidence," legitimacy is a central issue, and participants must attend not only to what they are doing but to appearances. The chapter presents certification theory clearly, touching on fundamental differences between business and educational organizations, the difficulties of responding to calls for instructional accountability, and the reasons why educators must attach great importance to others' perceptions.

12   Van Maanen, John, and Schein, Edgar H. "Toward a Theory of Organizational Socialization." In Barry M. Staw (ed.), *Research in Organizational Behavior.* Vol. 1. Greenwich, Conn.: JAI Press, 1979. Pages 3–39.

The theme of this theoretical discussion is that what people learn about their work roles in an organization is often a direct result of how they learn it. The article thus focuses on the receivers of organizational interpretations—the organization's members. It provides a framework for considering the dynamics and effects of organizational socialization. The authors offer a conceptual scheme that describes organizational domains, what individuals learn about their work, how they respond, and the organization's socialization tactics, together with propositions about the way these factors interrelate. The chapter provides a useful framework for research and for administrative thinking about such issues as why a given department or individual acts like an oddball or what may have given people unrealistic expectations of the organization.

Organization/Environment Focus

Linear

13 Cope, Robert G. *Strategic Planning, Management, and Decision Making.* AAHE/ERIC Higher Education Research Report no. 9. Washington, D.C.: American Association for Higher Education, 1981. 67 pages.

For a full description of this work, please see entry no. 174.

14 Shirley, Robert C. "Identifying the Levels of Strategy for a College or University." *Long Range Planning,* 1983, *16* (3), 92–98.

This article carries the concept of strategy from business, where it originated, to higher education organizations. Shirley's approach to strategy is linear in its step-by-step description. His definition of strategy is primarily adaptive, although he includes a linear, planning-oriented approach as well as specific attention to institutional mission, a more interpretive variable. According to him, the strategic variables for colleges and universities are mission, clientele, goals and objectives, programs and services, geographical service area, and desired comparative advantage relative to competing organizations. The article explains various levels of strategic decisions, using numerous examples from colleges and universities. It provides a framework for organizing a strategy effort and recognizing gaps, inconsistencies, and potential new avenues for action.

15 Whetten, David A. "Interorganizational Relations: A Review of the Field." *Journal of Higher Education,* 1981, *52* (1), 1–28.

Uncertain times, decreasing support, and increasing costs in higher education have led many organizations to cooperate through formation of consortia, resource sharing, or other means. This article reviews briefly the research on interorganizational relations and then focuses specifically on coordination among organizations. The author discusses various forms of coordination and specific prerequisites for coordination. He describes five steps for creating interorganizational coordination. He also considers potential consequences of coordination, some of which may be harmful. The article has high value for administrators who contemplate or participate in coordinated efforts with other organizations. It describes steps for implementation, potential pitfalls, and options for structuring coordinated arrangements.

Adaptive

16   Hardy, Cynthia, Langley, Ann, Mintzberg, Henry, and Rose, Janet. "Strategy Formation in the University Setting." *Review of Higher Education,* 1983, *6* (4), 407–433.

This article models the development of strategy in colleges and universities. After describing various kinds of strategy, the authors present a three-part model of decision making that focuses on professional judgment, collective choice, and administrative fiat. Their description of collective choice includes elements of collegial, political, rational, and organized anarchy models. Like Baldridge (no. 5), the authors assert that all three processes occur in higher education, each for certain decisions or situations. The authors derive numerous propositions about strategy making, concluding that university strategies show both remarkable stability and evolutionary change. The article provides a useful model that can help administrators diagnose their current processes of strategy making and recognize what processes might be most appropriate for future decisions.

★17   Hedberg, Bo L.T., Nystrom, Paul C., and Starbuck, William H. "Camping on Seesaws: Prescriptions for a Self-Designing Organization." *Administrative Science Quarterly,* 1976, *21* (1), 41–65.

The adaptive view of organizations emphasizes the importance of maintaining high levels of flexibility and responsiveness so that the organization is maximally attuned to its environment at all times. This article expands on that point, defines major problems organizations have in staying flexible, and suggests several components that help to maintain flexibility. The article also points out that organizations need to see changes in their environments as opportunities, rather than avoiding change. The article is a useful companion piece to that of Kerchner and Schuster (no. 392) for organizations facing crisis, letting them know what to expect and how to shape conditions in order to derive maximum benefits. Both articles also expand on the idea that stability is not necessarily a desirable goal, a point that many administrators and others find uncomfortable but one that has considerable value under the conditions many organizations face.

★**18**   Kerchner, Charles T., and Schuster, Jack H. "The Uses of Crisis: Taking the Tide at the Flood." *Review of Higher Education,* 1982, *5* (3), 121–141.

Please see entry no. 392 for a full description of this work.

★**19**   Quinn, James Brian. "Managing Strategic Change." *Sloan Management Review,* 1980, *21* (4), 3–20.

In a major study of the way business organizations manage strategic change, Quinn finds that strategic change is characterized by what he calls logical incrementalism, a multifaceted set of simultaneous processes that build gradually toward action. This practical article emphasizes interpersonal processes more than plans, analyses, or other technical functions. Quinn defines the patterns he found among approaches of businesses to successful strategic change, especially in creating awareness and commitment, and provides several examples from business organizations to illustrate his points. The article is straightforward and action oriented, although many of the actions described are abstract and complex. Top administrators who wish to foster large-scale organizational change over a period of years can benefit from these ideas.

20   Rubin, Irene. "Retrenchment, Loose Structure, and Adaptability in the University." *Sociology of Education,* 1979, *52,* 211–222.

This article is a qualitative, empirical study of the way five public universities made retrenchment decisions. Based in contingency theory, it examines a hypothesis implicit in Weick's work (no. 8) that looseness of organizational structure can increase an organization's ability to adapt. Rubin defines adaptability and various types of loose coupling. Then, after examining the behavior of universities, she concludes that the expected benefits of looseness did not generally occur. Rubin's study illustrates the difficulty of translating a biological model to organizations. It also brings to light the difficulties universities have in surveying their environments, evaluating their own units, and devising useful reallocation schemes. Although it does not develop its pragmatic implications, this article helps to explain why universities find it so difficult to deal constructively with decline.

★21   Starbuck, William H. "Organizations and Their Environments." In Marvin D. Dunnette (ed.), *Handbook of Industrial and Organizational Psychology.* Chicago: Rand McNally, 1976. Pages 1069–1233.

Starbuck provides a comprehensive scholarly review and synthesis of the literature on organizations and their environments through 1976. He includes several detailed tables of concepts and studies on the dimensions of organizational and environmental activities, the terms used in the literature to describe the environment, and the dimensions of organization-environment relationships. The chapter also discusses at some length the phenomena of adaptation and evolution and the arbitrariness of assuming that a definitive boundary exists between organizations and their environments. A great deal of valuable work in this area is necessarily excluded because it has appeared since the publication date of this chapter, but the review is a valuable map of the field and summary of early work. It provides a conceptual context for such topics as strategy, life cycles, and population ecology.

★**22** Zammuto, Raymond F., and Cameron, Kim S. "Environmental Decline and Organizational Response." In
Barry M. Staw (ed.), *Research in Organizational Behavior.*
Vol. 7. Greenwich, Conn.: JAI Press, 1984. Pages
223–262.

For a full description of this chapter, please see entry no. 397.

Interpretive

23 Cameron, Kim S., and Ulrich, David O. "Transformational Leadership in Colleges and Universities." In
John C. Smart (ed.), *Higher Education: Handbook of Theory
and Research.* Vol. 2. New York: Agathon, 1986. Pages
1–42.

For a full description of this work, please see entry no. 469.

24 Pettigrew, Andrew M. "Strategy Formulation as a
Political Process." *International Studies of Management and
Organization,* 1977, *7* (2), 78–87.

This article adopts a political view of strategy and also develops
the first discussion of strategy making as an interpretive process. Pettigrew sees strategy as a continuous process of partly
resolving environmental and organizational dilemmas, a process rooted in the context of organization, environment, and
history. He describes how demands for action arise, how power
is mobilized on behalf of demands, and how the management
of meaning connects demands with the capacity to mobilize
power. The article concludes with a call for attention to the importance of language, belief, myth, and symbolism. It provides
a useful framework for analyzing disputes about what an organization ought to do. It highlights the importance of legitimizing
a proposed course of action by placing it in the context of acceptable meanings. Pettigrew does not provide a full discussion
of the practical implications of these ideas, however.

★25   Pondy, Louis R., and Mitroff, Ian I. "Beyond Open System Models of Organization." In Barry M. Staw (ed.), *Research in Organizational Behavior.* Vol. 1. Greenwich, Conn.: JAI Press, 1979. Pages 209–264.

This chapter presents a cultural model of organization, emphasizing the use of language and the creation of shared meanings. It begins by showing the gaps and inadequacies of traditional open system theory. Using Boulding's (1956) framework for a general systems theory, the authors show that the open system model fails to acknowledge organizational participants' capacities for self-awareness, growth, use of language, and other human abilities. They discuss the role of language in social behavior and the importance of integrating the concept of language into formal organizational theory. The chapter concludes with implications for research and for management education. It does not draw out the action implications for administrators, but it does provide ideas that help to account for anomalies in organizations and suggest a new set of diagnoses and avenues for action.

26   Weick, Karl E., and Daft, Richard L. "The Effectiveness of Interpretation Systems." In Kim S. Cameron and David A. Whetten (eds.), *Organizational Effectiveness: A Comparison of Multiple Models.* Orlando, Fla.: Academic Press, 1983. Pages 71–93.

This chapter suggests that interpretation is a key function of organizations and is therefore a dimension of their effectiveness. Like Pondy and Mitroff (no. 25), the authors relate their contribution to the general systems framework proposed by Boulding and show its capacity to deal with organizations at a higher, cultural level of analysis. They define interpretation, describe how it occurs in organizations, and present a model of interpretation system types. The chapter asserts that interpretations provide stable frameworks within which participants can function. A section on the implications of these ideas for research and practice includes the claim that the job of management is to interpret, not get organizational work done. The discussion focuses attention on the importance of interpretation as a kind of organizational bottom line. (For a description of the book as a whole, please see entry no. 369.)

3

Robert O. Berdahl

State Involvement
in Higher Education

It is impossible to understand the complexities of institutional governance, particularly in the public sector, without some appreciation of the increasing role of state actions. The aim of this chapter is to enhance such appreciation.

The *state* role is emphasized here because even at the height of federal involvement in postsecondary education, during the 1970s, there was compelling evidence that the states had played and probably would continue to play the primary role in this area.

- *Historically,* individual colonies had given help to institutions of higher education within their boundaries even before the national government was created.
- *Constitutionally,* the Tenth Amendment to the U.S. Constitution established the principle that education in general was not under federal jurisdiction; thus it falls by default to state jurisdiction.
- *Legally,* institutions of higher learning, both public and independent, operate in a context of state law and normally must be licensed by state offices to operate.
- *Financially,* state tax dollars constitute the largest source of income for most public-sector institutions, and in some states they even provide a significant share of private-sector institutional funds.

Note: Susan Martin Studds's assistance with this chapter is gratefully acknowledged.

40

- *Politically,* it seems much more likely that politicians at the state level will interact intimately with institutions of higher education than that politicians at the federal level will do so.

The primacy of the state role in higher education is even more apparent in the 1980s, since the current administration favors a less extensive federal role and this inclination is reinforced by the prospect of a possible $200 billion annual federal deficit. Based on such perspectives, Clark Kerr once predicted that the federal era in higher education had ended and that new initiatives and new money for colleges and universities would come from the states instead of Washington.

The next section will briefly review the evolution of the state role in higher education and its related literature up to approximately 1980. Following sections will develop a framework for, and then annotate and comment on, the more recent literature.

Perspectives on State Actions and Related Literature

Before World War II the state role in the governance of higher education was exercised largely through the budget process, the appointment of members of public-sector governing boards, and occasional acts of licensing and regulation. This early state role was charted by Kelly and McNeely (1933) and by Brody (1935). With the massive expansion of postwar higher education, states found themselves spending vastly larger sums on their universities and colleges and, in addition, facing much more complex issues about which institutions, existing or new, should get which kinds and levels of academic programs. To aid themselves in sorting out budget fights and the role and mission issues, over thirty state governments during the 1950s or 1960s established some form of statewide board of higher education. These boards worked to try to achieve "orderly growth and development" of higher education by developing appropriate budget systems, long-range planning stressing diversity and articulation, and program and capital outlay review systems to implement the planning goals. The post–World War II state role was analyzed by Moos and Rourke (1959) and the development of statewide boards of higher education by Glenny (1959), Berdahl (1971, 1975), the Carnegie Commission on Higher Education (1971, 1973), and the Carnegie Foundation for the Advancement of Teaching (1976). M. M. Chambers wrote several monographs during this period that were critical of excessive state controls, including *Freedom and Repression in Higher Education* (1965). State planning was examined in Halstead (1974) and Palola, Lehmann, and Blischke (1970); state budgeting was extensively analyzed in a seven-volume series entitled *State Budgeting for Higher Education,* published from 1975 to 1977 by the Center for Research and Development in Higher Education at the University of California, Berkeley. The books in that series, by Glenny, Schmidtlein, Morgan, Bowen, Purves, and Meisinger, described budget practices in seventeen states. State program review practices were studied in Barak and Berdahl (no. 247).

The state role, then, broadened from a basically legal and financial relationship with public universities and colleges to an agenda that could include creating new institutions, determining role and mission for new and existing institutions, approving buildings and academic programs, agreeing to particular operating items (for example, student admission standards, tuition charges, and faculty salary scales), and appropriating the tax dollars to drive the whole system.

Private institutions have not been exempt from this growing state role. In many states, private-sector institutions are included in state planning activities and state student aid programs; in a few states, private institutions either by law (New York) or by voluntary practice (Minnesota and Maryland, for example) participate in state program review activities; and private institutions are often concerned with state policies that have an impact on the competitiveness of public-sector institutions. Relations between states and private or independent higher education were dealt with in four studies published within a two-year span: Education Commission of the States (1977); Carnegie Foundation for the Advancement of Teaching (1977); Breneman and Finn (no. 60); and Chronister (1978).

Paralleling this growth in state actions relating to higher education have been developments in state executive and legislative branches that also have important consequences for higher education. In many states there has been a steady strengthening of executive powers over recent decades. Governors' terms have been lengthened from two to four years; prohibitions against second terms have been removed; strong executive budgets have been instituted; item veto powers have been given; reorganizations of state activities have brought under executive control many independent and quasi-independent commissions and have converted some senior elective offices to gubernatorially appointed ones. Occasionally some limitations have been applied: for example, the item veto cannot be used on appropriations for the legislative or judicial branches. But basically the movement has been to give the governors increased powers to match their increased responsibility for achieving coherence in state programs.

As a countervailing force to this growth in state executive powers, legislatures in many states have moved to increase the staff assigned to their committees (particularly fiscal committees), have strengthened and broadened the post-audit function from its traditional concerns with fiscal and management audits to efforts to undertake performance audits, and have acted through groups like the National Conference of State Legislatures to generally improve their state efforts as solons.

As a consequence, universities and colleges in some states find themselves facing as many as three sets of increasingly sophisticated questioners: a statewide board, legislative committees, and executive agencies. The impact on institutional governance has been obvious. Glenny and Dalglish (no. 143) pointed out that in a few states public universities have constitutional autonomy, but for the most part, public institutions are subject to a broad set of state controls. Nor were all the state government developments limited to administrative issues. Those who talk policies also talk politics! Eulau and Quinley (1970) examined attitudes of state officials toward higher education, and Budig (1969), Goodall (1976), and Millett (1974) also wrote on various aspects of state policies and higher education. Usdan, Minar, and Hurwitz (1969) analyzed the political relations between elementary/secondary and higher education.

Another key development during this period was triggered by James Conant's book, *Shaping Educational Policy* (1964), which led (through the initiative of then-Governor Sanford of North Carolina) to the founding of the Education Commission of the States (ECS). This is a compact of the states in which many activities and studies are undertaken to improve state performance in education, both elementary/secondary and postsecondary. ECS published task force reports on the state role in higher education in 1973 and 1980.

Also active on the scene were three regional associations: the Southern Regional Education Board, the Western Interstate Commission for Higher Education, and the New England Board of Higher Education. Their purpose was to promote better relations between higher education and state governments.

A volume by Kent Halstead, *Higher Education Planning: A Bibliographic Handbook* (1979), provides an annotated bibliography covering many different aspects of state activities in this period. In particular, John Folger's chapter analyzes the main findings of many of the volumes just cited. In addition, Kaufman and Rabineau, with nine contributing editors, published in 1981 *Perspectives on Postsecondary Education: An Annotated Bibliography,* which covered a variety of "papers, proceedings and publications from Inservice Education Program State Leadership Seminars" from 1974 to 1980.

Framework for Analyzing the Literature

The literature on state actions that influence institutional governance is plentiful, although a great deal of it consists of "wisdom pieces" and commission reports. I shall comment later on the need for more effective policy research in this field.

To give some order and coherence to what would otherwise be a sprawling set of citations, annotations in this chapter have been grouped into five broad categories. Links to other chapters are noted where appropriate. With a few exceptions, citations have been limited to items appearing in the last eight years in order to emphasize material made available since the publication of Halstead's bibliography. The first and the fifth categories, both general ones, have the most citations, while the middle three (planning, budgeting, and program review) show only a modest amount of relevant work.

General Works on State Actions. Citations in this section include a new, comprehensive analysis of state impacts on higher education by an experienced author (no. 30), a report that deals with the state role as only one of several external elements (no. 27), three overviews of issues and related research (nos. 31, 32, 33), one detailed analysis of statewide coordination in three states (no. 29), an article urging systems theory and policy research on state issues (no. 28), and a special issue of the *Policy Studies Journal* devoted to just such policy research (no. 34).

State Planning. This category should be cross-referenced with relevant materials from Chapter Eight (Institutional Planning, Strategy, and Policy Formulation). In particular, that chapter treats the current emergence of strategic planning in a way that has not yet reached the literature on state planning. This latter literature has traced the evolution of planning from its early days of relative state neglect, through the heyday of state master planning in the 1960s and early 1970s, into the phase of rolling, tactical planning characteristic of the late 1970s. Such tactical planning can deal with any number of specialized issues, including enrollments, minority access, quality improvements, and higher education relations with business and industry. Halstead's massive 1974 opus was especially focused on statewide planning, but more often the relevant material must be found in chapters or sections of books dealing with broader topics, such as those of Glenny (1959), Berdahl (1971), or Millett (no. 33). Entries in this category include a few recent studies that deal explicitly and principally with state planning.

State Budgeting and Financing. As with planning, some relevant materials on state budgeting and financing can be found as chapters or sections within broader works, but this category includes several entries that deal explicitly and principally with the subject. In particular the University of Arizona annual conference proceedings, 1979–1983 (no. 39), constitute an impressive collection of relevant material. Other treatments of budgeting and finances are listed in Chapter Nine of this book.

Although most state budgeting has consisted of what have
been termed incremental budgeting and formula budgeting,
various analysts cited in this category also examine more ex-
otic variations such as PPBS (planning, programming, and
budgeting systems), ZBB (zero-based budgeting), and performance budgeting.

State Program Review. State planning and budgeting
tended to dominate the early writings on state actions, but the
topic of program review or evaluation has become a major source
of citations in the 1980s. Not all of them discuss the state role
as such, but nearly all have some relevance to this topic.

Early works in the area tended to pay great attention
to the more heavily traveled route of state approval of new
academic programs, but more recent works have included coverage of the state role in assessing existing programs. This shift
probably has been driven by concerns with retrenchment agendas, quality, or both. One general work on retrenchment (no.
410) and several works dealing with the state role in seeking
"quality in higher education" are listed in category five, which
deals with emerging issues. Other treatments of program evaluation can be found in Chapter Ten.

Recent and Emerging Issues. Obviously a category with
this title could include materials from many topics. In the interests of coherence, however, only three issues have been selected. In regard to the first issue, accountability, we note the
paradox that some of our citations point to a stronger state oversight role, while others emphasize increased management flexibility. A second set of issues concerns recent state efforts to improve quality in higher education through either mandated
assessment programs or financial incentives. A final set of issues
pertains to changing political dimensions, especially the increasing involvement of governors in state actions related to higher
education.

Commentary on the Literature

This field, as noted earlier, is still very much dominated
by "wisdom pieces" and commission reports. This reflects the

difficulty of moving beyond isolated case studies into any serious kind of theory building, given the present state of our knowledge in the area. There have not been many research efforts approaching the massive seventeen-state, multiyear study of state budgeting by Glenny (1976) and others, which did allow for some middle-range theory building.

Most social scientists studying phenomena connected with state governments soon learn that they are really engaged in exercises in comparative government and politics. Even though one may be able to hold national culture and language constant, the idiosyncrasies connected with particular structures, history, and personalities vary so much from one state to another that one could often wish to have anthropologists well grounded in ethnographic research on one's research team.

Crosson (no. 28) suggests that more coherence might be built into research on state issues if scholars adopted some variation of the open system theory or the state policy models she describes. However, there are so many possible relevant variables that it will be necessary to draw some qualitative distinctions among them before such an approach can move beyond mapping key actors and relationships into establishing some kind of predictive theory.

Glenny and Schmidtlein (no. 31) provide a splendid overview of the various issues and related research in the general area of state higher education policies. They also point to topics on which further research is needed.

Ideally, ways will be found to establish, fund, and maintain multidisciplinary teams of researchers who can examine state policy-making and its impact on institutional governance in depth. The field needs the insights of economists, political scientists, sociologists, psychologists, anthropologists, and historians and philosophers as well. Their impact will be greatest if they work together within some coherent conceptual framework.

Pending such desirable developments, we are left with a variety of case studies, wisdom pieces, and commission reports. This is by no means all bad, as individual case studies can build up over time into a body of knowledge from which it may be possible to derive important insights.

"Insights" is an important word here, for in this field it will be necessary to rely heavily for the foreseeable future on insights, also known as "wisdom" or *verstehen*. Guba and Lincoln (1981) have recently given methodological legitimacy to *verstehen* in the form of "naturalistic inquiry," and while good, tough empirical studies using statistical data will always be needed in this area, so too will qualitative approaches that recognize the indeterminate nature and variability of most state policy processes.

References

Berdahl, R. O. *Statewide Coordination of Higher Education*. Washington, D.C.: American Council on Education, 1971.

Berdahl, R. O. (ed.). *Evaluating Statewide Boards*. New Directions for Institutional Research, no. 5. San Francisco: Jossey-Bass, 1975.

Brody, A. *The American State and Higher Education*. Washington, D.C.: American Council on Education, 1935.

Budig, G. A. *Governance and Higher Education*. Lincoln: University of Nebraska Press, 1969.

Carnegie Commission on Higher Education. *The Capitol and the Campus*. New York: McGraw-Hill, 1971.

Carnegie Commission on Higher Education. *Governance of Higher Education*. New York: McGraw-Hill, 1973.

Carnegie Foundation for the Advancement of Teaching. *The States and Higher Education: A Proud Past and a Vital Future*. San Francisco: Jossey-Bass, 1976.

Carnegie Foundation for the Advancement of Teaching. *The States and Private Higher Education: Problems and Policies in a New Era*. San Francisco: Jossey-Bass, 1977.

Chambers, M. M. *Freedom and Repression in Higher Education*. Bloomington, Ind.: Bloomcraft Press, 1965.

Chronister, J. *Independent College and University Participation in Statewide Planning for Postsecondary Education*. Washington, D.C.: National Institute of Independent Colleges and Universities, 1978.

Conant, J. B. *Shaping Educational Policy*. New York: McGraw-Hill, 1964.

Education Commission of the States. *Final Report and Recommendations: Task Force on State Policy and Independent Higher Education*. Report no. 1. Denver, Colo.: Education Commission of the States, 1977.

Education Commission of the States, Task Force on Coordination, Governance, and Structure of Postsecondary Education. *Coordination or Chaos?* Report no. 43. Denver, Colo.: Education Commission of the States, 1973.

Education Commission of the States, Task Force on Coordination, Governance, and Structure of Postsecondary Education. *Challenge: Coordination and Governance in the 80's*. Report no. 134. Denver, Colo.: Education Commission of the States, 1980.

Eulau, H., and Quinley, H. *State Officials and Higher Education: A Survey of Opinions and Expectations of Policy-Makers in Nine States*. New York: McGraw-Hill, 1970.

Glenny, L. A. *Autonomy of Public Colleges.* New York: McGraw-Hill, 1959.

Glenny, L. A. *State Budgeting for Higher Education: Interagency Conflict and Consensus.* Berkeley: Center for Research and Development in Higher Education, University of California, 1976.

Glenny, L. A., and others. *State Budgeting for Higher Education: Data Digest.* Berkeley: Center for Research and Development in Higher Education, University of California, 1975.

Goodall, L. E. (ed.). *State Politics and Higher Education.* Dearborn, Mich.: LMG Associates, 1976.

Guba, E. G., and Lincoln, Y. S. *Effective Evaluation: Improving the Usefulness of Evaluation Through Responsive and Naturalistic Approaches.* San Francisco: Jossey-Bass, 1981.

Halstead, D. K. (ed.). *Statewide Planning in Higher Education.* Washington, D.C.: U.S. Government Printing Office, 1974.

Halstead, D. K. *Higher Education Planning: A Bibliographic Handbook.* Washington, D.C.: U.S. Government Printing Office, 1979.

Kaufman, M., and Rabineau, L. *Perspectives on Postsecondary Education: An Annotated Bibliography.* Report no. 141. Denver, Colo.: Education Commission of the States, 1981.

Kelly, F. J., and McNeely, J. H. *The State and Higher Education.* New York: Carnegie Foundation for the Advancement of Teaching, 1933.

Millett, J. D. *Politics and Higher Education.* University: University of Alabama Press, 1974.

Moos, M., and Rourke, F. *The Campus and the State.* Baltimore, Md.: Johns Hopkins University Press, 1959.

Palola, E., Lehmann, T., and Blischke, W. R. *Higher Education by Design: The Sociology of Planning.* Berkeley: Center for Research and Development in Higher Education, University of California, 1970.

Usdan, M. D., Minar, D. W., and Hurwitz, E., Jr. *Education and State Politics.* New York: Teachers College Press, Columbia University, 1969.

General Works on State Actions

27 Carnegie Foundation for the Advancement of Teaching. *The Control of the Campus: A Report on the Governance of Higher Education.* Lawrenceville, N.J.: Princeton University Press, 1982. 90 pages.

This report briefly surveys historical aspects of the traditions of university self-government and voluntary accreditation as bulwarks of autonomy, then examines the increasing roles of state and federal government and their court systems as major players in "the control of the campus." While the net assessment by this essay is that governmental intervention has been more helpful than hurtful, the authors also call for restoration of the vitality of self-governing aspects of university life in order to forestall excessive external controls. This discussion should interest readers concerned with the roles of faculty and trustees in governance, with regional and specialized accreditation, and with the uneasy policy interface between federal and state governments and the academic community.

28 Crosson, Patricia H. "State Postsecondary Education Policy Systems." *Review of Higher Education,* 1984, *7* (2), 125–142.

In this essay Crosson surveys the literature on systems theories and policy frameworks over the past twenty years and uses it to build a systems model and a policy model. She then applies each model to the Pennsylvania postsecondary education system as an example. She argues that more systematic approaches are needed if comparative studies across the fifty states are ever to be rewarding. While both models make it possible to envisage the many potential actors in state postsecondary education systems and some of their possible interrelationships, neither offers any guidance in making qualitative distinctions among the various linkages or presents any theories on the basis of which predictions can be made. It may be possible to make such distinctions and suggest such theories, however, by applying these models to specific circumstances.

29 Dressel, Paul L. *The Autonomy of Public Colleges.* New Directions for Institutional Research, no. 26. San Francisco: Jossey-Bass, 1980. 107 pages.

This study of autonomy begins with the assumption that absolute autonomy is neither possible nor desirable for educational institutions. It attempts to provide answers to four questions: (1) What is institutional autonomy? (2) What aspects of institutional autonomy are essential for a university to operate effectively? (3) What are the most serious present threats to university autonomy by government (state and federal)? and (4) What are the actual and potential implications for institutional autonomy of various forms of state coordination? The book analyzes these issues in the states of Ohio, Indiana, and Wisconsin. It does not come to any hard and fast conclusions but simply presents various factors that can influence an institution's autonomy. As the focus on accountability continues, this volume should be useful in helping administrators and other responsible parties determine a proper balance between autonomy and accountability.

30 Folger, John K. "Implications of State Government Changes." In Paul Jedamus, Marvin W. Peterson, and Associates, *Improving Academic Management: A Handbook of Planning and Institutional Research*. San Francisco: Jossey-Bass, 1980. Pages 48–64.

In this chapter Folger provides an excellent overview of changes in state governments and their implications for the higher education policy-making process. He reviews such items as public attitudes, the state political environment, changes in organization and procedures, and the increase in state responsibilities. He sees such changes increasing the state role in planning, budget review, and program evaluation in higher education institutions. He sees planning during a period of decline as both more difficult and more necessary—more difficult because traditional emphases on widespread participation are less successful when the agenda is retrenchment, and more necessary because "the consequences of every institution acting for its own short-run interest are predictably bad during a period of retrenchment." (For a description of this book as a whole, please see no. 553.)

31 Glenny, Lyman, and Schmidtlein, Frank. "The Role of the State in the Governance of Higher Education." *Educational Evaluation and Policy Analysis*, 1983, 5 (2), 133–153.

These two authors, both experienced in state coordination of higher education, have produced both a detailed inventory of

major research completed up to 1980 and a wide-ranging agenda
for needed future research. The areas they cover include state
budgeting, planning, program review, and information systems.
Among the trends and issues they survey are enrollment trends,
faculty trends, economic trends, and social trends. They consider the impact of these trends on four broad issues in higher
education: access, diversity, quality, and economy. This comprehensive overview of the state of the field as of 1980 merits
wide readership.

32   Millard, Richard M. "Power of State Coordinating
       Agencies." In Paul Jedamus, Marvin W. Peterson, and
       Associates, *Improving Academic Management: A Handbook
       of Planning and Institutional Research.* San Francisco: Jossey-
       Bass, 1980. Pages 62–95.

With some overlap with the Folger chapter in the same volume,
Millard reviews the evolution of state higher education boards,
describes their various types, outlines the major changes in conditions affecting them, and analyzes their responses to these
changed conditions. He then provides a detailed exploration of
the major functions of such state boards: planning, budget
review, and program evaluation. He urges that institutions and
state agencies reinforce each other more effectively, suggesting
that the alternatives may be either a Darwinian fight in which
few institutions will emerge stronger or more direct political
intervention that could destroy institutional integrity. (For a
description of the book as a whole, please see no. 553.)

★33   Millett, John D. *Conflict in Higher Education: State Govern-
        ment Coordination Versus Institutional Independence.* San Fran-
        cisco: Jossey-Bass, 1984. 285 pages.

This volume was written by John Millett with the aid of five
experienced collaborators. Members of the team evidently visited
and analyzed the structures of higher educational institutions
in twenty-five states where Millett's former employer, the
Academy for Educational Development, had earlier undertaken
studies. Millett, however, remains the principal author, and the
findings are vintage Millett. This means that an extended argu-

ment is made for the legitimacy of a strong state role in the coordination and governance of higher education; that tension is recognized as inevitable in the tug-of-war between autonomy and accountability and is seen as sharpened even further by the failure of leaders in higher education to understand the state role; and that fairly sharp distinctions are drawn between consolidated governing boards, seen by Millett as closer to the institutions, and coordinating and advisory boards, seen as closer to the state side. Although not all scholars of statewide systems and certainly not all institutional executives will agree with Millett's arguments, the book does move our understanding along considerably on the complex issues connected with state coordination and governance.

34 *Policy Studies Journal,* 1981, *10* (1), 19–70, 161–172.

Five articles cover state issues as a part of a journal issue devoted to higher education policy: L. R. Marcus and E. Hollander, "The Capitol and the Campus—Each in Its Proper Place"; D. Greer, "State-Level Coordination and Policy Implementation"; A. Rosenthal and S. Fuhrman, "Higher Education Leadership in State Legislatures"; M. Odell and J. Thelin, "Bringing the Independent Sector into Statewide Higher Education Planning"; and R. Craft, "Successful Legislative Oversight: Lessons from State Legislatures." Two articles cover the government/campus interface and describe a possible role for the statewide board as a buffer between them, not to eliminate conflict but to provide for orderly resolution. Another article describes the background of legislators who have become active in higher education policy. The third article focuses on the limited inclusion of independent colleges in statewide planning and advocates a shift to more reliance on the competitive market model. The final article takes a somewhat different look at the changes in legislative oversight of higher education. The articles do not build upon each other but rather provide a set of widely varying perspectives on state/higher education issues. They would be most appropriate to readers who already have an understanding of the state role in higher education and are interested in specific issues.

State Planning

35   Callan, Patrick M. "Evaluating Planning by Statewide
Boards." In Robert O. Berdahl (ed.), *Evaluating Statewide
Boards*. New Directions for Institutional Research, no.
5. San Francisco: Jossey-Bass, 1975. Pages 15–25.

This chapter in a volume about evaluating statewide boards
analyzes evaluation of planning as a method of evaluation that
does not result merely in tinkering with board structure. Although
now ten years old, this work retains basic importance. Callan
promotes the evaluation of planning as a step toward improved
board performance and also as a means to encourage states to
pay more attention to the planning function. He selects planning as a means by which to evaluate boards because of its
universal nature as a board activity. The focus of this type of
evaluation is on process as well as outcomes. This chapter could
be of use to legislative committees, blue-ribbon commissions,
academic groups, or boards themselves when they are charged
with evaluation.

36   Callan, Patrick M., and Jonsen, Richard W. "Trends
in Statewide Planning and Coordination." *Educational
Record*, 1980, *61* (3), 50–53.

This brief article outlines trends that appear as higher education moves from a period of growth to one of decline. It notes
that demographic changes, the fiscal health of states, and other
factors are likely to increase the reliance on and expectations
of statewide coordination and planning. Many issues are discussed in the context of the general state board duties of planning, budget review, and program review. The authors note
that the business of coordination is increasingly the business of
conflict. The article would be of interest to institutional personnel trying to determine how their self-interest can be served
through coordination, and also to coordinating agencies trying
to manage the interface between institutions and the political
branches of state government.

37   Floyd, Carol. *State Planning, Budgeting, and Accountability:*
           Approaches for Higher Education. AAHE-ERIC Higher Edu-
           cation Research Report no. 6. Washington, D.C.: Amer-
           ican Association for Higher Education, 1982. 51 pages.

In this monograph the author does a highly competent job of
reviewing a broad range of literature relevant to the topics of
state planning, budget review, and accountability (interpreted
largely in the form of program review). For each of these topics
she offers an analysis of the current state of the art as practiced
by statewide boards of higher education. Floyd finds that "the
interests of higher education institutions will be well served by
statewide boards being assigned broad functions and pursuing
these powers assertively while paying attention to the concerns
expressed by and maintaining amicable relations with the governor and legislature." Not all institutional leaders will agree, but
her detailed analyses are well presented.

State Budgeting and Financing

38   Caruthers, J. Kent, and Orwig, Melvin D. *Budgeting in*
           Higher Education. AAHE-ERIC Higher Education Re-
           search Report no. 3. Washington, D.C.: American As-
           sociation for Higher Education, 1979. 99 pages.

Please see entry no. 224 for a full description of this work.

★39   Conference Proceedings of the Annual Conference on
           Financing Higher Education.
           Harcleroad, Fred, *Financing Postsecondary Education in the*
           1980s, 1979, 126 pages. Leslie, Larry L., and Otto,
           Heather L., *Financing and Budgeting Postsecondary Educa-*
           tion in the 1980s, 1980, 90 pages. Leslie, Larry L., and
           Hyatt, James, *Higher Education Financing Policies: State/In-*
           stitutions and Their Interaction, 1981, 158 pages. Wilson,
           Robert A., *Responses to Fiscal Stress in Higher Education,*
           1982, 182 pages. Wilson, Robert A., *Survival in the 1980s:*
           Quality, Mission, and Financing Options, 1983, 291 pages.
           Tucson, Ariz.: Center for the Study of Higher Educa-
           tion, University of Arizona.

These volumes document the proceedings of five annual conferences on the financing of higher education in the 1980s. Participants, in addition to the Center for the Study of Higher Education at the University of Arizona, include the National Center
for Higher Education Management Systems (NCHEMS), the
National Association of College and University Business Offi-
ers (NACUBO), the Education Commission of the States (ECS),
and the State Higher Education Executive Officers (SHEEO).
The overall objective of the conferences was to enhance understanding and cooperation among the diverse players in postsecondary financing, and the various papers reflect this multiple
perspective. One volume specifically addresses state/institution
interactions and covers the topic in depth, giving examples from
specific states. State-level policy groups, institutional leaders,
and research and policy analysts provided the papers for the
volumes. Because of the breadth of participation these volumes
would be of interest to both practitioners and scholars concerned
with the financing of higher education.

40   Stampen, Jacob. *The Financing of Public Higher Education:
         Low Tuition, Student Aid, and the Federal Government*. AAHE-
         ERIC Higher Education Research Report no. 9. Wash-
         ington, D.C.: American Association for Higher Educa-
         tion, 1980. 88 pages.

In this monograph Stampen traces from the late 1960s through
the mid-1970s the national debate about the economic and social
consequences for access and equity of different policies concerning tuition levels and student aid programs. He competently
reviews a broad range of literature covering all sides of the debate
before concluding that a combination of low tuition in the public
sector and supplementary student aid programs offering mar-
ginally more support to students attending higher-cost private
institutions would best achieve the twin goals of access and equity.
He calls for needed research in several areas of these complicated
issues, which cut across federal, state, and institutional lines.
See also no. 47 under "Recent and Emerging Issues."

State Program Review

41   Barak, Robert J. *Program Review in Higher Education: Within and Without.* Boulder, Colo.: National Center for Higher Education Management Systems, 1982. 137 pages.

For a complete description of this work, please see entry no. 241.

42   Feasley, Charles E. *Program Evaluation.* AAHE-ERIC Higher Education Research Report no. 2. Washington, D.C.: American Association for Higher Education, 1980. 59 pages.

This report reviews and analyzes major contributions to the literature concerned with program evaluation. It discusses what is meant by program evaluation and describes nine ways that program evaluation is used. It examines three types of formal evaluation models that underlie program evaluation activities and looks at program evaluation from departmental to state legislative audit levels. The report discusses the purposes of program evaluation, the phases of the evaluation process, and the participants in the process. It also describes factors that influence the usefulness of evaluation reports. It concludes with speculation about the future of program evaluation. The report establishes a logical foundation for program evaluation and would be helpful to individuals developing plans for such evaluation.

43   Green, Kenneth C. "Program Review and the State Responsibility for Higher Education." *Journal of Higher Education,* 1981, *52* (1), 67–80.

This article discusses program review in terms of its contribution to accountability and assessment issues. It looks at the evolution of review of new programs into review of existing programs as demands for quality and accountability increased. The body of the article covers the definitions accorded to quality, state program review criteria, and the regulatory nature of program review. The author concludes that the state program review process has been the most sensitive to, and the most successful at, using multidimensional measures of program and institutional quality. The utility of the article lies in the applicability of the program review process as a measure of quality, as opposed to the traditional meritocratic viewpoint.

44   WICHE-NCHEMS. *Postsecondary Education Program Review, Report of a WICHE-NCHEMS Workshop and Study.* Boulder, Colo.: Western Interstate Commission for Higher Education, 1980. 176 pages.

This report on a workshop has as its focus the changing academic planning environment and the application of program review in responding to the need for quality in light of current pressures on higher education. It includes the results of a survey of institutions and state higher education agencies in the thirteen western states that examined issues involved in program review, approaches to program review, and clarification of differences in program review. The report presents a range from theoretical articles to those describing actual practice in the states and provides quantitative measures to evaluate quality. It emphasizes the relationship of state agency practices to institutional program review. The report will be of interest to decision makers at both the state and institutional levels.

45   Wilson, Richard F. "Institutional Participation and Reciprocity in State-Level Program Review." *Journal of Higher Education,* 1980, *51* (6), 601–615.

The article presents findings from a national study that looked at institutional program review relationships with state-level higher education agencies. It analyzes the nature of institutional participation, the relationship between agency structure and program review activities, and the public concern about reciprocal opportunities to review private college programs. Forty-five states were included in the study. A substantial part of the study was devoted to the way institutions were chosen for inclusion in statewide evaluations. The article is helpful in its observations about the relationship of agency structure to program review in private institutions and could assist decision makers contemplating structural changes in statewide agencies or statewide program review.

Recent and Emerging Issues

States, Accountability, Retrenchment, and Flexibility

46   Education Commission of the States. *Accountability and Academe: A Report of the National Task Force on the Accountability of Higher Education to the State.* Report no. 126. Denver, Colo.: Education Commission of the States, 1979. 40 pages.

The ECS task force, made up of institutional representatives, state higher education executive officers, state budget officers, accrediting agency representatives, governing board members, and legislators, examined the question of how higher education could best demonstrate its accountability and effectiveness in meeting statewide goals. The report begins with a definition of state accountability and outlines different processes that have been used in the past to measure accountability. It goes on to make eight recommendations for a process the commission feels that states should consider using, including problems they should avoid. This report should be useful to states in formulating policies that will lead to increased understanding and more effective accountability arrangements between state government and higher education.

47   Folger, John K. (ed.). *Increasing the Public Accountability of Higher Education.* New Directions for Institutional Research, no. 16. San Francisco: Jossey-Bass, 1977. 94 pages.

This volume includes separate chapters by Peterson and others on state performance funding in higher education; by Berdahl on state performance audits; and by Barak on state program

review. All three chapters are described by Folger as further
evidence that the states are reaching beyond traditional accountability concerns and making efforts to link the appropriations
process to outcome measures, to go beyond fiscal and management audits to evaluation of unit performance, and to evaluate
not only proposed new academic programs but existing programs
as well. Folger concludes that if collegiate institutions do not
develop more outcome measures themselves, they will be faced
with increasing state efforts to do so.

48   Mingle, James R. (ed.). *Management Flexibility and State
         Regulation in Higher Education.* Atlanta, Ga.: Southern
         Regional Education Board, 1983. 61 pages.

This volume includes an editor's overview of the scope and importance of increased management flexibility in higher education and case studies of such increased flexibility in Maryland,
Wisconsin, Kentucky, and Colorado. The authors convincingly
demonstrate that, particularly in times of fiscal austerity, local
campus management needs more administrative discretion to
help the institution adapt to changing conditions. Topics covered
include the rights to carry funds forward from one year to the
next, to expend excess income, and to invest funds; procure-
ment, contracting, and personnel policies; power to reallocate
funds; and "position control" issues. These well-analyzed studies
should be of interest to both state government and higher education personnel concerned with the never-ending pursuit of the
proper balance between autonomy and accountability.

★49   Mingle, James R., and Associates. *Challenges of Retrench-
         ment: Strategies for Consolidating Programs, Cutting Costs, and
         Reallocating Resources.* San Francisco: Jossey-Bass, 1981.
         394 pages.

For a full description of this work, please see entry no. 410.

50   Volkwein, J. Fredericks. "State Financial Control of Public Universities and Its Relationship to Campus Administrative Elaborateness and Cost: Results of a National Study." *Review of Higher Education,* 1986, *9* (3), 267–286.

This report of a research project examines the relationship between state fiscal control and the cost and elaborateness of administrative operations. The study covered eighty-eight public doctorate-granting research institutions in forty-nine states. Its statistical analysis provides a comparative picture of state financial control practices and illuminates the relationship between state financial and personnel control practices and university expenditures. The study found little evidence that freedom from state control encourages reduced overhead. It also found that campuses that are encumbered by state control are less likely to develop alternative sources of revenue. Although the findings presented are concrete and interesting, they are limited in their general applicability; the author cautions against generalizing to other types of institutions.

The States and Quality in Higher Education

51   *Change,* 1985, *17* (6), 11–48.

Under the editorial leadership of the American Association for Higher Education, a special issue of *Change* features six items on the theme "States and Quality": an editorial by Frank Newman, president of the Education Commission of the States; an interview with Thomas Kean, the education-minded governor from New Jersey; an interesting article on eleven professors who serve as state legislators; two articles on learning and assessment; and a roundtable discussion on Tennessee's experiment in performance funding by three persons in that state who had played key roles in the process. Taken together, these features should convince those who welcome greater state initiatives to achieve higher quality in postsecondary education and also warn those who fear such developments that more extensive state activity in this area is not a temporary phenomenon.

52   Ewell, Peter T. *Levers for Change: The Role of State Govern-ment in Improving the Quality of Postsecondary Education.* No. PS-85-2. Denver, Colo.: Education Commission of the States, 1985. 38 pages.

53   Education Commission of the States, Working Party on Effective State Action to Improve Undergraduate Educa-tion. *Transforming the State Role in Undergraduate Education: Time for a Different View.* No. PS-86-3. Denver, Colo.: Education Commission of the States, 1986. 40 pages.

These two monographs are part of a three-year project entitled "Effective State Actions to Improve Undergraduate Education." They explore how current resources can be used to improve undergraduate education and how states and state leaders can create a positive environment for institutional change. The first monograph provides a perspective on what states can do to im-prove the quality of undergraduate education, giving examples of approaches to such improvement at several institutions. The paper argues for a growing need for a state role in assessing and improving undergraduate education and discusses a number of possible initiatives that state governments can take to induce positive change. The second paper makes the case that states and state leaders can provide a creative external force for major change in institutions. It goes on to describe eight challenges in undergraduate education that are derived from an overall mismatch between educational needs and practice. It urges a transformation of the state role to meet these challenges and presents recommendations to state leaders. These papers should be useful to state and institutional leaders wrestling with ques-tions related to quality and assessment.

54   Folger, John K. (ed.). *Financial Incentives for Academic Quality.* New Directions for Higher Education, no. 48. San Francisco: Jossey-Bass, 1984. 99 pages.

This edited volume presents analyses of a host of techniques by which states (and other interested parties) can create finan-cial incentives for the enhancement of quality in higher education. It recognizes that many funding authorities are reluctant to provide additional funds, particularly during a period of stable or declining enrollment, without assurances that higher quality will result. Among the techniques examined are increased reliance on market forces; increased emphasis on specified performance standards; use of fiscal and symbolic incentives for "improved performance"; and categorized support for specifically recognized quality improvement measures. These studies should interest anyone working on the state/institutional border and especially the budget specialists on each side.

States, Politics, and Blue-Ribbon Commissions

55 Gove, Samuel K. (ed.). *Governors and Higher Education: A Partnership for the Future?* Papers prepared for Wingspread Conference, Racine, Wis., March 1985. 88 pages.

This volume contains eight preconference background papers defining changes that occur in the role of the governor as higher education increasingly becomes a state concern and as political rather than academic elements increasingly determine policy. Specific issues contained in the papers include budgets and financing, faculty salaries, financial aid, state aid to private institutions, innovative investment methods, coordination and governance, program review, and excellence and equity. The volume makes a convincing argument for the importance of the role of the governor in higher education and for the need for educators to become involved in the political process.

56 Hines, Edward R., and Hartmark, Leif S. *The Politics of Higher Education.* AAHE-ERIC Higher Education Research Report no. 7. Washington, D.C.: American Association for Higher Education, 1980. 75 pages.

The authors of this monograph analyze the relevance of over 300 bibliographical items to the understanding of the politics of higher education at the federal, state, and local levels. Their chapter on "The Politics of Higher Education at the State Level" covers the literature on statewide coordination, accountability and institutional autonomy, budgeting for higher education, and interinstitutional relationships (defined to include interinstitutional conflict, higher education and legislatures, higher education lobbying, and private higher education). The authors argue persuasively that much existing scholarship has been either too administrative/functional or too prescriptive/normative in its orientation. They suggest that proper recognition of the political dynamics inevitably present even in a field like higher education requires more theory-flavored, data-based studies to help transcend the limits of the many useful but limited case studies in the field.

57   Johnson, Janet R., and Marcus, Laurence R. *Blue Ribbon Commissions and Higher Education: Changing Academe from the Outside.* ASHE-ERIC Higher Education Research Report no. 2. Washington, D.C.: Association for the Study of Higher Education, 1986. 99 pages.

This monograph includes a systematic review of blue-ribbon commissions in the United States from 1965 to 1983 and looks at the number, purpose, authorizing bodies, composition, and recommendations of those commissions. It investigates the extent to which selected persons judge blue-ribbon commissions to be an effective vehicle for change in higher education. The report includes an in-depth study of two commissions (the Rosenberg Commission in Maryland and the Wassell Commission in New York), contrasting a commission whose recommendations led to a major restructuring of the state's educational system with one whose recommendations were largely ignored. This report should be useful to administrators looking for new ways to attack old problems.

4

John B. Lee

Federal Influences
on Postsecondary
Education

The federal government has become a pervasive partner in
higher education operations, and consideration of federal funding has become almost second nature to college administrators.
In 1985–86 it was estimated that the federal government provided a total of $16.2 billion for student aid and just over $6
billion in research funds. Federal funds pay for over one-fifth
of the estimated $100 billion higher education enterprise in this
country.

      The magnitude of federal funding and the pervasiveness
of regulations make federal policy impossible to ignore. Even
though states remain the largest provider of public funds to
higher education, the federal government plays a direct role in
almost every college in the nation. Unlike state funds, federal
dollars tend to be targeted and categorically restricted to particular goals or activities. The result is a complex web of federal
regulations that provide specific directions telling how each
federal program is to be managed on the campus. One of the
recurring themes in the literature is the degree to which colleges and universities are constrained by federal regulations.
Federal funding has had, for better or worse, a profound impact on the mission and operation of higher education in this
country.

65

It is difficult to classify federal higher education efforts as anything that resembles a policy. Rather than a single policy, there are hundreds of discrete programs aimed at achieving particular goals that range from environmental protection and employee safety to improved preparation of teachers and support of university agricultural extension programs. Other federal programs are not aimed specifically at higher education but nonetheless have a profound effect on it, including tax policy, health and environmental protection regulations, and social security programs.

The literature reflects a great deal of ambivalence about the federal role. In the long run, the federal government is perceived as having acted as a positive force for change. Federal research funds have fueled tremendous gains in university research capabilities; indeed, the growth and changing character of academic research since World War II have been among the most important effects of the federal presence in higher education. The other major federal effort has been in the area of student aid, designed to provide institutional access and choice for lower- and middle-income students. Federal student aid programs have been a critical factor in expanding the pool of students able to afford college.

Some analysts perceive federal government programs and regulations as intrusions into institutional autonomy and independent operation. One of the costs of accepting federal money definitely appears in commitments to abide by federal regulations that mandate policies and procedures, often including expensive reporting and accounting processes. There has been constant friction between institutions and the federal government in defining the character of this sensitive balance between the needs of individual institutions to carry out their missions to the best of their ability and the federal government's desire to use colleges and universities to achieve social goals that transcend the concerns of any single institution.

This chapter will review the literature pertaining to the relationship between the federal government and colleges and universities. The first part of the chapter will provide a historical framework that describes the development of federal policy and the attendant literature. The second part will offer a critical commentary on the state of the current literature relevant to higher education and the federal government. The third, and central, part of the chapter will be the annotated bibliography.

Historical Overview and Framework of the Literature

The federal government is not a newcomer to higher education. During America's earliest years, prior to the Civil War, the federal government provided land grants as incentives to develop colleges and universities in the states. Initially there was almost no federal oversight of these grants. It wasn't until 1862, with the first Morrill Act, that formal operational involvement of the federal government with higher education began.

Congress established the first office concerned with education in 1867. A part of the Department of the Interior, the office's only job was to initiate checks to land grant colleges and collect and publish education statistics. That simple role did not change appreciably until after World War II. In 1958, as part of the national response to Russia's *Sputnik*, Congress passed the National Defense Education Act (NDEA), which changed the federal role in higher education from a passive to an active one. The increasing federal involvement since then reflects the major role that higher education has come to play in an increasingly complex and sophisticated technological economy. Higher education has also become an important vehicle by which the government can improve economic opportunities for the poor, minorities, and women.

An increase in writing about federal higher education policy has paralleled the increasing involvement of the federal government in higher education. The concerns that stimulate legislation also result in publications. It is obvious that each of these activities influences the other.

The major theme of early authors in this field was the desire to protect institutions from undue federal intrusion (Gray, 1937; Willey, 1937). Such concern has continued into the 1980s, and many contemporary authors reflect this perspective.

A second issue that has attracted a number of writers is the role of federal policy in improving college access for the poor and minorities. The President's Commission on Govern-

ment and Higher Education (1947) suggested that the federal
government should institute student aid programs to help low-
income students attend college. Even though it was nearly fifteen years before the civil rights movement and President Johnson's War on Poverty began to address these issues, equity
became a central theme of a number of authors.

These two major themes are complemented by two more
minor ones. The first of these is the equality of federal treatment for diverse institutional types. Public and private, two-
year and four-year, and selective and nonselective are all institutional characteristics that need to be weighed as federal
policy is developed. A second minor theme is the federal role
in providing for adequate levels of trained manpower in certain fields, especially health, education, military, and science.
Some analysts have concluded that federal programs have resulted in an oversupply of certain professionals, for example
health professionals, while others argue that there is a continuing need for federal programs to help assure an adequate supply
and quality of highly skilled workers.

A number of publications cut across these main categories and include information appropriate to most or all of the
issues. This necessitates a category labeled General Introduction. Works in this category comment on the process or content of federal programs generally, as opposed to any single issue.

Federal Regulation. Federal control of higher education
has been a sensitive topic in this country since the federal government first rejected proposals for a federal university. A number
of authors, writing from different perspectives, continue to warn
us about the increasing intervention of central government into
matters that belong to educational institutions.

After 1972 there was an increase in the literature reflecting concern with excessive federal regulation of higher education (Seabury, no. 78; Sloan Commission, no. 79; Bender, 1977;
Shulman, 1978). Authors expressed a growing sense that regulations threaten the autonomy of higher education as well as increase the conflict between colleges and universities and their
funding agencies. The institutional cost of administering federal
programs had increased, by most reckoning, and these authors
were trying to identify the problems and suggest resolutions.

The literature revealed two major concerns in this period. The first was how to deal with the mandates imposed by civil rights laws that covered hiring, promotion, and admissions policy. The second was the call for increasing accountability for federal funds awarded to colleges and universities. Both of these efforts were perceived as posing threats to institutions of higher education by reducing their autonomy and flexibility.

Bender argues that it is not just the increase in the funding of federal programs that accounts for this fear of federal encroachment; there has also been a qualitative shift in the federal view of higher education. Congress has come to view colleges and universities as instruments of national policy, which is antithetical to the proposition that society is best served by autonomous institutions of higher education. A sharp decline in literature on this theme coincided with the election of Ronald Reagan, whose administration tried to reduce funding for programs supporting higher education and also to reduce the burden of federal regulations. The Republicans reemphasized the point that responsibility for education lies with local schools and the states, not with the federal government.

Only one study has attempted to document the costs and effects of federal regulations on colleges and universities. Van Alstyne and Caldren (1976) reported research showing that colleges faced rapidly escalating costs in administering federal programs.

The remainder of the work concerning federal regulation of higher education can best be classified as descriptive and anecdotal. Much of it is written by frustrated college and university administrators trying to cope with increasing regulations. Many of the reports conclude with recommendations for improving the relations between schools and the federal government.

Social Equity. Federal concern with social equity issues began to surface formally with the report of the President's Commission on Higher Education in 1947 (the Truman Report). The commission made strong recommendations to remove barriers of race, religion, economic status, and residence so that the nation could reach the goal of 50 percent of high school graduates entering college.

Authors in the 1950s and early 1960s supported expansion of federal aid beyond the support of scientific research in the university that had been established during World War II. The central theme of these works was the desirability of reducing the financial barriers to qualified and needy students (Babbidge and Rosenzweig, 1962; Moon, 1962; Rivlin, no. 72). These early works and others like them did not specify program characteristics but simply urged a general direction for federal policy. This direction was reflected in the development of need-based student aid programs in the Higher Education Amendments of 1965, the first act of Congress that authorized a set of programs aimed at the specific needs of higher education rather than just using higher education for the achievement of other goals.

During the late 1960s and early 1970s the Carnegie Commission reports took center stage. They recommended the guarantee of universal access and reasonable choice for students as an important federal role. Need-based aid should, in the commission's view, be balanced with federal fellowships for talented students and cost-of-education supplements to colleges and universities based on the number of federal grant recipients enrolled in the school (Carnegie Commission on Higher Education, 1972). The commission generally supported large increases in federal support for higher education (Mayhew, 1973).

The commission's recommendations were very influential, in large part because they reflected a consensus of diverse representatives of higher education. A second influential report, representing the Office of Education, was the 1971 *Report on Higher Education,* commonly called the first Newman report. This report argues that higher education has become increasingly organized and rigid and suggests that one way to encourage competition and innovation is to provide grants directly to students to pay tuition at the school of their choice. This report appeared one year prior to the authorization of the Basic Educational Opportunity Grant (currently called the Pell Grant), which was an embodiment of the concept of portable grants.

The *Second Newman Report* (1973) was published just after the landmark Higher Education Act Reauthorization of 1972. This act is the final definition of the federal commitment to student aid rather than institutional aid as the central mode of support for higher education. There have not been significant changes in federal higher education policy since that time. The *Second Newman Report* extended the arguments of the first. It marked the end of publications designed to define the appropriate federal role in higher education.

The mid-1970s saw a decided shift in literature on student aid. The earlier work had concentrated on defining federal policy position, an issue resolved with the Higher Education Amendments of 1972. The later work began to focus more on the empirical question of how effective student aid was in achieving its objective of increasing the number of low-income students attending college.

Early evaluation efforts analyzed effects on enrollment behavior that could be attributed to changes in the price of attendance. A series of studies carried out during the early 1970s (Corrozzini, Dugan, and Grabowski, 1972; Radner and Miller, 1970; Hartman, 1973) confirmed that price affects attendance but concluded that noneconomic variables are generally more important in the decision to attend college. The research is voluminous (for a good review of the student choice literature see Jackson, 1986) and not necessarily aimed at evaluating federal policy. It certainly cast light on the way student aid influences access and choice, but its results were mixed, and it did not have much impact on federal policy.

The other type of literature that became prevalent in the middle and late 1970s was aimed at improving the management and coordination of student aid. Rapid growth in federal programs, combined with a relative lack of standardized procedures, caused a number of program delivery problems. Fenske, Huff, and Associates (1983) produced the most recent book aimed at helping colleges and universities manage student aid programs.

In 1976 the National Task Force on Student Aid Problems, often called the Keppel Task Force after its chairperson, published its final report. This report suggests approaches to solving operational questions of defining student need, coordinating student aid programs nationally, and designing data forms acceptable to all the participants.

The National Commission on the Financing of Post-secondary Education was formed by Congress in 1972 out of frustration with the lack of available data and information regarding financing of higher education in general. Congress was not sure what form or amount of federal support for higher education was best. The final report of the Commission, *Financing Postsecondary Education in the United States* (no. 340), did not recommend a specific set of financing programs but rather developed a systematic method for choosing among the many alternatives placed before Congress.

In summary, the postwar literature on the federal government and equity shows a progression from works defining an appropriate federal role to a more technical literature that attempts to evaluate the effect of student aid and improve the management of federal programs.

Manpower Development. The federal government has always had a direct interest in assuring an adequate supply of trained professionals in certain fields, especially the sciences, the health professions, the military, and education. Each of these fields has developed its own programs and literature.

The Carnegie Commission on the Future of Higher Education (1970) argued that there was a shortage of key health care personnel and urged the federal government to provide financial support for education in this area, including forgivable loans to students and direct support for institutions providing the funds. By 1978, however, the problem had become an over-supply of medical personnel. The Carnegie Council on Policy Studies in Higher Education suggested continued federal support of medical and dental education but gave warnings against excessive regulation (no. 82).

Military education, which is largely funded by the federal government, involves higher education through the federally funded military academies and the Reserve Officers Training Corps (ROTC) on many campuses. Training of military personnel has never been a topic of major interest in the literature of higher education.

The federal government has taken a role in assuring the flow of qualified teachers, but its effort here has been subordinated to that of the states. There is relatively less literature dedicated to federal policy in teacher education than in the other manpower fields. Similarly, development of science manpower has been a part of federal policy but has never taken center stage in a major work. Efforts to increase science manpower are generally managed out of the various federal agencies and are related to funding research in a specific field. Support for graduate students is perceived as an ancillary outcome of funding for research. Several scattered programs are specifically aimed at manpower development, however, including the Fulbright Program for foreign study. Again, significant description or analysis of these programs has not appeared in the general higher education literature.

Institutional Diversity. The federal government has developed several programs that provide money directly to institutions of higher education. Examples include the Program for Developing Institutions, which provides money to underfunded schools serving low-income students. NSF provides grants to institutions to improve the teaching of science. The Fund for the Improvement of Postsecondary Education provides funding for innovative projects aimed at improving the educational experience of students. Federal funds have been made available to subsidize campus construction projects, buy materials for libraries, and purchase scientific equipment. Federal efforts in many of these areas have been very episodic, however, with programs being authorized and then coming to an abrupt end a few years later. Categorical institutional grants have been the favored mode of funding for these programs, and they have a long history.

Wolk (1968) provides a good description of federal categorical programs, including their strengths and weaknesses. Orwig (1971) edited a set of papers that outlines the rationale for different approaches that the federal government has used or might use in financing higher education. Throughout its history, the Carnegie Commission argued for a mix of student aid and categorical support for institutions that went beyond the traditional limited role. The commission even suggested (Carnegie Commission on Higher Education, 1972) that the federal government pay for a portion of college and university general expenses.

Since the early 1970s there have been very few publications commenting on the issue of federal support for institutions. This is due to the decision, reflected in the Higher Education Amendments of 1972, to support students instead of aiding institutions. Proponents of federal aid to institutions lost that argument and have been relatively quiet since then.

Critical Commentary

The diversity of federal programs has resulted in a variety of publications that are hard to categorize because they have little overall relationship. Most of the publications are relevant to a particular policy, and as the programs change, so does the currency of the material. Today's policy report becomes tomorrow's historical footnote. Because the material is usually content specific, there is no sense of cumulative development of knowledge.

Many of the reports were designed to influence policy and, especially when they supported programs that were not enacted, they quickly became dated. Their value is mainly that of a historical record, but some provide a resource that could be used in the resurrection of similar ideas at a later time. Examples of ideas that have never been enacted but have not disappeared are a federal student loan bank and the exchange of community service for educational financial support.

Most of the literature relating to interactions between the federal government and higher education is descriptive. It is based mostly on anecdotal examples rather than formal research. There has been very little development of theory or empirical investigation regarding the effects of federal programs on higher education.

Another characteristic that works against a cumulative and coherent literature is the isolation of different areas of federal policy from each other. For example, there is only marginal overlap between federal policy in medical education and federal student aid policy. As has been noted, there is no single federal policy concerning higher education, only a number of programs aimed at solving specific problems. Each of these problems involves its own constituency and develops its own literature. Even the Department of Education does little to coordinate, or even describe, the total federal effort in higher education (with the possible exception of student aid).

Some of the literature describes the dynamics of the policy process. Most programs receive a legislative review every five years or so. The policy process is fickle and inconsistent, being influenced by personalities, politics, and dollars. Several of the selections included in the bibliography for this chapter capture the character of the legislative process, most particularly Gladieux and Wolanin (no. 68), Finn (no. 62), and Bailey (no. 59). These works provide useful insights into the political process as well as information about the antecedents of current policy.

During the period of the Reagan administration very little has been written about the federal government and higher education. Most national reports have emphasized the importance of state and institutional policy in renewing higher education (National Endowment for the Humanities, 1984; National Institute of Education, 1984; Association of American Colleges, 1985). The optimism about the role of higher education in the nation's life and prosperity reflected in the literature right after World War II has been replaced with a much more limited vision. Instead of identifying a new or expanded role for higher education, there seems to be an implicit agreement to hold on to the existing federal programs and not ask for very much new.

The major exception to this is the 1985 publication of Frank Newman's *Higher Education and the American Resurgence* by the Carnegie Foundation for the Advancement of Teaching (no. 70). By renewing his call for a program of national service to allow students to repay their obligations for college costs, Newman is suggesting that it is time to reconsider the federal programs developed during the 1960s and 1970s and look for a new consensus regarding the federal government's responsibility toward higher education.

Future Topics. We need to use this pause in the expansion of federal programs to assess the overall impact of the federal government on higher education. There is evidence that the character of higher education has been changed as much by federal policy as by any other single influence. The emphases on academic research, training students for practical professions, and opening the doors of higher education to a broader clientele have all been, at least in part, major federal initiatives of the last 125 years, yet there is no broad description of the current impact of the federal government on higher education. A review of the development of the federal role in higher education since World War II, including the ways that specific programs have affected higher education, could tie together some of the diverse literature in the field. Such a work would help to introduce an overall perspective that is currently missing. A review of the relationship between higher education and the military and defense in general could help to increase our understanding of this critical area.

References

Association of American Colleges. *Integrity in the College Curriculum: A Report to the Academic Community.* Washington, D.C.: Association of American Colleges, 1985.

Babbidge, H. D., and Rosenzweig, R. M. *The Federal Interest in Higher Education.* New York: McGraw-Hill, 1962.

Bender, L. W. *Federal Regulation and Higher Education.* AAHE/ERIC Higher Education Research Report no. 1. Washington, D.C.: American Association for Higher Education, 1977.

Carnegie Commission on Higher Education. *Institutional Aid: Federal Support to Colleges and Universities.* New York: McGraw-Hill, 1972.

Carnegie Commission on the Future of Higher Education. *Higher Education and the Nation's Health Policies for Medical and Dental Education.* New York: McGraw-Hill, 1970.

Corrozzini, A. J., Dugan, D. J., and Grabowski, H. G. "Determinants and Distributional Aspects of Enrollment in U.S. Higher Education." *Journal of Human Resources,* 1972, *7,* 39–59.

Fenske, R. H., Huff, R. P., and Associates. *Handbook of Student Financial Aid: Programs, Procedures, and Policies.* San Francisco: Jossey-Bass, 1983.

Gray, W. S. (ed.). *Current Issues in Higher Education.* Chicago: University of Chicago Press, 1937.

Hartman, R. W. "The Rationale for Federal Support for Higher Education." In L. C. Solomon and P. J. Taubman (eds.), *Does College Matter? Some Evidence on the Impacts of Higher Education.* Orlando, Fla.: Academic Press, 1973.

Jackson, G. A. "Workable Comprehension Models of College Choice." Unpublished manuscript, Harvard University, 1986.

Mayhew, L. B. *The Carnegie Commission on Higher Education: A Critical Analysis of the Reports and Recommendations.* San Francisco: Jossey-Bass, 1973.

Moon, R. "Student Aid and the Federal Government." In C. Dobbins (ed.), *Higher Education and the Federal Government.* Washington, D.C.: American Council on Education, 1962.

National Endowment for the Humanities. *To Reclaim a Legacy: A Report on the Humanities in Higher Education.* Washington, D.C.: U.S. Government Printing Office, 1984.

National Institute of Education. *Involvement in Learning: Realizing the Potential of American Higher Education.* Washington, D.C.: U.S. Government Printing Office, 1984.

Newman, F. *Report on Higher Education.* Washington, D.C.: U.S. Government Printing Office, 1971.

Newman, F. *The Second Newman Report: National Policy and Higher Education.* Washington, D.C.: U.S. Government Printing Office, 1973.

Orwig, M.D. (ed.). *Financing Higher Education: Alternatives for the Federal Government.* Iowa City: American College Testing Program, 1971.

President's Commission on Government and Higher Education. *Higher Education for American Democracy.* Washington, D.C.: U.S. Government Printing Office, 1947.

Radner, R., and Miller, L. S. "Demand and Supply in U.S. Higher Education: A Progress Report." *American Economic Review,* 1970, *60,* 326–334.

Shulman, C. H. *Compliance with Federal Regulations: At What Cost?* AAHE-ERIC Higher Education Research Report no. 6. Washington, D.C.: American Association for Higher Education, 1978.

Van Alstyne, C., and Coldren, S. L. *Cost of Implementing Federally Mandated Social Programs.* Washington, D.C.: Policy Analysis Service, American Council on Education, 1976.

Willey, M. M. *Depression, Recovery and Higher Education.* New York: McGraw-Hill, 1937.

Wolk, R. *Alternative Methods of Federal Funding for Higher Education.* Berkeley, Calif.: Carnegie Commission on Higher Education, 1968.

General Introduction

58 Advisory Commission on Intergovernmental Relations. *The Evolution of a Problematic Partnership: The Feds and Higher Education.* Washington, D.C.: Advisory Commission on Intergovernmental Relations, 1981. 61 pages.

This report is part of a larger series that examines the role of the federal government in the American higher education system. The authors review the historical antecedents of current higher education policy and then present a review of issues current in the late 1970s. The report's final section develops a theory to explain the political dynamics of higher education. The publication also offers a summary review of federal funding and programs between 1787 and 1977. This short document has an ambitious agenda. It provides a quick reference to important historical policies and the debates that led up to them. The authors both catalogue the factors favoring expansion of the federal role and present an analysis of the constraints on continued growth. The work provides a description of both the content and the process of federal policy-making. An extensive bibliography makes up for the brevity of the work itself. The strength of the publication is that it provides both a quick orientation to key events relevant to the federal government's role in higher education and guidance to other, more complete publications.

★**59**   Bailey, Stephen K. *Education Interest Groups in the Nation's Capital.* Washington, D.C.: American Council on Education, 1975. 87 pages.

This monograph analyzes the development and function of education interest groups in the national federal policy process. It attempts to describe who these groups are, whom they represent, what they want, how they function, and something of the tasks they face in the near future. Bailey, a political scientist who was intimately involved in issues of higher education, believes that political decision makers rather than educators will shape education policy in the future. He describes the composition of the education lobbies and their roles in shaping national education policy. He points out that regardless of their differences, all lobbies need to protect their clientele from damage, induce rules and resources favorable to their clientele's perceived interests, and increase the group's respectability and recognition. He provides illuminating examples to demonstrate these different activities. Bailey's description of the operations of education lobbies in Washington remains true today. This monograph is useful to anyone who wants a realistic insight into the role of educational lobbies in shaping national higher education policy.

60   Breneman, David W., and Finn, Chester F., Jr. *Public Policy and Private Higher Education.* Washington, D.C.: Brookings Institution, 1978. 468 pages.

This book of essays describes different aspects of public policy that relate to private colleges. Three chapters are relevant to federal policy. The first, written by Lawrence E. Gladieux and Thomas R. Wolanin, traces the evolution of federal higher education policy from 1972 through the mid-1970s. It reviews the relations between Congress and the different groups representing private higher education after the 1972 amendments were passed. In the second chapter related to federal policy, Robert Hartman describes student aid programs and evaluates their effect on modifying price differences between public and private colleges, a goal he supports. His central policy suggestion is to develop federal programs to match state scholarship programs. Such federal programs will provide an incentive to attract state funding away from institutional subsidy and toward student aid, thus helping to equalize the cost of attendance at public and private colleges. The third relevant chapter, written by Emil M. Sunly, Jr., is a review of the several federal tax subsidies that benefit higher education. The author argues that they do not form a very coherent policy and also that they generally benefit the well-established schools and higher-income families. He reviews several alternatives for tax subsidies that might be considered. The chapter, even though it is dated by the recent changes in tax law, provides a clear overview and evaluation of the way tax policies operate as a subsidy to higher education. These chapters suffer from the fact that the specific policies that were under consideration in the mid-1970s no longer seem reasonable or possible in today's policy environment. However, the chapters do provide a sound framework for organizing federal policies and understanding their development.

61   Finn, Chester E., Jr. *Education and the Presidency*. Lex-
          ington, Mass.: Heath, 1977. 167 pages.

This is a case study of the White House's role in developing
education policy in the years 1969 and 1970. Chester Finn
writes from the perspective of a participant in the process.
His focus is on the formulation of policy in the White House
that led to the presidential message on higher education in
1970. Finn describes the dynamics of the process as the ideas
evolve and solidify. Information on the role of personalities,
the structure of the decision-making process, and the competition of national agendas for attention is combined in a
very readable book. The reader comes away with a deeper
appreciation of the way education policy is developed in the
executive branch. This is a good companion piece to the
Gladieux and Wolanin book (no. 68), which details the legislative
process during the same era.

★62   Finn, Chester E., Jr. *Scholars, Dollars and Bureaucrats*.
          Washington, D.C.: Brookings Institution, 1978. 238
          pages.

This volume provides an overview of federal higher education
programs, with special emphasis on student aid policies. Finn
makes the case that even though the federal government provides a great deal of financial support to higher education, it
has no comprehensive or purposeful policy in this area. Most
federal programs are relatively small and have specific purposes.
Finn presents the federal view of higher education as a means
to numerous ends rather than an end in itself. He worries that
institutions will distort their missions in order to receive federal
funds, which will become more critical during a decade of decline
in which external money can mean the difference between vitality
and decay. On the positive side, from Finn's perspective, Washington has provided something for nearly everyone; no one
federal policy goal has become dominant. Some of the content
of the book is dated by changes in programs and the chartering
of the Department of Education, but Finn's evaluation of the
problems with federal policy from the institutional perspective

remains relevant. It is a critical and significant review of the federal role in higher education.

63   Kerr, Janet C. "From Truman to Johnson: Ad Hoc Policy Formulation in Higher Education." *Review of Higher Education,* 1984, *8* (1), 15–54.

This study reconstructs the federal process by which the proposals of two public commissions and four internal task forces related to higher education were formulated. The review spans the years from 1946 to 1969 and describes the workings and attitudes of every administration from Truman through Johnson. The author concludes that proposals were likely to succeed if there was a precedent for the recommendations. Presidential support was more likely if the proposals were congruent with other policies and thrusts of the administration. The work suffers from its brevity, but it does provide an overview of the way several key programs evolved over the twenty-five years that marked the period of greatest development in federal higher education policy. The author uses primary sources and provides new information about each administration under consideration. In particular, she supplies information on the late Truman period and the Eisenhower presidency that is often overlooked. There was not much legislative activity during this period, but a great deal of consideration was given to the federal role in higher education. Ideas formulated at this time provided an important source that was drawn upon in the development of the NDEA legislation in 1958. This article provides a good review of these antecedents of current policy.

★64   Rainsford, George N. *Congress and Higher Education in the Nineteenth Century.* Knoxville: University of Tennessee Press, 1972. 156 pages.

This book examines the formative years of federal assistance to higher education, making clear the reasons for the composition and thrust of current programs. Rainsford sketches the colonial background of public policy toward higher education and then follows federal policy into the early twentieth century. This text is probably the best single historical overview of federal policy toward higher education. It focuses on the Morrill Acts of 1862 and 1867. The author presents an analysis of legislative and educational issues placed against the background of the political and social theories of each era and the major national events of the time. The book includes an extensive bibliography, a calendar of major education enactments, and a description of critical characteristics of the original land grants for higher education.

65 Wilson, John T. *Academic Science, Higher Education and the Federal Government 1950–1983.* Chicago: University of Chicago Press, 1983. 116 pages.

This book provides a relatively complete overview of federal programs that support academic research and student aid. The author perceives the historical relationship between government and higher education as a positive one that has furthered general social welfare. That positive relationship has become marked by more suspicion and distrust in recent years, however. Wilson first reviews the establishment of the National Science Foundation and then offers a description of the evolution of the Higher Education Act of 1965. In both sections he evokes the dynamics of issues, people, and environment to explain how policies evolved and changed. Wilson believes that the Reagan administration marks the beginning of a new federal policy toward higher education that is based on continuing concern for budgetary problems. This is a good book from which to gain a quick overview of federal policy in the years after World War II. It describes both problems and successes with clarity and wisdom. Wilson concludes with the argument that higher education must recognize and defend its true purposes, even though that might mean risking its relationship with the federal government.

Social Equity

66 Congressional Research Service. *Reauthorization of the Higher Education Act: Program Descriptions, Issues, and Options.* S. RPT 99-8. Washington, D.C.: U.S. Government Printing Office, 1985. 494 pages.

This publication was prepared at the request of the Senate Committee on Labor and Human Resources. It includes background information and a discussion of issues and options for each title of the Higher Education Act of 1965. Additional sections provide basic data about higher education in the United States, a summary of issues confronting higher education, and an overview of research and development activities being conducted in higher education institutions. The appendix contains a brief summary of the federal report "Involvement in Learning" and abstracts of the reports issued by the National Commission on Student Financial Assistance. The book provides a good introduction to this central piece of federal postsecondary legislation. The outline of policy issues, relevant data, and legislative history also makes it a handy introduction to federal higher education policy issues in general. The provision of national data on funding of programs, enrollment, and costs of attendance is a nice bonus for readers.

67 Froomkin, Joseph (ed.). *The Crises in Higher Education.* Proceedings of the Academy of Political Sciences, vol. 35, no. 2. New York: Academy of Political Sciences, 1983. 177 pages.

This book of readings is divided into three sections: "The Future of Institutions," "Student Aid Policies and Prospects," and "Trends in Enrollment and Financing." A number of the chapters are concerned with federal policy. Martin Kramer pictures the 1970s as the years of most significant growth in federal student aid programs. He does a good job of describing important issues, giving special emphasis to the needs test as a device for rationing limited public resources. Lawrence Gladieux reviews the role of student aid in a complex institutional, demographic, and political environment. Lee Hansen's paper argues that federal

student aid has made little or no contribution to increased access
for low-income students. Joseph Froomkin reviews the federal
role and rationale in financing graduate students. Stephen
Dresch reviews the effects of student aid and college enrollment
in light of longer historical and economic trends. Charles Saunders reviews the political realities that influence federal higher
education programs. All the contributors to this book are first
rate. Each chapter stands on its own, and in combination they
provide an excellent consideration of issues related to federal
policy and higher education. The book also includes a complete
topical index.

★**68**   Gladieux, Lawrence E., and Wolanin, Thomas R. *Con-
         gress and the Colleges.* Lexington, Mass.: Lexington Books,
         1976. 273 pages.

This book describes and explains the genesis, enactment, and
consequences of the 1972 amendments to the Higher Education Act of 1965. This was a significant legislative point in the
evolution of federal higher education policy. It decisively aimed
federal support toward student financial aid and away from
general aid to institutions. The book closes with generalizations
about the policy process. This case study was written by two
of the participants. They are able both to communicate the immediate feel of the process and to step back and use a more
detached, analytical approach that places the event in the context of trends, ideas, and movements of the time. This excellent
book should be useful to several audiences. Students and teachers
may find it interesting because it deals with federal programs
that directly affect them. Those with a professional interest in
the substance of federal higher education policy will find it a
useful reminder of an important debate that gave shape to current federal policy. Finally, social scientists who are curious
about the way government works will be interested in the book
as a case study in congressional decision making.

69   Manski, Charles F., and Wise, David A. *College Choice in America*. Cambridge, Mass.: Harvard University Press, 1983. 221 pages.

This book reports the results of an econometric analysis designed to identify the factors associated with college attendance. The authors consider many variables but are especially concerned with the effects of federally provided student grants on the decision to attend college. This is one of the few recent empirical studies on the effects of student aid on college attendance. The authors conclude that grants are important to low-income students enrolling in a school involving two years or less of study but have less effect on enrollment in four-year schools. The study's results are somewhat questionable, given that their base year for data collection, 1972, was the year before the Basic Grant Program was instituted. The authors had to modify the data and make a number of assumptions that weaken their conclusions. Nonetheless, the work is a good example of the type of approach that has been used to evaluate the effectiveness of federal student aid programs in reaching their goals. It is technical, but the authors provide a clear overview that is understandable to noneconomists.

★**70**   Newman, Frank. *Higher Education and the American Resurgence*. Princeton, N.J.: Carnegie Foundation for the Advancement of Teaching, 1985. 268 pages.

In this book Frank Newman calls for a fundamental review of national policy toward higher education. He believes that the political consensus supporting federal higher education policy has come to an end. Newman urges a reorientation of programs, shifting away from reliance on loans to students and toward community service in return for financial support. He calls for the expansion of federal student aid programs but prefers grants and work-study scholarships to loans. The central premise of the work is that loans drive students to seek jobs with higher pay, which works against student involvement in socially important but low-paying jobs. Newman also urges increased federal funding for university research, but his suggestions for research policy are more incremental in character than his revolutionary recommendations for student aid. The report raises basic questions about the long-term effect of current federal policy and suggests alternatives. This book provides an alternative point of view that should improve the debate about expanding loan programs. It is an important policy statement and should be widely read.

71 *Reports from the National Commission on Student Financial Assistance.*

The commission was established by Congress in 1980 to help provide information on a number of unanswered questions about student aid. It produced a number of background papers and reports, including nine major reports. Three of the reports were aimed at different aspects of the Guaranteed Student Loan Program. Others addressed topics such as the equity of student aid, graduate education, academic progress of aid recipients, problems in the delivery of aid, and a review of demographic trends that influenced higher education. This mixed bag of reports was utilized in the reauthorization hearings for what became the 1986 amendments to the Higher Education Act of 1965. They provide a record of some of the more intractable problems Congress faces in developing policy. They are useful to anyone who is interested in understanding the frustration Congress feels about the lack of information that could be helpful in their policy deliberations. The reports have never been widely distributed, but they are available through the ERIC Higher Education System.

★72 Rivlin, Alice M. *The Role of the Federal Government in Financing Higher Education.* Washington, D.C.: Brookings Institution, 1961. 179 pages.

This book reviews the history of federal concern with higher education to the early 1960s. The author also discusses fundamental questions about the future role of the federal government in financing higher education. She presents arguments both for and against government subsidies of higher education. The author considers the advantages and disadvantages of aid to students as compared to aid to institutions. She goes on to detail arguments regarding general versus categorical aid, student grants versus loans, and the appropriate level of education to receive aid. Her analysis concludes with an argument for federal aid to institutions to support teaching functions and a tuition scholarship program designed for bright students with need. The clarity and grace of this book make it accessible to a broad audience. It is a good introduction, providing a sense of history, an understandable policy perspective, and a context in which later work can be more easily understood. The work's definition of federal policy issues and evenhanded analysis hold up well over time: the same issues that were being considered in 1960 are still being argued today.

73 Wilson, Reginald. *Race and Equity in Higher Education.* Washington, D.C.: American Council on Education, 1982. 153 pages.

This book is the result of a conference on desegregation of higher education held in 1981 under the joint sponsorship of ACE and the Aspen Institute of Humanistic Studies. It contains five essays that lay out the demographic, political, and constitutional issues relevant to desegregation in higher education. Its authors hope it will improve what has become a long and arduous process. This book helps to untangle the historical and demographic issues, conflicts between white and black educators, limitation of funds available to address the problems, and even the definition of desegregation. It does not suggest how the problem can best be resolved, but it gives the reader a quick overview that improves understanding of the issues involved. Very little has been written recently about desegregation in higher education, and this book is a helpful reminder of the problem and its continuing presence.

Federal Regulation

74 Ad Hoc Committee on Government-University Relationships in Support of Science. *Strengthening the Government-University Partnership in Science.* Washington, D.C.: National Academy Press, 1983. 234 pages.

This work notes the continuing strain in the relationship between the federal government and the universities. The committee members are responding to what they believe is a long-term decay in the way the federal government relates to the academic research community. They feel that this issue, unless it is resolved, portends a steady loss of research capacity and a decline in the flexible, decentralized system of academic research that existed in the 1960s. The authors produce a list of specific policies that they believe would solve the problem. These recommendations reflect the position of a wide range of research groups. This report is a good statement of the increasing concern about the inflexibility of federal regulations and the shortsightedness of federal science policy in recent years.

75 Hobbs, Walter C. (ed.). *Government Regulation of Higher Education.* Cambridge, Mass.: Ballinger, 1978. 117 pages.

For a complete description of this work, please see entry no. 105.

76 Hodgkinson, Virginia Ann (ed.). *Impact and Challenges of a Changing Federal Role.* New Directions for Institutional Research, no. 45. San Francisco: Jossey-Bass, 1985. 83 pages.

The theme of these readings is that a new, more constrained federal funding policy is coinciding with the beginning of a demographic decline that will pose problems to institutions of higher education. This pessimistic publication is aimed at helping institutional researchers review some of the recent changes in federal policy and assess the impact of these changes on colleges and universities. Its topics include tax policy, civil rights enforcement, student aid, and new partnerships between business and higher education. The volume concludes with suggestions for campus institutional research agendas. This collection of articles provides a quick and current reference for administrators interested in the impact of federal policies on institutional research. It does not include information on the effects of federal regulation on academic research, however, nor does it provide a broad evaluation of federal policy. Nonetheless, given its limited purposes, it is a helpful document.

★**77**   Rosenzweig, Robert M., and Turlington, Barbara. *The Research Universities and Their Patrons.* Berkeley: University of California Press, 1982. 151 pages.

This report was sponsored by the Association of American Universities and reflects the concerns and recommendations of proponents of the research university. Topics of interest discussed here include graduate training, research libraries, industry-university collaboration, research facilities, and international area studies. The authors credit the federal government with being the main stimulus for the growth of the research university. They point out, however, that federal funding for research has become increasingly unpredictable in recent years as federal priorities have changed. This book covers a much broader area than just federal policy, since its authors feel that the federal role needs to be defined within the context of social and institutional needs. The book is very helpful in defining the mission of research universities and suggesting future goals that can be realized by careful consideration of the role that universities play in society.

78   Seabury, Paul (ed.). *Bureaucrats and Brainpower: Government Regulation of Universities.* San Francisco: Institute for Contemporary Studies, 1979. 171 pages.

This book of readings investigates the effect of federal regulation on institutions of higher education. The authors conclude that there has been an increase in the federal government's interference in colleges and universities and that this is thwarting the autonomy and integrity of higher education. At its worst, they say, federal regulation threatens academic freedom; at its best, regulation can improve the institution. Usually, however, regulations are expensive, burdensome, and a time-consuming drag on operations. Most of the federal regulations discussed here are applied to a broad range of institutions and cover issues such as social security and health and safety concerns. The authors note that it is the uniqueness of higher education institutions that causes the problems in many instances. For example, a university laboratory that handles small amounts of dangerous chemicals has to meet the same safety standards as a major chemical manufacturer, even though this may not be appropriate. The book's publication date marks the high tide of government regulation. The issues discussed remain important, but the deregulation that occurred under the Reagan administration has reduced the immediacy of these concerns.

79   Sloan Commission on Government and Higher Education. *A Program for Renewed Partnership*. Cambridge, Mass.: Ballinger, 1980. 309 pages.

This work includes a section on the role of the states but puts most emphasis on the issue of federal regulation, providing a detailed overview and analysis of the federal regulatory process. It has chapters on student financial aid, academic research, and the education of physicians. The report's useful analysis includes a good description of the problems associated with providing equal opportunity and the difficulty higher education has in dealing with such issues. Concern about the extent of federal regulation of higher education institutions is reflected throughout the work. The analysis of student aid policy is focused on very specific legislative decisions, as is the discussion of research funding, which reduces the report's long-term relevance to current decisions. The value of this report is in its definition of novel alternatives to current policy. Even though the specific recommendations are tied to the realities of the late 1970s, they may prove valuable as a resource for devising policy options in the future.

80   Smith, Bruce L. R., and Karlesky, Joseph J. *The State of Academic Science: The Universities in the Nation's Research Effort.* Vol. 1. New York: Change Magazine Press. 1977. 250 pages.

This volume focuses on the fact that, while university research in this country continues to produce work of the highest caliber, there are also signs of beginning deterioration. The authors believe that there will not be any dramatic signal marking the decline of American university research, only continued erosion. They support the need for substantial increases in the NSF budget, along with greater flexibility in the relationship between government and universities. They urge the federal government to view universities not as places to be tapped at will to produce findings of interest to federal agencies but rather as unique places for research. Specific federal demands for accountability have, in the authors' eyes, increased adversarial conflict with higher education as well as overhead costs. This publication was one of the earliest to call for restraint in federal regulations and an increase in funding. Its concerns are still relevant today, and the authors' suggestions for resolution remain useful.

81   Vanderwaert, Lois. *Affirmative Action in Higher Education: A Sourcebook.* New York: Garland, 1982. 259 pages.

For a complete description of this work, please see entry no. 420.

Manpower

82   Carnegie Council on Policy Studies in Higher Education. *Progress and Problems in Medical and Dental Education: Federal Support Versus Federal Control.* San Francisco: Jossey-Bass, 1976. 178 pages.

This was a second Carnegie report on medical education. The first, which appeared in 1970, warned of shortages of medical practitioners. It called for increased federal support, which was largely provided by legislation in 1971. This work, produced a mere six years later, found that the supply of medical practitioners was beginning to outstrip demand. The new problem is not one of supply, it says, but of getting practitioners to areas that are underserved. The authors suggest that the federal role should be to improve coordination among different groups and to emphasize development of primary care professionals instead of increasing the number of specialists. These recommendations define a steady-state federal role rather than one of expansion. Medical education has experienced more federal involvement than any other single professional field, and the results have been mixed. Federal policy has been ineffective and even counter-productive in trying to provide the correct level of trained pro-fessionals. This publication provides clear evidence of the prob-lem but also argues that continuing federal support is vital for health education. It is a valuable reminder of the difficulties of trying to anticipate the requirements for trained personnel in a decentralized planning environment.

83   Lovell, John B. *Neither Athens nor Sparta: The American Ser-vice Academies in Transition.* Bloomington: Indiana Univer-sity Press, 1979. 362 pages.

This book describes the growth and development of the military academies. Lovell presents the academies as significant success stories, evolving from narrowly defined trade schools into first-rate colleges. The book is divided into four parts. The first is a historical review of the academies; the second presents case studies of change in the institutions; the third provides an analysis of the determinants and consequences of change; and the fourth speculates on the future. Even though it provides a good review of military institutions in this century, the work is primarily an analysis of the factors that influence change. These institutions exist in a complex and unique political and bureaucratic environment, and the author is able to draw the complex factors together into a readable book that provides in-sight into the education of military officers.

5

Barbara A. Lee

Governance
and the Judiciary

If one were to list the various external influences upon the governance and management of academic institutions in order of the
magnitude of their effect on routine campus operations, the
judicial system would very likely lead the list. Over the past
twenty-five years, state and federal courts have considered the
application of the Constitution, common law, and state and
federal legislation to the management of colleges and universities and have, in many instances, found the colleges in viola-
tion of legal requirements. Court decisions have changed the
ways that colleges recruit and admit students; recruit, hire,
evaluate, and discharge faculty; allocate resources among programs; determine which units will be reduced in size or eliminated; and much more. Even so, the courts have been quite
deferential to the decisions of academics—faculty, administrators, and trustees—in matters pertaining to the evaluation of
students and faculty and to the manner in which an institution's
mission is implemented.

This chapter will review the literature pertaining to the
relationship between the courts and the campus. It will first examine the breadth of the courts' impact on campus management and the degree to which the literature addresses that
breadth. It will then describe the development of the literature
in this area and will characterize the literature's approaches and
goals. The chapter will analyze the degree to which the literature
has kept pace with legal developments and also the effectiveness

93

of various approaches taken by authors in this domain. Finally, the chapter will present a framework for analyzing the literature on what has come to be called "higher education law" and will present examples of important and useful contributions to that field.

The Field and Its Literature

Although litigation against academic institutions was not completely unknown prior to 1960, the few cases in which colleges were sued were generally resolved in favor of the colleges, and little legislation, on either the federal or the state level, existed to regulate college operations. However, the civil rights movement of the 1960s stimulated both Congress and the federal courts to take a closer look at institutional practices, particularly those involving faculty employment decisions and student disciplinary matters. State legislatures and courts followed their federal predecessors somewhat later, and state administrative agency regulation of higher education blossomed in the 1970s. The growth in judicial and executive branch oversight was paralleled by growth in the number of in-house counsel on college and university staffs and the retaining of outside counsel with expertise in higher education law and litigation.

Despite the significance of federal legislation for the management of colleges and universities, it is the courts, acting as interpreters and enforcers of the statutes, that have played the most dramatic role in changing administrative and academic practice. Courts have been asked to enforce the individual and group rights of faculty and students in circumstances where civil rights or liberties have been infringed, and they have declared entire state systems of higher education out of compliance with laws requiring the desegregation of public higher education. Litigation concerning a broad range of campus and system-wide issues means, in practical terms, that a campus-level decision challenged in court is not final until the last appeal is completed.

Although the impact of the judiciary has been greatest for public colleges and universities, private institutions have not escaped heightened regulation by federal and state administrative agencies and concomitant scrutiny by the courts. In some cases, private institutions have been found to have engaged in "state action" to the extent that, for regulatory purposes and in constitutional terms, they are treated as public entities and must comply with the additional restrictions that the Constitution places upon public institutions. Even those institutions not found to be engaged in "state action" have been obliged to adhere to the requirements of federal legislation under Congress's spending power (for example, federal student financial aid laws and regulations), federal and state civil rights laws, and state contract law regarding student rights under college catalogues and other institutional policies. Although many scholars have railed against the tendency of the courts to narrow the gap between public and private institutions (see the "Government Regulation and Institutional Mission" section of the annotated bibliography), others have welcomed the courts' recognition that student and faculty rights should not be totally predicated on the nature of the funding source of the institution.

The development of literature in this field paralleled the legal developments; thus, little was written prior to 1960. One early and prescient scholar, M. M. Chambers, first published a volume entitled *The Colleges and the Courts* in 1936 (with Edward Elliott). He updated this work periodically, increasing it from one to two volumes, between 1936 and 1972. Chambers also founded the National Association of College and University Attorneys in 1960. This association has grown from a small group of attorneys involved in legal matters related to higher education to the most important collective source of information and expertise on legal matters affecting colleges and universities in the country.

Writing about higher education law matters was sporadic during the 1960s. It focused primarily upon descriptions of individual judicial opinions, paying little attention to their implications for campus practice. As the quantity of litigation related to higher education increased during the 1970s, articles synthesizing and evaluating groups of cases became more frequent, and some literature began to appear that addressed the implications of a body of litigation for campus practice, although this approach was still more the exception than the norm. In the late 1970s, two texts appeared that reviewed the spectrum of higher education legal issues; one was a casebook, and the second was a narrative summary and analysis of trends in litigation and federal regulation of academe. Courses in higher education law had been developed in the mid-1970s, so these texts were a sorely needed resource for the current and future college administrators who took such courses. However, the primary approach of the literature remained descriptive and synthetic; only a few scholars studied the actual campus-level implications of legal trends or suggested ways in which institutions might seek alternatives to judicial review.

Framework for Organizing the Literature

The literature on the law of higher education is scattered through scholarly and practitioner journals, text and trade books, reference works and newsletters. It is difficult to name an issue in the management and governance of higher education that has not been addressed at least once by a state or federal court. The complexities of contemporary academic life, including problems of patents, copyrights, collaboration between industry and academe, and accountability to private and state funding sources, all have legal implications for academic governance, and all of these issues have been addressed by the courts. The categories of a framework to organize this wide array of topics and publication outlets thus must be very general, and overlap between categories is unavoidable. For the purposes of this chapter, the domain of higher education law has been divided into the following five categories:

General Background on Higher Education Law. Several excellent broad reference works give an overview of the range of legal issues affecting colleges and universities. Some summarize legal developments over the quarter-century of activity in this field, while others provide a comprehensive map of the domain of higher education law and its implications for institutional management.

Faculty Employment Matters. The individual most likely to litigate a college or university's decision is a potential, cur-

rent, or former faculty member. Faculty have challenged negative employment decisions under civil rights and contract law,
have attempted to overturn institutional regulation of outside
professional activities, and have frequently brought their collective bargaining disputes to court. Courts have also been asked
to settle disputes over the ownership of intellectual property,
the ability of faculty to enter business relationships with outside funding sources, faculty accountability for their professional
time, and the boundaries of academic freedom.

Student Academic and Disciplinary Rights. Litigation by
students against their institutions is nearly as frequent as faculty
litigation, and often as complex. The "student consumer movement" is credited with spawning much litigation concerning student contractual rights in connection with college catalogues and
other institutional policy documents. Students have also chal
lenged a wide array of disciplinary actions, including failure to
admit, academic probation and dismissal, and disciplinary probation and dismissal; privacy issues regarding dormitory use;
free speech rights in campus gatherings, student publications,
and student organizations; and defamation by professors and
administrators.

Resource Allocation at the Campus and State Levels. Congress and the courts have made a significant impact upon institutional autonomy in the control of resource allocation. Legislative "strings" attached to spending legislation have placed
sharp restrictions on institutional practices regarding student
financial aid, research funds, and other public funds. Federal
courts enforcing civil rights laws that prohibit segregation have
ordered the dismantling and reorganization of state systems of
public higher education in the South and Midwest. The Supreme
Court has interpreted the Constitution to require that public
colleges permit student religious groups to use campus facilities
for worship and has limited the right of unionized faculty to influence resource allocation decisions at the campus and state
levels. The significance of resource allocation decisions to the
management of colleges and universities, and the considerable
limitations on institutions' autonomy in resource allocation decisions, suggest the magnitude of legislative and judicial incur-
sion into this management responsibility.

Government Regulation and Institutional Mission. Literature in this category examines the impact of the legislatures and the courts on an institution's ability to develop and interpret its mission as its trustees, administrators, and faculty see fit. The writing in this area is more generic and less directed to specific problems than writing in the categories involving students and faculty. Scholars have examined such issues as the degree and propriety of government regulation of colleges and universities, the effect of legislatures and courts upon church-related colleges and universities, and the impact of state regulating agencies and accrediting associations on campus decision making.

These five categories cover the majority of the writing about the impact of the law on colleges and universities. A few specialized areas have not been included, primarily because their relationship to governance as such is limited. For example, articles on the role and responsibilities of the university counsel appear from time to time. The role played by the university counsel in campus decision making has indeed increased in importance over the last two decades; however, the literature in this area is written primarily for attorneys rather than for managers of academic institutions. Other literature directed primarily at occupants of a particular administrative post, such as the chief student personnel officer, sometimes involves legal issues but has not been included because of its role specificity. The resources listed in the previously named five categories focus primarily upon issues that have implications for the overall governance and management of institutions of higher education and touch on their basic purposes and functions.

Commentary on the Literature

The field of higher education law is still developing, and, in fact, is still in a relatively early stage of development. Most of the literature in the field is descriptive, some is analytical, and little is empirical. Scholars in this area have been criticized for their lack of interest in and attention to empirical investigation of the consequences of legislative and judicial actions for

campus practice (Zirkel, 1986). The most significant reason for
the lack of empirical research in higher education law is that
legal research is itself primarily descriptive and analytical. Legal
scholars analyze judicial opinions, legislative histories and interpretations of statutes, and trends in the development of a
specialized area of the law; most do not conduct empirical investigations or attempt to build or test theory. Nonlawyer
scholars writing about higher education law issues generally
analyze the implications of legal trends for administrative practice. Few have carried their investigations to the campus or state
level to determine what actual outcomes have resulted from
judicial rulings and legislative or administrative agency action.

     The literature in higher education law tends to follow
a predictable pattern. Most articles analyze one case or a few
related cases, addressing in some detail the legal claims of the
parties and the basis upon which the court decision rests. Some
articles stop at that point; others perform the case analysis and
then suggest implications for campus practice. This approach
is an important and useful one, for it notifies legal scholars of
new developments in the field and puts practitioners on notice
concerning potential necessary changes in campus procedures.

     Most of the literature in higher education law consists
of articles published in legal journals or in specialized journals
devoted to the study of education law. Although a few books
and monographs examine a particular legal issue in more depth
or examine the state of the law with regard to one area of
campus governance (for example, student admissions or faculty
hiring), fewer such publications have appeared than one might
expect, considering the number of issues there are to address
and the great significance they have for campus governance.
The rapidity with which the law changes discourages most
scholars from preparing book-length analyses of the state of
the law in one particular area, for the law is likely to change
between the time a manuscript is completed and the time of
publication. Authors of texts have found it necessary to make
substantial revisions to their works every two or three years in
order for the text to provide accurate information and not become obsolete.

Despite the difficulty faced by authors in this field, the appetite for sound, well-reasoned writing is sizable. Administrators and their attorneys seek analyses of legal problems and appreciate policy guidance and suggested approaches to resolving campus-level dilemmas before they result in legal consequences. For individuals interested in practical advice and recent trends, the current state of the literature in higher education law is probably satisfactory.

Scholars with wider interests in the governance and management of colleges and universities are likely to find the literature less satisfying, however. Little information has been published concerning the actual impact of judicial and legislative oversight of campus decision making. We know very little, for example, about the degree to which faculty collective bargaining has enhanced, limited, or otherwise changed the ability of faculty to participate in a meaningful way in institutional policy-making beyond their own academic departments. Little information is available concerning the impact of complex student disciplinary proceedings on faculty's willingness to follow up on cases of suspected academic misconduct. One cannot ascertain the real-life, campus-level consequences of a court opinion by reading that opinion or even by reading all the court opinions in a particular area of academic policy. Research inquiring into the campus-level reality of judicial decisions is time-consuming, expensive, and difficult to conduct; however, higher education law will not mature as a paradigm until such efforts are made on a regular basis. While case descriptions and trend analyses are important and useful sources of information, the larger consequences of the legal system for academic management and governance cannot be determined without empirical investigation.

Pressure at the federal level for deregulation will probably result in reduced federal oversight of academic decisions. However, state oversight is increasing in public precollegiate education and has now moved into the higher education arena. While the academic and disciplinary rights of students are fairly well established, and the parameters of the faculty employment relationship have been clarified over the last few years, many issues remain to be resolved. It is difficult to imagine that judicial activity in this arena will diminish, although its targets may shift somewhat. The field needs well-designed, comprehensive studies of the impact of the courts on the management of American colleges and universities. The law of higher education has matured over the past decade; the literature has yet to reach that state of maturity.

References

Elliott, E. C., and Chambers, M. M. *The Colleges and the Courts: Judicial Decisions Regarding Institutions of Higher Education in the United States.* New York: Carnegie Foundation for the Advancement of Teaching, 1936.
Zirkel, P. A. "Research in Education Law." *West's Education Law Reporter,* 1986, *29,* 475–481.

General Background on Higher Education Law

84 Edwards, Harry T., and Nordin, Virginia Davis. *Higher Education and the Law.* Cambridge, Mass.: Institute for Educational Management, 1979. 939 pages (with cumulative supplements covering developments in 1980, 1981, and 1982–83).

This book is a compilation of court decisions, laws, and regulations relevant to colleges and universities. The majority of its material is excerpts from legal opinions, although the authors provide commentary, discussion questions, and references to other important cases throughout each chapter. Chapters include an examination of the legal status of colleges and universities, with separate chapters devoted to private and public institutions. Other chapters focus on faculty employment issues (including collective bargaining), student rights and responsibilities, and the numerous sources of federal regulation of academic institutions. The book is especially useful as a text; it is less useful to nonlawyer administrators or policymakers, both because the authors perform little analysis or synthesis and because its updating ended in 1983. Nevertheless, the book and its supplements provide a comprehensive survey of the legal issues facing academic institutions. Despite its lack of currency, the information they contain is still accurate in most instances.

85 Gouldner, Helen. "The Social Impact of Campus Litigation." *Journal of Higher Education,* 1980, *51* (3), 328–336.

This article, written by an administrator involved as a defendant in several lawsuits against her university, examines the impact of litigation by faculty and students upon collegiality, peer review, and the campus community in general. She discusses the tendency of litigation to consume administrators' time and to dissuade faculty and students from serving on university committees and other self-governance groups that might become involved in litigation. The author notes that litigation has become part of the "business" of a college or university and that administrators must view it as a normal responsibility of academic management. Although the article stresses only the negative consequences of litigation and does not mention any possible positive effects, such as the remedying of inappropriate policies or unclear decision criteria, it is useful reading for individuals facing their first lawsuit or for those who need a fuller appreciation of the importance of practicing preventive law.

★86 Hobbs, Walter C. "The Courts." In P. G. Altbach and R. O. Berdahl (eds.), *Higher Education in American Society.* Buffalo, N.Y.: Prometheus Books, 1981. Pages 181–198.

This chapter provides a succinct and thoughtful summary of the divergent views concerning the role of the courts and the propriety of their scrutiny of higher education. Hobbs reviews the complaints of those who decry the "intervention" of the courts into academic affairs and then summarizes the opposing view that not only is the "intervention" justified, but important reforms have resulted from judicial review. The chapter then analyzes the doctrine of "academic abstention," the tendency of the courts to defer to the judgments of academics if those judgments appear to have been made fairly; reviews briefly some of the changes in campus procedures and policies resulting from judicial review; and concludes by stating that, although the courts have become more active in reviewing academic decisions, their deference to academic judgment has continued, and academic autonomy has seldom been compromised. The chapter provides a thoughtful and balanced analysis of the role of the courts in higher education and the various views of the propriety of the courts' actions.

*87 Kaplin, William A. *The Law of Higher Education: A Comprehensive Guide to Legal Implications of Administrative Decision Making.* (2nd ed.) San Francisco: Jossey-Bass, 1985. 621 pages.

This recent revision of the 1978 edition (which won the American Council on Education's award for the best book of that year) is a comprehensive summary of the legal issues affecting the management and governance of American colleges and universities. Some chapters focus on legal issues related to trustees, faculty, and students, while others analyze state and federal regulatory requirements and the legal relationship between institutions and accrediting associations. Important court cases, laws, and regulations are summarized, and their importance for academic management is discussed. The book is written clearly and is fully comprehensible to nonlawyers. It is a must for every college administrator, trustee, and educational policymaker, for it is the most comprehensive, thoughtful, and current work available.

88 Kaplin, William A. "Law on the Campus 1960–1985: Years of Growth and Challenge." *Journal of College and University Law,* 1985, *12* (3), 269–299.

This article provides an overview of the important legal issues facing American colleges and universities in the past quarter-century. The author examines the legal implications of social changes and modifications in educational policy, the evolution of the differing legal status of public and private institutions,

and developments related to religious institutions and the degree
to which such affiliations protect their autonomy. He also offers a brief description of institutional responses to heightened
judicial scrutiny and regulation. This article provides an excellent
introduction for administrators and policymakers to the development of several significant areas of higher education law.

89   O'Neil, Robert M. "Academic Freedom and the Constitution." *Journal of College and University Law*, 1984, *11*
(3), 275–292.

This article summarizes judicial treatment of the academic
freedom claims of faculty, students, and institutions themselves.
O'Neil traces case law developments that interpret the "core"
academic freedom issues of classroom discourse and extramural
speech. He then addresses the more troublesome issue of the
scope of academic freedom in five areas: university-based research, personnel decisions, admission of students, evaluation
of student performance, and use of university facilities. He cites
briefly some academic freedom issues that will trouble academics
and the courts in the years to come, including national security
restrictions, restrictions on communication among international
scholars, local regulation of certain research projects involving
controversial issues or procedures such as nuclear energy or
recombinant DNA, and continued regulation of the faculty-
administration relationship through collective bargaining.

Faculty Employment Matters

90   "The Academy in the Courts: A Symposium on Academic Freedom." *University of California-Davis Law Review*,
1983, *16*, 831–1088.

The summer 1983 issue of this journal is devoted to critical examinations of academic freedom and institutional autonomy.
Three articles on academic freedom address the courts' role in
providing access to scientific research during litigation, the boundaries of academic freedom in classroom lectures and discussion,
and the right of faculty to dissent. Three articles on employment discrimination discuss the application of Title VII of the

Civil Rights Act of 1964 to faculty employment decisions, secrecy in faculty personnel decisions, and judicial deference to academic autonomy in peer review decisions. This collection of articles provides a useful survey of critical legal issues for faculty and academic administrators. It also addresses the unresolved issues of the boundaries of academic freedom and the seemingly inevitable conflict between civil rights and the confidentiality of peer review judgments.

91   Baldridge, J. Victor, Kemerer, Frank R., and Associates. *Assessing the Impact of Faculty Collective Bargaining.* AAHE/ERIC Higher Education Research Report no. 8. Washington, D.C.: American Association for Higher Education, 1981. 55 pages.

This monograph analyzes longitudinal data collected by the Stanford Project on Academic Governance in 1974 and 1979 that are specifically related to unionized colleges and universities. It is one of a very small number of longitudinal, empirical investigations of the impact of faculty unionization on the governance and management of colleges and universities. The monograph examines the implications of bargaining for personnel decisions, administrative training and behavior, students, and traditional academic governance. It presents a good summary of institutions' early experience with unionization, finding fewer and more moderate consequences than early critics had anticipated. This monograph is a useful summary of the national experience with faculty bargaining in the 1970s, and administrators unfamiliar with a unionized setting may find it helpful for their local situations.

★92   Clague, Monique W. "Affirmative Action Employment Discrimination: The Higher Education Fragment." In John C. Smart (ed.), *Higher Education: Handbook of Theory and Research.* Vol. 2. New York: Agathon Press, 1986. Pages 109–162.

This chapter provides a penetrating, thoughtful analysis of the legal and practical issues involved in "affirmative action discrimination," or making preferential employment decisions

in order to increase the proportion of underrepresented groups
on a college faculty. Clague summarizes the controversy surrounding this issue, presenting the views of both the critics and
the proponents of race-conscious employment practices. She first
reviews cases involving single individuals who claimed employment discrimination, or "conventional" cases. Then she turns
to an analysis of voluntary "affirmative action discrimination,"
in which institutions justify preferential treatment of underrepresented groups by citing the importance of increasing the
proportion of minority individuals in their work force. Finally,
she reviews judicially mandated preferential treatment and its
potential to survive appellate review in light of pending litigation. This chapter is the most recent and best summary of the
issues involved in affirmative-action faculty employment decisions, and Clague's careful scholarship and thorough analysis
make it both thought provoking and useful for administrators,
faculty, and other policymakers concerned about the balance
between fairness to individuals and employment equity.

★**93**   La Noue, George R., and Lee, Barbara A. *Academics
       in Court: The Consequences of Faculty Discrimination Litiga-
       tion.* Ann Arbor: University of Michigan Press, 1987.
       295 pages.

This book, funded by a grant from the Carnegie Corporation
of New York, summarizes a three-year study of the impact of
discrimination litigation on plaintiffs and defendant faculty and
administrators. It synthesizes the results of nearly three hundred academic employment discrimination lawsuits in federal
court and then presents the findings of an empirical study of
five cases that assesses the implications for faculty personnel
policies and procedures, the personal consequences for faculty
plaintiffs and defendant faculty and administrators, and the implications of these cases for the legal system in general. The final
chapter suggests a series of questions that potential plaintiffs and
defendants should consider before entering the litigation process or deciding to defend against a lawsuit and addresses the
potential of nonlitigative mechanisms for resolving faculty em-

ployment disputes. Faculty, academic administrators, university counsel, trustees, and state-level policymakers will find this book a useful guide for assessing the potential consequences of litigation for an institution and its staff.

94   Olswang, Steven G., and Lee, Barbara A. *Faculty Freedoms and Institutional Accountability: Interactions and Conflicts.* ASHE-ERIC Higher Education Research Report no. 5. Washington, D.C.: Association for the Study of Higher Education, 1984. 77 pages.

This monograph addresses important issues in the conflict between faculty academic freedom and the legal responsibility of colleges and universities to be accountable to their funding sources, to state and federal regulatory agencies, and to institutional planning and management requirements. The authors examine the protections of academic freedom and institutional efforts to regulate faculty conduct by demanding full-time effort from faculty, inquiring into interactions with students, investigating allegations of scientific misconduct, resolving disputes over the ownership of intellectual property, and conducting periodic reviews of the performance of tenured faculty. The monograph is a useful guide for academic administrators caught between the external demands of government agencies and funding sources for accountability and faculty insistence on personal and professional autonomy.

95   Wright, Thomas H. "Faculty and the Law Explosion: Assessing the Impact—a Twenty-Five Year Perspective (1960–1985) for Colleges and Lawyers." *Journal of College and University Law,* 1985, *12* (3), 363–379.

This article summarizes several of the important consequences of the "law explosion" for college faculty and academic administrators. Wright enumerates the multitude of recent legal restrictions on faculty and administrative conduct in the areas of teaching, research, and the relationship between faculty and institution (particularly in regard to faculty employment decisions). He then assesses the impact of these restrictions on faculty

autonomy and the quality of faculty life. Academic administrators and policymakers will find this article helpful both for
its summary of the many legal forces affecting the academic
workplace and its comments on the success of academe in protecting the core functions of academic institutions—teaching and
research—from disruption by external intervention.

Student Academic and Disciplinary Rights

96 LaMorte, Michael W., and Meadows, Robert B. "Educationally Sound Due Process in Academic Affairs."
Journal of Law and Education, 1974, *8,* 197–214.

This article discusses the impact of the courts on faculty and
administrative decisions concerning student academic performance. It describes judicial review of the academic evaluation
of students, academic dismissals, and the enforcement of degree
requirements. The authors propose standards for "educationally
sound due process" to protect student rights, ensure fairness,
and permit decisions to withstand judicial review. Although the
article predates the important Supreme Court decisions in *Horowitz* and *Ewing,* its analysis of the law is still accurate, and its
suggestions for developing due process protections for students
remain appropriate. The article is useful primarily for new student personnel administrators who need a summary of the due
process protections that institutions, especially those in the public
sector, must afford students who challenge the academic judgments of faculty and administrators.

★97 Millington, William G. *The Law and the College Student:
Justice in Evolution.* St. Paul, Minn.: West, 1979. 629
pages.

This book is used primarily as a reference book for active administrators and a text for prospective administrators. Although
most law texts consist primarily of cases, the majority of Millington's text is a narrative summary of important legal issues
in student-institution relationships. He synthesizes a large body
of case and statutory law, examining social and historical influences on judicial review of student-institution relationships,

the substantive and procedural requirements imposed by the courts, and numerous areas of student rights (such as those related to speech, assembly, publications, admissions, and discipline). The book also devotes a section to the institutional implications of the body of law protecting student rights. Millington's work is a thoughtful, useful survey and analysis of the significant issues in student-institution relationships.

98   Nordin, Virginia Davis. "The Contract to Educate: Toward a More Workable Theory of the Student-University Relationship." *Journal of College and University Law,* 1981–82, *8,* 141–181.

This article examines judicial approaches to the student-institution relationship. The author examines a spectrum of issues related to student academic and social conduct and describes the approach taken by courts in reviewing the decisions of faculty and administrators. She also suggests how contract theory can be useful to administrators seeking to clarify the relationship between the student and the institution. Fully comprehensible to the lay reader, the article presents a useful framework for administrators concerned about the creation or revision of policies regarding student rights and responsibilities.

99   Stark, Joan S., and Associates. *The Many Faces of Educational Consumerism.* Lexington, Mass.: Lexington Books, 1977. 224 pages.

This collection of writings provides a clear and concise overview of federal, state, and accreditation influences on relationships between students and colleges. Student legal rights are summarized briefly, and chapters are devoted to federal regulation of student financial aid, the federal role in enforcing fair practices and access to information, the state role in monitoring educational quality and planning, and the regulatory role of regional accrediting associations. Model grievance systems and recommended procedural protections are included. This is a useful summary of the "student consumer" issue for new administrators, especially those who will be involved in planning for accreditation reviews or responding to state regulation.

Resource Allocation at the Campus and State Levels

100 Mingle, James R., and Associates. *Challenges of Retrenchment: Strategies for Consolidating Programs, Cutting Costs, and Reallocating Resources.* San Francisco: Jossey-Bass, 1981. 394 pages.

For a complete description of this book, please see entry no. 410.

★**101** Olswang, Steven G. "Planning the Unthinkable: Issues in Institutional Reorganization and Faculty Reductions." *Journal of College and University Law,* 1982–83, *9,* 431–449.

This article provides a thorough analysis of the legal parameters within which institutional managers must operate when planning for the reduction of academic programs and the retrenchment of faculty. Olswang analyzes the case law related to this topic and synthesizes the considerations and procedures necessary to prepare a retrenchment program that will withstand judicial review. He describes the rights of faculty, the procedural protections that must be provided, and the kind of proof of financial exigency that institutions must expect to offer. The article is helpful for administrators, trustees, and university counsel who are considering the need for and the planning necessary to accomplish institutional retrenchment.

102 Preer, Jean L. *Lawyers v. Educators: Black Colleges and Desegregation in Public Higher Education.* Westport, Conn.: Greenwood Press, 1982. 278 pages.

This book traces the legal and social history of segregation in public higher education from the 1890 Morrill Act to the current *Adams* litigation, which seeks to dismantle dual systems of public higher education. The strategy of the plaintiffs, the arguments of the defendant states and colleges, and the impact of the litigation on public higher education in the South are analyzed. The author uses historical documents and interviews with participants in the *Adams* litigation to examine both sides of a thorny issue: desegregation of public higher education versus maintaining a special identity and role for black colleges. The actions of both the federal courts and the federal enforcement agencies (especially HEW) are described, and their impact on the colleges is discussed. Preer's book is a useful and thoughtful account of an important issue of which all educators and policy-makers should be aware.

Government Regulation and Institutional Mission

103 Edwards, Harry T. *Higher Education and the Unholy Crusade Against Governmental Regulation.* Cambridge, Mass.: Institute for Educational Management, Harvard University, 1980. 51 pages.

This essay provides an important counterargument to O'Neil's 1975 article (no. 107). Edwards, a respected federal judge and higher education law expert, criticizes opponents of federal regulation of higher education. An especially significant section of his work describes judicial deference to academic decision making (the ''academic abstention'' doctrine) in faculty personnel decisions, institutional financial exigency, and student academic evaluation. Edwards points out that colleges prevail in most litigation, then analyzes the motives for higher education to resist regulation and the reasons why regulation is necessary. Although the essay has a strong point of view, it provides a balanced treatment, and it can help administrators and policy-makers be aware of the arguments made on either side of this important issue.

104 Gaffney, Edward McGlynn, Jr., and Moots, Philip R. *Government and Campus: Federal Regulation of Religiously Affiliated Higher Education.* Notre Dame, Ind.: University of Notre Dame Press, 1982. 248 pages.

This report of a foundation-funded study analyzes the impact of court decisions and federal laws on religiously affiliated colleges and universities. Issues addressed include using religious preference in employment decisions, student admissions and discipline, the rights of handicapped and addicted individuals, labor law issues, and a consideration of the implications for these institutions of Title IX's prohibition on classification or discrimination on the basis of gender. The book provides a useful overview of the impact of judicial and federal regulations on church-related colleges. It also raises troublesome issues of church-state separation, religious autonomy, the First Amendment's protection of the free exercise of religion, and other problems unique to church-affiliated colleges and universities. An earlier book by the same authors, *Church and Campus* (1979), examined the impact of judicial decisions on similar issues, while a later book, *State and Campus* (1983), provides a state-by-state analysis of state regulation of religiously affiliated colleges.

★**105** Hobbs, Walter C. (ed.). *Government Regulation of Higher Education.* Cambridge, Mass.: Ballinger, 1978. 117 pages.

This collection of essays examines the impact and implications of government regulation of colleges and universities from a spectrum of viewpoints. It provides an excellent synthesis of the arguments for and against government regulation, with particular attention to increasing institutional fairness and sensitivity to heretofore neglected individuals and interests while maintaining academe's ability to perform its educational, social, and cultural mission. Although government regulation has waned somewhat in the past few years, this book should be required reading for administrators and policymakers.

106 O'Neil, Robert M. "Private Universities and Public Law." *Buffalo Law Review,* 1969–70, *19,* 155–193.

The author discusses the legal distinctions between public and private colleges and analyzes the degree to which federal court decisions recognize the character and functions of private institutions. He examines the public purposes of private higher education and suggests an analytical approach for determining the degree to which courts may review decisions made by private institutions. The article is a useful discussion of the important distinctions between private and public institutions in terms of judicial review of institutional actions. It is especially significant for those policymakers who wish to become better informed concerning both the philosophical and the legal arguments for the autonomy of private colleges and universities.

107 O'Neil, Robert M. "God and Government at Yale: The Limits of Federal Regulation of Higher Education." *University of Cincinnati Law Review*, 1975, *44*, 525–547.

A college administrator/attorney examines constitutional limits on federal regulation of colleges and universities. The author examines the relationship between federal funding and regulation, the conflict of federal regulation with individual rights, and the collision between academic autonomy and federal regulation. He provides a good overview, fully comprehensible to nonlawyers, of the arguments to limit federal regulation. This article is probably the best known and most frequently quoted attack on excessive federal regulation of higher education, although it is not a polemic against all federal involvement. The article should be read in conjunction with the Edwards essay (no. 103).

6

Richard T. Ingram
Linda E. Henderson

Institutional Governing Boards and Trustees

More has been written about the roles and responsibilities of governing boards and of lay trustees, regents, curators, overseers, visitors, and governors within the past decade than was written during the preceding thirty-four decades of American higher education. College and university administrators, faculty, educational researchers, students of higher education and organizational behavior, and, happily, trustees themselves are all contributing to this growing body of literature. The reasons for this rapid growth are instructive, and we will explore them as we consider this unique feature of institutional governance and annotate some of the literature that has helped to describe it. We will also suggest some new directions for exploration, gaps where new research can make a difference.

At least three features of American higher education make it a distinctive enterprise in the world: its sheer magnitude and diversity, with more than 3,000 institutions of different types and sizes enrolling some 12 million students (8.8 million full-time equivalent); its emphasis on access and opportunity, whereby anyone with a high school diploma can secure admission to a college or university, usually within reasonable traveling distance and cost; and its form of control, in which some 2,237 governing boards and 48,000 men and women, who claim no special competence as educators, willingly share awesome responsibilities as unpaid volunteers for the institutions they serve. No country in the world has sustained this tradition of citizen-trustee

114

participation in virtually all of its institutions in both the non-profit and the for-profit sectors.

J. L. Zwingle, in his excellent summary of the evolution of lay governing boards (1980), reminds us that

> Even though history in itself may not prove anything, failure to understand the evolution of a system such as trusteeship can lead to false expectations about it or to misconceptions of alternatives to it. Thus the importance of lay trusteeship for American higher education arises from certain underlying principles that were present at the beginning of the American story and that bear on the future of education and the nation itself [p. 15].

Zwingle cites two basic principles in the American ethos that led to our reliance on external boards of control in education and other social institutions. The first of these is the belief that monopolization of power by anyone is a threat to the public good. The second is that education is too vital to the public interest to be allowed to rely totally on faculty for its governance.

Trustees and governing boards enjoyed a long period of relative obscurity before the 1960s, when students began to ask probing questions: Who are trustees? What are their purposes and their authority? What interests do they represent? How do we gain access to them? Students demanded answers to these and related questions, and boards found themselves involved in resolving disputes involving student behavior. Harold L. Hodgkinson's (1971) review of the literature on governance describes this period and marks the transition from the "old" to the "new" literature.

Development of the Literature

Prior to the early seventies, the literature focused extensively on the effects of student unrest and the Vietnam War on trustees, trusteeship, and institutional governance. Thereafter, a host of other demographic, economic, social, and political

factors came into play as educators and students of higher education probed the responsibilities of volunteer trustees and governing boards.

The sixties witnessed more of an increase in the number
of Americans aged fourteen to twenty-four than in the preceding
seven decades. The result was both a massive expansion of
educational opportunities and the requirement that trustees accept much more public scrutiny.

The seventies kept up the pressure on governing boards as
challenges from external sources multiplied in the face of competing demands for limited dollars. Government at all levels, the state
of the national economy, the courts, and new statewide coordinating commissions (as well as old ones with new muscle) all called
for greater accountability and more efficiency. Trustees found
themselves on the same hot seat as presidents and chancellors.

The eighties have brought more of the same, with the
added challenge of a downturn in student enrollment through
the early nineties. Trustees, along with their chief executives,
find themselves caught between internal dissent and continuing external pressures. Most recently, the literature reflects such
issues as the nation's penchant for open meeting laws in the
public sector (thanks largely to the fallout from Watergate) and
the liability insurance crisis.

The concept of lay trusteeship is a subject ripe for cultivation and thoughtful study as we seek the means to strengthen
an imperfect instrument that has nonetheless, on the whole,
served the public trust with distinction. How can trustees be
urged to reach for higher levels of performance and effectiveness
and at the same time support strong chief executive leadership?

Both friends and critics of lay trusteeship have tried in
their writing to explain the nature of "trusteeship" and suggest how it can be strengthened, but we must distinguish it from
the still popular term "governance." John Corson coined the
latter term more than twenty years ago in the revised edition
of *The Governance of Colleges and Universities*. He states that

> Use of the terms "govern" and "governance" is gen-
> erally reserved for consideration of the functioning of
> institutions of higher education. Those terms are used

to describe the process of "deciding" and of seeing to it
that the decisions made are executed. That process involves—in the college or university—students, teachers,
administrators, trustees, and, increasingly, individuals
and agencies outside the institution in establishing policies, rules and regulations, and in collaborating to carry
out those guides to action. The extensive diffusion of
authority and the consequent need for collaboration warrant the use of a distinctive term [1965, p. 20].

Trusteeship, then, is a part of the governance process
and therefore should not be considered synonymous with it. In
academic institutions we sometimes lose sight of the fact that
it is not only the trustees or the governing board who make decisions; many others are involved. Put another way, we must be
careful to distinguish between the study of trusteeship and the
study of governance. Both are important, but they are different.

Most of the literature on governing boards and trustees
is, unfortunately, descriptive rather than analytical. It is interesting to note that some 50 relevant doctoral dissertations were
abstracted in *Dissertation Abstracts,* and 122 articles and mono-
raphs are in the ERIC Clearinghouse on Higher Education
system, for the period 1981–1985. Their topics are diverse. Not
surprisingly, the method of data collection used in most of them
was the questionnaire survey.

Clearly, the subjects of trustees and trusteeship are much
more popular among writers and researchers than they used to be.
Hodgkinson's (1971) review of the governance literature prior to
1971, for example, cites 291 references—but only eight of them
employ the words "trustee" or "governing board" in their titles.

Framework

Surveying the new and growing literature related to institutional governing boards has required discriminating choices
among many strong contributions. We have chosen to include
only the more substantial and representative monographs and
books. Many of these have been published by the Association
of Governing Boards of Universities and Colleges.

The annotations in this chapter are grouped into five categories: Board Functions and Responsibilities; Types of Institutional Governing Boards; Board Membership; Board Organization; and Current Issues. We first offer some observations about each category to provide some context for the annotations.

Board Functions and Responsibilities. In this section we have placed literature that addresses the general responsibilities of governing boards. Particularly in the case of the citations marked with stars, it includes work that comprehensively summarizes the way trustees and boards fit into the larger governance process. Readers should note that both presidential search and performance assessment and the distinction between policy and administration are covered more fully in Chapter Twenty.

This section's citations stress that the fundamental responsibilities of governing boards are shared by trustees and boards across all types of institution; the important differences between institutions appear in the way those responsibilities are met. Some functions receive more or less emphasis depending on institutional setting, especially depending on whether the institution is publicly or independently controlled.

Types of Institutional Governing Boards. The public sector has at least four types of institutional setting and, therefore, styles of trusteeship: the two-year community college; the four-year college or university; the single-campus institution; and the multicampus institution or state system. Each has a character of its own. The independent or private sector has two major types: the nonsectarian college or university and the sectarian or church-related institution. It is true that the lines between "public" and "private" institutions, and between "church-related" and "nonsectarian" institutions, have become blurred. However, the conduct of trusteeship does vary significantly among these traditional categories, as the literature cited in this section illustrates.

Board Membership. The process of trustee selection and the composition of governing boards also vary by type of institution, particularly between the public and independent sectors. Key literature cited in this section covers students, faculty, and alumni trusteeship issues.

Board Organization. A board will be only as effective as the manner in which the trustees are organized to accomplish their work. Organization issues such as committee structure, bylaws, meetings, and the question of sunshine or open-meeting legislation are covered in this section. As the literature notes, board size and institutional settings often affect frequency of meetings and committee structure. For example, whereas the trustees of a medium-sized liberal arts college will typically meet quarterly as a full board, the smaller and very local board for a community college will most likely meet monthly. The former is likely to have an elaborate committee system, while the two-year college board is likely to operate as a "committee of the whole." The area of board organization is particularly ripe for more analytical study by students of trusteeship.

Current Issues. Of the many possible current issues that could be covered, we chose five that promise to be with us for some time to come. They are trustee liability and conflict of interest; the role of trustees and boards in coping with retrenchment and financial exigency; the board's role as a buffer in protecting the institution from unreasonable political intrusion; social issues such as divestiture and the South Africa situation; and the role of trustees in encouraging cooperation rather than conflict between public and independent institutions. We can expect to witness a growing body of literature in these areas as trustees and regents attempt to respond to new social and political issues that confront their institutions.

Commentary on the Literature

In spite of the extensive and growing literature on academic trusteeship, widespread misunderstanding about the functions and performance of governing boards remains. This confusion is shared by many trustees (although probably fewer than before), faculties, administrators, students, public policymakers, and the general public. Old stereotypes prevail, and a "we-they" antipathy between faculty and trustees or between students and trustees is not uncommon. Few trustees really feel good about the quality of communication between themselves and their constituencies. Can creative solutions to this problem be found that are acceptable to everyone, including chief executives? Can linkages between trustees and administrators be found or created without undermining executive leadership or trustee responsibility for final decisions on major policy issues?

The question of trustee-constituency communication is just one of many areas that could profitably be explored in future literature and research. For example, almost nothing has been done to document the amount of money trustees give annually to their institutions out of personal funds or how much they generate from other sources through their direct involvement. Not all trustees are able to or expected to give large sums, of course, but rising expectations in nearly every institutional setting call for trustees to give *something;* their example is important. The myths about trustee ''giving'' and ''getting'' should be studied. Which institutions are the most successful in fundraising, and what seems to make the greatest difference in success insofar as boards are concerned?

Many other issues also need to be addressed. Most of the time, the best trustees are the ones who are busiest in their own careers. How much can we expect of such persons? As institutions have grown larger and more complex, the responsibilities of trustees and boards for ensuring high quality in educational programs have become increasingly ambiguous. How can these responsibilities be clarified? With a continuing downturn in student enrollment and difficult budgetary conditions affecting so many institutions, chief executives realize that boards must be better informed and more willing to help make qualitative financial decisions. What information do they need? And what decisions should they make? In general, how are boards getting involved in academic affairs? How is their role changing, and how do these changes affect faculty, students, and the trustees themselves?

Accreditation is another important topic. Trustees today are better informed about the process of institutional and academic program accreditation than they used to be. It was common ten or twenty years ago for trustees not to see copies of final visiting team reports and recommendations, for example. Some regional accrediting associations now include carefully selected trustees on visiting teams, thereby potentially benefiting everyone, including the trustees and the institutions they serve. Although it remains the host chief executive's prerogative to decide whether a trustee should be added to the visiting committee, more and more CEOs see the value of such a practice. What are the experiences of trustees on accrediting teams thus far? How are issues of trusteeship and institutional governance addressed as part of the current accreditation process? What are accrediting associations doing to strengthen trustee and board performance, and is it working?

Trustees also face new ambiguities in the area of public policy. Especially in the independent college sector, presidents and chancellors have carried advocacy for their institutions to state and national capitols. Should trustees do the same? There is ample evidence that, of all the types of trustees and institutions, community college boards have been the most active politically—often with great success in past years. Witness, for example, their tendency to form their own state lobbying associations. To be sure, some chief executives and governmental relations officers have expressed legitimate concern about trustee assertiveness in this area; after all, unilateral trustee initiative "with friends in high places" can sometimes do more harm than good, and the trustees who have the greatest desire to move in political circles are sometimes not the best individuals to speak on behalf of their institutions.

Some institutions have selected influential trustees to act as public policy advocates. What have their experiences been? Have such board members improved public policy toward higher education as a whole, or has their successful involvement at the state level been confined to institutional or sector self-interest? How can trustees be more helpful as advocates for the entire industry?

Future contributions to the literature promise to be both interesting and useful in improving public understanding of the way trustees and boards function. Hopefully, too, they will be more prescriptive and less descriptive of sound policies and practices; more analytical and less theoretical; more reflective of what we now know about organizational and small group behavior, less independent of other disciplines.

More empirical research on the way boards and trustees ultimately make decisions will be particularly welcomed. We need current research with the thoroughness of the 1973 study by Paltridge and his associates (no. 120), which analyzed more than 7,000 individual actions as revealed in the minutes of some 100 meetings held by twenty governing boards of public institutions.

Trustees and their role in institutional governance provide a fertile area for thoughtful observation and study. Much remains to be done.

References

Corson, J. J. *The Governance of Colleges and Universities.* (Rev. ed.) New York: McGraw-Hill, 1965.
Hodgkinson, H. L. *Campus Governance: The Amazing Thing Is That It Works at All.* AAHE-ERIC Higher Education Research Report no. 11. Washington, D.C.: American Association for Higher Education, 1971.
Zwingle, J. L. "Evolution of Lay Governing Boards." In Richard T. Ingram and Associates, *Handbook of College and University Trusteeship: A Practical Guide for Trustees, Chief Executives, and Other Leaders Responsible for Developing Effective Governing Boards.* San Francisco: Jossey-Bass, 1980.

Board Functions and Responsibilities

108 Academy for Educational Development. *Improving Endowment Management.* Washington, D.C.: Association of Governing Boards of Universities and Colleges, 1985. 28 pages.

This study details endowment practices at twenty-three institutions and recommends strategies to strengthen endowment management policies. It concludes that strong trustee interest and involvement, the use of external professional investment managers, and the use of independent consultants to evaluate managerial performance are important factors in improving the management of endowments. The study's findings also indicate that institutions that employ independent consultants, multiple investment managers, and a systematic approach to policies and endowment management practices perform significantly better than do institutions that take narrower approaches. Illustrated with numerous charts and tables, this monograph considers the pros and cons of different investment strategies, offers suggestions for avoiding conflicts of interest, and discusses the advantages of disciplined spending plans. Its findings should assist trustees, business officers, development officers, and college and university auditors to monitor the performance of institutional endowments more effectively. It includes sample guidelines and illustrative questions that trustees should ask.

109 Association of Governing Boards of Universities and Colleges. *Pocket Publications Series.* Various authors, publication dates, and lengths.

The Association of Governing Boards (AGB) publishes a series of pocket publications, each of which focuses on a specific board responsibility. These publications summarize the major issues related to each topic and provide informed perspectives and advice from individuals knowledgeable about trusteeship and institutional governance. The series includes titles on trustee responsibilities, orientation and development programs, fundraising, resource management, the relationship between the board chairperson and the president, planning, endowment management, accreditation, advisory committees, improving board effectiveness, and many other subjects. These short treatises can serve as useful guides to board members, presidents, and others who desire to get a quick, general overview of specific trusteeship issues.

110 Association of Governing Boards of Universities and Colleges. *Self-Study Criteria for Governing Boards.* Washington, D.C.: Association of Governing Boards of Universities and Colleges, 1980. (Number of pages varies.)

This self-study questionnaire is designed to assist governing boards in assessing their membership, organization, and performance. Criteria focus on such issues as institutional mission and educational policy, board membership, board organization, institutional planning, financial support and management, board/chief executive relations, board/student relations, board/faculty relations, and the board as a court of appeal. The survey form includes a separate Trustee Audit to help individual trustees assess their own contributions to the board's work. Different versions of the criteria have been developed for independent and public colleges and universities, public multicampus systems, coordinating boards, community colleges, and theological schools. Although the questionnaire is intended for use by college and university boards of trustees, it can easily be adapted to meet the needs of other not-for-profit organizations and agencies.

111 Association of Governing Boards of Universities and Colleges and National Association of College and University Business Officers. *Financial Responsibilities of Governing Boards of Colleges and Universities.* Washington, D.C.: Association of Governing Boards of Universities and Colleges and National Association of College and University Business Officers, 1985. 114 pages.

This monograph examines the financial planning and management responsibilities of college and university governing boards. It traces the continuous flow of an institution's financial resources through its various programs, including acquisition of funds, allocation of operation expenditures, and protection and enhancement of capital. It stresses the use of financial accounting information for managerial rather than fiduciary purposes; notes the relevance of financial outcomes to program decisions; discusses policy matters relating to financial decisions; suggests ways to use accounting information for assessing performance in achieving objectives; and proposes some key financial indicators. A short guide to ''fund accounting'' is also included. Designed as a reference manual, this volume is directed foremost to members of governing boards, since it focuses on financial management at the policy level. However, chief business officers, campus chief executives, and others who provide financial information to their boards or are otherwise involved in making financial decisions in higher education institutions will also find it a useful resource.

★**112** Chait, Richard P., and Associates. *Trustee Responsibility for Academic Affairs.* Washington, D.C.: Association of Governing Boards of Universities and Colleges, 1984. 144 pages.

This study focuses on the board's responsibility for overseeing an institution's educational program. The authors examine the specific role and duties of the academic affairs committee; offer guidelines that define the committee's perspective on academic issues and its role in setting educational policy; review the need to establish sound faculty personnel policies; analyze academic program approval, review, and closure; and delineate the complex components of an academic budget. The monograph also includes highlights of a national survey of 600 college and university trustees and presidents on trustee involvement in academic affairs and summaries of eight in-depth case studies that examine different approaches to trustee participation in academic affairs. The book is tailored for college and university officials charged with overseeing academic programs, personnel, budgets, and policies. The authors definitely feel that boards of trustees should participate in academic affairs; the question is how they can do so most effectively.

113 Frantzreb, Arthur C. (ed.). *Trustee's Role in Advancement.* New Directions for Institutional Advancement, no. 14. San Francisco: Jossey-Bass, 1981. 103 pages.

This volume examines the importance of trustee participation in institutional advancement. Its various chapters focus on the responsibility of board members to both give on their own account and attract other private gifts; the role of trustees as ambassadors to important institutional constituencies; preparing the board and training it for action; identifying, selecting, and deploying financially strong and influential trustees; and understanding trustee giving and enhancing board motivation and

support. Specific suggestions for improving the working relationship among the governing board, the president, and the chief
development officer are offered, and illustrative guidelines,
checklists, and action steps are included to assist each figure in
realizing the importance of full trustee participation. Although
this book is intended for those persons most closely aligned with
an institution's fund-raising efforts, it should also be useful to
other administrators and students of advancement who desire
to more completely understand the amount of time, effort, and
board commitment needed to plan and execute a successful
development program.

★**114** Ingram, Richard T., and Associates. *Handbook of College and University Trusteeship: A Practical Guide for Trustees,
Chief Executives, and Other Leaders Responsible for Developing Effective Governing Boards.* San Francisco: Jossey-Bass,
1980. 514 pages.

This book provides a comprehensive resource on all aspects of
college and university trusteeship. It carries information on the
full range of trustee responsibilities, including institutional planning, fund-raising, resource management, academic program
review, tenure and personnel decisions, faculty bargaining, and
selection and assessment of the chief executive. It addresses issues
affecting governing board operation, including selecting and
orienting trustees, organizing the board, providing information
to board members, and strengthening relations between trustees
and administrators. In addition, it examines the major policy
issues facing trustees and administrators in the 1980s and beyond
and offers practical advice from legal authorities on avoiding
conflicts of interest and minimizing potential personal and institutional liabilities. This book is particularly valuable to both
new and experienced trustees, but it is also useful to chief executives, board secretaries, and other administrators who work
closely with the board. It synthesizes what is known about governing boards and how they fulfill their various obligations.

115 Kaiser, Harvey H. *Crumbling Academe: Solving the Capital Renewal and Replacement Dilemma.* Washington, D.C.: Association of Governing Boards of Universities and Colleges, 1984. 70 pages.

This book addresses the issues surrounding deferred maintenance of higher education's physical assets. Recommendations are offered both for policymakers at the national level and for administrators and governing boards at the campus level. Kaiser discusses the need to select priorities for capital renewal and replacement and presents three methods for establishing annual levels of funding: the annual operating budget, external sources, and creative financing alternatives. He concludes by offering suggestions for building constituencies and policy recommendations to secure financial support to meet higher education's capital renewal and replacement needs. This guidebook is written specifically to illustrate for trustees the range of their responsibilities to monitor and maintain their institution's physical plant and capital assets. Presidents, physical plant administrators, and business officers should also find it useful.

116 Mueller, Robert Kirk. *Behind the Boardroom Door.* New York: Crown, 1984. 242 pages.

This book describes life in the corporate boardroom. It is written in entertaining, witty, authoritative, and occasionally acerbic prose. Mueller reminds us that directorship is a distinctly human enterprise and is more art than science, more similar than dissimilar in different types of institutions, and more a matter of mystique than tangible. The same issues, the same misunderstandings of board functions, and the same public exaggeration of directors' freedom of action can be found in the for-profit and the not-for-profit sectors. Mueller suggests that no one model of organizational governance should be emulated, least of all the corporate, given its numerous shortcomings; the same ambiguities that shroud higher education trusteeship hang over corporate directorship. This special treatise on boardsmanship challenges the myth that higher education governance should closely imitate the corporate model. It is "must" reading for all college and university trustees and chief executives, in part because it confirms that what happens behind the corporate boardroom door is precisely what happens behind the academy's boardroom door.

★**117** Nason, John W. *The Nature of Trusteeship: The Role and Responsibilities of College and University Boards.* Washington, D.C.: Association of Governing Boards of Universities and Colleges, 1982. 114 pages.

This book examines the role and responsibilities of college and university trustees in the last quarter of the twentieth century and assesses the problems and opportunities now facing governing boards. It focuses on thirteen major trustee responsibilities and on fourteen organizational factors that define an effective board. Nason offers a brief history of lay trusteeship as well as a clarification of the demanding role of trustees. He also addresses the unique needs of state systems and coordinating boards as well as the legal liabilities of trustees. This volume is "must" reading for all trustees and chief executives. It is also an excellent primer for other academic administrators and researchers who seek a clearer understanding of the role lay trusteeship assumes in American higher education.

118 Nason, John W. *Presidential Assessment: A Guide to the Periodic Review of the Performance of Chief Executives.* Washington, D.C.: Association of Governing Boards of Universities and Colleges, 1984. 109 pages.

For a full description of this book, please see entry no. 523.

119 Nason, John W. *Presidential Search: A Guide to the Process of Selecting and Appointing College and University Presidents.* (Rev. ed.) Washington, D.C.: Association of Governing Boards of Universities and Colleges, 1984. 114 pages.

For a full description of this book, please see entry no. 524.

★120 Paltridge, James G., Hurst, Julie, and Morgan, Anthony. *Boards of Trustees: Their Decision Patterns.* Berkeley: Center for Research and Development in Higher Education, University of California, 1973. 90 pages.

This report examines the scope of trustee decision making at public four-year colleges, universities, and multicampus systems. Twenty governing boards, representing a cross-section of single- and multicampus institutions, were surveyed concerning the volume and range of board actions and decision-making patterns, as revealed through the minutes of approximately 100 board meetings. More than 7,000 individual trustee actions are classified into ten subject areas. Eighty percent of these fit readily into four categories: personnel, business and finance, physical plant, and academic programs. According to the authors, trustee decision making in public institutions is primarily pro forma and focuses on minutiae more often than on important policy matters. Paltridge and his colleagues include data on board and institutional characteristics; the volume and range of matters considered by boards; policy, including operating and delegated decisions; and board decision patterns. The findings of this analytical study should be particularly useful to those interested in learning more about the governing boards of public colleges and universities, how they function, and how they make decisions.

121 Pray, Francis C. (ed.). *Handbook for Educational Fund Raising: A Guide to Successful Principles and Practices for Colleges, Universities, and Schools.* San Francisco: Jossey-Bass, 1981. 442 pages.

For a full description of this book, please see entry no. 228.

122 Zwingle, J. L. *Effective Trusteeship: Guidelines for Board Members.* Washington, D.C.: Association of Governing Boards of Universities and Colleges, 1985. 45 pages.

This booklet is a concise introduction to the basic elements of lay trusteeship in higher education. Zwingle focuses on the essential duties of the individual trustee as well as on the responsibilities of the board as a whole. He addresses the important issues of board organization and bylaws, agenda setting, presidential assessment, policy and administration, and board self-assessment. In addition, he offers practical suggestions for improving various board functions and establishing good relationships with students, faculty, and the general public. This treatise reduces the ambiguities of board functions and thus is a valuable resource for trustees, college presidents, and other campus administrators.

Types of Institutional Governing Boards

123 Education Commission of the States. *State Postsecondary Education Structures Handbook, 1986.* Denver, Colo.: Education Commission of the States, 1986. 173 pages.

This resource includes the results of a survey of the legal structures, responsibilities, and membership of state coordinating and governing agencies and public institutional governing boards in postsecondary education. Tabular data and brief narratives are provided for each of the fifty states and the District of Columbia on the structure of each of the statewide coordinating/ governing boards; the scope of each agency's responsibilities; the legal bases for the agencies' authority; number of institutions governed; and general board membership and selection procedures, including involvement of students and faculty. The book is a valuable resource for students, faculty, state policymakers, trustees, and presidents. It includes in a single volume the data that researchers and practitioners seek in comparing legal structures, responsibilities, composition, and selection procedures for state coordinating and governing boards. The data are updated every three years.

124 Petty, Gary Frank (ed.). *Active Trusteeship for a Changing Era.* New Directions for Community Colleges, no. 51. San Francisco: Jossey-Bass, 1985. 114 pages.

This book examines the scope and limitations of trustee authority and provides guidance on using that authority. It offers advice to both the new and the experienced trustee in such areas as working with administrators and faculty; representing institutional interests to legislative agencies, accrediting boards, the media, and diverse college constituencies; and strengthening trustee selection and development through the aid of state and national community college associations. The authors stress the dangers of allowing the special interests of individual trustees to undermine the effectiveness of the board as a whole; explain why trustees should curtail their role in such areas as personnel decisions and collective bargaining; and highlight the growing representation of women and minorities on boards and the impact of their participation in community college leadership. This resource is helpful to trustees and presidents and to others who work closely with community college boards. It offers an overview of the qualifications needed by board members and delineates their proper roles and responsibilities.

★**125** Wood, Miriam M. *Trusteeship in the Private College.* Baltimore, Md.: Johns Hopkins University Press, 1986. 180 pages.

This study reports on fifty in-depth interviews with trustees and presidents from ten unnamed private liberal arts colleges located in four states. In confidential conversations with the president, the chairperson of the board of trustees, and three other members of each board, Wood develops a clear idea of what trustees actually do during the often substantial amount of time they devote to college affairs. The case studies also reveal each board's informal decision-making processes, power structure, and relations with the press. A brief overview of the trustee mandate and role and a summary of recent events that redefine that role are also presented. Wood focuses on president/board relationships, using illustrative case histories; discusses the board and its members as discrete subunits of their collegiate organizations; identifies three models of board behavior; and examines the ambiguous distinction between policy and administration. This volume is a valuable resource to trustees of private colleges and universities as well as to presidents and other administrators who work closely with the board.

Board Membership

126 Andersen, Charles. *AGB Special Report: Composition of Governing Boards, 1985: A Survey of College and University Boards.* Washington, D.C.: Association of Governing Boards of Universities and Colleges, 1986. 43 pages.

This study updates *Composition of College and University Governing Boards,* a similar survey published in 1977. Although it includes many of the same questions asked in the earlier study, this new volume was expanded to consider such characteristics as the professional background of board members; the types and number of other boards (both profit and not-for-profit) on which these people serve; and constituent representation. The report compares 1985 and 1977 data, highlights selected characteristics of board members, and shows that trustee demographics have changed only slightly over the eight-year period. This comprehensive study should be particularly useful to researchers and students of governance in reviewing the age, sex, race, occupation, and educational background of the 48,000 people who govern higher education. Numerous charts, graphs, and tables reinforce and highlight the narrative data.

127 Association of Governing Boards of Universities and Colleges. *Recommendations for Improving Trustee Selection at Public Colleges and Universities* and *Recommendations for Improving Trustee Selection at Private Colleges and Universities.* Washington, D.C.: Association of Governing Boards of Universities and Colleges, 1980. 54 and 46 pages, respectively.

These parallel reports by the Association of Governing Boards of Universities and Colleges offer recommendations on ways to improve the identification and selection of trustees at both public and private colleges and universities. The report for public institutions includes eighteen recommendations; the report for private institutions includes fourteen recommendations. Each offers an overview of the selection process currently used by the respective institutional type and recommends strongly that an effective nominating or screening committee be established and given clear responsibilities. Both reports are useful to those persons or groups responsible for appointing, electing, or recruiting prospective board members. The recommendations are presented as guidelines to assist governors, legislators, and self-perpetuating boards.

Board Organization

128 Association of Governing Boards of Universities and Colleges. *AGB Standing Committee Series.* Various authors, publication dates, and lengths.

AGB has nine new publications, similar in format to its *Pocket Publications Series,* that focus on the role and responsibilities of key governing board standing committees. These booklets, varying in length from ten to twenty pages, describe the specific duties of a board's typical standing committees and offer suggestions and guidelines for enhancing their effectiveness. The current titles are *The Executive Committee, The Nominating Committee, The Audit Committee, The Academic Affairs Committee, The Development Committee, The Buildings and Grounds Committee, The Investment Committee, The Student Affairs Committee,* and *The Finance Committee.* Reinforcing the concept that most of the work of governing boards should be accomplished in committee, these publications offer performance standards that trustees, key staff, and students of trusteeship will find useful.

129 Association of Governing Boards of Universities and Colleges. *Illustrative Bylaws for Independent Colleges.* Washington, D.C.: Association of Governing Boards of Universities and Colleges, 1980. 16 pages.

Bylaws are more than a legal formality—they are the framework upon which an institution is governed. AGB's *Illustrative Bylaws* offer sample wording on such matters as size of the board, length of term, mandatory retirement, emeritus or honorary trustees, and frequency of meetings for independent colleges and universities engaged in bylaw revision. Also included are longer, more detailed descriptions of the role and responsibilities of various standing committees and of the president, board chairperson, and other key board officers. Sample indemnification, conflict

of interest, and "discrimination prohibited" clauses are provided. This document is intended to serve primarily as a guide
regarding the kinds of issues and subjects that independent college and university governing boards should consider incorporating into their bylaws. Certain sections may also be useful
to public institutions and other not-for-profit boards. Professional staff, attorneys, chief executives, and members of bylaw
revision committees will find it valuable.

★**130** Cleveland, Harlan. *AGB Special Report: The Costs and
Benefits of Openness: Sunshine Laws and Higher Education.*
Washington, D.C.: Association of Governing Boards of
Universities and Colleges, 1985. 58 pages.

This study of the impact of sunshine laws on college and university governance assesses the expanding importance of information as a resource and provides a detailed explanation of the
key issues that are most directly affected by open meeting laws,
including presidential selection. Cleveland elaborates on the concept of the "trilemma": the inevitable conflict between the
public's right to know, the individual's right to privacy, and
the organization's mandate to do its job in the public interest.
The sunshine laws of all fifty states and their relative degrees
of openness are briefly annotated; relevant case laws and the
opinions of state attorneys general are surveyed; and summaries
of in-depth interviews with numerous individuals in six states—
Florida, Montana, Minnesota, Iowa, Texas, and Pennsylvania—
are provided. This monograph illuminates the debate about the
structure of openness, including such considerations as relative
costs and benefits, effectiveness in getting things done, and the
conflicting aims of people who seek both participation and privacy. It should be useful to members of public college and
university boards, state officials, and leaders in the news media
as they look at existing legislation and consider possible improvements.

Current Issues

131 Coons, Christopher A. *The Responses of Colleges and Universities to Calls for Divestment.* Washington, D.C.: Investor Responsibility Research Center, 1986. 148 pages.

Based on survey responses from 175 colleges and universities, this report examines the demands and directions of the student anti-apartheid movement, the responses of trustees and administrators, the divestment policies and actions of various institutions, and the reactions of corporations and alumni to divestment. Findings reveal that more colleges and universities adopted or revised their investment policies in 1985 than in all previous years combined. Coons offers commentary on the future of the divestment issue and the events and forces that could either end it or keep it current. This report is useful to trustees, presidents, students, and others concerned with apartheid and with divestment activities on American campuses. It is particularly valuable in illustrating the specific issues that are—or should be—of concern to board members.

132 Gardner, John W., Atwell, Robert H., and Berdahl, Robert O. *AGB Special Report: Cooperation and Conflict: The Public and Private Sectors in Higher Education.* Washington, D.C.: Association of Governing Boards of Universities and Colleges, 1985. 72 pages.

This monograph addresses the relationship between the public and private sectors of higher education. In the first chapter, Gardner provides a historical perspective on the recent conflict in some states; discusses the pluralism and diversity that have characterized American colleges and universities; and suggests that public-private college differences should be seen in the larger context of shared goals. Atwell provides a view from the national higher education associations in Washington and touches on federal policy. He discusses sources of institutional funding and competition for funds and for students. He also identifies a series of challenges that must be met effectively if harmony and mutual respect are to prevail. Berdahl reports on his findings from a survey of public and private colleges and universities in Pennsylvania, Illinois, Maryland, North Carolina, and New York. He provides information on the condition of relations between the sectors, the issues that join and divide the various institutions, and the policies and mechanisms that affect intersector relations at the state level. Using selected case studies, Berdahl offers several possible directions for action in the states that could lead to more constructive relations and reduce tensions and conflict. This report should be helpful to presidents, trustees, administrators, public officials, and others concerned about improving the relationship between public and private colleges and universities.

133 Johnson, Edward A., and Weeks, Kent M. "To Save a College: Independent College Trustees and Decisions on Financial Exigency, Endowment Use and Closure." *Journal of College and University Law*, 1986, *12* (4), 455–488.

This article examines the major legal issues surrounding trustee financial exigency decisions, the fiduciary duties of trustees to preserve institutional assets, and potential trustee liability for decisions to close an institution. The authors discuss each of these issues, including the ramifications and results of recent court decisions. According to the authors, actions taken by boards to resolve financial stress are increasingly being challenged in court; however, to date, relatively few lawsuits have evolved from trustees' decisions to declare financial exigency, terminate employment of tenured faculty, divert endowment income or principal for other purposes, or merge or close an institution. This article is of interest primarily to college and university trustees and to institutional legal counsel. Students, faculty, and other administrators will also benefit from the straightforward explanation of the board's basic fiduciary responsibilities.

134 Newman, Frank. *Choosing Quality: Building a Successful State-University Relationship.* Denver, Colo.: Education Commission of the States (forthcoming). About 80 pages.

This study focuses on the relationship between 125 major state universities and their respective states. Stressing that the relationships should be mutually constructive, Newman suggests that universities not only need adequate latitude and flexibility to achieve quality and preserve freedom of thought and scholarship; they also need a sufficiently active external force (in the form of the state) to ensure that they effectively meet the needs of the public in a changing society. Newman uses case studies that illustrate the complexities, risks, dangers, and idiosyncratic nature of the relationship between the states and their universities. He addresses such questions as these: How do the various states support their public universities, and how can those relationships be improved? What circumstances cause the failure of public policy and the diminishment of the quality and effectiveness of the university? What policies or strategies create a climate within which a state university will flourish? This study is of interest to trustees, chief executives, and other administrators of state institutions, as well as to state policy leaders, legislators, and others concerned with enhancing and improving state–state university relations. It encourages discussion, debate, and improved understanding of the various relationships among public universities and their states.

135 Weeks, Kent M. (ed.). *Legal Deskbook for Administrators of Independent Colleges and Universities.* Notre Dame, Ind.: Center for Constitutional Studies, University of Notre Dame, 1982. 400 pages.

This manual serves as a reference on a wide variety of legal matters that face administrators of independent colleges and universities. It emphasizes both preventive application of the law and problem solving, stressing the importance of intelligent planning to avoid costly litigation with private parties and needless confrontation with agencies of federal and state government.

Its primary focus is on such topics as governance, employment, physical facilities, students, and liability. Each chapter outlines a specific problem, identifies critical related issues, suggests some possible planning steps, and includes additional legal resources. This is a helpful resource for college and university administrators, higher education attorneys, and members of governing boards. It illuminates the litigious environment within which higher education functions and offers guidelines to help institutions avoid costly litigation.

7

Frank A. Schmidtlein

Administrative Structures and Decision-Making Processes

Following World War II, institutions of higher education in the United States grew rapidly in both numbers and size. Larger proportions of young people began to seek a higher education, the postwar rise in birth rates increased the potential number of students, and institutions expanded their research and public service roles. As campuses increased in number, size, and complexity, faculty and student roles in institutions changed, and states created multicampus systems and state-level coordinating and regulatory agencies to deal with the resulting issues.

Institutional growth was accompanied by an increasing interest in the effectiveness and efficiency of campus governance processes—the structures, policy formulation processes, and management practices employed to pursue institutional missions Around 1900, a literature on the character of organizations, primarily businesses and public agencies, had started to develop. Scholars and practitioners in higher education began to draw from this body of literature after World War II, employing its perspectives in descriptions and analyses of higher education governance and decision making.

Overview of the Field and Its Literature

This overview briefly traces the origins and development of the literature on higher education governance and decision

139

making and describes its current status. To begin with, the term *governance* has not been carefully or technically defined in the literature on higher education. Generally, the term has been taken to broadly encompass the structures, policies, and processes that institutions, or systems of institutions, employ to define and carry out their missions. Consequently, a comprehensive examination of the literature on governance could cover a broad range of topics, including organizational structures; policy formulation, planning, and decision-making processes; management techniques and processes; and finance arrangements. The term *decision making* typically is employed to describe the structures, processes, and techniques employed by persons in organizations to make choices among alternative policies and courses of action. Decision making, thus defined, is a subset of the area encompassed by governance. It is a primary focus of some higher education governance literature.

This chapter examines primarily those aspects of the literature that deal with governance structures and with decision-making processes that take place within such organizational contexts. These definitional restrictions still leave a large area for exploration, however—one that cannot be covered well in a single chapter. Consequently, the literature cited is that considered most important for understanding this topic. Readers should note that few other attempts have been made to organize and synthesize this body of literature, and many gaps exist in its coverage. Little attention has been given to linking notions of governance structures to concepts of decision making.

Evolution of Governance
Structures and Decision Processes

Institutions of higher education are among our oldest organizations. During their evolution they have developed distinctive patterns of organization and modes of decision making. Duryea (1973) traced the development of university organization from its medieval origins. Medieval universities instituted the use of many contemporary titles, such as *dean, provost, rector,* and *proctor*. They initiated the idea of formal courses and of the curriculum that leads to the baccalaureate and the master's and doctor's degrees. The corporate character of the university matured in England during the fifteenth and sixteenth centuries and served as a precedent for the organization of early colleges in the United States.

Historians such as Veysey (1965) and scholars such as Henry (1975) described major higher education organizational developments in the United States. These included development of both public and private institutions, authorization of land-grant colleges in 1862, and development of research universities in the late nineteenth century. In the twentieth century, following the Second World War, community colleges began to proliferate, multicampus systems emerged, and many states created coordinating agencies or statewide governing boards.

The growth of higher education enrollments after World War II produced a need for a larger number of institutions. Rather than establish more "freestanding" institutions, most states developed multicampus systems of higher education. These systems came about in two ways. In one pattern, a campus created satellite campuses in new locations, either establishing entirely new campuses or acquiring and transforming existing ones. These campuses reported to the administration of the "mother" campus or, more typically, to a central administration that was formed to govern the new system of campuses. The other pattern for developing campus systems was to create a new multicampus system headquarters to govern a group of existing freestanding campuses.

Clark (1963) noted four trends that accompanied higher education's growth: unitary forms of campus organization gave way to composite or federal structures, unified campus cultures gave way to multiple value systems, generalists gave way to specialized professionals, and decision making by consensus gave way to bureaucratic forms of coordination. The faculty became segmented through power flowing out toward departments. This individualism was enhanced by external agency grants and contracts that increased particular faculty members' leverage over the campus administration (Mooney, 1963).

During the post–World War II period, faculty power increased relative to that of the campus administration (Platt and Parsons, 1970). McConnell and Mortimer (1971) noted that faculty in many institutions obtained effective control over a wide range of academic affairs, including criteria for entrance to the profession; requirements for degrees; criteria for appointment, retention, and promotion; faculty work schedules; and course content. In recent years, moreover, faculty in a number of institutions have unionized, creating concerns about altering traditional forms of faculty organization and campus decision-making processes.

Institutions of higher education deal with sensitive beliefs and important public values. Consequently, their decision processes have been shielded to some extent from governmental political influences. This has been accomplished by interposing boards of trustees, with varying degrees of independence, between institutions and public officials. These boards of trustees have been given independence through various state constitutional and statutory provisions (Glenny and Dalglish, no. 143). In addition, concepts of academic freedom and institutional autonomy have been incorporated into laws that affect higher education. In recent years, a number of states have examined the autonomy and flexibility granted to institutions in response to concerns that they could not cope effectively with changing circumstances without the ability to react promptly to new opportunities and threats (Mingle and Associates, no. 49).

Sources of Governance and Decision Process Concepts

Writers on higher education governance and decision making have drawn their ideas primarily from earlier organizational literature that examined businesses and public agencies. Early writers such as Wilson (1887) and Gulick and Urwick (1937) were interested in organizational efficiency, which was typically defined in economic terms. Later authors such as Mayo (1933) took a broader view of efficiency, including noneconomic factors such as good human relations. Writers such as Simon (1945) viewed organizations as decision-making structures. Most early writers were heavily influenced by Weber's bureaucratic concepts of organizational structure (Gerth and Mills, 1946), but Ostrom (1974) criticized the bureaucratic assumptions underlying much of this literature. Describing what he termed "the intellectual crisis in American public administration," he contrasted concepts of bureaucratic efficiency with notions of controlling political power through systems of "checks and balances." Writers such as Katz and Kahn (1966) used the concept of "open systems," borrowed from the biological and physical sciences, to explain organizational governance and decision-making processes.

The literature on decision making in higher education draws heavily from writing in disciplines such as sociology, psychology, political science, economics, and applied mathematics. Historically, two broad strategies for decision making have emerged, one based on the paradigm of "marketplace" operations and the other on the paradigm of comprehensive organizational planning (Schmidtlein, 1974). Marketplace concepts have had a powerful influence on the way decision making is viewed in the United States, both in the economic sphere, with notions of free enterprise, and in the political sphere, with the idea of organizational checks and balances established to control the consequences of the "political marketplace."

In 1945 Herbert Simon produced his influential book, *Administrative Behavior*, which pointed out the time and knowledge constraints confronting administrators when they make decisions and the "satisficing" behavior that takes place as a result of these limitations. Since then, an extensive literature has developed on techniques for making "rational" decisions. This literature has been summarized by Friedland (1974). Georgiou (1973) criticized the notion that organizations seek goals, a tenet of much writing on decision making. Recent writings on decision processes stress their ambiguity (Cohen, March, and Olsen, no. 153) and the "loose coupling" among units that must act cooperatively (Weick, no. 8). A few authors have contrasted market and planning approaches to decision making, including Dahrendorf (1968), Etzioni (1967), and Schmidtlein (1974).

Development of Higher Education
Governance and Decision-Making Literature

Literature prescribing, describing, or analyzing the evolution and character of higher education governance and decision making appeared rather recently. Millett (no. 145) suggested that, in some respects, the story of college and university governance begins with Riesman's (1958) commentary about constraint and variety in American higher education. In 1960, Committee T on College and University Government of the American Association of University Professors set forth a statement of principles for faculty participation in university governance. That same year, Corson published a study of institutional practices. These efforts were followed by a good many commentaries, studies, and compilations of readings, among them Millett (1962); Perkins (1966); Demerath, Stephens, and Taylor (1967); Gross and Grambsch (1968); Goheen (1969); Howard and Franklin (1969); Hodgkinson and Meeth (1971); McConnell (1971); Baldridge (no. 344); Carnegie Commission on Higher Education (1973); and Perkins (1973). This literature tended to deal broadly with governance and decision making rather than dealing in great depth with organizational structures and decision processes.

Recent literature includes broad treatments of governance and decision making by scholars and practitioners such as Clark (no. 140) and Walker (no. 146); edited books with articles by various scholars, such as those by Sergiovanni and Corbally (1984), Bess (no. 159), and Peterson (1986); books reporting studies of governance structures, such as those of Helsabeck (no. 144) and Millett (no. 145); and books reporting research on various aspects of decision making, such as those by Cohen and March (no. 141) and Weick (no. 8).

In the 1960s, a great deal of attention was given to "rational" decision processes in organizations, borrowing techniques from microeconomics and applied mathematics. The development of computers and large data bases provided the means to utilize these techniques. Processes such as "program, planning and budget systems" (PPBS), "management by objectives" (MBO), and "zero-based budgeting" (ZBB) were designed to implement these decision-making perspectives and techniques. The Ford Research Program for Research in University Administration at the University of California, in the late 1960s and early 1970s, and the National Center for Higher Education Management Systems (NCHEMS), beginning in 1970, produced much literature on these approaches to decision making. Techniques for supporting decision making in higher education have been described by Hopkins and Massy (no. 303). By the 1970s, however, a reaction against "rational" decision processes became evident, based on problems in their implementation and on a growing body of literature on the constraints that affect decision making.

Framework for Organizing the Literature

The literature on institutional governance and decision making can be classified in many ways—for example, by stages of its development, theoretical perspectives and assumptions, and the numerous subtopics it addresses. The annotations in this chapter are somewhat arbitrarily divided into the following topics: (1) reviews of governance and decision process literature, (2) literature on campus governance structures, (3) literature on multicampus governance structures, (4) literature on campus faculty governance structures, (5) literature on institutional decision processes, and (6) books of readings on governance and decision making. These annotations do not include literature on the structure of governing boards, which is covered in Chapter Six. General comments on these categories follow.

Reviews of Governance and Decision Process Literature. No literature reviews exist that deal solely with campus organizational structures or campus decision-making processes. However, two recent reviews of higher education governance literature encompass, to a considerable extent, topics relevant to this chapter. One of these reviews is by March, a leading organizational theorist (no. 136), and the other is by Peterson, a noted scholar in the field of higher education governance (no. 137). These reviews discuss the principal literature in the field, the status of research in this area, and the need for integrated theories to guide further inquiry and scholarship.

Literature on Campus Governance Structures. This section contains a book by Helsabeck (no. 144), Millett (no. 145), and an article by Alpert (no. 138) that deal specifically with campus administrative organizational structures. A book by Cohen and March (no. 141) and a chapter from a book by Baldridge, Curtis, Ecker, and Riley (no. 139) describe metaphors used by administrators to picture campus structures and decision-making processes and also contain a broader discussion of governance. One chapter from a book by Etzioni (no. 142) examines the effects of a professional work force on organizational structure and decision processes. Two additional books, one by Walker, a practitioner (no. 146), and the other by sociologist and higher education scholar Clark (no. 140), provide broad descriptions of higher education governance and decision making. The first examines higher education governance systems around the world, utilizing a very comprehensive synthesis of current organization theory. The other draws on current organization theory and a broad range of experience to provide practical advice on campus governance. Another book, by Glenny and Dalglish (no. 143), describes the legal relationship between states and universities, which affects university governance structures and decision processes.

Literature on Multicampus Governance Structures. The literature on governance of multicampus systems is sparse and becoming dated. The most comprehensive and research-based literature on this topic is contained in the books by Lee and Bowen (nos. 147 and 148) included in the annotations.

Literature on Campus Faculty Governance Structures. There is relatively little literature on faculty governance structures, considering the importance generally given to the faculty's role in academic decisions. This section contains a statement on this subject by the American Association of University Professors (no. 149), books by Mortimer and McConnell (no. 152) and by Hodgkinson (no. 150) that report on studies of faculty governance, and an article by Kemerer and Baldridge (no. 151) that reports research on relationships between traditional forms of faculty governance and emerging campus faculty unions.

Literature on Institutional Decision Processes. The literature on higher education decision making has proliferated in recent years. Its focus has shifted from so-called "rational" decision making to concepts that place greater emphasis on the complexities and constraints that prevent fully considered decisions. This section contains primarily the more recent literature describing the complex, political character of decisions. One book (no. 155) describes the incremental character of decision processes, and two articles (no. 154, no. 158) describe limits to central control and "loose coupling" among organizational units. Another article (no. 153) describes the ambiguity and problematic nature of organizational decision making, and still another compares "incremental" and "comprehensive" concepts of decision making (no. 157). A book of readings (no. 156) describes strategic decision making, using examples drawn primarily from the business world.

Books of Readings on Governance and Decision Making. Several scholars have edited books of readings that encompass the areas covered in this chapter. Two of the best of these books (nos. 159 and 160) are included in the annotations.

Commentary on the State of the Literature

Recent literature on campus governance structures tends to attribute structural changes to environmental demands (Birnbaum, 1983; Cameron, 1984; and Tolbert, 1985). For example, increases in demand for education led to larger campuses, with more differentiated structures, and to multicampus systems. Growth in knowledge led to increasing specialization and development of departmental structures. Another body of literature, however, ascribes some change in governance structures to emerging theories of governance. Kauffman (1980) notes the controversy that began toward the start of the twentieth century when notions of business organization and management started to have an effect on college presidents' perceptions.

A few authors have attempted to set forth other factors that affect campus organizational design. Baldridge, Curtis, Ecker, and Riley (no. 139) listed differences in clients, technologies, worker skills, environmental vulnerability, and goal ambiguity as sources of variance in such designs. A political scientist, Redford (1969), noted that organizational structures are a means of allocating power among members. Therefore, organizational structures reflect contemporary notions of legitimate allocations of organizational power. Ostrom (1974), a sociologist, also described how concerns over allocating power influence the design of governance structures. Etzioni (1964), another sociologist, described effects on governance structures and decision processes when organizational authority is derived from one's professional knowledge rather than one's administrative position.

Many gaps exist in the literature on higher education governance and decision making (no. 136 and no. 137), and there have been few attempts to examine systematically the factors affecting design of campus governance structures that have been identified in literature from various disciplines. For example, research is needed on patterns of campus organization, including committee structures; faculty and student organizations; and actual institutional decision processes. Campus organization charts rarely show faculty governance structures or the extensive committee structures typical of most campuses. There is virtually no research on student governance structures, nor are there any comparative studies that systematically describe and analyze the governance structures of each principal type of institution. More research is needed on informal campus structures and processes and on the actual character of campus decision processes and the values and constraints that shape their nature.

References

American Association of University Professors. "Faculty Participation in College and University Government." *AAUP Bulletin*, 1960, *46* (2), 203–204.

Birnbaum, R. *Maintaining Diversity in Higher Education*. San Francisco: Jossey-Bass, 1983.

Cameron, K. S. "Organizational Adaptation and Higher Education." *Journal of Higher Education*, 1984, *55*, 122–144.

Carnegie Commission on Higher Education. *Governance of Higher Education: Six Priority Problems*. New York: McGraw-Hill, 1973.

Clark, B. R. "Faculty Organization and Authority." In T. F. Lunsford (ed.), *The Study of Campus Cultures*. Boulder, Colo.: Western Interstate Commission for Higher Education, 1963.

Corson, J. J. *Governance of Colleges and Universities*. New York: McGraw-Hill, 1960.

Dahrendorf, R. *Essays in the Theory of Society.* Stanford, Calif.: Stanford University Press, 1968.
Demerath, N. J., Stephens, R. W., and Taylor, R. R. *Power, Presidents, and Professors.* New York: Basic Books, 1967.
Duryea, E. D. "Evolution of University Organization." In J. A. Perkins (ed.), *The University as an Organization.* New York: McGraw-Hill, 1973.
Etzioni, A. *Modern Organizations.* Englewood Cliffs, N.J.: Prentice-Hall, 1964.
Etzioni, A. "Mixed Scanning: A 'Third' Approach to Decision Making." *Public Administration Review,* Dec. 1967, pp. 387–391.
Friedland, E. I. *Introduction to the Concept of Rationality in Political Science.* Morristown, N.J.: General Learning Press, 1974.
Georgiou, P. "The Goal Paradigm and Notes Toward a Counter Paradigm." *Administrative Science Quarterly,* 1973, *18,* 191–310.
Gerth, H. H., and Mills, C. W. *From Max Weber: Essays on Sociology.* New York: Oxford University Press, 1946.
Goheen, R. F. *The Human Nature of a University.* Princeton, N.J.: Princeton University Press, 1969.
Gross, F., and Grambsch, P. V. *University Goals and Academic Power.* Washington, D.C.: American Council on Education, 1968.
Gulick, L., and Urwick, L. (eds.). *Papers on the Science of Administration.* New York: Institute of Public Administration, 1937.
Henry, D. D. *Challenges Past, Challenges Present: An Analysis of American Higher Education Since 1930.* San Francisco: Jossey-Bass, 1975.
Hodgkinson, H. L., and Meeth, L. R. (eds.). *Power and Authority: Transformation of Campus Governance.* San Francisco: Jossey-Bass, 1971.
Howard, J. A., and Franklin, H. B. *Who Should Run the Universities?* Washington, D.C.: American Enterprise Institute, 1969.
Katz, D., and Kahn, R. L. *The Social Psychology of Organizations.* New York: Wiley, 1966.
Kauffman, J. F. *At the Pleasure of the Board: The Service of the College and University President.* Washington, D.C.: American Council on Education, 1980.
McConnell, T. R. *The Redistribution of Power in Higher Education.* Berkeley: Center for Research and Development in Higher Education, University of California, 1971.
McConnell, T. R., and Mortimer, K. P. *The Faculty in University Governance.* Berkeley: Center for Research and Development in Higher Education, University of California, 1971.
Mayo, E. *The Human Problems of an Industrial Civilization.* New York: Macmillan, 1933.
Millett, J. D. *The Academic Community.* New York: McGraw-Hill, 1962.
Mooney, R. L. "The Problem of Leadership in the University." *Harvard Educational Review,* 1963, *33* (1), 42–57.
Ostrom, V. *The Intellectual Crisis in American Public Administration.* University: University of Alabama Press, 1974.
Perkins, J. A. *The University in Transition.* Princeton, N.J.: Princeton University Press, 1966.
Perkins, J. A. (ed.). *The University as an Organization.* New York: McGraw-Hill, 1973.
Peterson, M. W. (ed.). *Organization and Governance in Higher Education.* (3rd ed.) Lexington, Mass.: Ginn, 1986.

Platt, G. M., and Parsons, T. "Decision-Making in the Academic System: In-
    fluence and Power Exchange." In C. E. Kruytbosch and S. L. Messinger
    (eds.), *The State of the University: Authority and Change.* Beverly Hills, Calif.: Sage,
    1970.
Redford, E. S. *Democracy in the Administrative State.* New York: Oxford University
    Press, 1969.
Riesman, D. *Constraint and Variety in American Education.* Garden City, N.Y.:
    Doubleday, 1958.
Schmidtlein, F. A. "Decision Process Paradigms in Education." *Educational Re-
    searcher,* 1974, *3* (5), 4–11.
Sergiovanni, T. J., and Corbally, J. E. (eds.). *Leadership and Organizational Culture.*
    Urbana: University of Illinois Press, 1984.
Simon, H. A. *Administrative Behavior.* New York: Free Press, 1945.
Tolbert, P. S. "Institutional Environments and Resource Dependence: Sources
    of Administrative Structure in Institutions of Higher Education." *Administrative
    Science Quarterly,* 1985, *30,* 1–13.
Veysey, L. R. *The Emergence of the American University.* Chicago: University of
    Chicago Press, 1965.
Wilson, W. "The Study of Administration." *Political Science Quarterly,* 1887, *2,*
    197–220.

Reviews of Governance
and Decision Process Literature

136 March, James G. "Emerging Developments in the Study
of Organizations." *Review of Higher Education,* 1982,
7 (6), 1–17.

This article reviews developments in the field of organization
theory. The author asserts that the classical view of organizations as hierarchical systems that seek goals is misleading. Recent theories of decision making, he points out, are examining
how people in organizations act on the basis of limited information and modest information-processing capacities. They examine how elements of a decision are ordered over time; the
role of rules and routines; and the interpretations, rituals, and
symbols used to make sense of organizations. Attention to these
organizational characteristics is changing views of management
information systems and organizational leadership and change

processes. The author concludes that future progress is likely to come from sensitive observers of natural processes who do not have a premature commitment to particular interpretations of events. This article, by a leading organizational theorist, is an excellent summary of organization theory's contributions to the understanding of institutional decision making. Students and scholars will find it a useful means to assess the current state of theory.

★**137** Peterson, Marvin W. "Emerging Developments in Post-secondary Organization Theory and Research: Fragmentation or Integration." *Educational Researcher,* 1985, *3* (14), 5–12.

This article reviews developments in theory and research on postsecondary institutions as organizations. Its author notes that studies have proceeded in many different directions, threatening to fragment this critical area of research. He examines major developments and identifies dilemmas in theory development, research methods, the organizational behavior context, and the relationship of theory to practice. He urges that these dilemmas be understood and addressed to assure continuing, integrated development of postsecondary organization theory and research. This article is the most recent and comprehensive examination of higher education governance theory and research. It is primarily of interest to scholars and students.

Campus Governance Structures

138 Alpert, Daniel P. "Performance and Paralysis: The Organizational Context of the American Research University." *Journal of Higher Education,* 1985, *56* (3), 241–281.

The author of this article argues that universities currently are facing hard times. Such times force them to look either at internal efficiencies or at innovations to increase effectiveness. Their tendency during previous periods of retrenchment has been to look toward internal efficiencies rather than consider-

ing changes in governance and purposes. The author also notes
that conventional organization charts do not accurately portray
campus structure. He suggests that institutions typically are
viewed in terms of a "linear model," whereas a better model
for dealing with current issues would be a "matrix model" that
facilitates looking across campuses by discipline rather than solely
within a campus across disciplines. The character and implications of the matrix model are discussed in some detail. Alpert
concludes that this model offers a starting point for universities
wishing to redefine their roles. This article is one of a very few that
explicitly address university organizational structure. Both
sophisticated administrators and scholars should find it of interest.

139 Baldridge, J. Victor, Curtis, David V., Ecker, George
P., and Riley, Gary L. "Alternative Models of Gover-
nance in Higher Education." In Gary L. Riley and J.
Victor Baldridge (eds.), *Governing Academic Organizations*.
Berkeley, Calif.: McCutchan, 1977. Pages 2–25.

The authors of this book suggest that academic institutions have
several unique organizational characteristics. They have ambiguous goals that often are strongly contested. They serve clients
who demand a voice in decision-making processes. They have
a problematic technology. They are professionalized organizations in which employees demand a large measure of control
over institutional decision processes. Finally, they are becoming more vulnerable to their environments. The authors feel
that these characteristics are not satisfactorily described by the
term "bureaucracy." They go on to describe three models of
academic governance that have received widespread attention:
the academic bureaucracy, the university collegium, and the
university as a political system. They discuss the images of
leadership and the management strategies that are implied by
each model. This chapter should be particularly helpful to senior
administrators seeking to enlarge their understanding of institutional governance and to students of higher education administration.

★140 Clark, Burton R. *The Higher Education System: Academic Organization in Cross-National Perspective.* Berkeley, Calif.: University of California Press, 1983. 315 pages.

This book's author, a leading scholar of comparative higher education, takes a cross-national look at institutional structures. Using an open systems approach as a theoretical framework, the book sets forth the basic elements of the higher education system from an organizational perspective and then demonstrates how these features vary across nations. The author contends that the American view of structure and organization has damaged the study of higher education because the United States postsecondary system, in its fundamentals, is a deviant system relative to others around the world. The book contains a very comprehensive and sophisticated examination of higher education organizational structures. Students and scholars interested in this topic will find it a provocative and useful work.

★141 Cohen, Michael D., and March, James G. *Leadership and Ambiguity: The American College President.* (2nd ed.) Boston: Harvard Business School Press, 1986. 290 pages.

This book, originally published in 1974, reports the results of four empirical studies of the presidency at forty-two four-year campuses. The book portrays colleges as "organized anarchies" and their leadership as constrained by ambiguous objectives, technologies, and experience. Major topics covered include presidential careers, metaphors of leadership and images of the presidency, processes and logic of choice, organization of time, presidential tenure, and leadership in the college setting. This book remains a classic description of college leadership, governance, and decision making. It has been somewhat controversial because it questions conventional notions of bureaucracy and decision making. However, its concepts, solidly based on research, are becoming increasingly accepted and studied. Administrators, scholars, and students should be familiar with its concepts of governance and decision making.

142 Etzioni, Amitai. "Administrative and Professional Authority." In Amitai Etzioni, *Modern Organizations*. Englewood Cliffs, N.J.: Prentice-Hall, 1964. Pages 75–84.

This chapter, from a short book on organizational theory, describes the effects of having primarily professional employees on an organization's structure and decision-making processes. The characteristics of authority derived from an administrative position are contrasted with those of authority derived from professional knowledge. Administration assumes a power hierarchy, while professional knowledge is largely an individual property that cannot be transferred from one person to another by decree. The author discusses the significance of line and staff distinctions and the question of whether an administrator or a professional should head a professional organization. Colleges and universities are particularly good examples of organizations made up of professionals. The governance issues discussed in this chapter should sensitize administrators, scholars, and students to a campus's special characteristics.

143 Glenny, Lyman A., and Dalglish, Thomas K. *Public Universities, State Agencies, and the Law: Constitutional Autonomy in Decline.* Berkeley: Center for Research and Development in Higher Education, University of California, 1973. 193 pages.

Although written in 1973, this book remains important for students and scholars interested in the legal relationship between the campus and the state. The authors sought to determine the substantive and procedural ways in which states relate to universities established by state constitution or statute. Four state universities (those of California, Colorado, Michigan, and Minnesota) with constitutional autonomy from state government were compared to four others (those of Hawaii, Illinois, Maryland, and Wisconsin) whose autonomy is based entirely on statutes. This analysis of the legal context of universities should be particularly helpful to university presidents and other staff who must deal with state governmental agencies and who are interested in better understanding the governance and decision-making implications of that relationship.

144 Helsabeck, Robert E. *The Compound System: A Conceptual Framework for Effective Decisionmaking in Colleges.* Berkeley: Center for Research and Development in Higher Education, University of California, 1973. 114 pages.

This monograph is based on the author's attempt to develop a college-based theory of organization and test it through research on four campuses. Helsabeck suggests that colleges are "compound systems" that contain elements of both centralized and decentralized structure. His theory attempts to link notions of structure and decision processes. He takes decision-making arrangements as the independent variable and organizational effectiveness as the dependent variable in his study and develops a formalized set of propositions. His study supports his hypothesis that decision-making arrangements vary by type of decision. This work is most useful to students and scholars of governance and decision making and to practitioners concerned with understanding relationships between bureaucratic and collegial forms of organization and decision making.

145 Millett, John D. *New Structures of Campus Power: Success and Failures of Emerging Forms of Institutional Governance.* San Francisco: Jossey-Bass, 1978. 294 pages.

This book seeks to put into perspective the changes that occurred in campus power structures during the turbulent 1960s, a period the author views as a time of innovation and change in campus governance. New structures and procedures were developed to extend participation to students, for example. The work describes governance patterns at thirty institutions representing different types of campuses (leading research universities, other universities, and general baccalaureate colleges). Four models of campus governance are reviewed: the dual-organization model, the academic community model, the political model, and the organized anarchy model. The author's recommendations include distinguishing campuswide governance from faculty and student governance, defining more precisely the scope of campuswide governance as an advisory process for the president, distinguishing campuswide governance from management, and asserting the leadership role of the president. This review of academic governance literature, with its descriptions of changes that took place on campuses during a crucial historical period, will be helpful to practitioners.

★**146** Walker, Donald E. *The Effective Administrator: A Practical Approach to Problem Solving, Decision Making, and Campus Leadership.* San Francisco: Jossey-Bass, 1979. 208 pages.

This book offers practical advice to higher education professionals on how to become more effective administrators. The author, himself a college president, explains the unusual nature of campus politics, examines the theoretical orientation of successful and unsuccessful administrators, and argues the wisdom of a diplomatic rather than autocratic approach to administration. The book draws on the author's experience and his considerable knowledge of organization theory literature. It should be very useful for both would-be and current administrators in colleges and universities. It is also a good practical guide for students of higher education administration.

Multicampus Governance Structures

★**147** Lee, Eugene C., and Bowen, Frank M. *The Multicampus University.* New York: McGraw-Hill, 1971. 481 pages.

This book reports the results of a study of nine multicampus university systems. The first part of the book reviews the nature and history of multicampus systems and the context in which they are developing. The second part examines governance structures: the governing board, the administration, faculty government, and student organization. The third part examines processes of governance: academic planning and programs, budget preparation and administration, handling of academic and administrative personnel, admissions and transfers, external relations, and business affairs. The fourth part examines problems, trends, and issues related to these systems. The authors view multicampus universities as one of the most significant recent innovations in governance but believe that their future depends on how well they resolve the new issues and deal with the new environments confronting higher education. This book is dated, but (with its companion volume, no. 148) it remains the only comprehensive treatment of this topic. Administrators, students, and scholars interested in these systems will find it useful.

148 Lee, Eugene C., and Bowen, Frank M. *Managing Multicampus Systems: Effective Administration in an Unsteady State.* San Francisco: Jossey-Bass, 1975. 172 pages.

This volume reexamines the nine multicampus systems studied in the authors' earlier book in light of changes taking place in the early 1970s. It focuses on academic affairs, budgeting, student admissions and transfers, and faculty staffing within the context of multicampus governance. Using, as before, a case study approach, the researchers describe and evaluate experiences the nine systems had in planning for and coping with limited growth, fiscal constraints, and possible retrenchment. They conclude that multicampus systems must have considerable flexibility if they are to make the most of their unique advantages. Such flexibility may be endangered by undue state intrusions, by their own too highly bureaucratized administration, and by too widely dispersed authority. This report is a valuable addition to the authors' earlier study.

Campus Faculty Governance Structures

★149 American Association of University Professors. "Statement on Government of Colleges and Universities." In *AAUP Policy Documents and Reports.* Washington, D.C.: American Association of University Professors, 1973. Pages 35–39.

This statement culminated many years of effort to prepare and refine statements on faculty and administrators' shared responsibilities for governing colleges and universities. It was jointly formulated with the American Council on Education and the Association of Governing Boards of Universities and Colleges, and all three organizations gave it their formal endorsement. The statement sets forth joint responsibilities for determining an institution's general education policy, internal operations, and external relations. Specific responsibilities for governing boards, presidents, and faculty are also described. All campus administrators and faculty should be familiar with this statement.

150 Hodgkinson, Harold L. *The Campus Senate: Experiment in Democracy.* Berkeley: Center for Research and Development in Higher Education, University of California, 1974. 151 pages.

This monograph reports the results of a national study of unicameral campus senates that surveyed 310 institutions concerning the origins, structure, and functioning of their campus senates. The survey was supplemented by case studies of four institutions, using participant/observer research teams and data from an Institutional Functioning Inventory (IFI) that was administered to representative samples of students, faculty, and administrators. The study revealed differences in faculty and administrators' perceptions, the need for senates to have a clear understanding of the campus mission, problems confronting senates having more than fifty members, and seasonal issues that must routinely be confronted. This study provides information on the development of campus senates and some issues they confront, together with recommendations to make them more effective. It should be useful to both administrators and faculty leaders.

151 Kemerer, Frank R., and Baldridge, J. Victor. "Senates and Unions: Unexpected Peaceful Coexistence." *Journal of Higher Education,* 1981, *52* (3), 256–264.

This article reports on the second of two studies that the authors made on the effects of faculty unionization on campus senates. Initially, they speculated that unions would undermine the existence of senates. However, their study revealed that faculty unions and senates were coexisting on a "dual track." Each had carved out its own sphere of influence, so the two generally did not conflict. Senates retained influence over academic matters, while unions were a primary influence on economic issues. The study also notes differences between faculty governance roles in two-year and four-year campuses. The authors speculate that unions may hesitate to become involved in retrenchment issues and that this could lead to tensions with senates in the future. This article provides information about a major concern related to the potential growth of faculty unionism. It helps to inform both administrators and faculty about trends in faculty governance.

★**152** Mortimer, Kenneth P., and McConnell, T. R. *Sharing Authority Effectively: Participation, Interaction and Discretion.* San Francisco: Jossey-Bass, 1978. 322 pages.

The authors of this book examine concepts of authority and legitimacy in American academic governance, looking at distribution of authority and at various claims for legitimacy. The book includes discussions of campus and system faculty senates, collective bargaining, faculty interaction with administrators and students, and faculty/trustee relations. In addition, it reviews governance issues related to central administrative leadership, accountability and external constraints, statewide coordination, and centralization/decentralization. The book draws upon the extensive research and experience of two leading scholars in the field of higher education governance. Administrators, scholars, and students alike will benefit from its insights.

Institutional Decision Processes

153 Cohen, Michael D., March, James G., and Olsen, Johan P. "A Garbage Can Model of Organizational Choice." *Administrative Science Quarterly,* 1972, *17,* 1–25.

The authors of this article propose that universities be viewed as a particular form of "organized anarchy." For some purposes, such organizations can be characterized as collections of choices looking for problems, issues and feelings looking for situations that require a decision, solutions looking for issues to which they might be an answer, and decision makers looking for work. The authors translate these notions into a computer simulation model of a "garbage can" decision process. They describe the implications of this model and then illustrate its possible applications by examining its predictions regarding the effects of adversity on university decision making. This influential article is rather complex and primarily of interest to scholars. Administrators, however, should be familiar with its basic concepts, which contradict conventional views of decision-making environments but are gaining currency among theorists.

★**154** Hunt, Pearson. "Fallacy of the One Big Brain." *Harvard Business Review,* 1966, *44* (4), 84–90.

The author suggests that too often schemes of analysis assume that problems are recognized, defined, analyzed, and solved by a unified organizational "brain" of enormous capacity that operates in a completely objective manner, searching for and comparing all possible alternatives in one thinking process and then arriving at the best possible answers. In reality, the author points out, organizations consist of many brains making many decisions at many levels. Minor decisions taken all along the line make certain conclusions inevitable, and major decisions evolve as a normal part of the system of doing work. Consequently, planning and creative thinking cannot be made the exclusive responsibility of a chosen few members of an organization. The author includes practical advice on the implications of dispersed decision making. Administrators and students will both benefit from reading this classic description of decision process structure.

155 Lindblom, Charles E. *The Policy-Making Process.* (2nd ed.) Englewood Cliffs, N.J.: Prentice-Hall, 1980. 131 pages.

For a full description of this book, please see entry no. 326.

156 Pennings, Johannes M. (ed.). *Decision Making: An Organizational Behavior Approach.* New York: Markus Wilner, 1983. 391 pages.

This volume is based on papers prepared for a symposium supported by the Office of Naval Research. Its twenty chapters, written by leading scholars of decision making, are organized under three rubrics: formulating strategy (the process and content of strategic decision making), implementing strategic change, and developing new approaches to strategy. The authors define strategic decision making as the making of fundamental decisions that significantly affect an organization's future. They approach this subject by describing various concepts of decision making, offering normative prescriptions, and pointing out the need for research to modify inaccurate conceptions of the decision process. This volume focuses primarily on the business world, but many of its concepts are relevant to higher education institutions. Both practitioners and higher education scholars should be familiar with this book.

★**157** Schmidtlein, Frank A. "Comprehensive and Incremental Decision Paradigms and Their Implications for Educational Planning." In George H. Copa and Jerome Moss, Jr. (eds.), *Planning and Vocational Education*. New York: McGraw-Hill, 1983. Pages 48–80.

This chapter is one of eleven written by planning theorists and vocational educators. Its author contrasts two concepts of decision processes that run through the literature: "comprehensive planning" and "incremental" or marketplace decision making. He describes these decision process paradigms by comparing the ways they deal with constraints of time, knowledge, resources, consensus, and role demands and their orientation to common value dilemmas confronting decision makers, such as choices between change and stability or between simplification and complexity. In practice, he concludes, decisions are made using elements from both concepts. Many persons in governmental positions, however, assume the validity of the planning concept of decision making, while the character of educational institutions more nearly approximates "incremental" assumptions. Schmidtlein suggests that this disparity in views is a major cause of public concern about institutional effectiveness. This article should help both practitioners and scholars reexamine assumptions about decision making.

★**158** Weick, Karl E. "Educational Organizations as Loosely Coupled Systems." *Administrative Science Quarterly,* 1976, *21* (1), 1–19.

For a complete description of this article, please see entry no. 8.

Books of Readings on
Governance and Decision Making

159 Bess, James L. (ed.). *College and University Organization: Insights from the Behavioral Sciences.* New York: New York University Press, 1984. 247 pages.

This book assembles nine articles by major organizational theorists. The articles are grouped in three categories: system states, personnel issues, and organizational processes and latent learning. The system states articles examine fundamental organizational characteristics. The personnel issues articles address motivation, job satisfaction, and role clarity. The organizational processes and latent learning articles examine leadership, decision style, strategy formation, and organizational socialization. The book should be of interest to higher education scholars and to administrators interested in current views on governance and decision making.

★**160** Peterson, Marvin W. (ed.). *ASHE Reader on Organization and Governance in Higher Education.* (3rd ed.) Lexington, Mass.: Ginn, 1986. 475 pages.

This book, assembled primarily for students taking courses on higher education administration, contains an outstanding collection of literature on higher education organization and governance. The twenty-nine readings are grouped into three topic areas: organization, governance, and responses to internal and external pressures. The book contains the best single compilation of literature on higher education governance.

8

Donald M. Norris
Nick L. Poulton

Institutional Planning, Strategy, and Policy Formulation

The formulation of plans, strategies, and policies has developed dramatically in higher education over the past thirty years, becoming a significant component of governance, management, and leadership. Techniques of planning have become more refined and are being applied with increased sophistication by educational leaders who are interested in taking initiatives to deal effectively with the challenging environment they confront. Consequently, a continually increasing demand for effective, sage applications of planning and management techniques has arisen.

This chapter deals with the ways colleges and universities monitor and respond to changes in their environment and how they develop strategies and policies that guide management initiatives. The resources identified in the chapter illustrate different approaches to institutional planning, strategy, and policy formulation; describe the current state of the art; and suggest new directions for the future. These resources also provide guidance in crafting an institution's relationships with major environmental forces of change, assessing the position of the institution, and establishing organizational goals. Our treatment of planning, strategy, and policy formulation is designed to link the issues identified in Part One of this volume with the management initiatives treated in Part Two.

163

Development of Planning, Strategy, and Policy Formulation

This chapter would be very different if it had been written five, ten, or twenty years ago. The challenges and conditions facing higher education have changed significantly over that period, resulting in changes in the nature of institutional decision making and changes in the techniques and applications of planning, strategy, and policy formulation that colleges and universities use to support those decisions.

Figure 1 examines different eras in planning and decision making in higher education, summarizing the relationships among various factors in each era. While the boundaries of the eras are somewhat artificial, they do suggest some interesting changes. The late 1950s and early 1960s witnessed the growth of pressures for departure from the incremental, nonparticipatory styles of planning and decision making that characterized the educational leadership of that period. Colleges and universities needed new approaches to deal with the tidal wave of new students and the growth of research and graduate study. During the 1960s, management science techniques were increasingly applied to higher education. Master planning and information-based decision making grappled with the challenges to facilities and programs posed by larger numbers of new students and new student clienteles. The growth in size and complexity of institutions was accompanied by more participatory decision making and some decentralization of power.

The overriding strategic planning issue in the 1970s, by contrast, was selective growth and retrenchment. This fueled the continued development and maturation of management science techniques. By the last half of the 1970s, resource allocation and redistribution challenges spawned the use of new sets of qualitative and quantitative analytical approaches that dealt with difficult choices and trade-offs among competing resource demands. Institutional research and planning grew to support these functions, and planners increasingly served as staff in developing formal, often comprehensive planning processes in many colleges and universities. But much of the thrust of planning was reactive, responding to environmental conditions only after they became clear.

By the start of the 1980s, decision makers had begun to embrace ''strategic management'' as a way of managing an organization with an eye to the environment. The condition of potential demographic decline has carried over into the 1980s, but colleges and universities are now confronted with additional challenges that require more enlightened action than merely dividing up pieces of a declining pie. These include changing student characteristics, investments in new information and telecommunications systems, joint economic development efforts with industry and government, and faculty shortfalls in growth areas such as business and engineering. These and similar issues have prompted leaders to take more proactive stances toward external developments and to seek alternate funding resources.

These recent changes have altered the focus of both current and future planning. Information and its analysis remain critical, but less importance is now placed upon technique, while more emphasis is given to distilling information to a manageable level and limiting its use in a manner appropriate for the given application. Planning support remains a staff function, but planning itself is a line function, the responsibility of institutional leaders. The institution/environment interface is more complex, and external factors are viewed as more manipulable, even controllable, than was previously thought. Institutional leaders now find themselves involved in strategic redirection, with planning and strategy development focused on quality, outcomes, and external relationships.

Literature and Research in the Field

Higher education has always drawn heavily from other disciplines to support its planning, strategy, and policy formulation endeavors. Many of the seminal articles and books on management applications in higher education were developed as specialized applications by economists, social psychologists, or political scientists examining higher education as an interesting and underdeveloped field of study.

Higher education has drawn ideas from many basic texts on business and corporate planning. Examples range from

Figure 1. Eras in Planning and Decision Making.

Era	Conditions	Primary Focus
1950s: Age Of Authority	o Relatively stable conditions o Goal consensus o New institutional types o Steady growth	o Facilities o New institution studies
1960s: Age Of Developing Quantitative Techniques	o Rapid growth in enrollment masking many problems o Expansion embracing new student clienteles o Student dissension	o Facilities o Institution self-studies o New programs o Student studies
1970s: Age Of Pragmatic Application	o Stabilizing enrollments o Revenue shortfalls o Need to reallocate resources to deal with imbalances caused by 1960s growth o Selective growth, retrenchment, and promise of decline in 1980s o Goal fragmentation	o Internal orientation o Existing programs o Resources o Efficiency o Recruitment o State relations
1980s: Age Of Strategic Redirection	o Substantial decline in numbers of traditional college cohorts o Decline in many institutions; substantial regional and institutional variations o Resource shortfalls o Changes in student characteristics o Need to invest large sums in computing, scientific equipment, and capital plant for research and graduate education	o External orientation o Effectiveness o Quality o Outcomes o Competitive advantage o Economic development o Telematics

Nature Of Institutional Decision Making	Nature of Planning, Strategy and Policy Formulation
o Less participatory, administrative fiat	o Continuation of traditional, less sophisticated modes of planning and strategy
o More participatory o Dispersal of power o Talk rational, but decision making predominantly incremental, political, nonrationalistic	o Physical master planning o Experimentation with management science techniques o Emergence of institutional research and planning o State system planning
o Reallocation mentality o Incremental, imperfect decision making o Some use of continued growth in late 1970s to prepare for 1980s o Some postponement of action until conditions get worse	o Comprehensive master plans o Program planning and evaluation o Resource reallocation o Management of decline o New techniques and advances in management science applications o Planning as staff function o Strategic management emerging in late 1970s
o Proactive relationship to environment o Internal decision making affected by external environment o Continued imperfections in decision making but harsh penalties for poor decisions or deferral of choices o Enhanced use of analysis and decision support systems o Emphasis is on information management	o Gain in popularity of strategic planning o Re-emergence of master planning o Selective focus on new clienteles, new partnerships, external relationships o Experiences with shortcomings of analysis and planning o Emphasis on applications rather than techniques o Planning as line function, dispersed through organization

Simon's *Administrative Behavior* (1957) to Schendel and Hofer's *Strategic Management: A New View of Business Policy and Planning* (no. 184). Management science applications to higher education have been made explicitly in several books, including Balderston's *Managing Today's University* (1974), Hopkins and Massy's *Planning Models for Colleges and Universities* (no. 303), and Lawrence and Service's *Quantitative Approaches to Higher Education Management* (1977). However, these applications have focused more on operational and managerial questions than on strategic issues.

Political science and public administration have yielded excellent works on public policy analysis, the importance of implementation, and the politics of the budget process. For example, Bardach's *The Implementation Game* (1977) and Wildavsky's *The Politics of the Budgetary Process* (1979) contain many lessons for higher education. From organizational behavior have come contributions such as Clark's "The Organizational Saga in Higher Education" (no. 9), Cohen and March's *Leadership and Ambiguity* (no. 141), and Havelock's *The Change Agent's Guide to Innovation in Education* (no. 356).

Relationships among the literature, research, and practice of planning, strategy, and policy formulation in higher education follow a pattern typical of the diffusion and adoption of innovations. Fundamental organizational research or new techniques originate in the social science or applied management disciplines, as we have noted. Problems and pressing issues in higher education then prompt inquiry and research on the application of the emerging concepts or techniques to the higher education setting. Leading institutions experiment with new ideas, an example being Stanford University's application of financial planning models and establishment of a computer-intensive environment. Articles on these pioneering applications gain attention. After results emerge and trends are identified, a major review highlights the developments of the era. Rourke and Brooks's *The Managerial Revolution in Higher Education* (1966) and Keller's *Academic Strategy* (no. 163) are two examples. These volumes prompt dissemination and provide interest in further research into higher education applications. As the area matures further, emphasis shifts to insightful application, and formerly new techniques become part of the accepted practice of higher education.

With the development of a growing cadre of higher education professionals who have great sophistication in planning techniques and applications, interest in developing and researching these applications will continue to increase. However, it is likely that new concepts will continue to come from the basic social science and management science disciplines, and the cutting edge will continue to be made up of educational leaders who experiment with applying new techniques in leading institutions. The true critical factor in successful planning, strategy, and policy formulation is insightful application, not technical virtuosity, and by the time an approach is ready for such application, it is part of the mainstream of planning, strategy, and policy formulation.

Framework for Study of Institutional Planning, Strategy, and Policy Formulation

Planning, strategy, and policy formulation cover a broad aggregation of activities, many of which overlap those described in the management and leadership parts of this book. The following framework groups the field's literature into categories that should assist readers in structuring their understanding and also provide links with other chapters.

General Planning/Planning History. A significant portion of the planning literature deals with basic definitions, theories and principles of planning, and/or the history of planning in higher education. Much of the general planning literature is prescriptive, normative, and unsuited to the higher education environment. The works we have selected here, however, provide both a sound definitional basis and a grounding in historical development that can serve as a road map in applying planning techniques to higher education. Literature on the organizational context of planning is covered in Chapter Seven.

Reflections on Planning/Criticisms of Planning. Over the years, a significant subset of the planning literature has evaluated and contrasted the potentials and limitations of planning practice. Such literature often arises from frustrations with the current state of the art. A number of excellent articles establish the relative strengths and weaknesses of incrementalism and strategic decision making, for example. This literature is essential to help the planner maintain a balance between desired outcomes and realistic expectations for current and future planning activities.

Strategic Planning/Strategic Management. An excellent set of books, monographs, and articles review the principles of strategic planning and provide guidelines for applying them to higher education. The reader should bear in mind, however, that strategic planning is only one of the three types of planning—strategic, tactical, and operational. Only strategic planning is dealt with in this chapter: operational and tactical planning are covered in the chapters of Part Two, Management.

Policy Formulation. A literature separate from public administration, political science, and policy studies provides an excellent grounding in the principles of policy. Special areas of emphasis in this literature include implementing policies, reconciling politics with science in policy analysis, and evaluating policies. Much of the work on policy analysis is inherently tactical in nature. However, understanding the strategic implications of the requirements for policy formulation is critical in establishing strategy. Our selections should help readers gain such an understanding.

New Directions. A final subset of the literature concerns the new directions in which the literature and practice of planning, strategy, and policy formulation are likely to move in the next several years. Selections in this category can direct the reader toward new developments and initiatives. References describing some of these new directions are included in this chapter, while others are discussed in other chapters of this volume.

Commentary

Clearly, the field of planning, strategy, and policy formulation is in a state of continuing flux. Figure 2 illustrates how changing environmental conditions are focusing planning attention on new relationships with the environment, new clientele, new sources of funding, and new partnerships with industry and government. Increased experience with planning and analytical support of planning has improved techniques, engendered an understanding of the limitations of various approaches, and directed attention to insightful applications. Finally, ongoing changes in the traditional feeder disciplines—business/corporate planning, policy studies/political science/public administration, organizational studies, and management science/operations research—continue to provide new and changing models for application. These factors are bringing about evolution and change in the current state of planning, strategy, and policy formulation and encouraging the emergence of a number of areas that are likely to become increasingly important over the next five years.

Figure 2 identifies a number of foci for strategic planning to which attention is being directed or is expected to be directed in the near future. These emerging areas will be important zones for practice, research, and planning. In the annotated bibliography that follows, references are included for the first three of these new directions, which are the ones closest to the processes of planning, strategy, and policy formulation. The remaining three areas are discussed in other chapters.

The futures research/environmental scanning/issues management area has been developing in the corporate world for a number of years. Through the efforts of James Morrison (no. 193) and other futurists, these techniques have now been applied to higher education and are being utilized in a number of institutions. The literature in this area is relatively well developed, but it lacks detailed case studies of successful applications. Such studies should appear in the next several years.

The competitive advantage literature is well developed in the business sector. The concept has also been applied to higher education in the area of student choice and institutional attractiveness. Case studies have been made of institutions, such as Carnegie Mellon, that have embraced the competitive advantage concept. Lacking, however, are examples of a broader set of applications of competitive advantage, as well as descriptions of emerging institutional cultures in complex settings that weave together the results and interrelationships of a number of individual measures of particular competing programs.

Figure 2. Areas of Emerging Importance in
Planning, Strategy, and Policy Formulation.

Changing Environmental Factors
• Increased external orientation
• Need for new sources of funding
• Demographic(s) changes and new
  clienteles
• Impending faculty manpower shortfalls

**Expanding Experience
and Developments**
• The practice of planning, strategy and
  policy formulation in higher education
• The higher education profession
  and literature

**Ongoing Developments in
Feeder Disciplines**
• Business/Corporate Planning
• Policy Studies/Public Administration
• Organizational Behavior
• Operations Research/MIS/
  Management Science

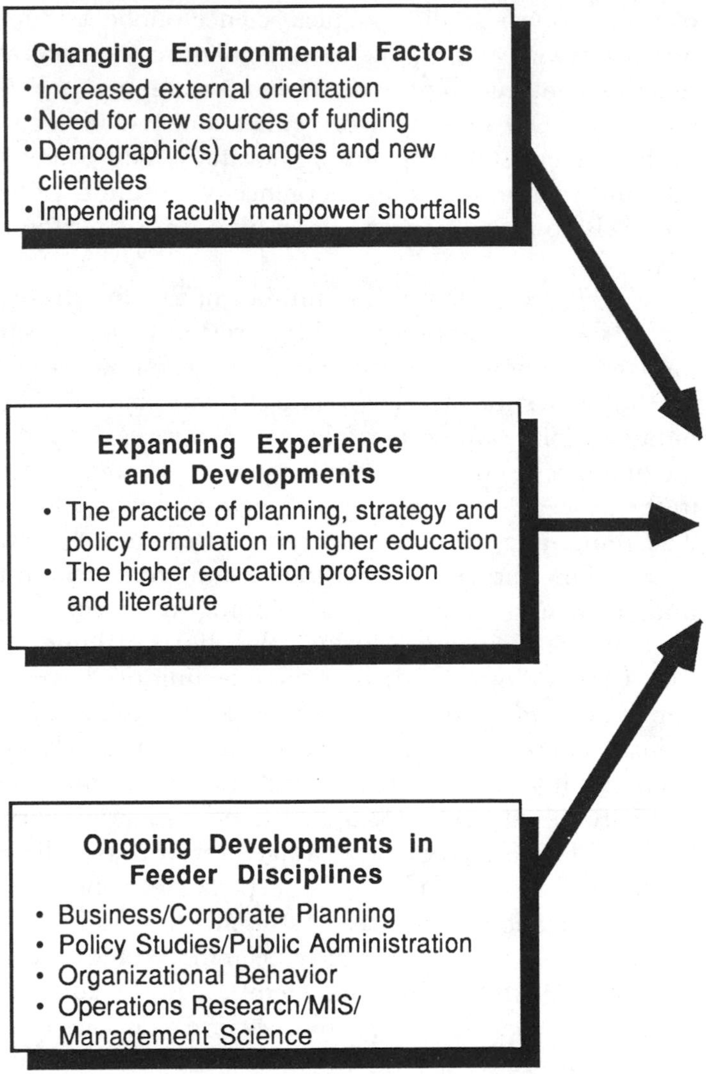

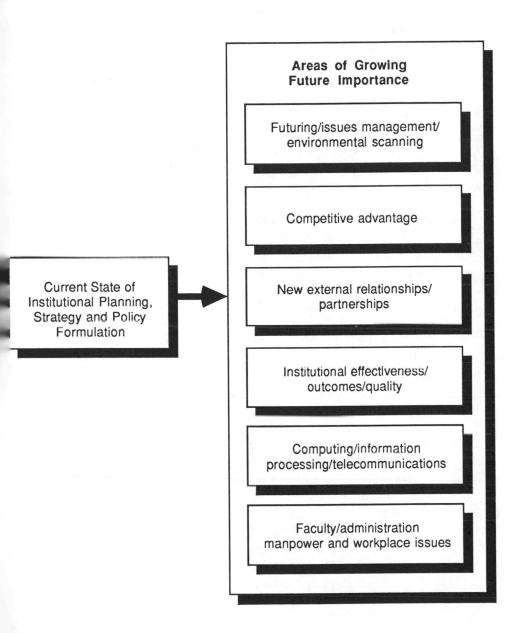

The literature on new external relationships is well developed in establishing the historical antecedents and the current and future reasons for education, industry, and government to join forces in new ways. Some reports also identify the kinds of initiatives that have worked in the past to establish research parks or other cooperative ventures. What is needed to help in future efforts are strategic evaluations that show which new organizational forms are working in the environment of the late 1980s and speculate on which of these will probably work in the future.

There is a growing literature on effectiveness/outcomes/quality. Most applications have dealt with relatively simple, small college settings. The aspects of overall institutional effectiveness in complex, large university environments remain to be treated in a satisfactory and comprehensive manner.

Technological changes in computing, information processing, and telecommunications are bringing the long-predicted "information society" closer to reality. These changes have significant implications for educational programming, delivery modes, access to student clienteles, facility needs, the nature of the library, and the nature of interactions among students, faculty, and staff. The literature has placed much emphasis on individual technological applications, uses, and potentials. More is needed on the integration of technological means into academic and administrative processes.

One of the important strategic challenges confronting institutions is the set of issues dealing with faculty/administration manpower and the workplace. The current faculty shortages in growth disciplines such as engineering are harbingers of coming shortages in other faculty disciplines. Administrators with the right training, experience, and attitudes are also likely to be in short supply. Furthermore, continuing fiscal constraints are likely to prevent the restoration of support services and adversely affect faculty and staff morale. The analytical techniques developed in the 1970s need to be applied creatively to these issues, which are likely to be a major force by the 1990s.

References

Balderston, F. E. *Managing Today's University*. San Francisco: Jossey-Bass, 1974.

Bardach, E. *The Implementation Game: What Happens After a Bill Becomes Law*. Cambridge, Mass.: MIT Press, 1977.

Lawrence, G. B., and Service, A. (eds.). *Quantitative Approaches to Higher Education Management*. AAHE-ERIC Higher Education Research Report no. 4. Washington, D.C.: American Association for Higher Education, 1977.

Rourke, F. E., and Brooks, G. E. *The Managerial Revolution in Higher Education*. Baltimore, Md.: Johns Hopkins University Press, 1966.

Simon, H. *Administrative Behavior*. New York: Free Press, 1957.

Wildavsky, A. *The Politics of the Budgetary Process*. (3rd ed.) Boston: Little, Brown, 1979.

General Planning/Planning History

161 Friedmann, John, and Hudson, Barclay. "Knowledge and Action: A Guide to Planning Theory." *Journal of the American Institute of Planners*, 1974, *40* (1), 2–16.

162 Hudson, Barclay. "Planning: Typologies, Issues, and Application Contexts." In George H. Copa and Jerome Moss, Jr. (eds.), *Planning and Vocational Education*. New York: McGraw-Hill, 1983. Pages 18–44.

These two articles trace the historical development of four major traditions of planning theory: philosophical synthesis, rationalism, organization development, and empiricism. The second article adds discussions of rationalism (synoptic planning) and the related approaches of incremental, transactional, advocacy, and radical planning. Each planning type is discussed by identifying its major themes and contributions, commenting on its primary weaknesses, and comparing it to the other types. Hudson also discusses criteria for evaluating theories and contexts for the theories' application, focusing particularly on the relationships of management to planning and of planning to evaluation. These articles provide essential insights and historical

perspectives on the relative merits and limitations of planning
theories in practice.

★**163** Keller, George. *Academic Strategy: The Management Revolution in American Higher Education.* Baltimore, Md.: Johns
Hopkins University Press, 1983. 177 pages.

This book resulted from a nationwide study of management
practices in a wide variety of colleges and universities in the
early 1980s. Keller describes the historical development of planning, management leadership in higher education, and the
emerging emphasis on academic strategy and strategic planning.
He describes academic strategies as a means of moving beyond
the limitations of normative, rigid planning on the one hand
and traditional incrementalism on the other. Keller provides
excellent discussions of the contextual and historical development of planning in higher education, the strengths and limitations of incrementalism and prescriptive planning, and the importance of leadership. The book's bibliography and references
are essential to any planner. Keller's characterizations of success factors for planning are good, though they are more abstract
than operational. His sense of new planning directions and
techniques is less successful.

164 Michael, Donald N. *On Learning to Plan—and Planning
to Learn: The Social Psychology of Changing Toward Future-Responsive Societal Learning.* San Francisco: Jossey-Bass,
1973. 341 pages.

Michael discusses the conditions needed to establish a process
for learning how to do long-range social planning, also called
future-responsive societal learning. He uses a social psychology
perspective in dealing with the individual potential for change
and for overcoming resistance to change. The book is not a "how
to plan" book; rather, it describes how individuals and organizations can learn to approach long-range social planning. Practicing planners will find very useful insights on learning how
to live with uncertainty, embrace error, accept ethical responsibility, live with role stress, and be open to change.

165 Norris, Donald M. *A Guide for New Planners*. Ann Arbor, Mich.: Society for College and University Planning, 1984. 46 pages.

This monograph provides an operational road map for new planners, institutional leaders attempting to start a new planning process or revive a moribund one, and planners interested in evaluating the success of their planning efforts. The focus is on practical observations and guidance derived from experience with both successful and unsuccessful planning ventures. Norris provides help in evaluating the existing environment for planning and avoiding the pitfalls of reflexive planning. He also presents a strategy for planning, a road map of the planning literature, a short list of critical references, sources of information and professional organizations, and a list of experts and consultants who will provide guidance to the new planner. This helpful guide focuses on operational and practical aspects of planning that are inadequately treated in many works on strategic planning.

166 Peterson, Marvin W. "Analyzing Alternative Approaches to Planning." In Paul Jedamus, Marvin W. Peterson, and Associates, *Improving Academic Management: A Handbook of Planning and Institutional Research*. San Francisco: Jossey-Bass, 1980. Pages 113–163.

This volume is a comprehensive handbook of planning and institutional research. (For a description of the book as a whole, please see no. 553.) Peterson's chapter provides the broad framework for the discussions of planning in all the chapters in the handbook. The chapter defines planning from several perspectives, presents the major theoretical models of and approaches to planning, and discusses the relationships among the environment, strategic planning, and tactical planning. It concludes by reviewing the major issues involved in developing an institutional planning function. This is one of the earlier resources in the higher education literature that provide the perspectives needed to extend planning practices from relatively formalistic and tactical approaches to the currently emphasized strategic planning and focus on environmental issues.

167 Peterson, Marvin W. "Continuity, Challenge and Change: An Organizational Perspective on Planning Past and Future." *Planning for Higher Education,* 1986, *14* (3), 6–15.

Trends in the past thirty-five years of planning in American higher education are summarized and then projected to the end of the decade. Peterson describes how techniques have become increasingly comprehensive and sophisticated, orientations have changed from reactive to adaptive, and practices have expanded in scope to include a complex array of situational factors. He then suggests that future planning efforts are likely to face continuing constraints and pressures from many constituents. Demographic, educational, telematics, and competitive "revolutions" are all predicted to cause adaptive changes in institutions. In managing these changes, Peterson sees planning becoming more proactive and future oriented; dealing with value-laden strategic choices, macro-change, and total context; and depending upon leadership that not only exercises strategic management but also provides vision and interpretation of changes for the organization. The forward-looking slant of this article makes it essential reading for all leaders and planners in higher education.

Reflections on Planning/Criticisms of Planning

168 Boulding, Kenneth E. "Reflections on Planning: The Value of Uncertainty." *Technology Review,* 1974, *77* (1), 8.

In this brief article, Boulding reflects upon his involvement with a university committee on planning and presents "twelve rather haphazard propositions." These range from several nontraditional views of the relationship between planning and decisions to a rather pessimistic view of the potential success of planning in universities. Boulding's views on decision agendas, valuation schemes, and uncertainty are very sobering for practicing planners. His concern that planning may produce illusions of certainty is countered by his advice to planners to widen the agendas and examine the values and valuc indicators of decision makers.

169 James, Barrie G. "Strategic Planning Under Fire." *Sloan Management Review,* 1984, *25* (4), 57–61.

This article examines key failures of strategic planning operations in the business sector. James contends that strategic planning approaches have been too growth oriented for application to declining markets, too narrowly focused on one or two aspects of a business for development of a central strategic theme, too often misapplied to changing situations, too focused on issue analysis rather than tactical implementation, and too self-centered, allowing techniques to become ends in themselves. No references are made to public or nonprofit sector applications, but the critique raises many issues that should be avoided in a strategic planning operation in any setting, including a college or university.

170 Mandelbaum, Seymour J. "A Complete General Theory of Planning Is Impossible." *Policy Sciences,* 1979, *11* (1), 59–71.

This essay proposes alternative definitions for *plan* and *planning* and discusses two criteria, brevity and neutrality, for developing a complete general theory of planning. Mandelbaum defines a plan as being "not a document stating intentions but a stable pattern of social interaction which variously constrains and encourages a set of subordinate behaviors" (p. 64). He discusses three dimensions of planning: the selection of a repertoire of behaviors, the process of adding to that repertoire, and the potential for structural transformation. He also comments on the role of planning professionals, presents several insights on the sources of resistance and the opportunities for professional planning, and discusses the uses of professional "dreaming." Although he is pessimistic about development of a general theory of planning, he encourages theoreticians and practitioners to continue the debate in order to learn more about the function of planning, which he contends is inherent in any social order.

171 Wildavsky, Aaron. "If Planning Is Everything, Maybe It's Nothing." *Policy Sciences,* 1973, *4* (2), 127–153.

The failures of national planning efforts around the world lead Wildavsky to question whether failure is integral to the very nature of formal planning. He explores this notion by discussing formal planning as future control, as cause, as power, as adaptation, as process, and as rationality. He concludes by discussing the costs and benefits of formal planning and the notion of planning as an article of faith. Although based on experience with formal planning in developing countries, the questions Wildavsky raises are applicable to any planning situation. Both complimentary and critical viewpoints on the application of formal planning are presented.

Strategic Planning/Strategic Management

172 Baldridge, J. Victor, and Okimi, Patricia H. "Strategic Planning in Higher Education: New Tool—or New Gimmick?" *AAHE Bulletin,* 1982, *35* (2), 6, 15–18.

This article begins with a critique of earlier long-range planning efforts and summarizes the stumbling blocks to effective planning. The authors conclude that earlier models of planning were not based on theories that reflected the real world of administrative decision making. They review strategic planning optimistically as a useful alternative that focuses on the organization's destiny and ultimate mission in the external environment. Conventional and strategic planning are compared along several aspects, including the arena of planning, who plans, time orientation, system and theoretical perspectives, and nature of outcomes. This brief article can provide a concise but comprehensive review of strategic planning alternatives for the university leader who is new to these concepts.

173 Chaffee, Ellen E. "Successful Strategic Management in Small Private Colleges." *Journal of Higher Education,* 1984, *55* (2), 212–241.

This valuable reference is based on a study of the way fourteen small private colleges dealt with financial decline. Two models of strategic management are presented and utilized to explain the results of the study, and extensive references in the literature are classified and compared in terms of the two models. The "adaptive" strategy model views the organization as an organism that changes products and services to maintain access to resources for survival. The "interpretive" strategy model, by contrast, views the organization as a social contract that is constantly changing and that requires the management of meaning, maintenance of credibility, and commitment of participants in order to survive. The author draws on the research to present both caveats and insights for practice. The conclusions drawn about the private colleges studied contain important messages for all institutions. For example, Chaffee notes that the more resilient institutions followed a combination of interpretive and adaptive strategies, with the former guiding the latter.

★174 Cope, Robert G. *Strategic Planning, Management, and Decision Making.* AAHE-ERIC Higher Education Research Report no. 9. Washington, D.C.: American Association for Higher Education, 1981. 67 pages.

175 Cope, Robert G. "A Contextual Model to Encompass the Strategic Planning Concept: Introducing a Newer Paradigm." *Planning for Higher Education,* 1985, *13* (3), 13–20.

These two publications present one of the most concise but complete available discussions of strategic planning and management as applied to higher education. The monograph contrasts the differences between long-range and strategic planning concepts, presents the intellectual foundations of strategic planning, discusses emerging techniques, and formulates a research agenda for studying the further application of strategic planning concepts to higher education. The 1985 article extends Cope's earlier discussions by advocating a contextual planning model that emphasizes the importance of the internal and external contexts of an organization. The model features six variables that lead to strategic choices: mission, opportunities, competition, strengths, commitment, and vision. These two publications are essential reading for both newcomers and experienced practitioners. Cope presents concepts succinctly and identifies resources for further investigation.

176 Forester, John. "Bounded Rationality and the Politics of Muddling Through." *Public Administration Review,* 1984, *44* (1), 23–31.

This article contends that determining and doing what is practical and what is rational depend upon the context. Forester develops a systematic scheme that identifies five layers of contextual complexity. This complexity is described as the type of boundedness of rationality, and it ranges from the rational-comprehensive ideal to the structurally distorted political-economic situation. For each level Forester describes conditions of administrative planning and action and the practical strategies that may need to be employed in taking actions. He outlines several complex strategies to replace simplistic approaches. Although this article is an abstract analysis of general public policy settings, the distinctions it makes are most valuable to planners who are attempting to determine the nature of their context and to assemble a mix of practical planning strategies likely to be successful in their particular setting.

177 Gluck, Frederick W., Kaufman, Stephen P., and Walleck, A. Steven. "Strategic Management for Competitive Advantage." *Harvard Business Review,* 1980, *58* (4), 154–161.

The formal planning systems of 120 companies in seven countries were studied to determine how these systems influenced major decisions shaping business strategies. The four-phase evolutionary model that emerged from this research has a direct correspondence to the development of planning techniques in higher education. The four phases are (1) basic financial planning, (2) forecast-based planning, (3) externally oriented planning, and (4) strategic management. Phase 4 involves the linkage of strategic planning to operational decision making. Three mechanisms to accomplish this link are described: a planning framework, a planning process, and a corporate values system. Most businesses and universities fall somewhere between phases 2 and 3. Therefore, phase 4 results present valuable implementation guidelines for both leaders and planning staff in higher education who desire to move toward strategic management.

178 Kotler, Philip, and Murphy, Patrick E. "Strategic Planning for Higher Education." *Journal of Higher Education,* 1981, *52* (5), 470–489.

The principles of strategic market planning found in the business literature are applied to higher education in this article. The authors review the strategic planning process model and illustrate it with a practical application in a small, private liberal arts college. They present modified business techniques for use in higher education and illustrate them with additional examples. The techniques include threat and opportunity matrices, academic portfolio analysis, and product/market opportunity analysis. The wide range of alternatives generated by these techniques is also illustrated. Since this article reports on some of the earlier efforts to apply marketing techniques to higher education, its discussion of techniques presents a bridge between early long- and short-range planning concepts and strategic thinking.

179 Mintzberg, Henry, and Waters, James A. "Strategies, Deliberate and Emergent." *Strategic Management Journal,* 1985, *6* (3), 257–272.

This essay is based on eleven intensive studies in both private and public organizations (including a university) of the way strategies are formulated. The authors define strategy as a "pattern in a stream of decisions." They characterize the relationship between intended and realized strategies as deliberate when the realized and intended strategies are identical and as emergent when a consistent pattern is present in the absence of intention. These strategems vary according to the precision and shared nature of leadership intentions, the degree of central control over organizational actions, and the benign, controllable, and predictable nature of the environment. Based upon the results of their research, the authors describe eight types of strategy along the continuum: planned, entrepreneurial, ideological, umbrella, process, unconnected, consensus, and imposed strategy. This is a valuable article for leaders and planning staff who are working with the often-neglected implementation aspects of strategic planning and policy administration.

180 Myran, Gunder A. (ed.). *Strategic Management in the Community College.* New Directions for Community Colleges, no. 44. San Francisco: Jossey-Bass, 1983. 121 pages.

This sourcebook deals with the emergent application of strategic management concepts to planning processes in the community college. Six areas are emphasized: external relations, internal communications and working relationships, financial resource development and allocation, program and service development, staff development, and strategic planning. Both strategic concepts and implementation approaches are discussed in this comprehensive review, making it a very useful reference for the practitioner in the community college. Particularly valuable are chapters on assessing and building relationships with groups in the environment, building internal consultation structures including collective bargaining units, and the role of the chief executive officer. The authors refer to many useful relationships that arise from the service role of the community college.

*181 Quinn, James Brian. "Strategic Goals: Process and Politics." *Sloan Management Review,* 1977, *19* (1), 21-37.

*182 Quinn, James Brian. "Strategic Change: Logical Incrementalism." *Sloan Management Review,* 1978, *20* (1), 7-21.

*183 Quinn, James Brian. "Managing Strategic Change." *Sloan Management Review,* 1980, *21* (4), 3-20.

This series of three articles reports on the results of extensive research on the management of strategic change in large organizations. It demonstrates why executives do not follow formal, textbook approaches. Instead, they are likely to use an integrative methodology that blends formal analysis, behavioral techniques, and power politics to achieve cohesive, deliberate movement. The author calls this approach "logical incrementalism." He argues that desired ends or strategic goals are conceived only broadly at the initiation of change; the goals are then refined and reshaped as new information is acquired. All three articles present guidelines on how to manage change processes, using actual examples. These results are also applicable to the higher education setting and are important for both leadership and staff support personnel. (For a full description of "Managing Strategic Change," please see entry no. 19.)

*184 Schendel, Dan E., and Hofer, Charles W. (eds.). *Strategic Management: A New View of Business Policy and Planning.* Boston: Little, Brown, 1979. 530 pages.

This volume is based on a collection of papers commissioned for a 1977 conference. The objectives of the conference were to define the dimensions and boundaries of business policy, strategic management, and planning; to identify opportunities and needs for research; and to help researchers, practitioners, and students better understand the implications of these new approaches to organizational integration. Ten topics are covered, including strategy and strategic management; goals and goal formation; strategy formulation, evaluation, and implementation; theory building and testing; and practitioners' views. Although the book is oriented toward business, one chapter is

concerned with not-for-profit organizations, including those in
higher education. References to the higher education literature
are dated. Nevertheless, this reference contains a blend of theory,
research, and practice and thus provides a useful source for those
seeking to understand the historical roots of strategic policy and
planning.

185 Shirley, Robert C. "Limiting the Scope of Strategy: A
Decision Based Approach." *Academy of Management Review,* 1982, *7* (2), 262–268.

186 Shirley, Robert C. "Identifying the Levels of Strategy
for a College or University." *Long Range Planning,* 1983,
16 (3), 92–98.

The first of these two articles deals with the failure of the literature to define adequately the character of strategic decisions.
Five criteria for distinguishing strategic decisions from other decisions are discussed, including the relationship between the organization and the environment, the whole organization as the
unit of analysis, the multifunctional nature of the decisions,
directional influence on activities throughout the enterprise, and
importance to success. In the second article Shirley outlines six
decision areas that accomplish the overall function of strategy
and discusses how they apply to the nonprofit sector, specifically
higher education. The six areas include basic mission, clientele,
goals, program/service mix, geographical service area, and comparative advantage. Shirley also contrasts the strategic level of
decision making with several other decision levels in the university. These two articles are very important for the planner and
institutional leader in that they provide an operational, decision-
based framework for organizing a strategic planning process.
(For a fuller description of the second Shirley article, please see
entry no. 14.)

187 Wortman, Max S., Jr. "Strategic Management and
Changing Leader-Follower Roles." *Journal of Applied
Behavioral Science,* 1982, *18* (3), 371–383.

The roles of leader and follower are described in this article,
with a specific focus on the strategic management functions of

executive officers. Wortman compares the role of the executive and his or her relationship with managers in two contrasting organizational settings, namely, organizations in which the executive is more concerned with short-term operating management and organizations in which the executive is more concerned with strategic issues. His comparisons cover leadership and followership behavior, personal style, follower reward structure, organizational structure, and problem-solving characteristics. His observations are based on literature contrasting American and Japanese corporate practices, but he also makes a case for applying them to government and nonprofit organizations. The content of this article is particularly important to executive officers in colleges and universities, governing board members, and officers in multicampus system administrations.

Policy Formulation

188 Brewer, Gary D. "Where the Twain Meet: Reconciling Science and Politics in Analysis." *Policy Sciences,* 1981, *13* (3), 269–279.

The role of policy analysis in social problem solving and strategic decision making is discussed, using a three-dimensional paradigm that combines science (explanation), analysis (contemplation), and politics (manipulation). Brewer applies the paradigm to bring out the purposes and uses (including nonuses) of policy analysis. Purposes range from brainstorming through planning and evaluation to scapegoating and blame sharing. Uses range from the analytical (narrowing options) to the political (postponement of action). This is a most valuable article for the planner, for it is one of the few resources that attempts to deal with both the scientific and the political dimensions of issues analysis. It also illustrates the inevitable tension that arises between rational analysis and political acts that lead to decisions.

189 Dror, Yehezkel. *Public Policymaking Reexamined.* (2nd ed.) New Brunswick, N.J.: Transaction Books, 1983. 420 pages.

This book is a republished version of a 1968 classic in policy sciences. Dror's analysis focuses on the interdependence of facts, values, and actions in public policy-making. His optimal model is qualitative rather than quantitative, contains both rational and extrarational components, includes metapolicymaking, and contains extensive feedback phases. Dror identifies improvements needed in public policy-making, including changes in knowledge, personnel, structure and process patterns, input and stipulated output, and the environment. Outlines of Dror's analysis and model are contained in comprehensive appendixes and are of great value to both the experienced planner and the newcomer. The references, however, are dated. More recent resources can be found in Dror's *Policymaking Under Adversity* (1986) and a third volume on "policy-gambling," which is in progress.

★**190** Elmore, Richard F. "Backward Mapping: Implementation Research and Policy Decisions." *Political Science Quarterly,* 1979–80, *94* (4), 601–616.

Elmore contends that most policy-making is flawed because it focuses on the front end of the policy-making process, which contends with goals, organizational intent, and hierarchy, rather than with the back end of the process, namely implementation, which is where 90 percent of the variation between policy intent and actuality occurs. As a cure, Elmore suggests "backward mapping," a process in which policymakers examine how and by whom policies will be implemented and then craft their policies to recognize the characteristics of the implementers and the variability and situational nature of the implementation environment. This is an excellent, context-establishing article that yields important insights on the difficulties of policy implementation. It should be very helpful to planners, who must deal with the uncertainties of extrapolating the impacts of plans on operating units and understand how strategy and tactics are translated and filtered by implementing units.

New Directions

Futures, Environmental Scanning, and Issues Management

191 Hearn, James C., and Heydinger, Richard B. "Scanning the University's External Environment—Objectives, Constraints, Possibilities." *Journal of Higher Education,* 1985, *56* (4), 419–445.

The Experimental Team for Environmental Assessment (ETEA) at the University of Minnesota was instituted in 1983 to test the applicability of the techniques of environmental scanning to a college or university setting and to "embrace uncertainty," among other objectives. This article provides a thoughtful analysis of the impediments to environmental scanning in a university environment and describes the structure, process, and interactions that characterized ETEA. The authors describe both immediate dividends and shortcomings of the environmental scanning technique. Hearn and Heydinger offer a handy set of hypotheses and findings and an excellent evaluative summary of the critical tensions in environmental assessment. These should be read by anyone thinking about conducting environmental scanning in a college or university. This article is an important complement to the other environmental scanning and futures literature.

192 Lozier, G. Gregory, and Chittipeddi, Kumar. "Issues Management in Strategic Planning." *Research in Higher Education,* 1986, *24* (1), 3–14.

This article discusses the technique of issues management as applied to the strategic planning process at Pennsylvania State University. Issues management is an ongoing organizational process that identifies issues that could affect the university, analyzes them to establish their relevance and the likelihood of their occurrence, and develops organizational responses to them. The technique was used as a strategy-oriented alternative to the ongoing institutional planning process, which was of necessity tied to the formal organizational structure. This article is extremely effective in demonstrating how an institution can link a macro-level, externally oriented, issues management process with a micro-level, internally oriented, formalistic planning process. The authors provide some excellent caveats and conclusions on the applications of issues management, on the "art" of planning, and on the importance of leadership in positioning institutions for the future.

★**193** Morrison, James L., Renfro, William L., and Boucher, Wayne I. *Futures Research and the Strategic Planning Process: Implications for Higher Education.* ASHE-ERIC Higher Education Research Report no. 9. Washington, D.C.: Association for the Study of Higher Education, 1984. 129 pages.

This publication presents a concise yet thorough development of a strategic planning process that combines the more traditional long-range planning cycle (goal setting, implementing, monitoring, and forecasting) with an environmental scanning cycle (scanning, evaluation/ranking, forecasting, and monitoring). The former maintains an internal perspective, while the latter is directed externally. The authors describe six components of the process, giving special attention to the techniques (including examples) of environmental scanning, issues evaluation, and forecasting. Their discussions cover scanning taxonomies, impact networks, the delphi technique, cross-impact analysis, scenario building, and many other topics. This is a valuable reference source for the leader, planner, or faculty member new to the applications of futures techniques. It also provides many citations that can help those who want to pursue techniques and applications in greater depth.

194 Zentner, Rene D. "Scenarios, Past, Present and Future." *Long Range Planning,* 1982, *15* (3), 12–20.

In this lucid article, Zentner presents a helpful explanation of the use of scenarios by planners. He traces the nature of the problems faced by planners, notes the failure of forecasting in meeting the needs for strategies to deal with uncertain futures, and discusses how to translate uncertainty into scenarios. Scenarios are characterized as "hypothetical sequences of events constructed for the purpose of focusing attention on causal processes and decision points.'' Zentner introduces methods for scenario development and describes how they can be used by planners. Several actual examples of corporate scenarios are provided in an appendix. This article is a cogent introduction to the use of scenarios, providing useful guidance on the why and how of scenario development and offering conclusions on the effective utilization of this technique.

Competitive Advantage

195 Ohmae, Kenichi. *The Mind of the Strategist: Business Planning for Competitive Advantage.* New York: Penguin, 1982. 283 pages.

This book explores the nature of strategic thinking and its difference from the formal planning process, the quantitative analysis and decision making that pass for strategic planning in many organizations. Ohmae presents four basic strategies for establishing competitive advantage and provides examples of their application in different settings. He suggests that choice of strategy should depend on whether the situation calls for utilizing existing, accepted concepts of the product/service or defining new concepts and also on whether or not it is wise to engage in head-to-head competition. This lucid, easily understood book is among the best introductions to strategic thinking and competitive advantage. While the examples are business oriented, the concepts are easily translated to higher education.

★196 Porter, Michael E. *Competitive Advantage: Creating and Sustaining Superior Performance.* New York: Free Press, 1985. 557 pages.

This book builds on Porter's earlier volume, *Competitive Strategy,* and applies his techniques for analyzing industries and competitors to creating and sustaining a competitive advantage. Porter deals with a variety of generic strategies, including cost, differentiation, and focus. He highlights the importance of coordinating the different stategies that units pursue within an overall framework for the organization. His concept of the ''value chain'' is

critical, enabling the planner to separate the activities of the organization and identify those that truly add the value from which
competitive advantage stems. This is an excellent book for the
planner who wants to focus in depth on the issue of competitive
advantage. The applications and examples are business oriented,
however, and the translation to applications in higher education
must be made by the reader.

197 Rowse, Glenwood L., and Wing, Paul. "Assessing
Competitive Structures in Higher Education." *Journal
of Higher Education,* 1982, *53* (6), 656–686.

This article focuses on the issue of "drawing power," which is another term for competitive advantage. Through analysis of enrollment patterns in New York colleges and universities, both public
and private, Rowse and Wing demonstrate the dependence of
high enrollment variability on competitive influences in addition
to demography and student participation. The authors discuss a
conceptual model for student choice, the results of a cluster analysis of New York institutions that identifies competing groups, a
summary of findings from the literature on competition, and a series of hypotheses about the way competition is affecting different
types of institutions. This article is an important reference for institutions seeking to assess their "drawing power." It provides
both qualitative and quantitative tools for evaluating the effects of
competition. It also gives a healthy sense of the complexity of dealing with the components of competitiveness in the real-world environment of enrollment management.

New External Relationships

198 Johnson, Lynn G. *The High Technology Connection: Academic
Industrial Cooperation for Economic Growth.* ASHE-ERIC
Higher Education Research Report no. 6. Washington,
D.C.: Association for the Study of Higher Education,
1984. 99 pages.

This monograph explores what is called "the high technology
connection"—cooperative endeavors involving academic and
industrial participants in technology transfer, or research and

development for economic purposes. Johnson provides several interesting typologies that allow the planner to view cooperative relationships from fresh perspectives. These focus on human resource and entrepreneurial aspects as well as on research and development outcomes. This is an excellent complement to the Matthews and Norgaard book (no. 199). Johnson deals in most cases with a different set of examples and focuses more closely on the developing partnerships among higher education, industry, and government. Institutional leaders and planners need to be aware of the implications of these developments for institutional planning, strategy, and policy formulation.

★**199** Matthews, Jana B., and Norgaard, Richard. *Managing the Partnership Between Higher Education and Industry*. Boulder, Colo: National Center for Higher Education Management Systems, 1984. 242 pages.

Drawing on a 1983 NCHEMS national assembly on the topic, this book explores the historical antecedents and current forces that are shaping new partnerships among higher education, industry, and government. It discusses the nature of these partnerships, the roles of different participants, and the risks and benefits to each, and offers conclusions about how to create and manage these relationships effectively. The content of this book has become even more salient with the growth of university/industry cooperatives and joint education/research ventures in the past several years. Matthews and Norgaard do an excellent job of placing these partnerships in the context of the growing proactive, external orientation of institutional leadership. This book provides the strategic planner with a guide to the scope and rationale of partnerships, though it does not deal much with the operational issues of making them happen.

9

Larry L. Leslie

Financial Management
and Resource Allocation

The ultimate "management instrument" of those who govern, manage, and lead is money. The way leaders and managers allocate and manage their financial resources often determines the effectiveness of their goal accomplishment. The experienced higher education observer knows that the true test of leadership's and management's intent is the pattern of their dollar allocation. To some, this observation may appear cynical; to those who understand how decisions are executed, it will be considered merely realistic. It has been said that in the end, all decisions are political. To this we would add that in the end, all political decisions are executed through some form of resource allocation or reallocation. The acts performed by managers in carrying out those political decisions will necessarily contain significant aspects of financial management.

This chapter reviews the literature pertaining to the ways resources should be and are allocated—beginning in the broadest policy sense—and the ways those resources should be and are managed once they arrive at the point of policy execution, which is usually the internal units of colleges and universities. To set the stage for viewing the more recent literature, the chapter begins with a historical sketch of this field's development. Toward

Note: I wish to express my gratitude to the members of the 1986 Higher Education Finance class at the University of Arizona and to graduate assistants Ellen Price, Nora Martinez, and Helen Garcia for their valuable assistance and suggestions in selecting and composing the annotations.

the end of this sketch, a simple dichotomy that has proved useful in organizing the annotations will be presented. The discussion then turns to the reasons why this literature has grown so dramatically in recent years. Employing the dichotomy just mentioned, I next offer a framework for viewing the annotations. The introduction closes with a commentary on the existing literature and, by implication, some new directions the literature might take.

How the Field Has Developed

The literature on higher education finance in contemporary times is often traced back to John Dale Russell, who, with F. W. Reeves, composed Volume 7, "Finance," in *The Evaluation of Higher Education* at the University of Chicago in 1935. Russell and Reeves's study of forty-four colleges served as a qualitative benchmark for unit cost studies for more than twenty years. Russell's was the premiere name in higher education finance during that entire time. However, the National Association of College and University Business Officers (NACUBO), the overarching professional organization in the field, traces the related professional literature back to William Rainey Harper's "The Business Side of a University" (1905). Other early landmark references cited by NACUBO are Trevor Arnett's *College and University Finance* (1922), W. B. Franke's "College and University Accounting" (1925), and T. L. Hungate's "A Study of Financial Reports of Colleges and Universities in the United States" (1930).

Financial management as a professional field clearly is of recent development, and the accompanying professional literature is of similarly recent origins. When the first edition of *College and University Business Administration (CUBA)* was published in 1952 by the American Council on Education, the field of financial management had not yet developed a completely separate identity. Indeed, it was not until the third edition, published in 1974, that specialists in the field wrested publication of *CUBA* from the American Council on Education, the umbrella organization for higher education. Prior to that time, a committee of college and university business officers had worked under council oversight to develop the first authoritative sourcebook on principles and policies for all areas of college and university business administration. With the third edition and continuing on to the fourth edition in 1982, however, NACUBO took over publication of *CUBA* and firmly established its preeminence in the field. Today, *CUBA* is "the bible" of business and financial administration in colleges and universities, and NACUBO seemingly possesses nearly total authority over formal procedures for business and financial management. In regard to the recency of literature in the financing field, it is instructive that the second edition of *CUBA*, published in 1955, listed fewer than a dozen references more than five years old in a bibliography of sixty pages.

How did higher education finance become an area worthy of the considerable attention it receives today? A principal explanation is simply one of changing scale. When higher education enrolled a few hundred thousand students and consumed a tiny portion of the gross national product (GNP), it did not seem to matter that resource management and allocation in this area were less than optimum. Today, however, with 12.3 million students enrolled and higher education costing $125 billion and consuming roughly 2.6 percent of the GNP, efficient and effective financing has become an important matter.

A corollary reason for the growth of the field's literature is that there is more to write about. With the growth of the higher education enterprise, many new financial management and allocation strategies and techniques have been advanced. Research and analysis have followed. Major changes have occurred in the way public subsidies are dispensed; the change to subsidies that permit low tuition from direct subsidies to needy students is one example. Another is in the structuring of direct subsidies to institutions, which has come to focus on such questions as these: How can government funding create incentives for improved educational quality and economic growth? How may state funding formulas be altered to stimulate achievement of specific social ends? What mechanisms may be established internally to further financial accountability and the capacity for change?

The introduction and growth of new strategies for financial management have been furthered by aberrations in financial support. Whether because of reduced government aid during periods of economic recession, declines in tuition receipts as enrollments recede, or other causes, institutional revenues ebb and flow. During prosperous years, higher education institutions raise salaries, begin new programs, purchase equipment, and commission new buildings; when revenue growth slows or revenue actually declines, stressful retrenchment steps are taken. Each occurrence brings about a new spate of literature, and a new, or more commonly old but newly relabeled, set of adaptive techniques usually emerges.

A third reason for the precipitate growth in this literature is that there are more people to write it. Some have argued that higher education degree programs are unnecessary—that collegiate administrators properly emerge from and gain experience only through the faculty ranks. Unnecessary or not, such degree programs have been created, particularly in research universities, and their faculties must research and write to gain academic acceptability. Their students, having been exposed to academic norms, assume administrative and academic positions and often thereafter feel a need to put their ideas and productive practices into print. Meanwhile, normal processes of professionalization are also at work. Like other specialists, college business officers increase in numbers, form professional organizations (NACUBO in this case), and begin to share ideas in written form. In time, subspecialties are created. Finance officers with different areas of expertise form substructures within larger organizations—for example, the Financial Management Committee within NACUBO—and create specialized publications, such as the *Journal of Education Finance* and the *Economics of Education Review*.

Framework

Taking the early 1950s as the beginning of the modern era in higher education financial management and resource allocation, one can identify two more or less parallel and distinct lines of research and scholarly development that are manifest in the literature. One line of development has been among applied researchers, administrators, and technicians. These were the faculty and graduates of the original three major Centers for the Study of Higher Education plus those of later centers; the vice-presidents and directors of or for budgeting, finance, and financial management; and staff members of offices of budgeting, institutional research, and planning. On occasion they were the staff members of state legislative committees or of national higher education associations. Somewhat more often they were the staff members of state coordinating and governing boards or of regional higher education associations. Most noticeably they were staff members of the National Center for Higher Education Management Systems (NCHEMS), of the Education Commission of the States (ECS), or of the State Higher Education Executive Officers (SHEEO).

As one might expect from such individuals, the line of research and scholarship they developed has had an applied or practical orientation. These researchers and writers largely have attempted to help solve problems, design schemes for better resource management and allocation, and generally provide ideas for the improvement of financial management practice. Examples annotated later in this chapter are Allen and Brinkman's innovative treatment of marginal costing techniques (no. 218), Anderson's juxtaposition of financial resources with institutional goal achievements (no. 213), and Hopkins and Massy's pioneering work on planning models (no. 303).

The second line of research and scholarship has been directed more toward broad policy. Examples annotated here are Breneman and Finn's treatment of the public responsibility for resource allocation to private higher education (no. 60), Breneman and Nelson's assessment of community college financing and related mission accomplishment (no. 203), and Leslie and Ramey's analysis of the relationship between state appropriations and enrollments (no. 208). Usually such writings have been more theoretical, or at least more theoretically based, than those in the first line, and there has been less concern with direct practice. In the first line of research and scholarship one may find, for example, writings on statewide allocation formulas and zero-based budgeting, whereas in the second line one may find dissertations on the concept of human capital theory and empirical estimates of internal rates of return to higher education. The first line is aimed primarily at practicing administrators; the second, at those involved in basic policy formation. Both groups are concerned with more efficient and effective resource decisions; however, the latter group's focus is on choices made in the allocation of societal resources among public ventures generally, while the former tend to focus upon efficient and effective use of resources already allocated to higher education.

This second, more theory-oriented group of researcher/scholars is composed primarily of graduates of economics departments rather than of higher education centers or management departments. Like the writings of the more applied group, higher education finance literature written by economists is a recent arrival. Although one may track the entry of economics into higher education finance policy to Alfred Marshall (1927) or even Adam Smith ([1776] 1985), economics did not really "arrive" in the public sector generally, and higher education in particular, until the Kennedy years. The writings of Mincer (1958) and Schultz (1960) on the concept of human capital and investment in education seem to have launched the economists' entry in contemporary times.

Resource Allocation Policy. The annotations that follow are grouped along the two lines of research and scholarly development just discussed. We present first the policy-based writings that are usually theoretical, often composed by economists, and tend to have as their primary aim the bringing of principles of marginal analysis to public finance. These writings look closely at resource allocation decisions in society overall and at allocation targets and forms within higher education itself. The material annotated in this area can be divided into about a half dozen policy areas. In this broad policy category, Bowen's book (no. 200) examines the value of higher education. Finn's book (no. 62) considers the financing role of the federal government, whereas the Sloan Commission work (no. 79) deals with government finance generally. Tuckman and Whalen's edited volume (no. 211) examines subsidies of all types, while the Carnegie

Council book (no. 204) focuses on tuition policies, and the Manski and Wise entry (no. 69) addresses student aid. The Leslie and Ramey paper (no. 208) concerns state appropriations to public institutions. Two other books annotated (no. 203 and no. 212) consider the financing of community colleges, and two relate primarily to private colleges (no. 60 and no. 206). Of the final two items, one (no. 207) discusses enrollment and tuition policy, and the other (no. 201) considers higher education costs in policy terms.

Internal Financial Management. The second major category of writings includes research and scholarship concerned with practical matters of internal financial management and allocation, both within institutions and within higher education systems broadly defined. Here the stress is upon improved financial operations, and traditional tests of rationality predominate: Through what means can organizational goals be met most effectively and at the lowest expenditure of resources?

The items annotated in this section cover several important financial management and resource allocation topics: (1) general financial management strategies and issues, (2) costing and resource allocation, and (3) other financial management functions. Five books and monographs discuss institutional financial management in broad terms (nos. 213, 214, 215, 216, 217). The same number of entries deals with techniques and uses of costing, particularly in resource allocation (nos. 218, 219, 220, 221, 222). In the third category, single entries address the topics of budgeting (no. 224), financial planning (no. 303), fundraising (no. 228), capital campaigns (no. 225), and accounting (no. 229). Campbell's book (no. 223) focuses on financial management practices in community colleges, whereas the Falender and Merson volume (no. 226) concerns practices in small colleges and specialized institutions.

Commentary

A major criticism of the resource allocation and financial management literatures is that the former is too political, whereas the latter is not political enough. When I began my higher education finance work with the Committee for Economic Development (CED) in 1970, I naively assumed that the CED effort to compose a national policy statement on the management and financing of colleges would be based on an objective analysis of the issues. Instead, I found that the CED task force appointed to examine the issues was composed almost exclusively of private college trustees whose single goal was to improve the competitive position of private colleges vis-a-vis public ones. The resulting document recommended a raising of four-year public tuitions to fifty percent of instructional costs—under the guise of expanding student opportunities. Such was my introduction to higher education finance policy-making. The CED policy statement (McMurrin, 1971) and a Carnegie Commission on Higher Education (1973) volume (*Higher Education: Who Pays? Who Benefits? Who Should Pay?*) were perhaps the most notorious examples of the many politically motivated policy documents of the decade.

None of us, of course, is ever completely free of personal values, and few policy writers escape the temptation to exercise them. This tendency is the major problem with higher education financing policy research and publications. If the reader is aware of an author's biases, little harm may be done; however, probably only the close observers of higher education are aware enough to exercise a judicious quantity of *caveat emptor*. Some writers identify their basic assumptions and what they seek to accomplish (for example, reallocating public resources to private institutions or moving resources from students to public institutions), but many do not. The unsophisticated reader may thus take some of the recommendations of these policy works without sufficient grains of salt. In sum, the finance policy analysis writings are useful primarily for building rationales for supporting previously held positions. Fortunately, most of the values held by the analyst/authors are consistent with prevailing social values.

In view of this politicization of the financial policy literature, the criticism that the financial management literature is lacking in attention to political realities must at first glance seem rather strange. The lack shows, however, in the fact that the

financial management literature too often proposes strategies
that are politically unrealistic. Those who toil in this field almost
uniformly employ a strict management science perspective and
judge financial management techniques on straight effective-
ness/efficiency criteria (achieving objectives at the lowest possible
cost) without consideration of political constraints. Zero-based
budgeting is a classic example of a politically unworkable technique foisted upon unsuspecting financial managers without any
attention to practicalities. The classic conceptual discussion of
conflicts between political reality and traditional management
rationality is contained in Aaron Wildavsky's (1984) treatment
of planning, programming, budgeting (PPB) and zero-based
budgeting (ZBB) techniques. In sum, the financial management
literature badly needs realistic field testing of management strategies, including examination of the practical constraints of
money, time, information, and politics.

References

American Council on Education. *College and University Business Administration.* (1st
    and 2nd eds.) National Association of College and University Business Of-
    ficers. *College and University Business Administration.* (3rd ed.) Edited by Abbott
    Wainwright. Washington, D.C.: National Association of College and Univer-
    sity Business Officers, 1974. National Association of College and University
    Business Officers. *College and University Business Administration.* (4th ed.) Edited
    by Lanora Welzenbach. Washington, D.C.: National Association of College
    and University Business Officers, 1982. Washington, D.C.: American Council
    on Education, 1952 and 1955.
Arnett, T. *College and University Finance.* New York: General Education Board,
    1922.
Carnegie Commission on Higher Education. *Higher Education: Who Pays? Who
    Benefits? Who Should Pay?* New York: McGraw-Hill, 1973.
Franke, W. B. "College and University Accounting." *Journal of Accountancy,* 1925,
    39 (3), 170–181.
Harper, W. R. "The Business Side of a University." In W. R. Harper, *Trends
    in Higher Education.* Chicago: University of Chicago Press, 1905.
Hungate, T. L. "A Study of Financial Reports of Colleges and Universities in
    the United States." Urbana, Ill.: National Committee on Standard Reports
    for Institutions of Higher Education, 1930.
McMurrin, S. M. (ed.). *The Conditions for Educational Quality.* Committee for
    Economic Development Supplementary Paper no. 34. New York: Commit-
    tee for Economic Development, 1971.
Marshall, A. *Principles of Economics.* (8th ed.) London: Macmillan, 1927.
Mincer, J. "Investment in Human Capital and Personal Income Distribution."
    Journal of Political Economy, 1958, *66* (4), 281–302.

Russell, J. D., and Reeves, F. W. "Finance." In J. D. Russell (ed.), *The Evaluation of Higher Education.* Vol. 7. Chicago: University of Chicago Press, 1935.

Schultz, T. W. "Capital Formation by Education." *Journal of Political Economy,* 1960, *68,* 571–583.

Smith, A. *Wealth of Nations.* New York: Random House, 1985. (Originally published 1776.)

Wildavsky, A. *The Politics of The Budgetary Process.* (4th ed.) Boston: Little, Brown, 1984.

Resource Allocation Policy

200 Bowen, Howard R. *Investment in Learning: The Individual and Social Value of American Higher Education.* San Francisco: Jossey-Bass, 1977. 507 pages.

In this book Bowen presents a comprehensive analysis of the value of American higher education in order to demonstrate why public resources should be allocated to the higher education function. He presents fairly the writings on such topics as human capital theory, how student attitudes change from freshman to senior year, how alumni view their college, and the measurability of the social benefits of higher education. His discussion includes efficiency and accountability in higher education, intended outcomes, cognitive learning, emotional and moral development, citizenship and economic productivity, societal outcomes from education and research and public service, and the views of social critics. Bowen's view is optimistic. Drawing on a profound knowledge of both the economic and the noneconomic aspects of higher education, he concludes that the historic growth of higher education in the United States has been beneficial to society and that future returns will be gained through widening access to higher education to include more people. The potential returns of higher education to society, he says, occur mainly in the augmenting of individual lives and the building of a sane society rather than in contributions to the gross national product. This book is a standard source for educators throughout the country.

*201 Bowen, Howard R. *The Costs of Higher Education: How Much Do Colleges and Universities Spend per Student and How Much Should They Spend?* San Francisco: Jossey-Bass, 1980. 287 pages.

Costs of higher education are determined by societal and institutional factors, Bowen points out. From society's perspective, the interaction between demand and cost determines the total expenditures allocated to higher education. From the institutional perspective, costs are set by the amount of money institutions are able to raise (Revenue Theory of Cost). Using time-series information, Bowen determines national cost trends in higher education. He concludes that educational costs per student have remained steady, but faculty compensation has depended on public attitudes. Actual costs at particular institutions reflect different desired outcomes, different expenditure patterns, and lack of a clear relationship between size and unit costs. Using both the national trends and the institutional information, Bowen estimates that in order to restore support of higher education to the 1969–70 level, the amount of money actually expended should rise 13 percent, to $2,500 per year per student in public institutions and $3,200 in private ones. This book is useful for understanding economic and financial concepts and for gaining a view of past, present, and future cost patterns in higher education and the underlying factors that explain them.

*202 Breneman, David W., and Finn, Chester E. (eds.). *Public Policy and Private Higher Education.* Washington, D.C.: Brookings Institution, 1978. 468 pages.

For a full description of this work, please see entry no. 60.

*203 Breneman, David W., and Nelson, Susan C. *Financing Community Colleges: An Economic Perspective.* Washington, D.C.: Brookings Institution, 1981. 222 pages.

This book is probably the most careful and scholarly analysis ever done on the topic of community college finance. The authors possess a broad understanding of higher education and a fairly good specific understanding of the mission of community colleges. The recurring theme of their book is the conflict that arises when community colleges strive to expand educational services while public resources are in relative decline. The authors examine the merits of public subsidy for the various functions of the community college, and several functions receive a negative evaluation. Most of the conclusions reached are substantiated by careful analysis, but exceptions are the beliefs that the transfer function should be removed and that remedial education should receive public support. Breneman and Nelson hold that the transfer function is not well served by community colleges and that students planning to earn a four-year degree should begin at a four-year school. The funding of remedial education, though defensible on other grounds, is not justified under their framework.

204 Carnegie Council on Policy Studies in Higher Education. *Low or No Tuition: The Feasibility of a National Policy for the First Two Years of College.* San Francisco: Jossey-Bass, 1975. 88 pages.

This report examines the feasibility of low or no tuition for the first two years of college. The report is primarily concerned with three issues: first, tuition policy in the fifty states and the effects of low or no tuition; second, whether the federal government should become involved in setting that policy; and third, if so, what the policy's objective should be. The report provides a brief history of tuition policies, beginning with the 1947 Zook Commission (which originally proposed that public higher education should be free during the freshman and sophomore years), and goes on to examine the feasibility of low or no tuition. Specific details and recommendations are given in the last chapter, including possible alternative tuition approaches. The council recommends that a new program of tuition equalization grants be adopted for students attending private colleges and universities. This report, though now dated, provides a useful reminder of the issues involved in setting tuition prices and what the long-term societal costs of present high and rapidly increasing prices may be.

★205 Finn, Chester E., Jr. *Scholars, Dollars and Bureaucrats.* Washington, D.C.: Brookings Institution, 1978. 238 pages.

For a complete description of this work, please see entry no. 62.

206 Hoy, C. John, and Bernstein, Melvin H. (eds.). *Financing Higher Education: Public Investment.* Boston: Auburn House, 1982. 200 pages.

This book is one of a three-part series developed by the New England Board of Higher Education for the purpose of investigating the relationship between higher education and the economy of New England. The primary aim of the book is to serve as a policy guidance handbook for state government and educational decision makers. It provides specific analysis of the effect of government and investment in higher education on the economy of the region. The entire collection of essays is based on the premise that the country's most persistent problem is inadequate investment in human capital through higher education. A penetrating but brief analysis of fiscal policies, including tax policies at the state level, is also provided, along with an examination of the implications of recent changes in federal tax laws regarding the treatment of private-sector contributions to higher education. Basically, the book provides a broad view of the national context of funding, giving specific emphasis to the New England region.

207 Ihlanfeldt, William. *Achieving Optimal Enrollments and Tuition Revenues: A Guide to Modern Methods of Market Research, Student Recruitment, and Institutional Pricing.* San Francisco: Jossey-Bass, 1980. 283 pages.

Ihlanfeldt has succeeded in writing a practical handbook that addresses the state of the student applicant market. Through a discussion of markets, yields, and pricing of educational programs, he outlines ways to plan marketing strategies. Another section of his book emphasizes the need for communication among different groups of people—staff, faculty, parents, alumni, and students—to facilitate the implementation of these marketing strategies. Ihlandfeldt offers several institutional case studies that provide relevant and useful information about the current state of marketing in higher education. This volume would be particularly valuable to presidents, deans, directors, and boards who have a practical orientation to problem solving. It is a "how to do it" book, not a theoretical treatise.

208 Leslie, Larry L., and Ramey, Garey W. "State Appropriations and Enrollments: Docs Enrollment Growth Still Pay?" *Journal of Higher Education,* 1986, *57* (1), 1–19.

Leslie and Ramey attack one of the most ubiquitous assumptions undergirding the financing of higher education in America: that enrollments are the key to financial health. They assert that during the period of financial stress and projected enrollment decline, institutional leaders based their management plan on enrollment maintenance or growth. They then proceed to demonstrate the fallaciousness of the enrollment-appropriation assumption. Utilizing 1965–1981 enrollment and state appropriations data for 439 public institutions, they show empirically that the states neither reward enrollment growth nor punish enrollment decline by adding or subtracting resources to any degree approaching the relative enrollment change. They conclude that state behaviors instead conform to normative political behavior. This article is fundamental to understanding the bases of state allocation of resources for public higher education.

★209 Manski, Charles F., and Wise, David A. *College Choice in America.* Cambridge, Mass.: Harvard University Press, 1983. 221 pages.

For a complete description of this work, please see entry no. 69.

210 Sloan Commission on Government and Higher Education. *A Program for Renewed Partnership.* Cambridge, Mass.: Ballinger, 1980. 309 pages.

For a complete description of this work, please see entry no. 79.

★211 Tuckman, Howard P., and Whalen, Edward (eds.). *Subsidies to Higher Education: The Issues*. New York: Praeger, 1980. 322 pages.

Tuckman and Whalen have edited a fifteen-chapter volume that addresses numerous topics related to the grants and subsidies supporting much of higher education. Subjects covered include financing patterns and sources of support, student grants and loans, faculty demand and compensation, subsidies in developing nations, federal regulations, unionization, and open admissions at the City University of New York. One of the most salient and controversial chapters is by William E. Becker, Jr., who argues that the scale of corporate giving to universities should influence the curriculum; for example, if a large corporation endows the university with a vast sum of money, it is in the university's best interest to advocate capitalism and discourage courses that are critical of that ideology. The ramifications of this proposal for institutional autonomy are far-reaching. Since the book covers such a wide range of topics, it should appeal to a diverse audience.

212 Wattenbarger, James L., and Cage, Bob N. *More Money for More Opportunity: Financial Support of Community College Systems*. San Francisco: Jossey-Bass, 1974. 122 pages.

This book on community college financing stresses that state funding is becoming a pervasive method of support for community colleges. The authors' research data were gathered from documents obtained from directors of community colleges in several states. They assert that local control and autonomy of the colleges must be maintained, for both philosophical and historical reasons. At the same time, an alliance between the state and local government is imperative if the mission of the comprehensive community college is to be carried out. This volume should be especially appealing to faculty members, boards of trustees, administrators, and politicians who are interested in community college affairs. It is a very concise treatment of a timely issue.

Internal Financial Management

General Financial Management Strategies and Issues

213 Anderson, Richard E. *Finance and Effectiveness: A Study of College Environments.* Princeton, N.J.: Educational Testing Service, 1983. 172 pages.

This work is the product of a study of financial and educational trends in American higher education. The study collected detailed financial, personnel, and other institutional data from ninety-three public and private colleges and universities every third year from 1967 to 1980. The Institutional Functioning Inventory (IFI) was used to measure campus climate on a variety of scales, such as concern for improving society, concern for undergraduate instruction, and concern for innovation. Visits were made to thirteen colleges to ascertain the accuracy of the financial and IFI measures, examine the context of the relationship between finance and functioning, and obtain a better understanding of whether administrative actions can keep financial trouble from affecting campus functioning. The author attempts to provide an evaluation of the financial trends in higher education and the changes in college functioning, as perceived by the faculty of the studied institutions. He then relates the changes in finance to the changes in functioning. This is one of a very few research studies into the internal operations of a broad sample of institutions.

214 Carter, E. Eugene. *College Financial Management.* Lexington, Mass.: Lexington Books, 1980. 201 pages.

Carter discusses several economic and financial concepts, including investment risk and risk premiums, short-term cash management, dormitory financing, tuition and student aid, and endowment management. He uses Georgetown University and Wichita State University as models in developing his points: endowment management and investment policies are described at Georgetown, while long-range planning, featuring the AAUP faculty planning model, is illustrated at Wichita State. The author presents his concepts in readable, nontechnical language. His book is ideal for administrators who have not been trained in professional financial management and are puzzled by the complex financial milieu they have entered.

215 Harcleroad, Fred F. (ed.). *Financing Postsecondary Education in the 1980s.* Tucson, Ariz.: Center for the Study of Higher Education, 1979. 126 pages.

This monograph is a collection of twelve papers presented at the fifth National Conference on Higher Education Finance. It includes penetrating analyses of costing and its relationship to planning and budgeting, the state role in financing and how it can be affected by postsecondary institutions, and the prospects for higher education finance in the 1980s. One article, "Financial Prospects for Higher Education in the '80s" by Larry L. Leslie, expresses a somewhat optimistic view of postsecondary financial prospects. Lyman Glenny, however, projects a much gloomier picture, based on declining enrollments and political machinations at the state level. One thread running through several articles is that educators must move from the ivy-covered environs of the academy into the tangled thicket of politics if they expect to obtain sufficient resources to sustain their institutions. The strength of these papers is in their breadth of coverage and their attention to political realities.

★216 Leslie, Larry L. (ed.). *Responding to New Realities in Funding.* New Directions for Institutional Research, no. 43. San Francisco: Jossey-Bass, 1984. 99 pages.

This volume of six chapters brings together the financial management and allocation strategies that originated during the enrollment and fiscal stress periods of the 1970s and early 1980s. Anthony Morgan's framework chapter, in which he organizes all the strategies developed since World War II, is probably the most useful essay ever written in identifying the common conceptual bases of financial management innovations. Paul Brinkman's chapter, on new state formulas, is the most thorough analytical paper written on this subject. Richard Allen brings together and illustrates the numerous incentive financing strategies developed to achieve particular goals, especially the improvement of quality. The chapter by Kenneth Mortimer and

Barbara Taylor is a report of their Lilly Endowment resource reallocation study, which identified and organized the numerous steps taken by institutions to increase efficiency and target goals. The editor's closing chapter utilizes Morgan's framework to synthesize the developments described in the four content chapters.

217 Lohmann, Roger A. *Breaking Even: Financial Management in Human Service Organizations.* Philadelphia: Temple University Press, 1980. 333 pages.

Lohmann's book presents a discussion and analysis of financial management in the context of human service organizations. Its predominant theme is the need to "break even" by acquiring capital to offset costs. Lohmann's model consists of a financial management process that includes fund-raising, budgeting, fiscal control, financial planning, and evaluation. This publication will appeal primarily to human services administrators and practitioners. It is an introductory text, presenting basic concepts and terminology in a very readable style. The student as well as the practitioner can profit from reading this "state of the art" human service financial management text.

Costing and Resource Allocation

★218 Allen, Richard H., and Brinkman, Paul T. *Marginal Costing Techniques for Higher Education.* Boulder, Colo.: National Center for Higher Education Management Systems, 1983. 80 pages.

Enrollment declines and fiscal shortfalls have created a renewed emphasis on using marginal rather than average costs to determine costs per student credit hour. This monograph examines three common methods of calculating marginal costs—the regression method, the incremental cost method, and the fixed and variable cost method. The regression method was found to be the simplest to use, but the authors judge it to be unreliable in determining specific costs. Its best use, they feel, is in determining the shapes and locations of cost curves. The incremental method was found to be the easiest of the three methods in computing variable costs, but because of an unstable relationship between costs and production, one can arrive at a negative marginal cost. The fixed and variable cost method was found to be most appropriate for higher education because it relies heavily on political processes for determining standard costs. The authors conclude that marginal costing techniques have a place in higher education, but more research needs to be done in this area to account for institutional differences. For those interested in developing marginal cost approaches to resource allocation, this publication describes the options and permits selection of the best approach.

219 Gamso, Gary. *An Approach to Cost Studies in Small Colleges.* Boulder, Colo.: National Center for Higher Education Management Systems, 1978. 83 pages.

This monograph provides the small college administrator, who may have limited access to or knowledge of computers, with a simplified approach to cost analysis. It supplies a set of guidelines for developing unit cost data, for either internal management or interinstitutional exchange, to complement management information that is already available. Detailed worksheets are used, so computers are not necessary. The author points out particular costing problems associated with small colleges. An extensive appendix provides an excellent, concise discussion of the caveats of cost studies as well as a description of the National Center for Higher Education Management Systems costing standards. Advances in computer technology have probably made this monograph less useful today than when it was published; however, its worksheets could be adapted for use with microcomputer spreadsheet programs.

220 Gonyea, Meredith A. (ed.). *Analyzing and Constructing Cost.* New Directions for Institutional Research, no. 17. San Francisco: Jossey-Bass, 1978. 108 pages.

This monograph deals with the Institute of Medicine model for determining cost per student and faculty resource allocation in health profession education, which, due to its complexity, has been largely excluded from traditional higher education cost analysis. The first article presents an overview of the pre– and post–Institute of Medicine model accounting problems and concludes that the model has had mixed success. It serves well in providing data to outside funding agencies but is of little value for internal management. The third article compares the Institute of Medicine model to other cost accounting models and questions why all give different values when using the same data sources. Other articles deal with the problems of determining student costs when using medical student equivalents compared to traditional student credit hours. The editor concludes that the Institute of Medicine model has applications in all areas of higher education, not only in health profession education. Medical costs have rarely been examined closely because existing models have not been appropriate, so the Institute of Medicine model, when perfected, could open a new area of financial management.

221 Levin, Henry M. *Cost Effectiveness, a Primer*. Beverly Hills, Calif.: Sage, 1983. 168 pages.

Levin uses examples and exercises to illustrate the concept of cost analysis and cost-effectiveness in policy analysis, particularly in program evaluation. His book presents an analytical framework for understanding cost analysis, the concept and measurement of cost, the assignment of values to program inputs, the implementation and analysis of program costs, and the distribution of program effectiveness. The book also discusses the proper and improper use of cost analysis. Levin's book is easy to read and is directed toward the policymaker and administrator as well as the program evaluator. The thorough discussion of marginal costs and the framework for allocating and distributing costs among constituencies are the two greatest strengths of the volume. The techniques described are necessary to but rarely found in academic program evaluation.

222 National Association of College and University Business Officers. *Costing for Policy Analysts*. Washington, D.C.: National Association of College and University Business Officers, 1980. 81 pages.

This report follows two previous higher education costing studies from the National Association of College and University Business

Officers. The report provides a guide for "cost behavior analysis," a dynamic approach to costing. It also offers insights and suggestions from administrators and analysts who have completed cost studies in specific areas. It identifies and describes factors that relate to dynamic cost behavior. A five-step procedure is given for cost behavior analysis, and four applications are provided: operation and maintenance at Denison University, use of faculty resources at Drake University, student service needs at Santa Fe Community College, and library fixed and variable costs at the University of Wisconsin. The report provides a simplified outline of cost analysis and a framework for beginning a cost study. It is not designed to stand alone as a costing tool, and unfortunately it provides no list of supplementary material.

Other Financial Management Functions

223 Campbell, Dale F. (ed.). *Strengthening Financial Management.* New Directions for Community Colleges, no. 50. San Francisco: Jossey-Bass, 1985. 130 pages.

This is a monograph of eleven articles on financial management in community colleges. Part One deals with the management functions of community college business officers—planning, cost accounting, purchasing, and financial aid. Part Two concerns the shifting role of the business officer, from that of an administrator and bookkeeper to that of a member of an entrepreneurial team. Part Three deals with issues and problems facing community college financial managers for the next ten years. Specific topics in Part One are the integration of academic planning into the budget process, the pros and cons of various cost accounting methods and the information that can be gained through their use, and new sources of revenues to replace declining federal and state aid. Part Two discusses ways to use community needs assessments as planning tools, tap private revenue sources such as alumni and corporations, and manage college investments. Specific topics discussed in Part Three include professional development programs for business officers. The last chapter is an abstract of community college finance articles currently available through the Educational Resources Information Clearinghouse for Community and Junior Colleges.

*224 Caruthers, J. Kent, and Orwig, Melvin D. *Budgeting in Higher Education.* AAHE-ERIC Higher Education Research Report no. 3. Washington, D.C.: American Association for Higher Education, 1979. 99 pages.

This monograph is known primarily for its description of budgeting alternatives in the unique environment of higher education. It is divided into six parts, the first of which examines budgeting to determine whether the process can be considered as political or technical in nature. The roles of the participants and the questions of centralization of authority and equity in distribution of funds are addressed in the second part. The third part examines the history of budgeting in higher education and its close ties to budgeting in government. Part Four details five budget-planning approaches: incremental, formula, PPBS, ZBB, and performance budgeting. The authors stress that rationality in budgeting may be dormant, but it is not dead. The fifth part of the monograph follows a budget cycle through all of its phases, from request to allocation and expenditure, and explores the strategies employed by the parties involved in the process. The sixth and concluding part is an attempt to peer into the future and predict the impact of forces that are likely to exert an influence on the budgets of institutions of higher education in the 1980s. This monograph is useful for those interested in considering and evaluating the available choices in budgetary approaches.

225 Coldren, Sharon L. *The Constant Quest: Raising Billions Through Capital Campaigns.* Washington, D.C.: American Council on Education, 1982. 128 pages.

In this follow-up to a 1977 study, the results of a 1979 survey of capital campaigns initiated by colleges and universities between 1974 and 1979 are summarized, along with plans for campaigns initiated between 1979 and 1984. Questions addressed include sources of funds, the role of pledges in the campaign, and modifications made in original goals. Institutions are sorted into twenty-two groups according to the Carnegie Classification System, thus enabling any institution to view its plans and experiences in relation to those of other, similar institutions. The survey found that the overwhelming majority of the colleges and universities achieved or exceeded their fund-raising goals. Research and doctoral institutions (which accounted for only 10 percent of the campaigns) received about one-half of all funds raised. Fifty-nine percent of all funds raised in the campaigns came from individuals. In general, the campaigns were seen as a manifestation of management reaction to crisis conditions. Since this volume provides detailed analyses of successful capital campaigns, it may be used to strengthen the hands of fundraisers negotiating for venture capital from institutional funds.

226 Falender, Andrew J., and Merson, John C. (eds.). *Management Techniques for Small and Specialized Institutions.* New Directions for Higher Education, no. 42. San Francisco: Jossey-Bass, 1983. 96 pages.

This sourcebook consists of eleven articles dealing with all facets of management for the small or specialized college, from revitalizing the public image of the college through funding and financial issues and the building of a board of trustees. It discusses the current challenges of limited resources, declining enrollments, higher fixed costs, and fewer new or expanded sources of income. While the articles presented are intended for managers of small colleges, the solutions they propose are equally applicable to departments in large universities and, to some extent, to larger institutions as a whole.

★227 Hopkins, David S. P., and Massy, William F. *Planning Models for Colleges and Universities.* Stanford, Calif.: Stanford University Press, 1981. 544 pages.

For a full description of this work, please see entry no. 303.

228 Pray, Francis C. (ed.). *Handbook for Educational Fund Raising: A Guide to Successful Principles and Practices for Colleges, Universities, and Schools.* San Francisco: Jossey-Bass, 1981. 442 pages.

This comprehensive handbook discusses the broad issues of philanthropic motivation and management of annual giving programs, capital campaigns, and the solicitation of major gifts. The book offers practical guidelines and specific recommendations for successful fund-raising at a variety of institutions, from small two-year colleges to large state universities. It contains contributions from over sixty authors. The case studies presented should prove useful to those designing fund-raising campaigns for higher education.

229 Scheps, Clarence, and Davidson, E. E. *Accounting for Colleges and Universities.* (3rd ed.) Baton Rouge: Louisiana State University Press, 1978. 379 pages.

This is an updated, authoritative sourcebook on current accounting policies and practices for colleges and universities. It contains clear explanations and over 100 example reports and schedules. About one-third of the book is devoted to the description and accounting of current funds. The balance of the book is a discussion of budgeting, purchasing, supply and equipment inventories, cost accounting, and financial reporting. The discussion is largely about standard, routine accounting techniques. Difficult or controversial issues are skirted; for example, cost accounting is covered in two pages, mostly listing difficulties and hazards of such activities. However, the book's particular purposes are well served.

10

Robert J. Barak

Program Planning, Development, and Evaluation

It is perhaps axiomatic that any effort concerned with the governance, management, and leadership of colleges or universities should include attention to the management of academic programs. From the Carnegie policy studies of the 1960s and 1970s, which by and large focused on the effectiveness, quality, and integrity of academic programs, to the most recent studies, such as the American Association of State Colleges and Universities' (AASCU) "The Role and Future of State Colleges and Universities" (1986), which asked for program management efforts "comparable to the Marshall Plan," all the national "blue-ribbon" panels have pointed to the need for improved academic program management. In fact, one could argue that without viable academic programs, all management and leadership activities in higher education are for naught.

This chapter will review the literature pertaining to the management of academic programs, including program planning, development, and evaluation. It will begin with a brief treatise on the growth and development of academic program management and corresponding developments in the literature. The chapter will then explore the different developments and maturity in the literature for major components of academic management. Finally, the chapter will present a framework for analyzing the literature and will present examples of significant and useful contributions to the literature on academic program management.

218

The Field and Its Literature

Often referred to under the general rubric of "academic programming," the management of academic programs comprises three distinct though highly interrelated components: (1) program planning—the conception and design of programs; (2) program development—the continuous process of developing and maintaining program vitality; and (3) program evaluation—the assessment of program worth. Each of the three components has its own distinct body of literature, which has developed in ways that parallel the development of the component itself.

Planning. Academic program planning can be viewed as a means of management control, as a means of enrichment and expansion of the curriculum, or as both. As a means of control, program planning (that is, the allocation of resources and the determination of program size, scope, and direction) is a relatively recent phenomenon in higher education. This view of program planning was conceived in the wake of the infusion of management science techniques (largely adopted from business, industry, and government) into higher education in the 1960s and 1970s. Consistent with its name, management science purported to make the management of colleges and universities a science. It placed heavy emphasis on systems and data analysis, forecasting, and simulation. For the purpose of this chapter, it is epitomized best by so-called programming, planning, and budgeting systems (PPBS), in which academic programs are viewed as similar to product lines in business. When PPBS was originally applied to higher education, in a form unaltered from that of its business origin, it met with little success. However, PPBS and other management science techniques were eventually modified to meet the specific needs of colleges and universities and then did contribute to more systematic approaches to college administration. The literature has followed this infusion of management approaches, even to the extent of replacing the term *college administration* with *college management*—much to the chagrin of some old-line administrators.

Not everyone views academic planning as a management function, however. To some, academic planning is primarily an opportunity for program enrichment and expansion. This view is primarily, but not exclusively, held by faculty who are planning new courses, programs, and other curricular offerings. This view of program planning can be traced back to colonial days and beyond. The literature on this subject shows clearly the gradual formalizing of the planning process. Whereas curricular planning used to be implemented at whim, it now is part of a formal planning process at most colleges and universities.

Development. Program development has a long past in higher education. Faculty and administrators have always sought to update, improve, or otherwise modify academic programs. Until very recently, however, the literature in this field has been plentiful but largely anecdotal, short on general management approaches to systematic program development. Fortunately, several recent works provide a strong basis for improving program development.

Evaluation. Perhaps the most mature of the three components of academic programming is program evaluation. This maturity is reflected in the quality and diversity of its literature. Growing out of the accountability movement that began in elementary and secondary education in the aftermath of *Sputnik,* program evaluation in higher education has progressed to the point where it now has a distinct name: program review.

The literature on program review is evolving rapidly. It began with fugitive papers from conferences put on by groups such as the Association for Institutional Research (AIR) and the Association for the Study of Higher Education (ASHE), which were based on limited personal experiences. The literature is now based on more extensive experience and research.

A related recent development is the growing interest in "assessment," a term usually used to mean evaluation in the broader sense, encompassing students, programs, and institutions. The assessment movement has been primarily aimed at "outcome measures," an attempt to assess the quality of the end products of education. While the literature on assessment is growing, sources related to the purpose of this chapter are limited.

Framework for Organizing the Literature

Like the field of academic programming itself, its literature can be divided into three major components: program planning, program development, and program evaluation. Each component is often found closely integrated into a larger concept. For example, much of the literature on program review is found in the broader body of literature on evaluation, and program planning and development literature is almost inseparable from that on curriculum planning and development. The literature on academic programming is scattered through scholarly and practitioner journals, as well as a few texts. Unfortunately, much of it is still "fugitive" literature.

The literature on program evaluation, as noted earlier, is the most prevalent of the three types. The bulk of this literature is broadly based, addressing all kinds of evaluations. With care, it is possible to extract that portion of the literature that relates to academic program evaluation in higher education; however, this is a time-consuming task for the practitioner. Fortunately, a few excellent recent publications and journal articles relate specifically to program review in colleges and universities. In this chapter's annotations, program evaluation literature is further divided into the following categories: general works on program evaluation, general works on program review in higher education, state-level program reviews, institutional reviews, and special aspects of program review.

Works dealing specifically with program development are least represented in the literature. Texts and articles dealing exclusively with this area are nonexistent. One has to consult references in the broader literature on curriculum planning to find good source documents on program development. Three excellent examples appear in the second major category of this chapter's annotations. Many personal accounts of curricular development are also available, but their application is limited.

The number of publications on program planning falls somewhere in between those on program development and evaluation. Books and journal articles on planning in higher education abound, but most address primarily institution-level planning rather than program planning. Published research on institution-wide planning has only limited application to planning of academic programs.

An important consideration in understanding the literature on academic planning is the interrelationship of its three components: planning, development, and evaluation. It is impossible to view any of these three aspects in a vacuum. Ideally, the three should be seen as integral parts of a cyclical process. Failure to view a component in this light may render it almost meaningless. The reader should keep in mind that the division of academic programming into three components in this chapter's annotations is merely a convenience.

Commentary

With the exception of that on program evaluation, the literature in the area of academic programming is limited. Few publications provide a comprehensive perspective that focuses exclusively on academic program planning and development. Research in these areas is sparse and often limited to dissertations, which frequently are difficult to locate and are of limited value to the practitioner. Far too many publications are normative and descriptive, mere "show-and-tell" exercises with very limited broader application—though this has not deterred people from trying to apply them. The author knows of far too many disastrous attempts to implant someone else's "success" story in an environment where it just doesn't fit.

Academic program planning and development would seem to be ripe with opportunities for comprehensive works based on research. Since there has not been much theory building in academic programming, much work needs to be done on that aspect as well.

Program Planning

230 Armijo, Frank, and others. *Comprehensive Institutional Planning: Studies in Implementation.* Boulder, Colo.: National Center for Higher Education Management Systems, 1980. 350 pages.

This monograph details three case studies of experience—at Willamette University, Lorain County (Ohio) Community College, and Ohio University—in developing, implementing, and revising the planning process described in two other publications by the authors, *A Handbook for Institutional Academic and Program Planning* (1978) and *Academic Planning: Four Institutional Case Studies* (1978). The publication is valuable because it places program review and planning in a broader context (that of institutional planning) and describes the developmental and evaluative process in such an endeavor. This book should be useful for those seeking examples of planning in these three types of institutions and those with a general research interest in the topic.

★231 Bergquist, William H., Gould, Ronald A., and Greenberg, Elinor Miller. *Designing Undergraduate Education: A Systematic Guide.* San Francisco: Jossey-Bass, 1981. 332 pages.

This book provides ideas and resources for curricular development in the undergraduate program. Six primary dimensions of undergraduate curricula are identified: time, space, resources, organization, procedures, and outcomes. The authors systematically present each of these dimensions and describe it with reference to the alternative ways in which colleges and universities have designed undergraduate curricula. They also propose a basic curricular taxonomy. Their concluding chapter describes the use of "curriculum option analysis" (COA), a four-step methodology for exploring the six dimensions, in an engaging and creative manner. This book is a most helpful guide to those planning and developing academic programs.

★**232** Conrad, Clifton F. *The Undergraduate Curriculum: A Guide to Innovation and Reform.* Boulder, Colo.: Westview, 1978. 213 pages.

This volume proposes a conceptual framework for curricular planning and identifies trends and innovations that represent various approaches to undergraduate education. The first two chapters provide the framework, while the remaining four chapters focus on the major trends and innovations in undergraduate education within four broad categories of innovation. These last four chapters are particularly valuable for those seeking innovative approaches to planning undergraduate programs. The author includes a discussion of the strengths and weaknesses commonly associated with different types of innovations.

★**233** Heydinger, Richard B. "Planning Academic Programs." In Paul Jedamus, Marvin W. Peterson, and Associates, *Improving Academic Management: A Handbook of Planning and Institutional Research.* San Francisco: Jossey-Bass, 1980. Pages 304–326.

While wisely not prescribing a particular approach to planning, the author describes a taxonomy of thirteen different planning styles and compares these styles across a set of common dimensions. The taxonomy is designed as a diagnostic tool with which administrators and institutional researchers can locate the planning style that best meets their needs. The author also makes suggestions for improvements in program planning in light of the constraints facing education. The thirteen styles noted include knowledge development, entrepreneurial, administrative, curriculum committee, governing/coordinating board, formal democratic, problem focused, needs assessment, program data, program review, program development fund, incremental budgeting, and economic incentives. (For a description of the Jedamus book as a whole, please see entry no. 552.)

234 Mayhew, Lewis B. "Curriculum Construction and Planning." In Asa S. Knowles (ed.), *Handbook of College and University Administration: Academic.* New York: McGraw-Hill, 1970. Pages 2-36 to 2-52.

This chapter in a handbook on academic administration is intended to serve as a practical guide that contains basic information and procedures for curriculum construction and planning. It includes very useful information on approaches to curriculum construction, techniques and mechanisms for curricular change, and long-range curricular budget making and planning. It also has a section of definitions of common terms. It could be especially helpful to the novice or the person not closely associated with academic administration who wants to quickly gain some background knowledge on academic planning.

Program Development

★235 Chickering, Arthur W., Halliburton, David, Bergquist, William H., and Lindquist, Jack. *Developing the College Curriculum: A Handbook for Faculty and Administrators.* Washington, D.C.: Council for the Advancement of Small Colleges, 1977. 171 pages.

This handbook has been accurately described as a "mine of information on current curriculum theory." It is in fact much more, since it also demonstrates how these theories have been given expression in concrete applications. The volume consists of four parts: curricular rationale, curricular design, curricular practice, and curricular implementation. In addition, an extensive three-part appendix provides curricular models, innovations, and planning tools. This volume should be particularly valuable for practitioners looking for a single sourcebook on curricular development.

236 Dressel, Paul L. *College and University Curriculum.* Berkeley, Calif.: McCutchan, 1971. 325 pages.

This volume is a classic. Although now somewhat dated, it remains one of the few books that deal exclusively with the curriculum in colleges and universities. It covers the gamut of the subject, including basic considerations of curriculum development, discussions of curriculum peculiarities in various disciplines and levels, and curriculum evaluation and review. It should be of value to anyone interested in the background literature on curriculum evaluation, and it is "must" reading for students of the field and others interested in gaining a comprehensive background in the area of curriculum and program planning and development.

Program Evaluation

General Works on Program Evaluation

237 Adelman, Clifford. *Assessment in American Higher Education*. Washington, D.C.: Office of Educational Research and Improvement, U.S. Department of Education, 1986. 82 pages.

This volume will be of assistance to those striving to develop and carry out better means of assessment (defined broadly to include program evaluation, testing, surveys, and so on). It consists of five sections, which summarize recent trends in assessment in higher education and describe a number of promising institutional efforts. The papers address topics such as the growing interest in measuring educational achievement, assessing outcomes, the costs of assessment, and assessment in career-oriented education.

★238 Alm, Kent, Miko, Marina-Biihler, and Smith, Kurt. *Program Evaluation*. Washington, D.C.: American Association of State Colleges and Universities, 1976. 207 pages.

This is a directory of program evaluation practices at colleges and universities in twenty-one states. Practices are reported alphabetically by state. Each institution's practices are described on the basis of self-reports by the institution. The book provides an excellent source of information regarding institutional practices, from which persons interested in developing a program evaluation system can pick individual aspects to adopt for local use.

239 Craven, Eugene (ed.). *Academic Program Evaluation.* New Directions for Institutional Research, no. 27. San Francisco: Jossey-Bass, 1980. 119 pages.

The authors of this volume provide a perspective on the historical context, current status, and potential future directions of academic program evaluation. They list a variety of approaches to academic program evaluation and make recommendations for effective practice to assist institutional research persons and others seeking a broader perspective on program evaluation. Authors and contributions include Fred Harcleroad on the history of evaluation, Barry Munitz and Douglas Wright on institutional approaches to program evaluation, Donald Smith on multicampus approaches, E. Grady Bogue on state agency approaches, Kenneth Young and Charles Chambers on accrediting agency approaches, and a concluding perspective by Eugene Craven.

240 Miller, Richard I. *The Assessment of College Performance: A Handbook of Techniques and Measures for Institutional Self-Evaluation.* San Francisco: Jossey-Bass, 1979. 374 pages.

This volume provides guidelines for developing better criteria and procedures for institutional appraisal, including appraisal of academic programs. It identifies measures, policies, and procedures that can help to ascertain the extent to which an institution and its programs are going where they want to go. The volume advocates an assessment style that strikes a balance between that recommended by some humanists, who believe that the most significant facts about educational programs cannot be measured numerically, and that of the systems analysts and cost-effectiveness experts, who scorn "soft" evidence. Chapter Five provides useful guidelines for the evaluation of existing and planned academic programs and support services.

General Works on Program Review

★**241** Barak, Robert J. *Program Review in Higher Education:
        Within and Without.* Boulder, Colo.: National Center for
        Higher Education Management Systems, 1982. 137
        pages.

Based on the experiences of the author and an extensive study
of program review in colleges, universities, and external agencies, this volume provides practical advice to those interested
in designing program reviews or seeking a better understanding of academic program review. Separate chapters address
changing patterns in the underlying purposes, participants, and
procedures for approving and reviewing new and existing programs at the institutional and state levels. Basic principles of
good review and key steps for implementing them are presented.
The volume concludes with a discussion of controversial issues
surrounding program review.

★**242** Barak, Robert J. "Seven Common Myths on Program
        Review." *Educational Record,* 1986, *67* (1), 52–54.

This article discusses seven common myths that have developed
in recent years regarding program review. The author refutes
myths regarding cost savings, selection of criteria, the use of
"model" approaches, and others. Since these "myths" have
become part of our knowledge of the program review process,
it is important that practitioners and others with an interest in
the area be aware of alternative perspectives on certain key
issues.

243 Ohio Board of Regents. *Developing a Process Model for In-
        stitutional and State-Level Review and Evaluation of Academic
        Programs.* Columbus: Ohio Board of Regents, 1979. 171
        pages.

This is a useful monograph for those interested in development
of models for program evaluation. While use of such models

can result in processes that do not fit a particular institution or state, especially if the models are adopted wholesale, they can be handy in outlining an evaluation approach that can be used by many institutions and can provide some suggested review components.

★**244** Warmbrod, Catharine, and Persavich, Jon J. *Post-Secondary Program Evaluation.* Columbus, Ohio: National Center for Research in Vocational Education, 1981. 272 pages.

This handbook presents a process that can be used to evaluate postsecondary occupational education programs. If applied selectively, it can also be useful for colleges and universities. The volume includes materials designed to gather information from a number of sources. Each chapter that deals with these sources contains subsections on goals and objectives, procedures for administration, procedures for data analysis, and model instruments and documents. Two additional sections deal with cost analysis and preparing and reporting evaluation results.

245 Wilson, Richard F. (ed.). *Designing Academic Program Reviews.* New Directions for Higher Education, no. 37. San Francisco: Jossey-Bass, 1982. 110 pages.

This volume consists of nine chapters, each by a different author. They include "Alternative Evaluation Strategies" (House), "Review as an Adaptive System" (Petrie), "Values in Decision Making" (Dressel), "Assessing Program Quality" (George), "Evaluation Systems Are More Than Information Systems" (Braskamp), "Planning for an Evaluation Network" (Smock), "Process Issues in State-Level Reviews" (Wallhaus), "Evaluating Administrators" (Hoyt), and "Concluding Statement" (Wilson). The title of the book is misleading: those looking for a "how-to" guide will be disappointed. More knowledgeable reviewers will find the readings and perspectives of the authors valuable, however.

246 Wilson, Richard F. (ed.). "Critical Issues in Program Evaluation." *Review of Higher Education,* 1984, *7,* 143–157.

This article identifies five major issues in evaluating academic programs, including the dilemma of multiple purposes, the value of criteria, overscheduling, the decision-making linkage, and evaluating process effectiveness. Effective program evaluation requirements are outlined. Practitioners and professional evaluators will find these perspectives useful in instituting program review.

State-Level Program Reviews

★247 Barak, Robert J., and Berdahl, Robert O. *State-Level Academic Program Review.* Denver, Colo.: Education Commission of the States, 1978. 141 pages.

This is a basic volume on state-level program review, based on research and the experience of the authors. It provides a general status report on state-level review activities and specific review responsibilities in the fifty states. It also provides specific criteria for evaluation, case studies of several states, a proposed general model for state-level review and monitoring, and an analysis of key issues associated with state board activities in the sensitive area of academic programs. This basic work in the field has been updated periodically since its original 1978 publication.

248 Barak, Robert J., and Miller, Richard I. "Rating Undergraduate Program Review at the State Level." *Educational Record,* 1986, *67* (2–3), 42–46.

This article presents the results of a joint study by the two authors concerning the undergraduate program review activities of state higher education boards. The results of their survey indicate considerable activity in this area and a generally favorable rating of it by representatives of the state boards. It is likely that a similar survey of institution-based people would be less favorable. The article contains suggestions for improvement and advice to states considering activities in this area.

Institutional Reviews

★249 Arns, Robert G., and Poland, William. "Changing the
University Through Program Review." *Journal of Higher
Education,* 1980, *51* (3), 268–285.

This article describes program review approaches used at Ohio
State University and the University of Vermont for the purpose of program improvement. It points out the importance of
the process, which the authors regard as being at least as important as the reason why reviews are done. In this case, the
process links the reviews with budgeting and "term planning."
The latter is a process that projects resource requirements, fund
sources, and enrollments for a one to three-year period and uses
the result as a basis for daily decisions. This article is particularly
recommended for those interested in a model that links review
with planning and budgeting at major research universities.

250 Clark, Mary Jo. *Program Review Practices of University
Departments.* GRE Board Research Report, GREB no.
75-7aR. Princeton, N.J.: Educational Testing Service,
1977. 12 pages.

This report provides the results of a survey of 454 university
department heads concerning the most recent self-study of program review in their departments. It describes the heads' judgments about the importance of collecting each information element for each of three purposes: internal department use for
program planning and improvement, university use for departmental monitoring and decisions about resource allocation, and
judgments by external groups such as accrediting agencies or
state coordinating boards. This volume is useful for those interested in understanding the unit role in program review. It
also provides good suggestions for information collection.

★251 Conrad, Clifton F., and Wilson, Richard F. *Academic Program Review: Institutional Approaches, Expectations and Controversies.* ASHE-ERIC Higher Education Report no. 5. Washington, D.C.: Association for the Study of Higher Education, 1985. 93 pages.

This report is an analysis of pertinent literature on program review at the institutional level. It provides an examination of the central issues and reflects on ways in which program review might be improved. It begins by sketching the historical antecedents and growth of program review, goes on to describe the diverse approaches and major issues of the field, and concludes with proposals for improving program review. These latter include the following: (1) the delineation of a single driving purpose that is well understood; (2) regular reviews linked to, but separate from, planning and budgeting processes; (3) selective use of features from several models; (4) flexibility; (5) cyclical reviews; (6) multiple indicators of quality; (7) reasonable judgments of programs; (8) use of outside reviewers only in certain reviews; (9) linkages between reviews and other processes; and (10) prevention of reviews from driving other processes.

252 Gentile, Arthur C. "A Model for Internal Review." *Communicator,* 1980, *12,* 4–7.

This article is not so much a description of a model per se as it is a good-sense resource for developing a program review plan. It accurately points out many of the pitfalls in plan development and contains considerable advice on the elements of a good review process. The author notes the importance of repetitive reviews, utilization, administrative support, clear lines of responsibility, the division between graduate and undergraduate reviews, open communication, care in preparation of reports, the process itself, and specifying goals. The article should be useful for those developing a review process or evaluating a process already in place.

253 Heydinger, Richard B. "Does Our Institution Need Program Review: A Framework for Answering This Question." Paper presented at the Association for Institutional Research Annual Forum, Houston, Texas, May 1978.

A central question that needs to be answered by those considering the development of a program review process is whether such a process is really needed. This article provides a four-part framework for evaluating the necessity and feasibility of establishing a review process. It presents the criteria for making this decision and provides the essential outcomes of the decision on the purposes, scope, and implementation strategy for the review process.

254 Kuh, George D., and Ransdell, Gary A. "Evaluation by Discussion: An Evaluation Design for Post-Secondary Programs." *Journal of Higher Education,* 1980, *51* (3), 301–313.

This article describes an alternative evaluation approach called Evaluation by Discussion (EBD). This process can be used for evaluating certain aspects of an academic program, such as academic or student service units. As described, the approach is flexible in that its character can change depending on the style and composition of the evaluation team; the scope, size, and complexity of the program being evaluated; the number and degree of interactions among program audiences; and the nature of the issues to be discussed.

255 Simpson, William A. "Easing the Pain of Program Review: Departments Take the Initiative." *Educational Record,* 1985, *66* (2), 40–42.

This brief article describes a department-based program review process and argues that because colleges and universities pose unique and difficult fiscal problems, department-level program reviews offer numerous advantages over university-level reviews. These advantages include defusing the effects of reduction, eliciting more input from those affected, and taking advantage of attrition in permanent budget reductions.

256 Sparks, David S. "The Four C's of Graduate Program Evaluation." *Communicator,* 1980, *13* (3), 1-2, 7-8.

This article describes the four "C's" associated with the assessment of quality in master's program evaluation: criteria, credibility, cost, and consequences. For the purposes of the author's discussion, programs are grouped into categories called traditional, specialized, and nontraditional. Traditional indices of quality suffice for traditional programs, but specialized and nontraditional programs are more difficult to evaluate. The author recommends more attention to responsibilities to students, consideration of alternative ways to develop and deliver programs, increased attention to content, a more certain basis for comparison, and improved capacity for planning.

Special Aspects of Program Review

★257 Barak, Robert J. "The Role of Program Review in Strategic Planning." *Association for Institutional Research Professional File,* 1986, *26,* 4-7.

This research-based article explores the complicated relationship between program review and strategic planning. The author identifies and describes general types of relationships, then presents implications for colleges and universities. The contributions of program review to the planning and other decision-making processes are also described. This article would be of value to those interested in integrating comprehensive program reviews into a strategic planning process.

258 Cochran, Thomas R., and Hengstler, Dennis D. "Political Processes in an Academic Audit: Linking Evaluative Information to Programmatic Decisions." *Research in Higher Education,* 1984, *20* (2), 181-192.

This article describes the significant role of political considerations in academic program evaluations. The authors identify six factors that were important in linking the information gathered from the evaluation to decision making: the reasons for the evaluation, involvement of the participants, communication of the results, organizational context, recognition of subjectivity, and the role of the institutional research office. These considerations are all important for persons responsible for program evaluation.

★259 Davis, Carolyn K., and Dougherty, Edward A. "Guidelines for Program Discontinuance." *Educational Record,* 1979, *60* (1), 68–77.

Noting that across-the-board reductions in academic programs can potentially weaken academic quality, the authors argue that each institution should establish priorities among its various academic programs. Such priorities can be used as a basis for more selective reductions by phasing out programs and adding accrued resource savings to other programs. Such an approach will be likely to maintain or even enhance the quality of an institution's programs. The paper describes the development of program discontinuance guidelines and their implementation at the University of Michigan. It provides a good, common-sense approach to the use of evaluation for setting priorities and allocating resources.

★260 Franchak, Stephen J. *Using Evaluation Results: Guidelines and Practices for Using Vocational Evaluation Effectively.* Columbus, Ohio: National Center for Research in Vocational Education, 1981. 88 pages.

This handbook provides some very valuable guidelines for utilizing the results of evaluation, a major area of difficulty in program evaluation. While developed primarily for vocational institutions, it can be useful (when applied selectively) to four-year colleges and universities as well. The book includes sections on utilization of evaluation, communication, decision making, innovative ways of promoting utilization, and preparing and reporting evaluation results. It also includes a selected, annotated bibliography.

261 Hodgkinson, Harold, Hurst, Julie, Levine, Howard, and Brint, Steve. *A Manual for the Evaluation of Innovative Programs and Practices in Higher Education.* Berkeley: Center for Research and Development in Higher Education, University of California, 1974. 201 pages.

This sourcebook should be useful to those interested in evaluating innovative programs. The authors describe it correctly as the "first step in providing an evaluating 'Yellow Pages'" for innovative programs. The volume consists of two basic sections: a description of the major evaluation instruments available and a list of then-current innovative programs and practices.

★**262** Long, James P., Minugh, Carol J., and Gordon, Robert A. *How to Phase Out a Program.* Columbus, Ohio: National Center for Research in Vocational Education, 1983. 47 pages.

This is a very valuable volume for those anticipating or experiencing program closure. While written for vocational programs, its many practical suggestions regarding the problems, concerns, and procedures involved in phasing out a program are applicable to colleges and universities as well. The aspects of closure covered include reasons for phaseout, alternatives to phaseout, making the decision to phase out, obtaining the necessary approvals and support, and implementing the phaseout. Several model approaches (which should be used with caution) as well as related readings are included.

★**263** Melchiori, Gerlinda A. *Planning for Program Discontinuance: From Default to Design.* Washington, D.C.: AAHE-ERIC Higher Education Research Report no. 5. American Association for Higher Education, 1982. 48 pages.

This monograph carefully analyzes and synthesizes the major literature on program reduction and discontinuance. It also provides a framework for developing long-range organizational plans to meet the need for program reduction while minimizing the potential disruption caused by program discontinuance.

The monograph describes program discontinuance as a proactive, realistic tool for retrenchment in that it can potentially change curricula and reduce budgets. The author reinforces the important point that the earlier an institution or system plans for systematic program discontinuance, the less traumatic the actual reduction and change will be.

★**264** Shirley, Robert C., and Volkwein, J. Fredericks. "Establishing Academic Program Priorities." *Journal of Higher Education,* 1978, *29* (5), 472–489.

This article has provided the bases for discussion in the literature regarding the strategic uses of program review in setting priorities among programs and reallocating resources. The key to this use is the "matching" process in which external needs, opportunities, and constraints are matched with the institutional mission and program reviews to make strategic decisions on program offerings and priorities. The authors delineate specific criteria to consider, such as program quality, need, and cost. The section on integrating decisions on priorities with decisions on resource allocation, an area of considerable complexity, is particularly valuable. This article should be especially useful for those interested in using reviews for broad purpose within an institution.

Ray T. Fortunato
Joseph A. Greenberg
Geneva Waddell

11

Human Resource Development and Personnel Administration

Interwoven throughout governance, management, and leadership processes in higher education is the interaction of people and the impact of their effectiveness or ineffectiveness on these processes. A contextual overview of human resource development and management (personnel administration) is particularly important to this guide to key resources because of these often unpredictable interactions. This chapter is based on the idea that some human resource development and management responsibilities belong to most people involved in these processes in higher education institutions, regardless of their position or function.

The purpose of this chapter is to present the most recent and valuable literature related to human resource development and management and also to offer a framework for conceptualizing these fields and their related literature. Since development of human resources has received substantial attention in the literature recently because of increasing organizational and human needs in this area, we focus attention on human resource development first, including a contextual overview of the field and its related literature and then a commentary on the literature and on future trends and issues. Secondly, we present an overview and commentary on the literature related to human resource management (personnel administration). We conclude with annotations of the most recent and valuable references in both fields.

238

Contextual Overview of the
Human Resource Development Field

Human resource development (HRD) as a field is growing, and a variety of patterns relevant to higher education institutions are emerging in the process. The field and the literature
have not paralleled each other in growth, however, because the
literature remained dispersed among other disciplines and fields
for many years after HRD itself began to emerge as a separate
field—which happened as recently as 1969 (Nadler, no. 269).
As Nadler and Wiggs (no. 270) suggest, a book on managing
a human resource unit could not have been written a decade
ago. The roots of the field can be found in behavioral sciences,
adult education, and personnel management. Complexities of
the work force, technological advances, and legal requirements
have all contributed to the growth of human resource development as a field. Recognition of the need for specialists to manage
these changes, increasing emphasis on productivity improvements, and added recognition of the impact a trained work force
can have on the economy have also contributed to this growth.
Significant contributions to the professional literature
on human resource development in the past decade were made
by Leonard Nadler and others (nos. 281, 269, and 270) and
Robert Craig (no. 265). Patricia McLagan's *Models for Excellence,*
done for the American Society for Training and Development
(no. 268), is also a major contribution to the professionalism
of HDR practitioners and consultants. Additionally, Malcolm
Knowles's adult education guides and models (nos. 278 and 280)
and Patricia Cross's models and synthesis of research findings
(no. 274) made considerable contributions to the adult education field that continue to strengthen human resource development efforts.

Framework for Organizing the HRD Literature

Human resource development can be seen as a process
of identifying needs, designing and delivering programs, and
evaluating results. Within this process, most of the literature

has focused on designing and delivering programs—possibly as a result of the difficulties presented by needs identification and the skills and knowledge required for realistic evaluation. For purposes of this overview, the term *development* will be used to include education, training, and other human resource development efforts. We will discuss the HRD field and its literature in terms of specific needs related to development of faculty, administrators, staff, and possibly trustees.

Faculty Development. In the 1950s professional development programs for faculty included professional meetings, sabbaticals, released time, retreats, and programs established to encourage faculty to publish. Student activism in the 1960s led to the creation of a few developmental programs aimed at instructional improvement. By 1974, faculty development had become a topic for serious discussion, research, publication, and negotiation. The 1970s witnessed a limited acceptance of faculty development as a legitimate response to individual and institutional needs, and during the late 1970s and early 1980s the need to consider changes in the careers of faculty either through organizational and/or program changes or through personal development and graduated retirement programs grew greatly.

Today, in the mid-1980s, most educational institutions have an increasing need to acclimate faculty to new markets, to help them keep pace with technology and its effects on their disciplines, to assist them in increasing their productivity by appraising the value of each of their development efforts, and to guide them in making calculated choices in planning for future development (Chait and Gueths, no. 273). The literature of the late 1980s can address these needs by keeping pace with issues such as faculty workload, institutional environment, and post-tenure review (Licata, no. 275), as well as technology changes and ways for evaluating efforts and techniques related to faculty development.

Appropriate incentives can create the motivation for many faculty members to continue to be vital within their organizations and can provide the necessary stimuli to those in need of revitalization. Although individual faculty members are motivated by different incentives, intrinsic factors related to altruism and love of one's job have usually proved more significant in increasing vitality than extrinsic rewards (McKeachie, 1979).

Administrator Development. Individual institutional development opportunities for college and university administrators have grown from the same embryonic stage as those available to faculty in the 1950s. Nonetheless, these opportunities, generally characterized as "professional development," frequently are unsophisticated and focus on breadth rather than depth issues. Many of the development activities suggested for faculty by Centra (no. 272) and Bowen (1985) are just as appropriate and useful for administrators, and they could greatly improve the quality of administrative development programs. For example, the need for personal development that focuses on team-building and interpersonal skills and for organizational development programs that increase competence and awareness of trends goes well beyond the commonly available institution-based administrator development menu. All too often we hear pithy aphorisms like "education is a business, run it like one," or "the fate of an effective teacher is to be promoted to an administrative position." These references, in some instances, reflect organizational realities, and they underscore the need for substantive, needs-based development activities for college and university administrators as well as literature that informs the field of programs, processes, and accomplishments. Individual institutions may need to implement or strengthen organizational development programs by involving administrators, faculty, students, and staff in planning short- and long-range activities that improve the efficiency and effectiveness of their operations.

National and regional opportunities for administrative professional development do abound in the 1980s, as evidenced in the regular "Calendar of Events" in the *Chronicle of Higher Education* and the *Wall Street Journal National Business Employment Weekly*. Fisher and Coll-Pardo in the American Council on Education's *Guide to Professional Development Opportunities for College and University Administrators* (no. 499) and Fortunato and Keiser in *Human Resource Development in Higher Education Institutions* (no. 277) also provide numerous examples of such opportunities. Programs such as those of the Institute for College and University Administrators, established at Harvard University, and the administrative intern program at Boston University provide an intensive orientation for recently appointed presidents, vice-presidents, deans, business officers, and student personnel administrators.

In the mid-1980s, administrative professional development needs center around budget provisions, overcoming barriers of cost and time, empirical evaluation of existing programs, new programs for developing entrepreneurial skills, marketing techniques for maintaining or increasing student enrollments, methods for conducting future-oriented research, and programs for developing analytical and synthesizing skills to handle information overload. The literature of the late 1980s can contribute to these developmental efforts by focusing on improving evaluation of existing programs, professionalizing the existing and future cadre of administrators and managers, and reporting methods for conducting future-oriented research.

Support Staff Development. Although literature specifically on development of support staff in higher education is sparse (partly because of the limited number of development activities), some of the literature on faculty development (as well as many of the activities comprising personal, instructional, and professional development) can be applied to support staff, as can much of the literature in the training field.

Many colleges and universities need to strengthen their investment in support staff development. Bouchard, in *Personnel Practices for Small Colleges* (no. 282), points out that "Colleges and universities historically have been labor intensive, investing up to 70–80 percent of operating budgets in human resources," and have been "dilatory in recognizing that the development of human resources, as well as the creation of an organizational climate conducive to development, directly relates to attainment of institutional mission and goals" (p. 178). According to Bouchard, the breadth and scope of training and development on college campuses "appear to be directly related to institutional size, administrative commitment, and program budget, and range from informal on-the-job training to formalized, com-

prehensive multipurpose programs for all classes of employees''
(p. 122).

Supervisory training, technical skills training, and techniques for handling student inquiries and telephone calls are
the most common types of training provided to support staff
in higher education institutions. A variety of methods and techniques are useful in support staff training and development (see
nos. 279, 280, and 281 for examples).

Some special development needs of support staff can best
be met by apprenticeship programs or mentoring, according
to Fortunato and Keiser (no. 277). The Federal Bureau of Apprenticeships and Training or equivalent state agencies can help
in developing apprenticeship programs, or such programs can
be developed independently.

Commentary on the Human
Resource Development Literature

Professional literature on human resource development
in higher education is dispersed among many disciplines and
functions. Although literature on faculty development became
exhaustive in the 1970s, professional literature specific to the
needs of other higher education groups and to human resource
development as a higher education field is less frequently found.

Some references from the business literature, especially
in the areas of cost-benefit analysis and evaluation of training,
can be useful to those responsible for evaluating HRD efforts.
For example, Kirkpatrick (no. 267) provided a collection of
valuable writings on evaluation of training, and Kearsley (no.
266) provided a practical guide describing and illustrating a set
of models for applying cost-benefit analysis to training systems.
While Kearsley's work contributes to the training and development profession in a substantial way, he admits that ''even
though you may have conducted an outstanding cost-benefit
analysis that is convincing beyond the shadow of a doubt, there
are always good reasons why you still may not succeed'' (p. 196).
One of these reasons usually is ''more demands for a fixed
budget than can be satisfied.'' Kearsley suggests that one should

find a solution that allows for synthesis of the needs making the demands on the budget rather than partly funding a program, since partial funding may be insufficient to have any real effect.

Further advances in evaluation techniques and applications are wanted to meet the special needs of the higher education environment. Improved and refined evaluation of the results of human resource development programs can be useful in gaining support for future development activities and for supporting human resource development functions in general.

Key questions that remain to be answered in regard to evaluating human resource development programs and activities in higher education include these: Is the gain to the institution in terms of increased performance sufficiently greater than the cost of the training or development effort to justify the investment? Were the specified professional development needs met with available resources? In the long run, can the needs be met at a lower cost?

Much of the current literature will become outdated quickly because HRD is a rapidly growing and changing field. Quantitative and qualitative research is needed in the areas of program planning and evaluation.

Issues and Trends in HRD. Some of the future trends and issues in the field of human resource development relate to contributions to productivity improvements, redefining the role of international training and education, placement of the HRD function in the organization, career ladders for HRD professionals, and mechanisms for sharing technological resources.

Additionally, environmental factors will continue to exert much influence on the nature of human resource development activities in higher education institutions. Among these factors is major legislation in the area of equal employment opportunity/ affirmative action, which significantly affects training and development programs. Questions will be constantly raised about whether training is conducted in a nondiscriminatory manner and to what extent it contributes to the attainment of affirmative action goals and timetables. Legislation uncapping the mandatory retirement age may also lead to some retraining and reassignment of existing staff. Such legislation, as well as numerous other environmental factors, overlaps the human resource development and management fields.

Overview of Human Resource
Management (Personnel Administration)

Decisions to give one person more pay than another or to pay someone absent for illness are personnel decisions, whether or not a formal personnel office exists. Thus, human resource management (formerly called personnel management or administration or services in higher education institutions) has always existed in any organization with several employees, higher education institutions included. However, the complexity of legislative requirements, coupled with increasing numbers of faculty and staff, and the need for consistency in administering policies and practices have created the need for formal human resource administration offices to service and coordinate plans and programs institutionwide. The need for improved human resource planning to assure that adequate numbers and kinds of people are appointed to move higher education institutions in directions that will most effectively meet the needs of changing clients has also led to growing demands for formal personnel administrative services. So have such factors as public employee collective bargaining acts in many states, unharnessed proliferation of lawsuits, unemployment compensation legislation, the Health Maintenance Organization Act, the Fair Labor Standards Act, the Employee Retirement Income Security Act, and, more recently, the Consolidated Omnibus Budget Reconciliation Act.

Prior to 1970, personnel administrative offices usually provided full services only for support staff, with faculty services being limited to benefits matters only. Since then, some institutions have begun to look to these offices for assistance in such faculty personnel matters as tenure, promotion, and retrenchment. Where faculty unionization has taken place or has been attempted, even greater numbers of requests for assistance have resulted (see College and University Personnel Association, no. 283).

Framework for Organizing the HRM Literature

Human resource management/personnel administration can be divided into three major categories—positions, people, and processes—for purposes of organizing the literature and conceptualizing the field (see Fortunato and Waddell, no. 285).

Positions. How many faculty and staff positions are needed and at what levels are key questions in this first major human resource management area. Controlling the number of positions needed was not as crucial during the era of rapid growth as it has become today. Because of enrollment and funding problems, institutions have become keenly aware of the need for position and rank control. During the late 1970s and early 1980s, positions were retrenched mostly through attrition or a variety of other methods while institutions considered budget cuts. Complex systems for evaluating requests for new positions have been developed, and program and budget planning have received increased attention as institutions redistribute scarce resources to enhance effective programs and meet new needs. Selective resource enhancement programs have become essential to efficient operations and, in some cases, survival.

Financial parity and salary projections are integral parts of position creation and control. Salary surveys conducted by individual institutions and by associations such as the College and University Personnel Association can be useful tools in providing salary control data (see nos. 288 and 289).

Most of the literature related to the position category is found in journal articles and textbooks under headings such as job analysis, job evaluation, salary structures, compensation, retrenchment, and comparable worth. Literature of the late 1980s can be useful by keeping pace with related legislation and court decisions and by focusing on effective ways to plan and control the numbers and kinds of positions needed.

People. How higher education institutions can recruit or appoint and retain the people best qualified to meet their current and future needs is a critical question in the people category. This category incorporates recruiting, appointing, orienting, motivating, communicating, developing/training, evaluating,

and dismissing faculty and staff. Recruiting faculty and staff
has become very complex because of regulations related to affirmative action, equal employment, and uniform selection.
Uniform procedures for promotion have become essential,
whether the promotions involve academic rank or support staff
positions. For additional information on equal employment opportunity and affirmative action, see Chapter Seventeen of this
volume and entry no. 291 in the present chapter. For information on performance evaluation, see Chapter Nineteen of this
volume.

A substantial part of the budget of any institution is expended on benefits, both mandated ones and optional ones provided in an attempt to retain qualified people. Planning for and
carrying out benefits programs are usually part of the work of
a human resource administrative office. Medical benefits have
recently presented a special problem. During the past several
years, the cost of medical delivery systems has increased at a
rate greater than the rate of inflation. This has caused substantial drain on institutional financial resources and has led to severe
cost containment, cost avoidance, and cost transfer actions (no.
292).

Literature on subjects in the people category is dispersed
throughout journals, textbooks, newsletters, monographs, and
newspapers and covers topics ranging from recruiting to dismissing people. Literature of the late 1980s that keeps pace
with legislative activity and court decisions will be the most
useful.

Processes. Personnel processing questions include what
policies should be developed, who should review and approve
policies, and how those policies should be disseminated, implemented, and evaluated. Policies are needed to govern the
severance of employment that may occur as a result of retirement, resignation, dismissal for cause, retrenchment, death, illness leading to disability, or temporary layoff. Policies regarding sabbatical leaves, definitions of academic ranks, emeritus
rank, and free (public) or paid (private) consulting are needed
as well (see no. 293). Faculty and staff are usually provided with
mechanisms to appeal any institutional actions or inactions that

they feel are unfair. Usually, appeals on matters of tenure denial or promotion are limited to procedural fairness. The processes for granting or denying tenure have become more elaborate as higher education enrollment and staffing have leveled off, however. Some institutions with heavily tenured-in faculties are exploring various alternatives.

Electronic data management systems now enable human resource managers to conduct essential planning studies much more easily and maintain a variety of faculty and staff records more efficiently. Administrative offices can also use such things as applicant tracking systems, talent banks, and hiring reports (see nos. 286 and 287 and Meyer, 1984). Additional programs designed to meet specific needs have been developed at many institutions as well. These include wellness, awards, preretirement counseling, financial planning, and employee assistance programs.

Literature of the late 1980s related to processes in human resource management could be most useful by providing samples of policies that are working in higher education institutions and by keeping pace with technological advances that can improve productivity and effectiveness.

Commentary on Human Resource
Management Literature

Professional literature generally has not kept pace with what is happening in the field of higher education human resource management because practitioners have not had the time or incentive to document their work or findings. Personnel practitioners have been inclined to make studies for use within their institutions rather than for general public use. Examples of such studies include studies by discipline of the ratio of tenured to nontenured faculty members and studies by discipline of the various awards of probationary tenure granted upon appointment. Additionally, sometimes practitioners have been reluctant to disclose the strategies they used in reaching their goals. For example, once a practitioner successfully negotiates a contract with a union, he or she normally will not wish to make a public disclosure of the "wins" and "losses" that took place during the process. Therefore, much of the human resource management/personnel administration literature has been written about less controversial subjects. Research in this field has also left much to be desired because of the need for improved statistical techniques for measuring people functions.

Issues and Trends. The issue of comparable worth versus equal pay has been heavily debated. Under equal pay law, individuals doing equal work in the same type of position (for example, males and females coaching or performing laboratory functions at the same level) should be compensated similarly. The comparable worth philosophy would have the pay equalized for males and females whose work is judged to be equal, regardless of the type of positions compared. The comparable worth concept implies that the marketplace should not be a factor in setting pay, while the equal pay law does permit the marketplace to be a factor. The comparable worth issue remains unresolved.

Collective bargaining is a governance issue in some institutions. For example, when unionization takes place, questions are raised regarding the status of department chairpersons and other faculty. Governance changes to some extent when collective bargaining takes place, depending on the legal limitations of the bargaining process (see no. 284).

Other issues and trends in human resource management include flexibility in academic staffing, linking of personnel and fiscal management planning, productivity improvement and contributions, wellness programs to reduce benefits costs, and employment-at-will practices. Institutions have already begun to look for flexibility in academic staffing through setting strict standards for tenure, creating alternatives to tenure, controlling academic positions at time of termination, using more part-time people, creating early retirement programs, and retrenchment. Productivity improvement programs in some institutions now include providing more effective performance reviews that are related to predetermined standards. The high cost of benefits has caused institutions to begin looking for more cost-effective health care management systems, including self-insurance, establishment of preferred provider organizations, introduction of wellness programs, and redesign of health care plans.

References

Bowen, Z. P. "Tangible and Intangible Faculty Incentives." In Roger G. Baldwin (ed.), *Incentives to Enhance Faculty Vitality*. New Directions for Higher Education, no. 52. San Francisco: Jossey-Bass, 1985.

McKeachie, W. J. "Perspectives from Psychology: Financial Incentives Are Ineffective for Faculty." In D. R. Lewis and W. E. Becker, Jr. (eds.), *Academic Rewards in Higher Education*. Cambridge, Mass.: Ballinger, 1979.

Meyer, G. J. *Automating Personnel Operations*. Madison, Conn.: Bureau of Law and Business of Madison, 1984.

Human Resource Development

General

★265 Craig, Robert L. (ed.). *Training and Development Handbook: A Guide to Human Resource Development*. (2nd ed.) New York: McGraw-Hill, 1976. 866 pages.

Fifty-nine authorities developed the forty-seven chapters of the second edition of this classic, sponsored by the American Society for Training and Development. Covering sections on the training and development function, program development, applications and media, and methods, it has served as a road map for training and development professionals in business and education for more than a decade. The book is useful to both new and seasoned trainers and educators, as well as managers of human resource development programs. A forthcoming update, strengthening the evaluation- and technology-related chapters, will be even more helpful.

266 Kearsley, Greg. *Costs, Benefits, and Productivity in Training Systems*. Reading, Mass.: Addison-Wesley, 1982. 199 pages.

Kearsley's guide describes and illustrates a set of models for applying cost-benefit analysis to training systems. It provides what one needs to know to plan, conduct, and evaluate such an analysis. The case study provided is especially useful in illustrating how the models fit together. A major weakness of this form of analysis is the tendency of some who use it to oversimplify by reducing results to formulas and graphs. However, like statistics, cost-benefit analysis can be useful as a decision-making tool.

★**267** Kirkpatrick, Donald L. (ed.). *Evaluating Training Programs.* Washington, D.C.: American Society for Training and Development, 1980. 318 pages.

This reference is a collection of sixty articles and other materials that have appeared in the *Training and Development Journal.* It provides in one source several broad approaches and specific techniques of evaluation and is useful to those responsible for evaluating training and learning activities.

★**268** McLagan, Patricia A. *Models for Excellence: The Conclusions and Recommendations of the ASTD Training and Development Competency Study.* Washington, D.C.: American Society for Training and Development, 1983. 208 pages.

This report is an important tool for categorizing and systematizing the professional development of training and development practitioners and educators. It lists and explains 15 roles, 31 competencies, and 102 outputs of human resource development professionals. The behavior models it describes can be used as a standard of professional performance by educational institutions, HRD departments, and individuals practicing or expecting to practice in the HRD or adult education field.

★**269** Nadler, Leonard (ed.). *The Handbook of Human Resource Development.* New York: Wiley, 1984. 872 pages.

This handbook, designed to eliminate confusion and clarify HRD models and concepts, provides a useful glossary of terms and a comprehensive account of the HRD field. It also details program areas, international areas of HRD, and human resource areas related to HRD and offers commentary on the future of HRD. It is useful to HRD practitioners and managers of HRD programs who need a detailed account of the field and a guide for implementing programs.

*270 Nadler, Leonard, and Wiggs, Garland D. *Managing Human Resource Development: A Practical Guide.* San Francisco: Jossey-Bass, 1986. 294 pages.

This practical guide provides advice on designing a human resource development unit so that it enhances organizational mission. Describing illustrative cases, the book also offers advice on hiring, supervising, and facilitating career development of HRD practitioners, administering a budget system, and planning and implementing a variety of HRD activities. The book is useful to managers of HRD units as well as line and general managers with human resource development accountability.

Faculty Development

*271 Baldwin, Roger G. (ed.). *Incentives for Faculty Vitality.* New Directions for Higher Education, no. 51. San Francisco: Jossey-Bass, 1985. 121 pages.

This monograph, one of many fine resources from the New Directions series, focuses on the range of faculty incentives available in higher education. Baldwin has collected a series of articles that reflect faculty development practices at selected colleges. He uses the theme of faculty vitality to present the important issues surrounding career growth and satisfaction. Articles on intrinsic and extrinsic incentives emphasize the need of faculty to maintain their love of profession as a basic element of satisfaction and suggest that the number and types of development opportunities be expanded throughout the span of a faculty member's career.

*272 Centra, John A. "Types of Faculty Development Programs." *Journal of Higher Education,* 1978, *49* (2), 151–162.

This article presents a framework for organizing faculty development activities into logical programs and provides many examples of each type of program. Centra suggests that faculty development should include four distinct areas: personal development, instructional development, professional development, and (an especially critical component) organizational development. His design yields valuable suggestions for administrative and support staff development as well as faculty development.

★273 Chait, Richard P., and Gueths, James. "Proposing a Framework for Faculty Development." *Change,* 1981, *13* (4), 30–33.

This article considers faculty development as one of several responses to change in higher education. Chait and Gueths propose design criteria for and discuss essential steps of and direct rewards from faculty development. They suggest that faculty development will always be a risk to some degree and the only greater risk is to do nothing. The framework they propose should be useful to those responsible for "doing something" about faculty development.

★274 Cross, K. Patricia. *Adults as Learners: Increasing Participation and Facilitating Learning.* San Francisco: Jossey-Bass, 1981. 300 pages.

This book describes and synthesizes research findings and constructs two explanatory models, one for understanding and motivating adult learners and one for organizing knowledge about their characteristics and circumstances to help decision makers devise new roles and formats for higher education in the 1980s. The book should be especially useful to adult educators and higher education consultants. Trainers in business also can benefit by understanding adults as learners.

★275 Licata, Christine M. *Post-Tenure Faculty Evaluation: Threat or Opportunity?* ASHE-ERIC Higher Education Research Report no. 1. Washington, D.C.: Association for the Study of Higher Education, 1986. 105 pages.

Licata has done an exhaustive literature review of the posttenure faculty evaluation issue, including recent research findings, to support her contentions. This monograph reflects the serious problems that face higher education as the professoriate grows older and the opportunities for evaluation and development diminish. The issues of budgetary constraint, steady-state re-allocations, declining enrollments, and retrenchment that pervade the entire enterprise of higher education are also important in posttenure evaluation. The implications for administrative practice and conclusions that Licata offers can assist the reader in understanding this vital issue and in designing, developing, and evaluating strategies to combat the problems it presents.

Administrator Development

276 Fisher, Charles F., and Coll-Pardo, Isabel (ed.). *Guide to Leadership Development Opportunities for College and University Administrators.* Washington, D.C.: American Council on Education, 1979. 197 pages.

For a full description of this work, please see entry no. 499.

★277 Fortunato, Ray T., and Keiser, Dennis W. *Human Resource Development in Higher Education Institutions.* Washington, D.C.: College and University Personnel Association, 1985. 80 pages.

This work provides background information needed for establishing a human resource development program in higher education institutions. It includes information on assessing needs, setting goals, staffing, funding, gaining support, finding and working with instructors, mentoring, assessing effectiveness, and offering alternatives to classroom instruction. Descriptive samples covering over seventy courses of the types currently used in higher education are displayed, and the authors also include detailed information on establishment of apprenticeship programs. This book should be useful to anyone responsible for establishing faculty, management, or staff development programs. The sample programs, all actually in use in higher education, provide ideas for planning.

★**278** Knowles, Malcolm S. *The Modern Practice of Adult Education*. Chicago: Association Press, 1980. 400 pages.

This practical guide to adult education and practice spells out some new thinking in education, shifting the accent from teaching to learning, and focuses on the concept of lifelong learning as well as differences between adult education and learning. Techniques of teaching, contract learning, and designing and managing learning activities are thoroughly covered, as are techniques for designing a learning environment, diagnosing needs, and evaluating programs. Especially useful are the thirty-two exhibits and appendixes of policy statements, sample program designs, tools for operating programs, evaluation materials, and tools for conducting learning activities. Educators and trainers can benefit greatly from this guide.

Support Staff Development

279 Carnevale, Anthony P., and Goldstein, Harold. *Employee Training: Its Changing Role and an Analysis of New Data*. Washington, D.C.: American Society for Training and Development, 1983. 92 pages.

This work, which was developed in response to increased interest in the role of training in the American national economy, asserts that the United States underinvests in human resources. It also provides an analysis of the impact of high technology on the work force. It lends support to human resource development activities in education as well as in business.

★**280** Knowles, Malcolm S. *Using Learning Contracts: Practical Approaches to Individualizing and Structuring Learning*. San Francisco: Jossey-Bass, 1986. 262 pages.

In this book, Knowles explains the benefits and limitations of learning contracts in adult learning. His twenty-three examples of contracts should be useful to HRD professionals, adult educators, and managers trying to enhance quality and effectiveness of contractual processes with adult learners. Community college educators will find the examples especially applicable to their needs.

★**281** Nadler, Leonard. *Designing Training Programs: The Critical Events Model.* Reading, Mass.: Addison-Wesley, 1982. 252 pages.

Nadler's book explains unique features of the "critical events model" and shows how to use it in program design. The model uses continuous involvement of managers and supervisors in the design process and provides for constant evaluation and feedback to test the relevance of what is being done. The book can be useful to those responsible for skills and technical training, including new trainers, subject matter experts, and faculty involved in curriculum design for vocational and technical subjects. The model fits best for skills and technical training for support staff.

Human Resource Management

General

282 Bouchard, Ronald A. *Personnel Practices for Small Colleges.* Washington, D.C.: National Association of College and University Business Officers/College and University Personnel Association, 1980. 178 pages.

This joint effort for NACUBO and CUPA provides a descriptive overview and exhibits of five areas of personnel administration in small colleges. Its major contribution is the fifty-two exhibits, which include sample policies, procedures, position descriptions, personnel forms, and related articles. The book can be useful to business officers in small colleges who are responsible for personnel functions, directors of personnel, personnel specialists, and generalists in medium-sized colleges and universities. The book covers staff personnel administration only.

283 College and University Personnel Association. *Tenure and Retrenchment Practices in Higher Education: A Technical Report.* Washington, D.C.: College and University Personnel Association, 1980. 226 pages.

This comprehensive study of tenure and retrenchment policies and practices was conducted with a Ford Foundation grant by a committee assembled by CUPA. It provides data from 1,058 institutions on such items as the meaning of tenure, formulation of policies, notification of eligibility, governance roles, and relationship to funding sources. This study is useful to individuals responsible for formulating policy and to scholars studying in those areas. The data are aggregated and also broken down by Carnegie Classification—doctorate-granting institutions, comprehensive universities and colleges, liberal arts colleges, and two-year institutions.

284 College and University Personnel Association. *Journal of the College and University Personnel Association,* 1985, *36* (2), entire issue. 58 pages.

This journal volume provides nine articles on collective bargaining in higher education. Written by academic personnel, employee relations practitioners, a lawyer, a president, and a dean, the articles include perspectives, imperatives, and projections for collective bargaining in the year 2000. The information they contain is useful to those involved in collective bargaining in higher education institutions.

★285 Fortunato, Ray T., and Waddell, D. Geneva. *Personnel Administration in Higher Education: Handbook of Faculty and Staff Personnel Practices.* San Francisco: Jossey-Bass, 1981. 384 pages.

This handbook of faculty and staff personnel practices is a comprehensive guide to all facets of a fully integrated academic and staff human resource management program. The book is divided into three major sections—positions, people, and processes—and covers topics ranging from recruiting to dismissal of faculty and staff. Seventy-three exhibits demonstrate policies, forms, and legal references. The book offers an excellent guide to personnel practitioners and to faculty and students in higher education administration who want to understand and work with human resource management and development.

★**286** Heneman, Herbert G., Schwab, Donald P., Fossum, John A., and Dyer, Lee D. *Personnel/Human Resource Management*. Homewood, Ill.: Irwin, 1986. 745 pages.

This nine-part graduate-level text is a comprehensive account of P/HRM functions in a variety of organizations. Its case studies, model, and up-to-date legislative breakdowns make the text useful to faculty, students, and practitioners in business as well as in higher education.

★**287** Ivancevich, John, and Glueck, William. *Foundations of Personnel/Human Resource Management*. Plano, Tex.: Business Publications, 1986. 825 pages.

This detailed text suggests a diagnostic approach to understanding personnel/human resource management and provides up-to-date information on planning and staffing, performance evaluation and compensation, training and development for better performance, labor relations, safety and health, work scheduling, and evaluation of personnel/human resource management functions. Cases and diagrams make it useful to faculty and students for practical learning as well as to practitioners who are new to the field. Although the book was written primarily for the business and government community, much of its information is applicable to higher education.

Positions

★**288** American Association of State Colleges and Universities/
College and University Personnel Association. *1985–86
National Faculty Salary Survey by Discipline and Rank in State
Colleges and Universities.* Washington, D.C.: American
Association of State Colleges and Universities/College
and University Personnel Association, 1986. 45 pages.

This study provides national data showing faculty salaries by
discipline and rank. The data cover 38,890 faculty members
at 440 private institutions and 63,623 faculty members at 262
public institutions and include forty-six disciplines. Average,
low, and high salaries are shown by rank. Public institutions
that have participated in each of the five years of the survey
may request special salary trend studies by selected disciplines
and institutions, as may private institutions that have participated in the first and fourth studies. All institutions may request data on any ten or more institutions. These data should
be useful to anyone responsible for faculty salaries. A strength
of the survey is that it provides data by ranks within disciplines;
a weakness is that it deals in averages.

★**289** College and University Personnel Association. *1985–86
Administrative Compensation Survey.* Washington, D.C.:
College and University Personnel Association, 1986. 134
pages.

This work contains up-to-date salary information from 1,612
higher education institutions on the 99 primary positions and
69 secondary positions most common to higher education institutions. Information on salaries for presidents and for academic,
administrative, and student services personnel is included. A
special feature is the inclusion of small studies tailored to meet
the needs of specific institutions. The data should be of interest
to anyone responsible for salary administration. They offer a
useful guide to salaries in the marketplace.

290 College and University Personnel Association. *1985–86 National Faculty Salary Survey by Discipline and Rank for Private Colleges and Universities.* Washington, D.C.: College and University Personnel Association, 1986. 38 pages.

This study is described under no. 288, American Association of State Colleges and Universities. This study provides the same information for private colleges and universities.

People

291 College and University Personnel Association. *Journal of the College and University Personnel Association,* 1984, *35* (4), entire issue. 52 pages.

This journal volume includes seven articles on affirmative action in colleges and universities. The articles were written by practitioners, faculty, and legal counsels. Especially useful is a summary of nondiscrimination regulations that affect institutions of higher education.

*292 Herzlinger, Regina, and Schwartz, Jeffrey; Herzlinger, Regina, and Calkins, David. "How Companies Tackle Health Care Costs." Parts I, II, and III. *Harvard Business Review,* 1985–1986, *85* (4), 68–81; *85* (5), 108–120; and *86* (1), 70–80.

This study on the growing costs of health care is based on a survey of more than 200 large companies. Most of the companies have tried to cut costs by redesigning their insurance policies and by changing suppliers of health care services. However, the result has been mere cost shifting rather than solving of basic problems related to costs and delivery systems. The articles provide examples of options such as wellness programs, insurance options, health promotion, use of community resources, and preventive programs. The authors' survey gives a clear picture of what is happening in this important high-cost area. Those responsible for benefits programs should find this a useful set of articles.

Processes

293 Elliott, James M., Fortunato, Ray T., and Pezzoni, John V. *College and University Personnel Models.* Washington, D.C.: College and University Personnel Association, 1980. 129 pages.

This book provides samples of partial policy statements in eighteen major policy areas, taken from policies in use at twenty higher education institutions. A strong feature of the book is that each policy is broken down into its basic elements, and suggested policy statements are shown for each element. The breakdown by elements causes the user to analyze a policy's purposes prior to committing the policy to writing. Personnel practitioners and members of committees charged with reviewing and/or recommending policies should find this to be a very useful tool. Its strength lies in the fact that policy statements displayed are in actual use. Some important policy areas are not included, however.

294 Meyer, Gary J. *Automating Personnel Operations: The Human Resource Manager's Guide to Computerization.* Madison, Conn.: Bureau of Law and Business of Madison, 1984. 200 pages.

Meyer presents background information on why an organization should automate in the first place, what personnel tasks should be automated, and what steps are required to plan and execute an automation project. The book includes lists of software vendors and products as well as text, figures, and glossaries. It should prove useful to anyone beginning the process of automating or updating an existing system. Although some of the material will become outdated quickly, the basics of planning and implementation it covers make this a useful resource.

295 Schrodt, Phillip A. *Microcomputer Methods for Social Scientists.* Beverly Hills, Calif.: Sage, 1984. 96 pages.

This work provides a basic introduction to microcomputer concepts, languages, and applications. It covers both data base management systems and graphics and provides basic descriptions for general operating procedures as well as suggestions for advanced application and troubleshooting. It should be useful to help beginners avoid major errors in setting up economical personnel systems in small colleges and should also be a handy tool in conducting a variety of studies.

12

Bernard S. Sheehan

❦❦❦❦❦❦❦

Decision Support Systems and Information Technology

Decision support is the use of computers to assist management and decision making. This has been an important field for some time, but now its potential for higher education management is enhanced by the widespread availability of new information technologies. Current literature in the field describes the changing information technology and deals with applications of computers and telecommunications to decision support in higher education management.

The most recent advances in computers hold renewed promise for the use of decision support technology in the collegial and collective decision processes traditional to higher education and increasingly common in business. Those working in higher education governance, management, or leadership can use computers as personal tools for decision support activities ranging from report generation (including graphics as well as text) to data calculation and retrieval. Even more important, computers are increasingly being used for communications, a vital aspect of governance, management, and leadership. Group decision support systems and the use of computer-assisted meetings (computer conferences) to expedite committee work are further examples of the pertinence of decision support to higher education.

The Development of the Field and Its Literature

The literature of decision support in higher education and its parallel literature in management and business yield

263

insights related to both people and technology. The foundations of the study of decision support lie in many academic disciplines and human undertakings. Scott Morton (1971) was one of the first to pull together two important roots of decision support: the use of data and models on interactive computers and an organizational approach that emphasizes analysis of important decisions and provision of support to decision makers. As Scott Morton points out, "This support is possible in complex, unstructured, problem situations and can be used by the manager in conjunction with his intuitive 'feel' for the problem and its solution" (p. 1). The research on organizational decision making done at the Carnegie Institute of Technology and associated with Simon (1960), Cyert and March (1963), and others, as well as the technical work on interactive computer systems carried out mainly at the Massachusetts Institute of Technology by Licklider (1960) and MIT's Project MAC, are basic to understanding those roots.

The place of decision support in the overall field of computer-based management information systems can be clarified by the following summary analysis, quoted from perhaps the most influential book in this field, that of Keen and Scott Morton (no. 298):

1. Computer science: creates technology, both hardware and software. This is a necessary but not sufficient contribution to information systems.
2. Management science: represents the analytical viewpoint in structuring problems and develops the models so often necessary to drive information systems.
3. Behavioral science: provides insights into the implementation process and the human and organizational context of the system.
4. Data processing: builds the application systems the organization finally uses.
5. Management: understands the realities of decision making and thus which systems can be effective.
6. Decision support: focuses attention on building systems in relation to key decisions and tasks, with the specific aim

of improving the effectiveness of the manager's problem-solving process.

The effectiveness of decision support in higher education depends on the ability of people to understand and trust a process that transforms inquiries into measurements—that is, into management information—in a practical context that permits knowledgeable and purposeful choices among alternatives. This notion of the generation of information for decision support, sometimes referred to as the ''Berkeley approach'' to decision support systems (DSS) and associated with Churchman and others, is another important theoretical root of decision support. The essential relationship between managers and the data provided by decision support systems is summarized by Mason and Swanson (1981) as follows:

1. The reports presented by a DSS should be based on those measures that promote the most effective management decisions.

2. The managers who receive reports from a DSS should be able to criticize the management data intelligently. They must be skilled at uncovering the underlying assumptions of the data and at recognizing the limits of the inferences that may be drawn from them.

The literature on decision support in higher education was influenced by the early research on the use of computer models in university planning and administration that was done for the Commission on the Financing of Higher Education (the Bladen Commission) in Canada. A report to the commission (Judy and Levine, 1965) illustrated the first CAMPUS model. The authors referred to the work of Robert McNamara, McKean (1958), Hitch and McKean (1960), the Rand Corporation, and others. Their report notes, ''The system simulation model does not 'automate' any decisions. Its role is entirely that of a tool that can greatly improve the information with which university planners and decision makers work'' (p. 11). Over the next decade, users around the world gained experience with (Hussain,

1976) and a healthy skepticism about the application of management science to higher education.

Some of the problems of early models arose because data adequate for input and for specifying model parameters were often hard to come by, and the output was hard to use, especially in the form in which it came out of the computer. Large models were expensive to build and maintain. Because they were also difficult to explain, they often were not trusted by decision makers, who usually had little direct contact with the models and their builders. But just as management information systems (MIS) have overcome the setbacks caused by not living up to early expectations and by the doubt of some about the value of applying information technology to ill-defined management processes, decision support has also regained the confidence of many users. "This resurgence is the result of the confluence of five factors: institutions' current need for improved decision making, the learning about the do's and don't's of modeling that has taken place during this period, the widely publicized success of modeling at Stanford University, the improvement of modeling system software, and, finally, the availability of new delivery systems" (Updegrove, 1981, p. 61).

A Framework for Organizing the Literature

The three organizing principles that seem to provide the best basis for a taxonomy of today's decision support literature are DSS as a type of MIS, decision support as associated with "end user computing," and the communications aspects of decision support. Since there is also a body of the literature that provides underlying fundamentals and roots shared by all three categories, it is useful to add a foundations component to the framework.

Background and Foundational Readings. The decision arts, sciences, and technologies are the elements of decision support in all organizations, including those of higher education. Hence, some of the basic texts on management information systems, decision support, and the general use of information technology in higher education management contain materials fundamental to a full appreciation of decision support in higher education management, even though they are not part of the literature written especially for this field.

The Management Information System Tradition. The concept of MIS as a federation of many functional subsystems (associated, especially in the 1970s, with large centralized computers and professional electronic data processing or EDP staffs) is a useful frame of reference for understanding decision support. This perspective sees decision support systems as a class of management information system lying at or near the end of an EDP continuum that begins with transaction processing and moves on to operational control, management control, and strategic planning. A more informative continuum is one that classifies problems faced by decision makers. These range from structured, almost programmable choices to highly unstructured problems for which no straightforward solution techniques are known, such as those one may encounter in student appeal cases. DSS are helpful in dealing with problems near the unstructured end of this spectrum. Since decision support "grew up with" MIS, the two have a shared organizational and technological heritage, including large computers, large applications (usually of institutionwide significance), outputs used by many people in the institution, and a system run and controlled by professionals. Thus it is not surprising that a category of DSS literature draws on concepts and experiences that sprang from MIS.

The Emergence of End User Computing. According to some writers, one of the important differences between decision support systems and other management information systems is the centrality of the user to the system. The user's view of the decision and its context, the user's judgment on what information, alternatives, and solutions are appropriate, and even the user's personal technology greatly affect DSS results. This sharp shift from an organizational, professional MIS bias to the personal values and desires of the decision maker (user) is addressed in a second category of DSS literature.

A few years ago, the more personal approach of DSS might have been associated with emerging microcomputer technology, while standard MIS would have been connected with mainframe technology. Now the availabilty of "mainframe" software, such as fourth-generation languages (4GLs) that are easily accessible to the user without the help of programmers or other data processing professionals, means that the emphasis on personal values of end users need no longer be associated with any one type of technology. (Fourth-generation languages are increasingly used by data processing professionals to develop end user applications, by decision support intermediaries on campuses to prototype and build DSS for specific decision makers, and indeed by end users themselves when they wish to quickly build a personal system on a mainframe, access a data base, build a data base, format reports, or use graphics and text processing. James Martin (1982) has popularized 4GLs.) The widespread use of the microcomputer as a workstation connected to a campus mainframe also means that emphasis on end users is possible with both microcomputer and mainframe technology.

Still, especially for the novice user, "there is something less forbidding about a small, personal computer as compared with a terminal tied to a large computer" (Sprague and McNurlin, 1986, p. 337). Thus, the personal computer (PC) is still the main force behind end-user-oriented computing. Decision makers and decision support intermediaries see the microcomputer as personal, private, responsive in a friendly and interactive way, easy to use but powerful and expandable or connectable to other systems, reasonably priced, and steadily improving in price and performance. For the first time most decision makers can not only access the data they feel they need but also represent knowledge, manipulate data, seek insights through experiments with their own models, and formulate and test arguments and alternative decisions. Decision support activities that can be carried out on PCs include analysis, data retrieval, forecasting, text processing, and testing "what-if" hypotheses. Most can be done with standard software such as data base managers, spreadsheet generators, word processors, communications software, graphics packages, planning simulations, and expert systems packages.

Questions related to the management and implementation of end user computing have not been given the prominence in the higher education literature (Jedamus, 1984) that they have in the more general management literature. One of the initial organizational responses to the flood of microcomputers was the information center (IC), which is staffed by several people with some technical expertise and who are also good communicators, educators, and listeners. The number of these units has grown enormously in the past five years, and their role has also grown to include training on PCs, computer literacy education, user assistance, consulting, marketing and evaluation of information technology products, DSS prototype development, and help with computer networking problems. Information centers in business are described by Gerrity and Rockart (1986), and proposals for the role of ICs in higher education can be found in the proceedings of the 1984 CAUSE national conference (Sholtys, 1985), Stevenson and Walleri (1983), and Sheehan (1985).

Expert systems, arising out of the field of artificial intelligence, will be likely to play an important future role in decision support in higher education management. However, little experience with them has been reported. Luconi, Malone, and Scott Morton (1986) is a good general source on expert support systems, which are described as "computer programs that use specialized symbolic reasoning to help people solve difficult problems well. This is done by pairing the human with the expert system in such a way that the expert system provides some of the knowledge and reasoning steps, while the human provides overall problem-solving direction as well as specific knowledge not incorporated in the system" (p. 4).

Communications. The convergence of computing and telecommunications not only as technologies but also as organizational units, administrative issues, and services is one of the most significant developments in information technology in this decade. Sometimes referred to as telematics, this merging of information technologies has profoundly influenced decision support by bringing to institutions a whole new range of office and communications systems. Since decision support applications using networks are relatively novel, it is possible and convenient to classify literature describing them as separate from "MIS" and "end user computing." We refer to this classification as "communications" rather than telecommunications in order to emphasize both the technology and the human aspects of the use of telematics in decision support. A current challenge to designers and users of decision support is to realize the full potential of this technology by building on the lessons learned in the last two decades.

New telecommunications services that have potential decision support applications in higher education include text and messaging communications, data communications, new voice communications such as voice mail, information retrieval using videotex, and image transmission for teleconferencing and facsimile. It is too early to judge which of these technologies will make contributions of long-term significance. However, since communication goes to the heart of the decision maker's task, it is reasonable to assume that this area of decision support technology will receive much attention in the immediate future.

Commentary on the Literature

The literature on decision support in higher education management will be judged more or less adequate depending on the extent to which one is prepared to "sweep in" the vast and explosive literature in closely related foundation fields and applied areas. Certainly, the rapid evolution of decision support technology makes it difficult for higher education management literature to reflect a current picture of the state of the art. Many of the pieces specific to decision support in higher education management are conference proceedings, often reporting local experience. Not many comprehensive, theoretical, or empirical studies have yet appeared. Field practice is clearly ahead of the literature.

A glance at general trends in decision support technology may be useful in predicting specific effects in higher education. Such trends suggest that more people in higher education management will be using improved versions of spreadsheets, data base management systems, and graphics packages. The real power of group decision support systems may be realized as the "critical mass" is reached in the number of people who use local area networks or national/international computer-based network services for electronic mail and conferencing (Huber, 1984). Since the communication technology for teleconferencing is really in place now (Jennings and others, 1986; Chew, 1986; Oberst and Smith, 1986), its future may depend mostly on the way human and organizational issues related to it are resolved in the next few years. The currently very popular ''integrated'' software, which provides several capabilities (data base, spreadsheet, communications, graphics, and so on) in a single package, is almost sure to be made more powerful in its functions, slicker in its integration, and more friendly and intelligent in its dialogue interface with the user. Perhaps the promise of artificial intelligence will be realized here. In the longer term, DSS are likely to be powerful expert systems that include speech recognition. The applications they will see in higher education and elsewhere are impossible to predict.

References

Chew, R. L. ''Value-Added Network Services for Universities.'' In *1995–Planning and Managing the Odyssey*. Boulder, Colo.: CAUSE, 1986.

Cyert, R. M., and March, J. G. *A Behavioral Theory of the Firm*. Englewood Cliffs, N.J.: Prentice-Hall, 1963.

Gerrity, T. P., and Rockart, J. F. ''End User Computing: Are You a Leader or a Laggard?'' *Sloan Management Review*, 1986, *27* (4), 25–34.

Hitch, C. J., and McKean, R. N. *The Economics of Defense in the Nuclear Age*. Cambridge, Mass.: Harvard University Press, 1960.

Huber, G. P. ''Issues in the Design of Group Decision Support Systems.'' *MIS Quarterly*, 1984, *8* (3), 195–204.

Hussain, K. M. ''Comprehensive Planning Models in North America and Europe.'' In T. R. Mason (ed.), *Assessing Computer-Based System Models*. New Directions for Institutional Research, no. 9. San Francisco: Jossey-Bass, 1976.

Jedamus, P. ''The Case for Decision Support Management.'' In W. L. Tetlow (ed.), *Using Microcomputers for Planning and Management Support*. New Directions for Institutional Research, no. 44. San Francisco: Jossey-Bass, 1984.

Jennings, D. M., and others. ''Computer Networking for Scientists.'' *Science*, 1986, *231*, 943–950.

Judy, R. W., and Levine, J. B. *A New Tool for Educational Administrators*. Toronto: University of Toronto Press, 1965.

Licklider, J. C. R. ''Man-Computer Symbiosis.'' *IRE Transactions on Human Factors in Electronics*, 1960, *1*, 4–10.

Luconi, F. L., Malone, T. W., and Scott Morton, M. S. ''Expert Systems: The Next Challenge for Managers.'' *Sloan Management Review*, 1986, *27* (4), 3–14.

McKean, R. N. *Efficiency in Government Through Systems Analysis.* New York: Wiley, 1958.

Martin, J. *Application Development Without Programmers.* Englewood Cliffs, N.J.: Prentice-Hall, 1982.

Mason, R. O., and Swanson, E. B. *Measurement for Management Decisions.* Reading, Mass.: Addison-Wesley, 1981.

Oberst, D. J., and Smith, S. B. "BITNET: Past, Present and Future." *EDUCOM Bulletin,* 1986, *21* (2), 10–17.

Scott Morton, M. S. *Management Decision Systems.* Cambridge, Mass.: Harvard University Press, 1971.

Sheehan, B. S. "Telematics and the Decision Support Intermediary." In M. W. Peterson and M. Corcoran (eds.), *Institutional Research in Transition.* New Directions for Institutional Research, no. 46. San Francisco: Jossey-Bass, 1985.

Sholtys, P. A. "Bootstrapping the Information Center." In *Information Management Basics in a New Technological Era.* Boulder, Colo.: CAUSE, 1985.

Simon, H. A. *The New Science of Management Decisions.* New York: Harper & Row, 1960.

Sprague, R. H., Jr., and McNurlin, B. C. *Information Systems Management in Practice.* Englewood Cliffs, N.J.: Prentice-Hall, 1986.

Stevenson, M., and Walleri, R. D. "Institutional Research and End User Computing: The Development of an Information Center." Paper presented at the 23rd annual forum of the Association for Institutional Research, Toronto, May 1983.

Updegrove, D. A. "Using Computer-Based Models." In N. L. Poulton (ed.), *Evaluation of Management and Planning Systems.* New Directions for Institutional Research, no. 31. San Francisco: Jossey-Bass, 1981.

Background and Foundation Readings

★296 Davis, Gordon B., and Olson, Margrethe H. *Management Information Systems: Conceptual Foundations, Structure and Developments.* (2nd ed.) New York: McGraw-Hill, 1985. 693 pages.

This is the second edition of the 1975 textbook that helped to define management information systems. MIS is defined to be an integrated, user-machine system for providing information to support operations, management, and decision-making functions in an organization. The system utilizes computer hardware and software; manual procedures; models for analysis, planning, control, and decision making; and a data base. The book describes decision-making processes, concepts of information, information technology, humans as information processors, support systems for management of knowledge and information system requirements, development, implementation, and management. This is an essential foundation reference for any student of decision support in higher education.

297 Hopkins, David S. P., and Schroeder, Roger G. *Applying Analytic Methods to Planning and Management.* New Directions for Institutional Research, no. 13. San Francisco: Jossey-Bass, 1977. 117 pages.

This monograph is concerned with the practical use of operations research in institutions of higher education. It covers faculty resource planning, student enrollment forecasting, financial modeling, departmental faculty scheduling, cost analysis, and management systems design. In the last chapter, Schroeder defines a management system as ''an interrelated collection of information, decision procedures, and people who direct the operation of an organization'' (p. 99). He examines six false assumptions said to underlie the design of management systems for colleges and universities. This is a useful volume because of its many experience-based examples of decision support applications.

★298 Keen, Peter G. W., and Scott Morton, Michael S. *Decision Support Systems: An Organizational Perspective.* Reading, Mass.: Addison-Wesley, 1978. 264 pages.

This volume formalized decision support as a separate field by describing and prescribing how the design, implementation, and evaluation of information technology ought to articulate with decision makers' problem-solving processes and needs. The literature on management information systems and decision making for the previous twenty years is integrated from this new perspective, and examples of practical DSS are also provided. The authors differentiate computer-based support for management decision making from data processing, MIS, and other uses of information technology by stressing that DSS must be useful to managers and that the decision process starts with the manager's definition of the key decision problems to which interactive computer systems should be applied. This book, although published a decade ago in a field profoundly influenced by rapidly changing technology, is still a basic reference and the inspiration for much of what has followed.

299 McCredie, J. W. (ed.). *Campus Computing Strategies*. Bedford, Mass.: Digital Press, 1983. 316 pages.

These institutional case studies are a valuable source of experience in creating strategic plans for computing and communications use in higher education. Schools described include Dartmouth College, Carnegie-Mellon University, Stanford University, the University of Minnesota, the California State University System, and five others that participated in a 1981–82 EDUCOM study. The planning processes reported indicate that large amounts of financial and human resources—a combination of new resources and reallocated older ones—will be needed to realize the new technologies' potential. This book is useful to readers interested in the impacts of converging information and communications technologies on higher education. The book does not treat decision support directly, but many aspects of decision support technology planning are included.

300 Mason, Thomas R. (ed.). *Assessing Computer-Based System Models*. New Directions for Institutional Research, no. 9. San Francisco: Jossey-Bass, 1976. 112 pages.

This monograph provides an early evaluation and description of the use of computer models as tools for planning, management, and policy making in postsecondary education, drawing on experience from the previous decade. The volume includes results of a survey of college and university model users, some basic elements of models then in use (such as the "induced course load matrix"), modeling at statewide and national levels, and a comparison of models used in North America and Europe. It is a useful early sourcebook for students of decision support in higher education.

301 Sheehan, Bernard S. (ed.). *Information Technology: Innovations and Applications.* New Directions for Institutional Research, no. 35. San Francisco: Jossey-Bass, 1982. 121 pages.

The purpose of this volume is to provide information on computer and communications technologies. Since institutional planning for effective use of information technology should be based on an appreciation of the underlying technology, such information is valuable to decision makers. The volume presents the elements of an analysis that allows the generalist to evaluate current and anticipated applications of these technologies to higher education. It discusses human information processing and the human interface with the machine, then moves from a treatment of chips and other components to devices and networks of devices. Topics covered range from office automation to instructional technology and from the strategic planning issues of computation, communication, and information to the insights of research on planning for telematics.

The Management Information System Tradition

302 Adams, Carl R. (ed.). *Appraising Information Needs of Decision Makers.* New Directions for Institutional Research, no. 15. San Francisco: Jossey-Bass, 1977. 106 pages.

This is a critical assessment of the information needs of decision makers and of the effectiveness of management information systems in higher education. Chapter authors suggest improvements in the development and implementation process related to different aspects of decision support and to different types of institutions and educational systems. Adams notes that "our expectations of future use of a growing information technology must be tempered by our knowledge of persistent problems" (p. 79), and he concludes that "achieving the promise offered by information technology will require adopting the corrective measures suggested by decision makers" (p. 86). This volume is noteworthy because it articulates many of the issues of the MIS debate of the late 1970s as they apply to higher education.

★303 Hopkins, David S. P., and Massy, William F. *Planning Models for Colleges and Universities.* Stanford, Calif.: Stanford University Press, 1981. 544 pages.

This comprehensive survey of planning models is carefully written to be equally valuable and accessible to those interested in technical design aspects and to practical administrators concerned with the sensible use of modeling. The authors' perspective is that "models do not 'produce' plans or decisions, good or bad. People do." Their volume is based on a decade of experience at Stanford and other universities. It presents the case for planning models and then offers specific types of models for budget projections, student flow, costing, and human resource planning. Theoretical topics necessary for a mature understanding of planning models, such as microeconomics, financial planning under uncertainty, and the make-or-buy decision, are also covered. The excellent discussions of philosophical and methodological problems make this volume a standard reference on decision support.

304 Moore, Laurence J., and Greenwood, Allen G. "Decision Support Systems for Academic Administration." AIR Professional File, no. 18. Tallahassee: Association for Institutional Research, Florida State University, 1984. 9 pages.

This pamphlet in the informal AIR Professional File series introduces the idea of DSS and discusses how DSS might be useful to academic administrators. The authors define DSS and sketch its historical development as the outgrowth of a convergence of rapidly developing technologies and other bodies of knowledge. They then present an application of DSS in university administration as an illustrative example. Although the pamphlet is intended for an audience with some computer background, even readers lacking such background will gain insight into the DSS notion and development process from the description of an example system that analyzes tuition-and-fee policy. The extensive references are drawn mostly from the management literature rather than the higher education literature.

305 Poulton, Nick L. (ed.). *Evaluation of Management and Planning Systems.* New Directions for Institutional Research, no. 31. San Francisco: Jossey-Bass, 1981. 102 pages.

This monograph compiles examples and other important information on the use and effects of management and planning techniques and systems in colleges and universities. The chapter authors conclude that the primary product of these systems is an improved ability to store and analyze information and better bases for taking action. Topics covered include environmental assessment, master plans, resource allocation, program review, computer models, and management development. There is a short annotated bibliography on each of these topics. This is a compact, readable volume with a good deal of practical information.

★306 Sprague, Ralph H., Jr., and Carlson, Eric D. *Building Effective Decision Support Systems.* Englewood Cliffs, N.J.: Prentice-Hall, 1982. 329 pages.

This book tells how to develop a decision support system. It does not have a higher education focus, but it is often quoted in the higher education literature. DSS technologies are described in three levels: specific DSS, DSS generators, and DSS tools. The book also discusses human roles associated with DSS: manager (user), intermediary, DSS builder, technical supporter, and toolsmith. Design approaches are illustrated as well. DSS technology is treated as the interaction of three components: dialogue, data, and model. The authors' systems analysis approach is firmly rooted in decision makers' requirements and perspectives and thus deals with concepts such as representations of information, operations on these representations, memory aids, and user controls rather than the "bit and byte" type of topic that might appear in more technical books on information systems.

The Emergence of End User Computing

307 Brown, Kenneth C. *The Administrative Use of Microcomputer Systems*. Washington, D.C.: American Association of University Administrators, 1983. 6 pages.

This concise booklet in the American Association of University Administrators' *Administrative Update* series describes the use of microcomputers to improve productivity of administrators in four function areas: decision support, communication, personal assistance, and task management. Electronic spreadsheets, graph and chart formatting aids, and data base management systems are said to be the most valuable types of decision support aids for both novice and experienced micro users. Since administrators spend so much of their time communicating, the author proposes the technology for office automation as a growth area. Administrators may also use electronic mail systems to improve communications on campus or between institutions. This short piece gives the busy administrator an overview, some steps to take, and some cautions.

308 Glover, Robert H. "Designing a Decision-Support System for Enrollment Management." *Research in Higher Education,* 1986, *24* (1), 15–34.

This recent article illustrates the philosophy, design, and building of a decision support system for complex applications in higher education management by describing how the University of Hartford DSS for enrollment management was developed. This DSS is comprehensive, both in the range of enrollment-related topics and issues its models and data bases support and in the types of hardware and software used by the university's Office of Planning and Institutional Research to build it. Its progress in satisfying user requirements is attributed to a development process that makes use of integrated, user-friendly, fourth-generation software tools and a prototyping implementation approach. The paper is one of the few in the literature that provides practical insights into the state of decision support by describing the actual conceptual framework, design, and implementation of a DSS currently in use.

309 Hammond, Lynn W. "Management Considerations for an Information Center." *IBM System Journal,* 1982, *21* (2), 131–161.

This paper suggests what should be done in setting up an information center (IC). The IC notion, which is closely linked to the technical aspects of decision support, is defined, and questions of IC mission, initiation, organization, position, and staffing are detailed. While the paper is about business, the IC concept it describes could also be applied to higher education. An IC is a small unit that provides education, technical support, usable tools, data, and systems access to users in a manner that the users can recognize as worthwhile. Readers familiar with the user-oriented traditions of many academic computer service units will see the IC as a natural means to promote the implementation and effective use of decision support technology.

310 Rohrbaugh, John, and McCartt, Anne Taylor (eds.). *Applying Decision Support Systems in Higher Education.* New Directions in Institutional Research, no. 49. San Francisco: Jossey-Bass, 1986. 121 pages.

This recent paperback covers a broad range of topics related to decision support systems, including tactical decision making, Markov-based decision support applications, formal decision models, strategic decision making, decision conferencing, group decision support systems, resource allocation models, system dynamics simulation models, and evaluation of alternative decision processes. These approaches are illustrated with higher education management examples such as pricing, budgeting, tenure processes, and space allocation. A very important contribution of the volume is that it demonstrates and documents from the literature the enormous scope of issues that must be addressed in successful DSS applications. While the chapter authors do not always weave DSS convincingly into the higher education management fabric, this sourcebook, which assumes no prior knowledge of DSS, will help its target audience of institutional administrators and planners learn about DSS.

★311 Tetlow, William L. (ed.). *Using Microcomputers for Planning and Management Support.* New Directions for Institutional Research, no. 44. San Francisco: Jossey-Bass, 1984. 103 pages.

The purpose of this sourcebook is to provide an overview of the "chaotic, volatile, and rapidly changing computer revolution" and its applications to decision support. Topics covered include evolution of the use of computer-based information systems in decision support, institutional research and telecommunications applications of microcomputers, essential facts about microcomputers and their use for distributed information processing, factors in the cost of computing, the nature of effective decision support management, and many other issues pertinent to the successful use of microcomputers in this field. Tetlow sums up their promise and peril as follows: "Microcomputer technology is direct, personal, and especially well suited for the task of decision support. Perhaps the only thing that exceeds its usefulness is the expectation of a new or potential user" (p. 93). This monograph is a must for the library of the decision support practitioner in higher education.

Communications

★312 Hiltz, Starr Roxanne, and Turoff, Murray. *The Network Nation: Human Communication via Computer.* Reading, Mass.: Addison-Wesley, 1978. 528 pages.

This is one of the most quoted comprehensive works on group communications via computerized conferencing systems (CCS). CCS use computers to "structure, store, and process written communications among a group of persons." This early volume treats many CCS topics that have remained practically and theoretically important, such as related technologies; social and psychological processes; potential applications and impacts on managerial and staff functions; CCS for public use and for traditional research communication processes; projecting the future, the economy, the utility of the technology and its regulation and of the human-machine interface; and the societal impacts of computerized conferencing. It is still an essential reference for those interested in higher education applications of computer conferencing.

313 Jamieson, Derek M., and MacKay, Kenneth H. "Using Microcomputers for Distributed Information Processing." In William L. Tetlow (ed.), *Using Microcomputers for Planning and Management Support*. New Directions for Institutional Research, no. 44. San Francisco: Jossey-Bass, 1984. Pages 53–62.

Recognizing that communicating is a people-oriented activity and that people resist change, this chapter explains how the microcomputer can nonetheless contribute to communications in higher education. Its topics include word processing, DSS, electronic spreadsheets, electronic messaging systems, computer conferencing, intelligent terminals, electronic forms, and local area networks. The authors stress and illustrate the need for careful technical planning and coordination among the many institutional organizational units involved in order to maximize the communications benefits of microcomputers. This short, highly readable piece presents the essence of this new and important topic on the basis of the authors' campus experience. (For a description of this handbook as a whole, please see entry no. 311.)

★314 Quarterman, John S., and Hoskins, Josiah C. "Notable Computer Networks." *Communications of the ACM*, 1986, *29* (10), 932–971.

This comprehensive, comparative survey of computer networks will be useful to the increasing number of higher education administrators who must decide and manage issues related to sets of interconnected computers and the resultant services, costs, and benefits. The authors use a taxonomy of five network types: research, company, cooperative, commercial, and metanetworks. They compare more than thirty-five networks in terms of characteristics including purpose, administration, funding, protocols, services, speed and reliability, naming, addressing, routing, size and scope, and access. Social and legal issues as well as a sketch of the history of the networks compared are also included. A brief bibliographical note introduces a valuable set of nearly 100 references.

13

Cameron Fincher

Policy Analysis
and Institutional Research

Governance and management in institutions of higher education are both directly related to the formation and implementation of policy. Governing and managing are not the same functions, however, and governing boards are not merely policy-making bodies that leave the implementation of policy to dedicated administrators. Both governing boards and institutional leaders are actively involved in policy development, and members of both groups can benefit from the clarification of policy, its formation, and its implementation in institutional settings. Policy is thus a unifying concept for institutional governance and management, as well as a concept that is central to the common concerns of corporations, governments, and universities.

In institutions less complex than American colleges and universities, policy might still be regarded as the primary function of governing, coordinating, or advisory boards. Such boards would establish guidelines for administrative actions and decisions and then give competent administrators the autonomy and freedom needed to carry out institutional programs and services. Some observers still believe that policy is the primary responsibility of governing bodies and would insist that policy, in the form of rules and regulations, should not be too restrictive on administrative decisions: policy should guide administrative action, but it should not be a rule book that is consulted before every decision. Such observers regard policy as a rationale for actions and decisions that require some degree of administrative discretion.

282

Analysis of public and institutional policies affecting the governance and management of higher education is the most effective means of clarifying policy issues, reshaping or redirecting policy, and establishing a less confused policy-making process. The development of more effective methods and skills for policy analysis, in turn, is the most challenging issue in institutional research. The purpose of this chapter is to provide an overview of public and institutional policy as each influences academic governance and management and is in turn influenced by institutional and policy analysis research and literature.

The chapter emphasizes public policy, as opposed to institutional policy, because the former has been the more potent force during the past quarter-century. Changes in public policy have altered radically the administration and governance of institutions that have usually been outside the mainstream of public policy issues and concerns. In higher education this happened with the Servicemen's Readjustment Act of 1944, the National Defense Education Act of 1958, the Higher Education Act of 1965, and the Educational Amendment Acts of 1972. It should be noted, however, that federal and state legislation can alter institutional policy and practices only when there is a change in the demands and expectations of the public. Access to higher education by women, minority groups, and low-income students has been facilitated by federal and state legislation, but legislation is not solely responsible for the many changes observed in educational opportunities beyond high school. Changes in public policy, in many respects, are like John Adams's conception of the American Revolution: they take place in the minds of American citizens long before they take place on literal or figurative battlefields.

Public Policy and Policy Analysis

The analysis of public policy is, in most respects, the separation of various policy issues into smaller, more manageable problems for purposes of interpretation and implementation. Having broken out the embedded issues and concerns in policy, the policy analyst then has the task of reassembling the parts into a functional or organized unit.

Policy analysis, as frequently practiced, is indeed a process of rational analysis and/or reasoning. The assumptions, objectives, preferences, and expected results of policymakers are often concealed in the public policy-making process, however. One challenge to the policy analyst is to identify these implicit, unstated, or obscured features. The implicit objectives of policymakers may be quite different from the stated or avowed objectives of the policy itself. The actual outcomes of the policy, furthermore, may differ from both explicit and implicit objectives.

Many methods are available to policy analysts. Analyses of public and institutional policies may be historiographic, comparative, longitudinal or developmental, sociological, legalistic, political, economic, technological, or a mixture of these and other possibilities. Analysis may be focused on purposes, objectives, and legislative intent; strategies, priorities, programs, and other process variables; costs, benefits, impact, residual effects, and other outcomes; or policy development as a process of interest in its own right. Rather than being comprehensive, most policy analyses concentrate on examining specific antecedents, alternatives, consequences, or (sometimes) side effects or by-products of a policy.

In the early 1970s, concerted efforts were made to recast the study of policy formation to reflect planning, management, and evaluation techniques developed in other organizational settings. PPBS (planning, programming, and budgeting systems) management by objectives, zero-based budgeting, and other specific techniques were transferred to government and higher education from aerospace industries, the military services, and other technologically oriented enterprises. Similarly, applications of systems analysis, operations research, and management science were strongly advocated from both within and without in government agencies and on college campuses. The highly specialized, technical features of these approaches, however, proved to be not sufficiently sensitive to the historical, cultural, social, political, and personal dimensions of public policy. Administrators learned that techniques developed in different organizational settings could not easily replace older, more familiar concepts and methods of policy planning, formation, and implementation.

In higher education the state of policy analysis currently is promising but not highly sophisticated. Occasional doctoral dissertations provide analyses of policy issues, and occasional reports from institutes or centers of higher education deal with policy-related problems and concerns. Much of the literature on policy analysis, however, is ephemeral, often lost in reports that are quickly dated and just as quickly out of print. Thus, this chapter concentrates on books that are likely to be in most college and university libraries, public policy studies that are regarded as classics in traditional or behavioral disciplines, and published studies that clarify both the substance of policy issues and methods of inquiry and analysis. National commission reports that are long on policy recommendations and short on policy analysis, as well as ad hoc institutional studies that are short on substance, method, and general interest, have been excluded.

Institutional Research and Policy-Related Research

Institutional research is (or should be) a systematic, objective method of inquiry and analysis that has excellent promise as a research specialty related to the formation, implementation, analysis, and evaluation of institutional policy. Institutional research also is (or should be) an invaluable contributor to the formation and study of public policy in higher education. This specialty should no longer be confined to routine statistical analyses and reports or to ad hoc studies commissioned to bolster administrative decisions. Institutional researchers should not hesitate to insist that policy analysis and policy research are essential to the study of institutions as invaluable and unique sociocultural parts of our pluralistic society.

A happy marriage between policy analysis and institutional research is usually forestalled by the conceptual difficulties of policy, not by lack of the competencies and skills required for methodologically sound institutional research. Public policy is too often perceived as something that happens to an institution, and institutional policy is too often regarded as an unquestioned necessity or the lesser of several evils. Many observers believe that institutional researchers have long had the analytical capabilities and research skills needed to make larger, more significant studies of institutional structure, functions, and effectiveness. They further believe that analysis, interpretation, and evaluation are not widely recognized functions of institutional research because such responsibilities are jealously guarded by others.

The clarification of policy as a unifying concept in administration, governance, and institutional research could make a substantial contribution to effectiveness in all three areas of responsibility. Institutional and program planning is seldom possible without analytical studies of institutional goals, program objectives, and their related outcomes. Self-studies are required by virtually all regional accreditation agencies and accrediting professional associations. Program and project evaluations are now required by virtually all funding agencies as well.

In many respects institutional research provides a mode of inquiry that is complementary to policy analysis. Institutional characteristics and summarized information on faculty, students, facilities, finances, and programs are often the grist for analytical mills, and the successful implementation of policy is always reflected, to some extent, in the institutional, administrative, faculty, and student data with which institutional research deals. The historical development of institutions can be studied and compared more objectively with the recorded data and information that institutional research often provides. Comparative, longitudinal studies of the development of policy are also more feasible when accurate and reliable institutional records are available for analysis and interpretation.

Multiple regression and correlational methods now provide means for analyzing effects that are particularly relevant to policy-related research. The effects of specific policy changes can be analyzed in terms of their particular antecedents and/or determinants, and the magnitude of expected effects can be estimated. More important for many policy studies, these analyses may permit a better appreciation of cause-and-effect relationships in policy issues marked by complexity and resistance to systematic study.

The combined application of policy analysis and institutional research to the study of policy issues holds great promise. Where weaknesses do exist, they are often attributable to the conceptual limitations of analyst or researcher, not to the limitations of method. Computing capabilities on most college campuses and in most policy arenas now exceed appreciably the analytical models developed by researchers and the historical/comparative data available for analysis, interpretation, and evaluation.

Commentary on the Literature

The literature on policy analysis has been dominated by the behavioral and social sciences. Economists, political scientists, sociologists, and specialists in public administration have contributed the most substantive analyses of public policy issues, and their work constitutes most of the classics in policy analysis. The content and methods of such classics are only partly applicable to the analysis of policy in higher education, however. Many studies deal with issues only slightly related to the management and governance of colleges. Nonetheless, they demonstrate a conceptual and methodological sophistication that policy analysts in higher education should have. Familiarity with the published work of Bauer (nos. 317, 318), Boulding (no. 319), Coleman (no. 321), Lindblom (nos. 320, 326), Wildavsky (no. 329), and others may be as important as knowledge of the work of Bowen (nos. 200, 201, 333), Bailey (no. 316), and others that is more directly related to institutional policy in higher education.

The annotations provided in this chapter are intended more as an introduction to the literature of policy analysis and institutional research than as a guide or a critique. The policy analysis and institutional research literature related to institutional management and governance is indeed voluminous, and the references chosen for annotation serve primarily to orient prospective researchers and practicing administrators. Students of policy analysis and institutional research should gain an appreciation of both fields' historical development.

   The chapter's annotated references should make clear
that rational, analytical modes of inquiry and empirical, quantitative methods of research are complementary. They should
also underscore the dependency of policy analysis and institutional research on the kinds of institutional data and information that are available—and on the methods by which such data
and information are commonly processed. They should make
evident that the analytical and interpretative competencies of
institutional researchers and academic administrators can be
enhanced by more sophisticated methods of policy analysis.

   Most of all, the annotated references should clarify the
role of policy as a unifying concept in institutional management
and governance. Public and institutional policies are the common threads in the fabric of policy analysis, institutional research,
academic administration, and academic governance. The clarification of policy issues, the more systematic development of public
policy, and the more intelligent and intelligible study of institutional policy are essential to the continued development and advancement of institutions of higher education.

Public Policy and Policy Analysis

315 Ackoff, Russell L. *The Art of Problem Solving: Accompanied
by Ackoff's Fables.* New York: Wiley, 1978. 214 pages.

Although written with a light touch, this volume by an experienced systems scientist gives good insight into the resolution
of policy issues. Ackoff distills many years of experience by using brief and often telling examples of practical problems that
have been solved by restructuring the problems or recasting objectives, variables, or expected outcomes in different terms. In
many respects, his approach could be regarded as insightful
learning or cognitive restructuring. Applications of the approach
are given in Part Two of the book, and the relevance of several
applications will quickly be appreciated by knowledgeable policymakers and researchers.

316 Bailey, Stephen K. *Congress Makes a Law: The Story Behind the Employment Act of 1946.* New York: Columbia University Press, 1950. 282 pages.

Known much later as vice-president of the American Council on Education, Stephen Bailey should be better recognized for this classical study of congressional policy-making. It traces the development of congressional efforts to establish a national policy of full employment in the post–World War II era and the eventual passage of legislation that resulted in the National Council of Economic Advisors. Bailey provides an excellent case study in federal legislation, the participation of congressional leaders, and the influence of "political brokers." Although dated, his book can be read for its insights into the legislative process as it relates to public policy.

★317 Bauer, Raymond A., and Gergen, Kenneth J. (eds.). *The Study of Policy Formation.* New York: Free Press, 1968. 392 pages.

One of the more informative books on policy-making, this book addresses several major issues in public policy and the contributions of behavioral and social scientists in clarifying those issues. Bauer's introductory chapter deals with the complexities of the policy-making process, research strategies, and the need to study individual actors in the policy process. Zeckhauser and Schaefer consider public policy in the context of normative economic theory; Bauer gives an informative overview of decision theory as it relates to public policy; Furash provides good insight into the problems of technology transfer; and Gergen discusses the methods used in studying policy formation. Other chapters deal with specific policy areas, such as urban transportation and foreign aid, and the state of the art in policy studies. One underlying theme of the book is the inappropriateness of viewing policy formation as another form of decision making. The complexities of policy preclude a single set of utility preferences, complete knowledge of alternatives and consequences, and a single, best solution.

★318 Bauer, Raymond A., Pool, Ithiel de Sola, and Dexter, Lewis D. *American Business and Public Policy: The Politics of Foreign Trade.* (2nd ed.) Chicago: Aldine-Atherton, 1972. 499 pages.

Bauer, Pool, and Dexter provide an excellent case study in public policy-making, the role of self-interest and ideology, the influence of pressure groups, and the importance of public opinion and attitudes. Their study begins with the renewal of the Reciprocal Trade Act in 1953 and closes with the Trade Expansion Act of 1962, but it covers much more than the political processes of foreign trade. In many respects, the authors view the public policy-making process as a process of social and political communication in which attitudes, opinions, and beliefs are most influential. Policymakers in higher education may be reluctant to read a book on business and foreign trade, but they can learn much from Bauer, Pool, and Dexter's insights concerning communication and policy-making as a social process. A prologue to the second edition is particularly appealing in its discussion of reactions to the first edition, which won the American Political Science Association's Woodrow Wilson Award in 1963 for the best book published on government, politics, or international affairs.

319 Boulding, Kenneth E. *Principles of Economic Policy.* Englewood Cliffs, N.J.: Prentice-Hall, 1958. 440 pages.

Policy is defined by Boulding, an economist, as principles that govern actions directed toward given ends. In policy there is an active concern with ends, means, and the nature of the organization or group that is involved. As Boulding puts the questions, what do we want, and how do we get it? Elsewhere in his book, Boulding compares policy to a small-scale map of the world in which we live. Like a map, policy does not give guidance in detail, and it should not be confused with reality. Economic problems are solved, Boulding says, partly by sheer ignorance and partly by a curious process of pressure, propaganda, and compromise. Policy is shaped by the hammer of organized pressure groups striking the anvil of electoral opinion. No one pretends that political process produces perfect policy; never-theless, politics is the process by which policies are produced. Boulding also equates policy with a deliberate distortion of the ecosystem in ways that favor the objectives of the policymaker. Every new policy interferes with the equilibrium of the previous state of affairs. Finally, Boulding points out that policy is never confined to a single objective. For example, economic policy pursues the multiple objectives of stability, progress, justice, and freedom—objectives that are seldom compatible and sometimes are in violent opposition.

★320 Braybrooke, David, and Lindblom, Charles E. *A Strategy of Decision: Policy Evaluation as a Social Process.* New York: Free Press, 1963. 268 pages.

The strategy of disjointed incrementalism is presented in this volume as the method of policy analysis most often used by those who work in the fields of policy evaluation and decision making. The objectives of policy analysis are to improve present conditions, policies, and objectives by obtaining more information. Such improvements are usually marginal or incremental, and they seldom are perceived as substantive or enduring. Policy analysis is thus seen as a matter of adjusting objectives, strategies, or priorities. These adjustments will seldom result in radical change because they will be made under conditions that do not permit a high degree of understanding. Analysts continue to use a strategy of disjointed incrementalism because of limitations in their knowledge, the costliness of extended analysis, the absence of a completely rational system of analysis, the openness of policy issues, and the diversity of forms that policy problems take. In other words, analysts cannot be comprehensive in their resolution of policy issues, so they accept a lesser challenge. In addition to their clarification of incrementalism as a means of policy-making, Braybrooke and Lindblom provide a useful distinction between preemptive and meliorative values (or rules) in policy analysis. Many policies are intended to make the current situation better, but some policies do indeed preempt certain choices or decisions.

321 Coleman, James S. *Policy Research in the Social Sciences.*
Morristown, N.J.: General Learning Press, 1972. 23
pages.

According to Coleman, there is no comprehensive methodology
for the study of public policy as an aid to the development of
future policy. If the social sciences are to serve as policy sciences,
they must develop a more coherent and self-conscious methodology. Policy research must bridge the world of academic disciplines and the world of public action. The latter world operates
on a different schedule, has its own language, and involves vested
interests, controlled resources, and conflict. Policy research must
take into consideration that timely partial information is more
helpful in crucial actions than complete information after the
fact. Parsimony and elegance may serve well in academic disciplines, but accurate predictions and redundancy will be more
valuable to decision makers. Users or consumers of policy research will not be social scientists, and they will expect research
findings that are related to user or consumer problems. The
values of users will determine the formulation of policy research
problems, Coleman concludes, although the canons of scientific research must continue to govern the ways in which policy
research is conducted.

322 Etzioni, Amitai. "Policy Research." *American Sociologist,*
1971, *6,* 8–12.

Policy research is regarded by Etzioni as more encompassing
than applied research and more concerned with the goals of the
organization for which policy is researched. The difference between policy research and applied research, he says, is much
the same as the difference between strategy and tactics. The difference between policy research and basic research is the difference between strategy and theory; the former is less abstract
and more closely tied to specific courses of action. Neither policy
research nor applied research can claim neutrality, but policy
research should avoid specific assignments that serve only client
needs. Where applied research is instrumental, policy research
is much concerned with values, clarification of goals, and the
relations among goals and means. To be effective, policy re-

search should be conducted in special organizational units that communicate their findings to policymakers, produce practical or usable knowledge, and develop a language that both practitioners and policymakers can use.

323 Fincher, Cameron. *The Purpose and Functions of Policy in Higher Education.* Athens: Institute of Higher Education, University of Georgia, 1973. 22 pages.

Policy is defined in this brief monograph as a general, overall, rational canopy for specific actions, procedures, or operations. Fincher makes distinctions between policy and administration, policy and legislation, policy and ideology, and policy and theory. The functions of both public and institutional policy are identified as decisions, plans, and programs. Two schema for policy-making are presented and discussed: one deals with public policy, in which feedback is permissible through appellate courts and organized influence, and the other deals with institutional policy, in which decisions, plans, and programs are evaluated and moved closer to synthesis or modified by policy review and revised inputs to policy issues.

324 Fincher, Cameron. *Technology Transfer and Political Decision-Making: The Conflict in Models.* Athens: Institute of Higher Education, University of Georgia, 1975. 23 pages.

The two models presented in this monograph are both highly relevant for analysis and research. The first is a synoptic model for general problem solving, in which seven stages of problem solving are depicted in the sequence most often recommended by problem-solving theorists and researchers. The second is a heuristic model for political decision making, which is presented as transactions among participants who direct their inquiries to leaders or authorities who, in turn, seek to stabilize the situation and maintain the decision-making structure that has already been established. The dominant feature of the first model is sequence, and it directly implies that problems are solved by taking one step at a time. The other model is transactional; it implies that equilibrium is the desired outcome, but inputs to policy issues can be modified and recycled.

★325 Janis, Irving L., and Mann, Leon. *Decision Making: A Psychological Analysis of Conflict, Choice, and Commitment.* New York: Free Press, 1977. 488 pages.

Janis and Mann provide a conflict model of decision making that should be of particular interest to policy analysts. Because people are reluctant decision makers, the necessity of making certain decisions is often the source of stress or personal anxiety. Decisional conflict is especially evident when decisions have important consequences and require appreciable commitment over a period of time. Five sequential stages of decision making are depicted in terms that make good sense in policy-making: (1) appraising the challenge—a stage in which the decision maker is unable to remain complacent about goals and courses of action currently pursued; (2) surveying alternatives—a search for more acceptable courses of action; (3) weighing alternatives— a consideration of pros and cons, costs and benefits; (4) deliberating about commitments—second thoughts about implementing a decision and the personal costs involved; and (5) adhering to the decision despite negative feedback—a period of reconsideration after experiencing some degree of both success and disappointment. A pattern of decision making that is particularly relevant in policy decisions is described by Janis and Mann as defensive avoidance. Such a pattern is often observed when decisions are difficult and it is possible to shift blame to others.

326 Lindblom, Charles E. *The Policy-Making Process.* (2nd ed.) Englewood Cliffs, N.J.: Prentice-Hall, 1980. 131 pages.

This volume presents a summary of Lindblom's thinking on the making of public policy. He sees policy-making as a political process remarkable for its complexity and apparent disorder. He criticizes conventional views of the policy-making process as misleading because they depict policy as the product of a single governing mind. Public policy is not formed through the careful analysis of alternatives and the judicious weighing of costs and benefits, he insists. Rather, it is the product of negotiation, bargaining, and compromise among competing interest groups in a political arena. For the most part, policy decisions result only in incremental adjustments that reduce—temporarily—

the conflicts among political parties, interest groups, and other organized groups seeking public resources. Lindblom sees policy analysis as specialized or technical attempts to examine rationally and/or empirically the various underlying issues that influence particular policies.

327 Neustadt, Richard E., and May, Ernest R. *Thinking in Time: The Uses of History for Decision-Makers.* New York: Free Press, 1986. 329 pages.

Two distinguished historians present in this book their views on the uses of history in policy decisions. They draw both examples of success and examples of failure from the nation's recent history, and they analyze the influence of historical consciousness and/or memory on specific actions and decisions as case studies in national policy. The gist of Neustadt and May's method is a delineation of a situation in terms of what is known, what is unclear, and what is presumed. Past events are then analyzed in terms of their likenesses and differences with the current situation, problem, or issue. When the comparisons of past and present are reasonably clear, the next step is to define the objective. It will help, the authors contend, to ask, ''What's the story?''—to put time lines on key events and to plot key trends—and to raise the questions that journalists would normally ask in such situations: when, what, where, who, how, and why? The decision maker should then be in position to place personalities and organizations, a process that implies a reexamination of presumptions and a reconsideration in light of results. Neustadt and May's method need not be accepted to appreciate the emphasis they place upon historical knowledge and understanding in the resolution of public policy issues. Unexamined memory may be the poorest guide of all.

328 Peltason, J. W., and Burns, James M. (eds.). *Functions and Policies of American Government.* Englewood Cliffs, N.J.: Prentice-Hall, 1962. 450 pages.

Politics is defined in this book as conflict among interest groups, and policy is regarded as the product of that conflict. Changes in policy, in turn, are viewed as producing interest groups. Politicians and public officials are the obvious mediators in interest group conflict and the beneficiaries or victims of successful policy solutions, the authors of this introductory text suggest. Among the cautions they issue is the insight that in a democratic society the absence of policy may be as important as the presence of policy; policy by acquiescence is policy nonetheless. Further, in the absence of clearly stated public policy, private or personal policy will be substituted. In economics, as the classical example, what the government does not regulate, the market will—and the market will reflect the policies of those ready to compete in the absence of policy.

★**329** Wildavsky, Aaron. *Speaking Truth to Power: The Art and Craft of Policy Analysis.* Boston: Little, Brown, 1979. 418 pages.

A political scientist who now regards himself as a political economist, Wildavsky in this volume pulls together his insights and viewpoints on policy analysis. Policy is viewed throughout Wildavsky's writing as both a process and a product. As a process, policy is concerned with what is and what ought to be. It is a reordering of priorities in an attempt to serve the public interest. Policy analysis is a craft that calls for creativity, Wildavsky says. Analytical craftsmanship can be stimulated by theory and sharpened by practice, but competence in the craft is learned, not taught. Policy solutions can be viewed as a temporary and partial reduction of tension, as programs negotiated by claimants to limited public resources, and as hypotheses about "what works" and makes sense. In essence, policy analysis is the art of problem solving; operationally, it is the comparison of alternatives, programs, objectives, resources, and outcomes. Many of the views expressed in the volume have been published elsewhere, but they are placed in perspective by interconnecting passages that further clarify Wildavsky's concept of policy analysis.

Institutional Policy and Policy-Related Research

330 Balderston, Fred E., and Weathersby, Georgia B. "PPBS in Higher Education Planning and Management: Part III, Perspectives and Applications of Policy Analysis." *Higher Education,* 1973, *2* (1), 33–67.

Balderston and Weathersby make a convincing argument that use of PPBS (planning, programming, and budgeting systems) in higher education is precluded by higher education's organizational and political environments. They do not see academic collegiality and strict organizational accountability as compatible, and they do not believe that colleges and universities have the technical and analytical competencies to support PPBS. They present policy analysis as an alternative approach, one in which decisions instead of activities are used as organizing principles. The analysis of policy decisions should bear incrementally on institutional problems and assist in building planning and management systems on a case law basis. The authors contend that policy analysis structures institution-specific information, focuses on institutional decision variables, and then restructures institutional decision making in an effort to anticipate key decisions. The analytical base of institution-specific information is developed from specialized models for enrollment forecasting, student flow, faculty staffing and activities, physical facilities, and so on.

★331 Bowen, Howard R. *Investment in Learning: The Individual and Social Value of American Higher Education.* San Francisco: Jossey-Bass, 1977. 507 pages.

For a full description of this work, please see entry no. 200.

★332 Bowen, Howard R. *The Costs of Higher Education: How Much Do Colleges and Universities Spend per Student and How Much Should They Spend?* San Francisco: Jossey-Bass, 1980. 287 pages.

For a full description of this work, please see entry no. 201.

★333 Bowen, Howard R. *The State of the Nation and the Agenda for Higher Education.* San Francisco: Jossey-Bass, 1982. 212 pages.

In this brief volume Bowen raises policy issues that others have avoided. He asks questions like these: What kind of people do we want our children and grandchildren to be? What kind of society do we want them to live in? How can education be guided and shaped to help nurture such people and to create that kind of society? Bowen believes that a majority of American adults can become well educated in the next fifty or sixty years. His concept of well-educated adults is people who are open to ideas and free from prejudices and dogma; people who appreciate our social and cultural heritage and who think maturely about the meaning of human existence; people who maintain a broad outlook on life and a deep concern for the betterment of human beings. In addition, well-educated adults have mastered, in some depth, a field of study and maintain both a desire and a capacity for continued learning. They are self-reliant and continue to develop both physically and intellectually. Finally, they are prepared to live interesting and fulfilling lives. The policy implications of Bowen's book are profound. Bowen is optimistic about the future of higher education.

334 Carnegie Commission on Higher Education. *Priorities for Action: Final Report of the Carnegie Commission on Higher Education.* New York: McGraw-Hill, 1973. 109 pages.

This volume is the best single source of information about the Carnegie Commission on Higher Education and its work from 1967 to 1973. The commission issued twenty-one special reports, including policy recommendations for American higher education, and published over eighty special studies dealing with policy issues of the late 1960s and early 1970s. In concluding its work, the commission identified six priorities for public and institutional policy: (1) the clarification of educational purposes, (2) the preservation and enhancement of quality and diversity, (3) the advancement of social justice, (4) the enhancement of constructive change, (5) the achievement of more effective governance, and (6) the assurance of public resources and their more effective use. The usefulness of the volume is enhanced by chronological listings of commission reports and sponsored studies, technical notes on enrollment projections and minority access, and selected details of commission meetings and membership. Numerous recommendations of the Carnegie Commission are now established policy, and the relevance of its final report is still substantial.

★335 Carnegie Council on Policy Studies in Higher Education. *Three Thousand Futures: The Next Twenty Years for Higher Education.* San Francisco: Jossey-Bass, 1980. 439 pages.

Although issued as the final report of the Carnegie Council on Policy Studies in Higher Education, this volume is more appropriately regarded as a prospective view of higher education in a period following unprecedented development and growing pains. The policy implications of societal and institutional trends are discussed in terms of their impact on the nation's 3,000 institutions of higher education. The increasing dependence of colleges and universities on public resources, uncertain enrollment projections, aging faculty and student populations, and increased governmental regulation are trends that will affect all institutions adversely and some, perhaps, fatally. The strength of the report lies in the council's enrollment projections, its identification and discussion of trends, and its efforts to encourage serious thought about the future of higher education.

336 Firnberg, James W., and Lasher, William F. (eds.). *The Politics and Pragmatics of Institutional Research.* New Directions for Institutional Research, no. 38. San Francisco: Jossey-Bass, 1983. 104 pages.

The obvious influence of politics on public and institutional policy is the focus of the eight chapters contributed to this sourcebook in the New Directions for Institutional Research series. The book makes clear that policy-making at federal, state, and institutional levels is affected by the competing objectives of participants in the process, the decision styles of administrators and policymakers, the nature and comparability of data and information used, and the institutional researchers who collect and report many of the data that feed directly or indirectly into policy decisions. Implied throughout the volume is an increasing need for institutional researchers and policy analysts to understand the political setting in which they work.

337 Frances, Carol. "Influence of Federal Programs." In Paul Jedamus, Marvin W. Peterson, and Associates, *Improving Academic Management: A Handbook of Planning and Institutional Research*. San Francisco: Jossey-Bass, 1980. Pages 20–47.

This chapter provides an excellent summary of the federal legislation influencing higher education since the Northwest Ordinance of 1787. The evolving role of the federal government is considered, and the impact of federal support and regulation on American colleges and universities is discussed. Frances gives two models of the federal government's policy development process: one, linear and somewhat truncated, depicts the current approach made by the federal government, while the other suggests an improved approach to policy analysis and development. (Entry no. 553 describes this handbook as a whole.)

★338 Jedamus, Paul, Peterson, Marvin W., and Associates. *Improving Academic Management: A Handbook of Planning and Institutional Research*. San Francisco: Jossey-Bass, 1980. 679 pages.

For a full description of this work, please see entry no. 553.

339 Manning, Thurston E. "Academic Policies and Standards." In Asa G. Knowles (ed.), *Handbook of College and University Administration*. Vol. 2. New York: McGraw-Hill, 1970. Pages 2–3 to 2–14.

This chapter in Knowles's two-volume handbook of administration offers an informative discussion of academic policies as traditionally viewed in academic administration and governance. Manning treats policy as a written statement that provides a guide for individual actions within an organization. Specifically, he sees academic policy as setting academic standards—the preferred performance sought by administrators in their various decisions and actions. The purpose of academic policies is to guide behavior within the institutional setting, Manning maintains. Thus, the bounds of discretion should be well defined, and the identity of individuals exercising discretion should be clear. Policy-making authority in American colleges and universities, almost without exception, is vested in a governing board (or board of control) and delegated in specific ways to administrators through an institution's president or chancellor. The board's authority in educational policy may be delegated completely or partially to the faculty as a collective entity. Manning gives assistance in determining which policies are usually regarded as faculty matters.

340 National Commission on the Financing of Postsecondary Education. *Financing Postsecondary Education in the United States*. Washington, D.C.: U.S. Government Printing Office, 1973. 442 pages.

Mandated by the Educational Amendments of 1972, this study of financing is a significant example of policy-making inquiries at the national level. Given the impossible charge of studying the impact of past, present, and anticipated private, local, state, and federal support for postsecondary education, the commission made a commendable effort in developing a framework for analyzing national policies, in considering alternative plans, and in making recommendations with policy implications. Among the commission's recommendations was continuing federal leadership in the development of standard procedures for calculating instructional costs per student, by level and by field of study. Also recommmended was the adoption of an analytical framework, similar to the one used by the commission, that would employ objectives and criteria, general policies to accomplish the objectives, and financing mechanisms to implement the chosen policies. The proposed analytical framework was to include a set of measurements to describe the achievement of societal and national objectives and means whereby judgmental reviews of financing mechanisms could be made with regard to specified objectives.

★341 Peterson, Marvin W., and Corcoran, Mary (eds.). *Institutional Research in Transition*. New Directions for Institutional Research, no. 46. San Francisco: Jossey-Bass, 1985. 117 pages.

This volume commemorates the twenty-fifth annual forum of the Association for Institutional Research and provides a commendable perspective on the development of institutional research as a much-needed institutional function and responsibility. Contributors to the volume discuss the practice and profession of institutional research in higher education, its status as a practicing art or professional specialty, related changes in the external environment, strategies for changing institutional governance and management, and the important role of communications and computation in supporting policy and planning decisions. Running through the six chapters is an appreciable optimism concerning the progress institutional research has made in a quarter-century and its promises for the future.

14

Robert C. Nordvall

Innovation,
Planned Change, and
Transformation Strategies

Over the last few decades the calls for widespread change in higher education have been constant, albeit based upon varying rationales. In the 1960s the quality of the academic preparation of students generally was rising, and arguments for curricular reform were often premised upon the need to provide less structured requirements so that students could become more independent learners. The high rate of inflation of the 1970s caused resource allocation problems for higher education, and an emphasis upon accountability arose. The 1980s have seen a spate of reports about the undergraduate curriculum that propose more attention to the quality of undergraduate teaching and the cohesiveness of the undergraduate curriculum.

Changes that occur on individual campuses are often a response either to these general calls for change or to internal pressures that may parallel national concerns. (Occasionally change is simply imposed by external forces; for example, a state agency may mandate a new budget system.) Almost always, too, evolutionary change is occurring: new courses are added to the curriculum, new programs arise, new people occupy key positions and introduce new procedures and emphases.

The focus of this chapter is on change that is planned, major (not small-scale evolutionary change), and not imposed by the fiat of an external group. Such planned change illustrates the full range of the change process, from the articulation of

303

a need through the formulation of a response to the adoption and implementation of an innovation.

There is a rich body of literature on various types of planning for an organization—long range, strategic, tactical, and so on. Planning processes should form an important part of the introduction of major change, but instead, discussions of the planning process usually center upon how an institution can respond in an organized way to the shifting demands of its external and internal environments. The emphasis is upon determining wise responses, not upon carrying them out. Although it often discusses the diagnosis of organizational problems, the literature of planned change, in contrast, primarily emphasizes the process of the acceptance and implementation of new ideas.

Models of Planned Change

Since colleges and universities share features of other complex organizations, writers about change in higher education draw upon a variety of organizational perspectives, including those of business organizations, lower schools, and political communities. There is also a substantial body of literature on the diffusion of innovations in noneducational settings.

Most studies of innovations and changes in higher education feature the practical. They often present advice about how to successfully launch and sustain an effort to change some aspect of the institution. This practical advice ordinarily is presented within one of the major theoretical models of planned change in higher education. These models are research, development, and diffusion (rational planning); social interaction; problem solving; political; and linkage and adaptive development.

The research, development, and diffusion model's key feature is convincing people to change by means of rational arguments. It begins with basic and applied research to develop a useful innovation. This innovation is then disseminated through means such as writings, conferences, and films. These means convince people on campuses of the wisdom of the innovation; they use it themselves and convince others to do so. The Keller Plan of Personalized Instruction, the PLATO system of computer-assisted instruction, management by objectives (MBO), and planning, programming, and budgeting systems (PPBS) are examples of innovations that were disseminated in this way.

The social interaction model similarly concentrates on how new ideas are adopted. Its emphasis is less on the research and development stages and more on the diffusion stage, however. Rather than depending primarily upon the strength of the rational arguments in favor of adoption, this approach concentrates on making sure these arguments are targeted to the persons in the organization who are the most likely to adopt new ideas. The model attempts to identify the characteristics of such persons. Once the innovators and early adopters within the group use a new idea, its use spreads in a predictable way throughout the group. This model grows primarily out of empirical research on the diffusion of agricultural innovations and medical advances.

The problem-solving model, in contrast, is not premised upon introducing change through rational arguments. Although it begins with a stage of diagnosing problems and generating alternative solutions, this model concentrates upon improvements in communications, trust, and individual and peer group relations within the organization as the key elements in a change effort. The emphasis is not only on adopting a change to solve a current problem but also on building organizational capacity to solve future problems. The problem-solving model uses applied behavioral psychology as developed by the human relations school of business administration.

The political model also concentrates on the people within the organization as the key to change, but it is less sanguine about the possibilities of reducing conflict through increased trust, better communications, and improved group relations. Intraorganizational conflict and division into interest groups are natural, according to this model. Change occurs as these groups forge coalitions to get what they want. These groups use their political power to influence those with authority to institute the changes desired. The political model stresses the use of influence and power to affect the actions of key individuals and elites within the organization; its literature calls upon studies of the exercise of power in political communities. J. Victor Baldridge (nos. 344, 345, and 354) is the leading proponent of this model.

The linkage model and the related adaptive development model are syntheses of the other models. In these models, rational planning is employed to develop new ideas (as in the research, development, and diffusion model). As in the social interaction model, these ideas are introduced through social networks; the interpersonal and intergroup relations that are barriers to change must be confronted in the process (problem solving). The political aspects of influencing those with power and authority are not overlooked, either.

The term "linkage" refers to the importance this model places on linking those interested in change both to sources of innovation outside the institution and to persons with similar interests within the institution. "Adaptive development" means that the ideas that are imported from outside the college or university must be modified to fit local circumstances. Planned change is a local process that is, nevertheless, stimulated and guided by adapting innovations from elsewhere (rather than inventing new ones). Jack Lindquist (no. 347) is a primary proponent of the adaptive development model, which he bases on his empirical studies of change in higher education institutions.

Framework for Organizing the Literature

Although the models of planned change provide a useful overview of the field's theoretical perspectives, they do not provide a similarly useful way to categorize the literature on planned change, because many descriptive works contain synopses of all the major perspectives on change in higher education.

Articles and books about change often begin with a review of prior literature in the field. Some works are primarily literature reviews and attempt this task in a comprehensive manner. Others move beyond the literature review to a case study or studies that are analyzed in terms of theories in the literature. Such an analysis may lead to the formulation of a model to explain planned change. When a case study is not the focus, the author may nevertheless formulate a model based upon the literature review. A common feature of most writings on planned change is a discussion of the strategies recommended for a successful change effort.

Thus, the literature on planned change can be divided into four categories, as follows:

Reviews of Literature. This category is reserved for items that are primarily literature reviews, rather than works that merely include such a review.

Models of Planned Change. This category includes works that focus primarily on the formulation or application of a model of the change process. The application of a model can, of course, involve a case study, but the focus of the books and articles in this category is upon the model itself.

Case Studies. The number of institutions examined in these case studies ranges from 1 to 115, but most of the studies involve fewer than 10 institutions. The case studies often conclude with a discussion of one or more models of planned change and a list of advice for change proponents, but the emphasis is more on the empirical study of the change process than on the formulation or validation of a model or the provision of advice.

Strategies for Change. The emphasis in these articles and books is on practical advice. They are the sources to which a reader would turn when trying to decide what steps to take to plan a change effort. Suggested strategies often appear in the form of lists or an agenda for the implementation of change.

Commentary on the Literature

Clearly, there is no single accepted theory of the way change occurs in higher education that can be easily applied to all change efforts. Models of change in higher education that synthesize various perspectives are more comprehensive than models with a narrower viewpoint, but comprehensive models do not aid in determining the importance of different elements in the environment. For example, the political environment at a college or university is an important factor in any efforts to introduce change, but in what types of situations is the political factor likely to play a truly major role? A comprehensive change model does not answer this question. Even a more focused model of change, such as the political one, often does not explain how one can tell which political factors are the most vital ones to address. Similarly, a case study that argues for the importance of manipulating political factors may provide valuable guidance for some change programs, but for which ones? Thus, the various models point out important factors to be considered in mounting a change effort, but they cannot indicate either the balance among these factors in a particular situation or the importance of any particular factor in this situation.

At a more abstract level, there is the question of how to apply lessons and findings about change in other contexts to change in higher education. Discussions of change on campus draw upon works that analyze change in other settings, such as businesses, communities, and elementary and secondary schools. There are certainly analogies between these contexts and higher education, but the strength of the analogies is not always immediately apparent.

Applications of findings from other types of organizations or even other colleges and universities can depend upon what these findings determine to be the key factor for successfully instituting change. If the key factor is seen to be changing the attitudes and values of individuals, the universal lessons are more likely to be found. Discussions of why individuals resist change do not distinguish between reasons for resistance among college professors and reasons applicable to employees in other types of organizations. Perspectives on the change process that emphasize building trust and better communications in the workplace similarly do not view these needs as depending upon the type of employer. In contrast, a political perspective on change must draw distinctions between a corporation and a university. There is no group of employees in the typical corporation that is analogous to the professoriate, for example. Thus, change models that focus upon organizational structures are not easily given universal application. A criticism of the social interaction model is that it concentrates upon the propensity of individuals to adopt innovations and does not properly consider the environment in which they work. A farmer or a docter who is attracted by an innovation can adopt it for his or her personal use much more easily than a curriculum committee can institute an educational reform.

The search for a unified theory to explain how change occurs in all organizational contexts may be a vain one. Even if such a theory could be created, it is doubtful that it could provide detailed steps to guide all change efforts. At best, such a theory could provide a list of factors that have been proven critical in a broad range of change activities. This list would most likely be similar to the compilations of practical advice that already are frequently found in the literature about introducing innovations and change. The list derived from a unified theory would, at best, eliminate the inconsistencies found in current practical discussions about change; it would not provide a simple, universal scheme to achieve change.

Furthermore, the inconsistencies in the lists of practical advice are not extensive. Instead there are areas of broad agreement. The first of these is that change cannot simply be ordered by top administrators. Their role, at best, can be to establish procedures that facilitate change and to respond thoughtfully to change proposals made to them. Second, successful programs of change should be based upon institutional research that allows for a proper analysis of the problem to which the change proposal responds. Third, regardless of what the institutional research shows, change will not occur unless the need for it is perceived both by a broad group and by at least some people with the authority or influence to implement the change successfully. Finally, there is agreement that the emphasis upon achieving change often overlooks the stage of ongoing implementation. The losing side in the debate on whether to make a change is often strong enough to block the change's successful implementation. Therefore, support for the new idea must be sustained after it is instituted.

As has been noted, there are many models of the change process. The more comprehensive models are necessarily more general and therefore do not provide concise guidance on producing change in a particular environment. Similarly, advice about change strategies is often so broad that it is difficult to determine how to apply it to specific situations. There is a recognized need to move to more empirical studies that analyze how change models operate in different settings. For example, Conrad (no. 349) examined the sources and processes of curricular change at four institutions. Ross (no. 352) tested the importance of three factors suggested by the literature by reviewing the introduction of innovations at 115 institutions. Lindquist (no. 347) examined the application of research and theories on planned change to case histories of change processes at seven institutions. Such empirical studies offer the best hope for refining the findings about change in higher education so that the literature can move beyond the often repetitive discussion of models to test theories about change and to provide guidance for applying these theories to different types of change efforts and to various environments.

Reviews of Literature

342 Lindquist, Jack. "Political Linkage: The Academic-Innovation Process." *Journal of Higher Education,* 1974, *45,* 323–343.

Lindquist lists seven kinds of research and theoretical works that offer perspectives on the innovation process in colleges and universities, including case histories, research on academic governance, how-to-do-it guides for change, works on innovation diffusion, accounts of planned change in lower schools, works on political power and decision making, and discussions of the decision process in business and industry. He next discusses seven factors that form obstacles to academic innovation: the threat to secured positions, the extreme differentiation of groups and fields of knowledge on campus, the pluralistic power structure, traditional academic values, the difficulty of proving that an innovation provides improved education, the isolation of college and university members from new teaching-learning information, and simple organizational inertia. The article proposes a political linkage model that deals with the sources of academic innovation, the diffusion of these innovations to members of the campus community, and the process by which decisions about innovation go through the institutional governance system. Lindquist also provides practical advice clearly grounded in change-process theory. This article provides a good short overview of the literature and guidance for applying the findings in it to a campus environment.

343 Nordvall, Robert C. *The Process of Change in Higher Education Institutions*. AAHE-ERIC Higher Education Research Report no. 7. Washington, D.C.: American Association for Higher Education, 1982. 49 pages.

This report reviews the literature on planned change in colleges and universities in order to serve as a guide for persons wishing to change their own institutions. It considers both theoretical models of the change process and practical advice about orchestrating that process successfully. As background to the theoretical models, the report discusses different conceptions of the decision-making process on a college or university campus. The major theoretical change models identified include rational planning, problem solving, social interaction, political, linkage, and adaptive development. Since organizational receptivity to change is an important influence on the success of a change effort, the report reviews the characteristics that mark an organization open to change. The section on practical advice about change begins with advice on building an organizational climate that is receptive to change. Other practical advice topics include formulating the change proposal, mounting a campaign to secure its approval, and assuring that it is completely implemented. This overview is primarily for administrators who want a brief summary of the theory and practice of change in higher education institutions.

Models of Planned Change

344 Baldridge, J. Victor. *Power and Conflict in the University.*
New York: Wiley, 1971. 238 pages.

Baldridge begins by reviewing three models of university governance: political, bureaucratic, and collegial. He argues for a
political model, based upon political science studies and sociological analysis of complex organizations. He tests his model
through an empirical analysis of policy changes at New York
University in the 1960s. He discusses the organization and attitudes of what he terms partisan groups. The resources (power
bases) available to these groups are bureaucratic, professional,
coercive, and personal. Cohesive, disciplined, and well-organized partisan groups are more likely to use these resources to
achieve changes, he says. This book is a useful guide for those
who want to muster the political forces within a university to
make a change.

345 Baldridge, J. Victor. "Organizational Change: The Human Relations Perspective Versus the Political Systems
Perspective." *Educational Researcher,* 1972, *1,* 4–10, 15.

Baldridge sees the goals of the human relations approach to improved organizational functioning as reduction of conflict within
the organization; integration of the needs of individuals with
the needs of the organization; and emphasis on a more democratic, sensitive, and humane organization. He doubts that these
goals, even if reached, will automatically result in improved functioning of the organization. He argues instead for an approach
that seeks to understand and use the political processes within
the organization. His approach sees conflict within the organization as natural. Interest groups are inevitable, and one should
study how they articulate their goals and seek to influence the
decision-making process. The ideal leader of a change effort,
according to Baldridge, would understand sociological and political theory. He or she would use political and rational strategies
rather than psychological ones to achieve change. Satisfaction
of the organization's staff would be secondary to achievement

of organizational goals. This article is a concise statement of many of the criticisms of a human relations approach to organizational functioning and thus is useful to scholars studying this approach and to practitioners considering using it.

★**346** Dill, David D., and Friedman, Charles P. "An Analysis of Frameworks for Research on Innovation and Change in Higher Education." *Review of Educational Research*, 1979, *49* (3), 411–435.

The authors place the processes of purposive change and innovation within the broad category of organizational change. They then derive four basic frameworks for describing change in higher education: complex organization, conflict, diffusion, and planned change. They compare these four in terms of customary research methodology, common unit of analysis, prescriptive or descriptive intent, common dependent variables, and loci of impetus for change. They develop causal models for each of the four, identifying the key variables in the framework and the relationships among them. Finally, they provide a discussion of general variables that are common to two or more of the frameworks. The authors argue that combinations of these four frameworks should be used as the basis for research on change and innovation in higher education. The article's purpose is to provide a more sound conceptual basis to guide this research. This theoretically sophisticated article is aimed at scholars in the field of change research.

★**347** Lindquist, Jack. *Strategies for Change.* Berkeley, Calif.: Pacific Soundings Press, 1978. 268 pages.

Growing out of the Strategies for Change and Knowledge Utilization project, this book first reviews the theory and research of planned change and then applies this research to case histories of change projects at seven higher education institutions. A model of planned change—the adaptive development model—is formulated on the basis of these case histories. The adaptive development model calls for adaptation of external innovations that are developed to fit the local context of the organization.

This model is an extension of the linkage model of change proposed by Havelock (no. 356). The discussion of the model is followed by extensive practical advice about how to implement change successfully. This study is an excellent introduction for persons wishing to understand both how planned change works at a college or university and how to introduce successful innovative change at a higher education institution.

348 Rogers, Everett M. *Diffusion of Innovations*. (3rd ed.) New York: Free Press, 1983. 512 pages.

Rogers is the major investigator of diffusion of innovations, and in this book he responds to criticisms that his diffusion model applies only to individuals by including a chapter on innovation in organizations. The book summarizes diffusion research, including a discussion of key features of innovations that affect their rate of adoption: relative advantage, compatibility, complexity, trialability, and observability. These features can be important for the adoption of innovations in an organizational setting. This work also contains chapters on determining the characteristics of persons most likely to adopt innovations and on the role of the change agent in the innovation process. Even though the social interaction model of change (based upon the diffusion paradigm) has been criticized as not particularly applicable to higher education, this work attempts to deal with the criticisms of the model and broaden its relevance for organizational change. This book provides the understanding of Rogers's work that is necessary for anyone who wants a broad overview of change theory.

Case Studies

★349 Conrad, Clifton F. "A Grounded Theory of Educational Change." *Sociology of Education*, 1978, *51*, 101–112.

Conrad examines four institutions that recently had undergone curriculum changes to discover answers to two questions: What are the major sources of academic change? What are the major processes through which academic change occurs? The major sources of change are identified as external and internal social structural forces that threaten the status quo. The major stages in the change process are conflict and interest group formation, administrative intervention, the policy-recommending stage, and the policy-making stage. Administrators function both as brokers among interest groups and as a vested interest group in themselves, Conrad says. He sees his theory as closer to the political model of change than to other perspectives he discusses (complex organization, planned change, and diffusion of innovation). All these perspectives are useful in explaining some part of the change process, but the political model, as augmented by the grounded theory of this article, is seen as having the greatest explanatory power. This article is one of the few that empirically test various change theories; thus it is of special interest to scholars of the change process.

★**350** Levine, Arthur. *Why Innovation Fails*. Albany: State University of New York Press, 1980. 224 pages.

This book is primarily a study of the history of a number of experimental colleges at the State University of New York at Buffalo from 1966 to 1975. Despite the title, the innovative colleges did not all fail. Most, however, had to change to conform more closely to university policies and norms. The key factors that mark a successful innovation, according to Levine, are profitability (the innovation meets the needs of the whole institution) and compatibility (the innovation is congruent with the norms and values of the institution). The histories of the experimental colleges are analyzed through an assessment of these two factors. An incompatible innovation might be altered to greater conformity, but an unprofitable one will be terminated. The work concludes with a study of its implications through a review of the literature on planned change. Although this work is primarily about the theory of change, the two-page synthesis of theories on planned change provides a useful checklist for anyone leading an effort to institute a change within an organization.

351 Martorana, S. V., and Kuhns, Eileen. *Managing Academic Change: Interactive Forces and Leadership in Higher Education.* San Francisco: Jossey-Bass, 1975. 240 pages.

The authors' theory of interactive forces evolves from their analysis of reports on innovations from two dozen institutions. The three types of forces that interact are personal (decision makers, implementers, and consumers), extrapersonal (for example, facilities, policies, trends), and goal hiatus (the discrepancy between the aspiration toward a particular institutional goal and the achievement of it). The book presents postulates about how these forces interact. The authors also develop a matrix for assessing the impact of the forces during the stages of the development of an innovation. In addition to this theoretical analysis of the introduction of innovation, they develop lists of strategies and tactics for successfully effecting change. This book presents a quantitative approach (not typical in this theory-oriented literature) for measuring the probability of successful change. Practitioners can use this quantitative framework in estimating the prospects for a successful change effort.

★352 Ross, R. Danforth. "The Institutionalization of Academic Innovations: Two Models." *Sociology of Education,* 1976, *49,* 146–155.

Drawing on a study of innovations at 115 colleges and universities, Ross examines the importance of three factors that the literature on academic change has deemed important for introducing innovations: resources to start new programs, pressures to innovate, and the institutional authority structure. For the introduction of departments in emerging standard disciplines (for example, biophysics, linguistics, computer science), resource availability proved to be the only one of the three factors that was predictive. For new programs in urban and ethnic studies, resource availability, student pressure, and a certain type of authority structure (decentralized, with a president who spends much of his or her time on academic affairs) all seem to contribute toward program adoption. This article moves beyond studies that attempt to find factors that contribute to or inhibit change in general to an analysis of different kinds of academic change that may require different factors to encourage their institutionalization. It will be of major value to persons interested in the empirical study of the innovation process.

353 Sikes, Walter W., Schlesinger, Lawrence E., and Seashore, Charles N. *Renewing Higher Education from Within: A Guide for Campus Change Teams.* San Francisco: Jossey-Bass, 1974. 184 pages.

This book grew out of a project of the NTL Institute titled "Training Teams for Campus Change." Action-research teams of faculty, students, and administrators were established at eight institutions to serve as change agents on their campuses. The action-research approach is an application of the problem-solving model of change. It uses the systematic collection of data to diagnose the causes of dissatisfaction. Goals are set for improvement, and group action is devised to achieve the goals. On the basis of the case histories of the teams, the authors draw conclusions about the circumstances that are most favorable for the successful use of this approach to change. The volume concludes with a manual for change teams. The teams at the eight institutions achieved some successes, but their experiences were certainly not all positive. The experiences of these teams and the authors' discussion of these experiences provide an excellent starting point for anyone who wishes to assess the usefulness of the action-research team approach for a particular change effort.

Strategies for Change

354 Baldridge, J. Victor. "Managerial Innovations: Rules for Successful Implementation." *Journal of Higher Education,* 1980, *51,* 117–134.

This article is based on a study of the Resource Allocation and Management Program (RAMP), which granted awards to forty-nine private liberal arts colleges to introduce modern managerial practices. The key elements for success were administrative and

faculty support, generous funding, and skillful project directors.
The first step in the adoption of the managerial innovation
should be a needs assessment. Baldridge discusses factors that
often block such an assessment. He then reviews the dimensions
of the political processes on campus and proposes rules for
building effective political support for the innovation. The rules
concentrate upon framing the issues, building evaluations of support, and wisely navigating the proposal through the organization's bureaucracy. These rules are important for success in
the second step of the process—introducing the new project.
Baldridge stresses that plans need to be made for the evolution
and institutionalization of the innovation, because the initial enthusiasm for it will eventually end. Although its conclusions are
not unusual for any article stressing the political aspects of introducing change, this study is based upon a larger sample of change
efforts than is typical. Thus, it provides important evidence for
researchers about change. It also has important implications for
those planning to implement changes, especially at liberal arts
colleges.

355 Bennis, Warren G. "Who Sank the Yellow Submarine?"
Psychology Today, 1972, *6* (6), 112–120.

Subtitled "Eleven Ways to Avoid Major Mistakes in Taking
Over a University Campus and Making Great Changes," this
article is based on the author's key role in the effort in the late
1960s to transform the State University of New York at Buffalo into a major multiversity. The effort was a failure, as promises outstripped resources and plans for change proliferated without a solid base. The eleven principles for change that Bennis
proposes on the basis of his experience at Buffalo include the
following: recruit with scrupulous honesty, guard against the
crazies, build support among like-minded people, plan for
change from a solid conceptual base, do not settle for rhetorical
change, do not allow those who are opposed to change to appropriate such basic issues as academic standards, know the territory, appreciate environmental factors, avoid future shock,
allow time to consolidate gains, and remember that change is
most successful when those who are affected are involved in the

planning. The principles are not new, but this very informal account shows that they cannot be replaced by good intentions and charismatic leadership. This is a good, short, practical guide to avoiding mistakes when planning major change.

356 Havelock, Ronald G. *The Change Agent's Guide to Innovation in Education.* Englewood Cliffs, N.J.: Educational Technology Publications, 1973. 304 pages.

This is a manual for change agents—persons who facilitate planned change or planned innovation. It presents a model of the stages in planned change: building a relationship with the client, diagnosing the problem, acquiring relevant resources, choosing a solution, gaining acceptance of the solution, stabilizing the innovation, and generating self-renewal. For each stage, Havelock presents suggested strategies for success. The book also summarizes the strategic orientations of various approaches to educational innovation: problem solving; social interaction; research, development, and diffusion; and Havelock's synthesis of these, linkage. The volume concludes with an annotated bibliography of major books relevant to educational change. This work is aimed at educators in elementary and secondary schools. It is a good summary of both theory and practical steps for successfully introducing an innovation into any educational organization.

357 Hipps, G. Melvin (ed.). *Effective Planned Change Strategies.* New Directions for Institutional Research, no. 33. San Francisco: Jossey-Bass, 1982. 135 pages.

The nine essays in this collection cover the need for planned change, general suggested strategies, and three institutional case studies. Whereas much of the writing about change discusses how to overcome institutional blocks to a particular change, this volume focuses on ways to institutionalize a continuing process of change within the organizational structure. For example, Philip Winstead presents a model for planned change with components of organizational development, information systems, and a formal office of institutional planning. He also discusses the implementation of the management planning model at Furman

University. The summary chapter extracts the common elements
from the three case studies of planned change. This volume provides a useful overview of planned change, with brief case studies
to place the overview in a context. Administrators responsible
for determining an institution's planning process will find the
book helpful.

358 Kirkpatrick, Donald L. *How to Manage Change Effectively:
Approaches, Methods, and Case Examples.* San Francisco:
Jossey-Bass, 1985. 280 pages.

This book provides an excellent summary of both the philosophical approaches and the practical advice about change that
are contained in business management literature. Especially useful is the summary in Chapter Three of writings about change by
a number of the major management authors. Common themes
from these writings (for example, empathy, communication, and
participation) provide the basis for Part Two of the book, which
discusses specific approaches for making changes and having
them accepted. The book closes with a number of case studies.
This book presents a comprehensive overview of management
principles and approaches that the educational administrator
should both understand and be able to adapt to the educational
environment.

359 Klein, Donald. "Some Notes on the Dynamics of Resistance to Change: The Defender Role." In Warren
G. Bennis, Kenneth D. Benne, and Robert Chin (eds.),
The Planning of Change. (4th ed.) New York: Holt, Rine-
hart & Winston, 1984. Pages 498–507.

This article points out that resistance to change is not always
the undesirable element it appears to be in studies made from
the perspective of people seeking change. Those seeking change
see only its benefit to them, not its effect upon the whole organization. The defender can provide the broader perspective. Re-
sisters to change often defend the self-esteem, competence, and
autonomy of people in the group. Change agents often differ
in their values and information from those for whom they are

planning. Change agents may keep the change process secret until the time of unveiling the change plans and action recommendations. The ultimate clients of the change may realize that at this point they can have little effect upon the details of the plan; their only source of influence is to defeat the plan in open conflict. This article makes the useful point that those opposing changes are not necessarily backward-looking people but may have legitimate reasons for their opposition. People dedicated to making changes will find that this article provides a perspective that they need to understand.

360 Wattenbarger, James L., and Scaggs, Sandra. "Curriculum Revision and the Process of Change." In Arthur M. Cohen (ed.), *Shaping the Curriculum*. New Directions for Community Colleges, no. 25. San Francisco: Jossey-Bass, 1979. Pages 1–10.

This short article proposes primarily a political strategy for introducing curricular change into a community college. It contains a synthesis of advice from various studies on change efforts but goes beyond these studies to note the importance of an often overlooked barrier to the implementation of change—lack of budgetary information on the part of the change advocates. The authors recommend a complete understanding of the budgetary process as a first step in an effort to introduce change. The political campaign for change that the authors describe is meant to respond to the three stages of Kurt Lewin's theory of change—unfreezing current attitudes, inducing the change, and refreezing the new attitudes. Although it is aimed at community college personnel, this article's advice is not limited to the particular organizational features of community colleges.

15

Kim S. Cameron

Improving Academic Quality and Effectiveness

The evaluation of quality and effectiveness in higher education has a long history, probably over 200 years (see no. 390). Systematic and scientific assessments, however, were not present in the published literature until shortly after the turn of the century—around 1910—when James McKeen Cattell published the first quality ranking of colleges and universities based on the accomplishments of renowned scholars (see no. 382). Since that time, two separate literatures have emerged, one focusing on "quality" and the other on "effectiveness" in higher education. The effectiveness literature has emerged more recently than 1910. It developed mainly among organizational researchers studying private- and public-sector organizations and then later was applied to colleges and universities. A review of publications referring to both effectiveness and quality, therefore, necessitates a search of independent streams of writing, even though at first blush the terms seem almost synonymous. It also necessitates choices about the boundaries to be drawn around these two ambiguous terms. Because neither word has an objective referent, and neither has been defined precisely in the literature, neither has been measured precisely nor consensually. In fact, the major controversy in the literature on these two terms is on how to measure them accurately. There are no clear guide-

Note: Karen Bantel's assistance in the compilation of bibliographical information in this chapter is gratefully acknowledged.

322

lines for deciding what items to include in a review such as this one, since many proxy terms have been used and many levels of analysis and referents have been applied in the literature.

This introduction will attempt to explain why, despite their ambiguity, these two concepts hold a place of central importance in the higher education literature and lie at the heart of college and university research and administration. It will also attempt to differentiate the two terms from each other and from commonly used proxies. Finally, it will point out why confusion and disagreement still permeate the literature and will identify the boundaries that have been drawn to limit the literature in the chapter's annotations.

The Importance of Effectiveness and Quality

Few topics in higher education have generated as much attention and controversy recently as the quality and effectiveness of colleges and universities. Despite the numerous difficulties and paradoxes associated with the study of quality and effectiveness (see no. 364), the search for relevant criteria by which to measure these remains a primary activity of college and university administrators and researchers. There are theoretical, empirical, and practical reasons why this is so.

Theoretically, the construct of effectiveness lies at the very center of all organizational models. That is, all conceptualizations of organizations have embedded in them notions of the nature of effectiveness or of the differences that exist between effective and ineffective organizations. Similarly, quality of outcomes and institutional functioning lies at the center of theories of educational administration, outcomes, governance, financing, and performance. The need to distinguish between high and low levels of quality is a driving force in these theories.

Empirically, the constructs of effectiveness and quality are assumed to be the ultimate dependent variables in institutional research. Evidence for effectiveness or quality appears (albeit in rather imprecise ways) in most investigations of college and university processes, governance, and outcomes. The pursuit of evidence that one academic program, structure, reward system, administrative style, curricular design, or whatever is better than another makes effectiveness and quality central empirical issues.

Practically, the need to evaluate quality and effectiveness in higher education is important both because it is so common and because it is increasingly being mandated. To begin with, individuals are constantly faced with the need to make judgments about the effectiveness or quality of institutions. For example, decisions as to which institution will receive an NSF grant, which college will be recommended by a guidance counselor, or which department will be required to retrench are all based at least partly on judgments of institutional effectiveness or quality.

Accountability for effectiveness and quality has also become the watchword of a variety of higher education constituencies in light of environmental factors such as a diminishing college-age population, decreased federal funding, changing student preferences, and poor U.S. showings in international comparison tests. When resources are tight and questions are prevalent regarding their judicious use, more attention is bound to be paid to effectiveness and quality—evidence that constituencies are getting adequate "bang for the buck."

Definitions of Effectiveness and Quality

As has been noted, disagreement remains regarding the meaning, and especially the measurement, of effectiveness and quality. This is hardly surprising. Obviously, effectiveness and quality are constructs—abstractions used to interpret reality. They have no objective existence (see no. 365), and it is impossible to identify a necessary and sufficient set of indicators for them. Common usage—and the specific usage of particular writers in particular circumstances—determines their meaning. Any attempt to define them reflects the biases of the definer as much as the inherent meaning of the words. However, the inclusion of a chapter on effectiveness and quality in a book such as this suggests that some such attempt is required. The following definitional boundaries are offered, therefore, to help guide readers through the annotated references that appear in the chapter.

Effectiveness and quality differ from one another primarily in the institutional phenomena to which they refer. They also differ in the precision with which they are used in the higher education literature. For example, in the literature on private- and public-sector organizations, quality almost always is relatively precisely defined as the absence of errors. High-quality products, for example, are those that work without having to be repaired. Low quality is indicated by faults or mistakes. In such settings, "quality" can be objectively counted and observed. In higher education, however, *quality* has become a catchall term that has few, if any, reliable quantifiable indicators. It has been used to refer to almost any condition that is valued or desired by some constituency. In contrast, *effectiveness* is used as a catchall term in the organizational literature, but it has developed a more refined meaning in connection with higher education.

One way to understand the difference between these two terms in the higher education context is to consider a college or university as an organization composed of two different communities—a campus community and a disciplinary community. The campus community consists of the activities and attributes within the boundaries of the institution, including its structure, governance, information/communication system, patterns of faculty-student interaction, pedagogical procedures, and so on. The disciplinary community, on the other hand, consists of activities associated with professional or scholarly responsibilities, generally outside the institution's boundaries. Publishing, attending professional meetings, maintaining collegial networks in the discipline, obtaining research grants, and so on are examples of disciplinary activities.

Effectiveness is associated with the campus community, quality with the disciplinary community. An institution is effective if its campus community performs successfully. An institution is of high quality if its disciplinary community performs successfully. Therefore, institutions can be effective without being of high quality, or they can be of high quality without being effective.

Other words that are sometimes substituted for quality or effectiveness in the literature are less comprehensive. For example, "efficiency" is a ratio of inputs to outputs. An efficient institution is one that has little waste and few uncommitted resources. Efficiency is associated with the campus community and is subsumed by the construct of effectiveness. That is, an institution can be efficient without being effective, but it cannot be effective without being at least moderately efficient. Efficiency and quality, on the other hand, may exist independently, since they generally apply to different communities within higher education. Similarly, such proxy terms as *worth, value, productivity,* and *excellence* may be subsumed by effectiveness and/or quality (see nos. 363 and 384).

Because the definitions of effectiveness and quality are so broad in scope, they permit, even encourage, a wide variety of types of performance and attributes to be developed in institutions of higher education. The pursuit of effectiveness and quality in colleges and universities is not a pursuit of the one right answer or the single best criterion. It is, instead, the pursuit of a wide variety of criteria, none necessary and sufficient, that serve to guide the judgments of multiple evaluators.

Organizing Framework and Literature Selection

The distinctions in definition just referred to arise from common usage in the higher education literature. The literature on effectiveness has remained attached mainly to the performance of colleges and universities as organizations, or to subunits such as academic departments, while the literature on quality has focused mainly on indicators of the scholarly or academic attainment of individuals or units. The most prominent procedure for assessing effectiveness, for example, has been to assess organizational activities and attributes (campus community). The most prominent procedure for assessing quality has involved reputational ratings based primarily on faculty productivity or student achievement (disciplinary community).

The literature on effectiveness and quality in higher education is not completely dichotomized by this "community" distinction, however. A more complex categorization scheme is therefore presented to help readers more quickly identify annotations of interest. The categories were formed after a survey of some 300 key references in the effectiveness and quality literatures. The two major dimensions used in the scheme are the central concept used in the reference (effectiveness or quality) and the content focus of the reference.

In the literature emphasizing effectiveness, four different areas of content are present: (1) department or program performance, (2) institutional performance, (3) methodological issues, and (4) frameworks or models of effectiveness. In the quality literature, the content areas receiving the most emphasis are (1) undergraduate student or instructor performance, (2) undergraduate institution performance, (3) graduate department or program performance, and (4) higher education system performance.

Obviously, only a small number of the important references in the literature can be included in this chapter. The reader therefore should know of several biases that guided my selections. First, I have tried to include a variety of types of publications that have appeared under each of these major concept/content headings. In the effectiveness literature, types of publications include (1) books containing literature reviews and new models, (2) critiques and reviews of issues, (3) proposed effectiveness frameworks, and (4) empirical studies of effectiveness. In the quality literature, main publication types are (1) extensive reviews of the quality literature, (2) proposed dimensions or criteria of quality, (3) empirical studies of quality, (4) investigations of correlates of quality ratings, and (5) recommendations and policy implications regarding quality.

A second bias is an inclination toward the institutional/organizational level of analysis. I have included only a very small sampling of the literature on individual student outcomes or faculty productivity, for example, and only a sampling of the department or program literature. References that use departmental or program assessments to make statements about the college or university as a whole are included, but not those that maintain an individual focus. This bias toward a more macro level of analysis is driven by the fact that several other chapters in this sourcebook focus on outcomes and performance on more micro levels of analysis—students, faculty, departments, programs, and so forth.

A third bias is toward references that are cited often, are well known, or are important because they represent a unique point of view. I tried to select the best-known citations; therefore, many high-quality books or articles are omitted either because a more well-known reference is included or because too many other representatives of that topic are in the list.

A fourth bias is toward references that contain extensive citations, surveys of the literature, and/or conceptual models, approaches, or (rarely) theories. Readers can find an extensive literature on many topics by starting with the references included in this chapter. My annotations are intended merely to be springboards to further investigation, not a comprehensive listing.

Commentary on the Literature

Too little progress has been made toward a cumulative, progressive literature related to quality and effectiveness in higher education in the last decade or so. Additional articles appear regularly, but the traditional debates about definition and appropriate criteria continue. In short, the literature on quality and effectiveness in higher education is characterized by diversity, conflict, and fragmentation.

The diversity that characterizes the literature is caused by the fact that different publications select different levels of analysis for investigation (for example, student outcomes, programs, departments, institutions, or state systems), different time frames (for example, short-term ''snapshot'' assessments, medium-range trend analysis, or long-run ecological or population analyses), different constituencies' perspectives (for example, those of top administrators, students, faculty, accreditation teams, trustees, or state boards), different purposes (for example, national commission polls or academic research), different referents (for example, past performance, goals, peer institution or colleague performance, ideal standards, or constituency demands), and many more, without acknowledging that such differences are crucial in explaining results. Diversity in approach and perspective is not undesirable in writing and research, but if a cumulative literature is to be developed, each approach must acknowledge its perspective relative to others. So far, too few careful comparisons have appeared.

The conflict in the literature is characterized by the debates that continue to surround objective versus subjective measures of quality, for example, or the differences in judgments that result when program quality measurements are compared to student or institution quality measurements. Some authors argue that certain objective indicators (especially faculty publication counts) are powerful predictors of subjective quality assessments, while others argue that such relationships are discipline or institution dependent or not even present at all. Similarly, some authors argue vehemently for assessing quality and effectiveness at the student outcomes level, while others argue for program or department assessment and still others advocate institutional evaluations. Recent research indicates, however, that quality and effectiveness on one of these levels is not related to quality and effectiveness on the other levels. A few recent articles are beginning to address these conflicts directly, but for the most part, these unacknowledged conflicts continue to hamper development of a cumulative literature.

The fragmentation typical of the quality and effectiveness literature is mainly a product of the absence of consensual models and definitions. The fact that colleges and universities are variously characterized as collegiums, hierarchies, political arenas, organized anarchies, loosely coupled systems, psychic prisons, disciplinary consortia, markets, clans, adhocracies, professional bureaucracies, and so forth illustrates another reason why a cumulative literature has not emerged. An effective hierarchy is conceptualized very differently than is a high-quality clan, for example. Moreover, because the constructs of effectiveness and quality have developed independently in higher education, the literatures describing them hardly overlap at all. Divergent streams of research and theorizing continue with little reference to one another. This kind of fragmentation of definition and perspective contributes to the slowness of cumulative development typical of these literatures.

Organizational Effectiveness

Department or Program Performance

361 Bare, Alan C. "The Study of Academic Department
Performance." *Research in Higher Education,* 1980, *12,*
3–22.

This paper proposes a systems model of academic department
performance and reports an empirical test of the model in a set
of twenty departments. Departmental input and process variables were related to the following eight departmental outcomes:
(1) student satisfaction with overall learning experience, (2) student satisfaction with faculty, (3) student satisfaction with academic advising, (4) student graduate school admissions ratio,
(5) student employment in field ratio, (6) faculty satisfaction
with departmental research quality, (7) faculty job satisfaction,
and (8) degrees conferred per faculty member. These eight
departmental outcomes were found to be largely independent
of one another and were predicted by relatively unique patterns
of departmental characteristics. Salient among the correlates of
departmental outcomes were faculty workload, tenure pattern,
and disciplinary differences.

★362 Pfeffer, Jeffrey, and Salancik, Gerald. "Administrator
Effectiveness: The Effects of Advocacy and Information
on Achieving Outcomes in an Organizational Context."
Human Relations, 1977, *30,* 641–656.

This paper reports the findings of a study of a sample of academic
departments in a large state university on the subject of resource
allocations. The effects of the following three variables were examined: (1) information about the distribution of subunit influence, (2) information about the subunit's standing on various
dimensions, and (3) the effects of advocating that allocations
be based on dimensions favoring the subunit. Results indicate
that advocating the use of criteria favorable to the subunit was
positively related to allocations, particularly for more powerful
subunits and less critical and scarce resources. Knowledge about

the organization's political structure primarily benefited the allocations of less powerful departments. These results held for resources allocated through committees of department representatives. For general fund allocations made through an administrative decision process, however, advocacy tended to decrease resource allocations, especially for high-power departments.

Institutional Performance

★**363** Cameron, Kim S. "A Study of Organizational Effectiveness and Its Predictors." *Management Science*, 1986, *32* (1), 87–112.

This study demonstrates why organizational effectiveness studies are crucial in certain types of organizations, especially colleges and universities, and suggests ways to remedy many of the weaknesses and criticisms of past investigations. The results of this study of twenty-nine colleges and universities in the northeastern United States indicate that certain managerial strategies are strongly associated with high static effectiveness scores and with improving effectiveness over time. Managerial strategies, in fact, were found to be more important than four other factors selected as predictors of organizational effectiveness (external environment, structure, demographics, and finances). Proactive strategies and those with an external emphasis are more successful than internal and reactive strategies.

364 Quinn, Robert E. (ed.). "A Symposium on the Competing Values Approach to Organizational Effectiveness." *Public Productivity Review*, 1981, *5*, 103–200.

This symposium is the result of several years of attempts by individuals at the Institute for Government and Policy Studies to clarify issues surrounding the notion of organizational effectiveness. Emerging from this work is a conceptual framework known as the competing values approach. Five papers are presented that explain and develop this framework. Kim Cameron reviews the recent literature and demonstrates the need for the line of research presented. Robert Quinn and John Rohrbaugh report the study from which the approach originally emerged. John Rohrbaugh describes how the framework has been operationalized in a set of public organizations. David Anderson demonstrates the theoretical potential of the framework. In the final paper, Michael Thompson, Michael McGrath, and Joseph Whorton discuss practical applications of the competing values approach.

Methodological Issues

★**365** Cameron, Kim S. "Measuring Organizational Effectiveness in Institutions of Higher Education." *Administrative Science Quarterly,* 1978, *23* (4), 604–632.

This study examines the concept of organizational effectiveness in institutions of higher education. Some obstacles to the assessment of the concept in this setting are discussed, specifically criteria problems and the unique attributes of colleges and universities, and criteria choices are outlined. Criteria were generated from dominant coalition members in six institutions, and nine dimensions of organizational effectiveness were derived from the criteria. The author tested reliability and validity of their dimensions and found evidence for certain patterns of effectiveness across the nine dimensions. He concludes that effectiveness possesses multiple dimensions that must be operationalized in different ways.

366 Ghorpade, Jaisingh (ed.). *Assessment of Organizational Effectiveness.* Pacific Palisades, Calif.: Goodyear, 1971. 256 pages.

One of the earliest to focus on the issues inherent in studying organizational effectiveness, this book responds to a lack of a firm analytical base and unavailability of universally acceptable criteria in this literature. One purpose of the book is to contribute to the clarification and resolution of the basic issues in this field of inquiry. Another is to present several of the classic pieces of research done on effectiveness over the previous fifteen years. This book is divided into four parts. Part One addresses the broad theoretical and conceptual issues involved in the study of organizational effectiveness. Part Two is concerned with criteria of organizational effectiveness. Part Three discusses empirical research in the area. Part Four deals with methodological considerations. Each part begins with a discussion of issues and continues with readings that elaborate upon and exemplify the points raised. Additional references, with commentary on some of the key works, follow each section.

★367 Kanter, Rosabeth Moss, and Brinkerhoff, Derick. "Organizational Performance: Recent Developments in Measurement." *Annual Review of Psychology,* 1981, *7,* 321–349.

This article is a review of the literature on performance measurement. It confirms the emerging political model of organizations, which views organizations as battlegrounds for stakeholders, both inside and outside, who compete to influence the criteria for effectiveness in order to advance their own interests. Models that recognize the complexity of the organizational effectiveness construct tend to differentiate at least three kinds of "effectiveness": goal attainment or task effectiveness, appropriate organizational structure and process, and environmental adaptation. The authors examine critical issues in each of these three areas, addressing both public-sector and individual effectiveness. They conclude that finding universal dimensions for organizational effectiveness is no longer important in the literature. The new focus is on how particular measurement systems arise, whose interests they serve, and how (or whether) they function to guide or shape an organization's activities.

★368 Van de Ven, Andrew, and Ferry, Diane. *Measuring and Assessing Organizations.* New York: Wiley-Interscience, 1980. 552 pages.

This book is written for organizational researchers, consultants, and practitioners who diagnose, evaluate, and take action to solve problems in the design and performance of organizations. It is concerned with the development of a scientifically valid and practical approach for assessing the performance of a complex organization in relation to the way it is organized and to the environments in which it operates. Based on the results of a longitudinal research program called Organization Assessment (OA), in progress since 1972, the OA framework identifies the organizational and environmental characteristics that are important for explaining the effectiveness, efficiency, and quality of working life for organizations, work groups, and jobs. The authors propose a set of measurement instruments and process guidelines for understanding and improving work in organizations.

Frameworks or Models of Effectiveness

*369 Cameron, Kim S., and Whetten, David A. *Organizational Effectiveness: A Comparison of Multiple Models.* Orlando, Fla.: Academic Press, 1983. 292 pages.

The main purpose of this book is to address directly the issues of nonintegration and noncomparability in the literature on organizational effectiveness. Different perspectives of organizational effectiveness are presented by various contributors, and each is systematically compared with the others in order to highlight its basic assumptions, its strengths and weaknesses, and the trade-offs necessary in using it. None of the models is considered to be universally applicable; the basic assumption underlying the book is that it is important to understand the relative contributions of several different models and how these models relate in order to appreciate the meaning of the construct. Practical suggestions for improving effectiveness are also included.

*370 Goodman, Paul S., Pennings, Johannes M., and Associates. *New Perspectives on Organizational Effectiveness.* San Francisco: Jossey-Bass, 1977. 275 pages.

The stated purpose of this book is to delineate the major theoretical and methodological issues pertaining to organizational effectiveness and to suggest some points of resolution. The ultimate goal is to move research on organizational effectiveness in a more analytical and cumulative direction. The book is organized around a set of five original essays by major contributors to organizational theory and research (John Campbell, W. Richard Scott, Michael Hannan and John Freeman, Johannes Pennings and Paul Goodman, and Karl Weick). Each essay is followed by a smaller paper that reacts to and builds upon the major essay. The book's unique contribution is that it brings together an interdisciplinary group of researchers who attempt to provide a direction for future research.

371 Keeley, Michael. "Impartiality and Participant-Interest Theories of Organizational Effectiveness." *Administrative Science Quarterly*, 1984, *29*, 1–25.

This article introduces the "harm-based" approach to evaluating effectiveness in organizations. Keeley analyzes the concept of organizational effectiveness, showing how it might be formulated to impartially reflect the various interests of organizational participants or constituents. In this way his perspective is similar to the "strategic constituencies" or "resource dependence" approaches to effectiveness developed by others. The article compares and contrasts these various participant-interest approaches (as well as other commonly used models of effectiveness, particularly the goal model) but differentiates itself from them by pointing out the advantages of defining effectiveness by incorporating a principle of justice: the minimization of regret of the least-advantaged constituency. Essentially, Keeley says that organizations should be judged effective if they do no harm or if they minimize the harm done to the group that has least power to get what it wants from the organization.

★372 Pfeffer, Jeffrey, and Salancik, Gerald R. *The External Control of Organizations: A Resource Dependence Perspective.* New York: Harper & Row, 1978. 300 pages.

This book is a major contribution to the organization theory area called resource dependence. Theorists in this area emphasize that the environment of an organization contains scarce and valued resources required by the organization for its survival. As a result, the organization is dependent upon a variety of interest groups, individuals, and other organizations, each of which has its own particular set of preferences that is applied to the outputs or activities of the organization in an evaluation process. Organization effectiveness is thus an external standard and a multifaceted concept. Since criteria of effectiveness conflict, effectiveness is inevitably defined only with respect to the assessment of a particular group. The authors contrast the concept of organization effectiveness with that of efficiency, defined as an internal standard of performance that measures output per unit of input. Efficiency and effectiveness are independent standards for evaluating organizations, they conclude. In addition to its contribution to theory, this book is intended as a guide to the design and management of organizations.

373 *Review of Higher Education,* 1985, *9* (1). 130 pages.

In this special issue of the *Review of Higher Education,* authors illustrate the diversity associated with effectiveness in higher education by approaching the topic from several different viewpoints. They discuss effectiveness using students, faculty, administrators, societal culture, peer assessment, and organizational theory as criteria. All of these authors were asked to address the same two questions at the end of their articles in order to provide a point of comparison among their various perspectives and guidelines for those wishing to pursue the perspectives in research or practice. The two questions are as follows: (1) What administrative principles can be derived from your perspective? and (2) What research implications are suggested by your viewpoint? There are six major articles in this review issue.

374 Steers, Richard M. *Organizational Effectiveness: A Behavioral View.* Santa Monica, Calif.: Goodyear, 1977. 204 pages.

This book considers ways that the relative degree of organizational effectiveness can be assessed and what managers can do to facilitate such assessment. Steers's approach to the study of effectiveness is to integrate organization-level factors, such as structure and technology, with individual-level factors, such as employee motivation, attachment, and performance. This approach is based on the belief that any dynamic model of organizational effectiveness must examine the processes by which individual effort and behavior influence subsequent organizational performance. Steers examines four categories of what he feels are the most important determinants of organizational effectiveness: organizational characteristics, environmental characteristics, employee characteristics, and managerial policies and practices. In all, several hundred studies are reviewed. The book's final chapter summarizes and integrates the various findings into a statement of the major processes involved in effectiveness.

375 Zammuto, Raymond F. *Assessing Organizational Effectiveness: Systems Change, Adaptation, and Strategy.* Albany: State University of New York-Albany Press, 1982. 181 pages.

This book proposes an evolutionary model of organizational effectiveness and explores how judgments of effectiveness are related to the continued viability of organizations and society as a whole. This perspective is presented as one of many possible explanations that exist in the literature; the author also discusses a number of other perspectives, all of which offer insight into the concept. Zammuto's model considers three distinct elements and their interaction: (1) the role of constituent preferences in defining the preferred direction of social evolution, (2) the role of constraints in creating niches within which organizations exist, and (3) the effect of time on organizational performance. Effective performance requires that an organization satisfy evolving constituent preferences through niche expansion over time, Zammuto concludes. This increases adaptability of the organization to its environment. Two case studies are presented to illustrate the application of the evolutionary approach.

376 Zammuto, Raymond F. "A Comparison of Multiple Constituency Models of Organizational Effectiveness." *Academy of Management Review,* 1984, *9* (4), 606–616.

This article reviews four sets of multiple-constituency models of organizational effectiveness. The models employ relativistic, power, social justice, and evolutionary perspectives, respectively. Comparison of these perspectives shows that the construct of organizational effectiveness is both value based and time specific. The author integrates generalizations concerning values and time in an extended definition of the organizational effectiveness construct. This definition specifies that constituent preferences for organizational performance are the raw materials on which evaluations of organizational effectiveness are based. These preferences can change over time; new preferences can emerge to replace ones that were satisfied by the previous outcomes of organizational performance.

Institutional Quality

Undergraduate Student or Instructor Performance

★377 Pace, C. Robert. *Measuring Outcomes of College: Fifty Years of Findings and Recommendations for the Future.* San Francisco: Jossey-Bass, 1979. 188 pages.

The intent of this book is to address three highly related questions: What do we know about students' achievement during college? What do we know about achievement after college? What do we know from surveys about institutions of higher education? The author draws evidence from landmark studies and lines of inquiry, data obtained from large-scale testing programs and surveys, information about thousands of students and alumni from hundreds of colleges and universities, and surveys of institutions made at different periods of time over the past forty to fifty years. His concern is with tendencies central to many institutions and consistent over time. The author concludes with recommendations for the future assessment of educational outcomes.

Undergraduate Institution Performance

★**378** Astin, Alexander W., and Solmon, Lewis C. "Are Reputational Ratings Needed to Measure Quality?" *Change,* 1981, *13* (7), 14–19.

In this report, the authors explore a number of questions concerning academicians' judgments about the quality of undergraduate programs. Their data come from a large-scale pilot attempt to rate undergraduate departments in seven selected fields. The focus in this article is on the objective correlates of undergraduate quality ratings, state or regional biases, and other methodological issues relating to reputational ratings of undergraduate quality. A central part of the analysis examines the correlation between objective institutional measures of quality and subjective ratings for six quality criteria and for seven undergraduate fields. The results indicate that such objective characteristics as relative size, selectivity (hence prestige) of a department, expenditures, and field and degree-level concentrations are good predictors of raters' subjective judgments of quality for most fields and on most of the quality criteria. Differences between results of ratings surveys and "objective" measures may reflect rater bias rather than real differences in quality.

379 Kuh, George D. *Indices of Quality in the Undergraduate Experience.* AAHE-ERIC Higher Education Research Report no. 4. Washington, D.C.: American Association for Higher Education, 1981. 41 pages.

In this monograph, the author attempts to bring about greater clarity in defining the quality of student experience by identifying and reviewing specific indices of quality. Based on an eclectic perspective that encompasses elements of both quantitative and qualitative approaches, Kuh analyzes literature in three important areas: the multiple properties of quality, the utility of different methodological approaches to quality assessment, and the opinion and empirical research about quality in the undergraduate experience. The author organizes his discussion with a framework that places quality indices in four categories: context indices, representing institutional characteristics that remain stable over time; input indices, reflecting characteristics of entering students; involvement indices, characterizing the interaction between and among students and faculty; and outcomes indices, reflecting intended products or unintended effects associated with college attendance. This framework is intended to assist administrators and faculty in their evaluation of the quality of undergraduate education.

★380 Lawrence, Judith K., and Green, Kenneth C. *A Question of Quality: The Higher Education Ratings Game.* AAHE-ERIC Higher Education Research Report no. 5. Washington, D.C.: American Association for Higher Education, 1980. 76 pages.

This report examines the question of quality in higher education by considering how quality has been measured in the past. The authors first review studies that analyze the reputation of graduate education and professional programs. They conclude that the definition of quality varies with the context, including who is doing the assessment, by what means, and for what purpose. Following this examination, they identify quantifiable indicators of quality applied to undergraduate education then discuss quality in relation to accreditation and state program review. They present several conclusions as to how quality in higher education might be better defined and how methods of assessing quality might be improved.

★381 Webster, David S. "Advantages and Disadvantages of Methods of Assessing Quality." *Change,* 1981, *13,* 20–24.

Webster discusses six alternative methods commonly used for assessing quality in colleges and universities. He points out the weaknesses, even the inappropriateness, of each method by showing examples of misleading or inaccurate assessments that it has led to. The six alternatives are reputational rankings; faculty awards, honors, and prizes; citations in citation indexes; student achievements in later life; scores of entering students on standardized tests; and institutional academic resources. Webster argues that the ideal academic quality ranking should be multidimensional; based on achievements of all students and faculty, not just a few outstanding ones; based on per capita, not aggregate, figures; and based on how much students learn.

382 Webster, David S. "James McKeen Cattell and the Invention of Academic Quality Rankings, 1903–1910." *Review of Higher Education,* 1985, *8,* 107–122.

The contributions of James McKeen Cattell to the evaluation of academic quality are chronicled in this article. Cattell's work predated that of all other researchers, although most current literature considers Hughes's *Study of Graduate Schools of America* (1925) to be the first study of college and university quality. The author points out that Cattell's invention of academic quality ranking arose from his work in studying the educational backgrounds and achievements of men of science. By identifying the institutional affiliations of eminent scholars and aggregating them, he produced in 1910 the first quality ranking of American institutions of higher education.

Graduate Department or Program Performance

★383 Beyer, Janice M., and Snipper, Reuben. "Objective Versus Subjective Indicators of Quality in Graduate Education." *Sociology of Education,* 1974, *47,* 541–557.

Various investigators have been interested in establishing objective correlates with the Cartter report ratings of quality in graduate education. None, however, has concentrated on the way these correlates might differ across disciplines. Using both original data and data from published sources, this study examines the relationship of the rated quality of university departments to other possible quality indicators in two physical science and two social science departments. Results from discriminant and multiple regression analysis indicate that different variables were found to be the best predictors of departmental quality for different fields. No objective measure was found to be linearly, or even monotonically, related to the Cartter ratings across fields. An important conclusion from these findings is that the structure of knowledge within a scientific field or discipline has implications for attempted measurement of quality.

★384 Conrad, Clifton F., and Blackburn, Robert T. "Program Quality in Higher Education: A Review and Critique of Literature and Research." In John C. Smart (ed.), *Higher Education: Handbook of Theory and Research.* Vol. 1. New York: Agathon, 1985. Pages 283–308.

The major purpose of this article is to review and critique three lines of research on the assessment of program quality and to examine the implications of each for future research. The paper is divided into four major sections. The first section provides a context for the discussion by looking at the multiple meanings of quality. The second section examines program evaluation research that is based on a "reputational" approach; the third reviews research based on "objective" indicators; and the fourth looks at research on the quantitative correlates of program quality. Each section reviews the pertinent literature and its major findings, examines major criteria and methodological procedures, and offers a critique of the limitations and strengths of the approach as a foundation for some recommendations for future research. This article provides a thorough and comprehensive literature review and analysis on program quality.

385 Conrad, Clifton F., and Blackburn, Robert T. "Correlates of Departmental Quality in Regional Colleges and Universities." *American Educational Research Journal,* 1985, *22* (2), 279–295.

This article isolates correlates of departmental quality at the master's and doctoral level in regional colleges and universities. The forty-five departments in the sample represent fourteen public institutions in two states and include departments in biology, chemistry, education, history, and mathematics. In addition to simple correlation, the analysis is based on multivariate linear regression. Departmental quality is found to be correlated with individual and combined measures of faculty (scholarly productivity, grantsmanship, age and tenure status, geographical origin of highest degree, and teaching workload), students (number and ability), program (proportion of institutional degree programs at the advanced graduate level and curricular concentration), and facilities (library size). The findings suggest that the factors associated with graduate departmental quality are more multidimensional in regional colleges and universities than in highly ranked research universities.

386 Drew, David E., and Karpf, Ronald. "Ranking Academic Departments: Empirical Findings and a Theoretical Perspective." *Research in Higher Education,* 1981, *14* (4), 305–320.

Evaluations of academic departments through peer review rankings have assumed great importance. This article reviews the history of these highly publicized rankings and subsequent attempts to identify empirical correlates of the ratings. The authors present new findings that indicate that the American Council on Education (ACE) subjective rankings can be predicted almost perfectly (r = .91) with one measure—departmental rate of publication in highly cited journals. These findings both support the notion of peer ranking and reveal some inherent weaknesses in the academic assessment process. The authors suggest that present studies confound quality and quantity, effective measures of teaching quality are needed, and the most useful assessment technique for future policy-making consists not of unidimensional rankings but rather of multidimensional indicators of departmental structure and function. Finally, the authors propose that concepts from social stratification theory can illuminate understanding of evaluation in higher education.

Higher Education System Performance

387 Morgan, Anthony W., and Mitchell, Brad L. "The Quest for Excellence: Underlying Policy Issues." In John C. Smart (ed.), *Higher Education: Handbook of Theory and Research.* Vol. 1. New York: Agathon, 1985. Pages 309–348.

Major national studies of secondary education have been undertaken by various foundations, commissions, and independent researchers in response to an increase in public concern about the quality of education. This article reviews thirteen of these reports, selecting policy issues common to most of them and assessing the contributions of each to long-standing policy debates. Drawing upon these reports and a host of supporting literature, the authors present an overview of six distinct perspectives on defining educational excellence: the political economy approach, the productivity approach, the value-added approach, the producer-consumer quality approach, the content approach, and the eclectic approach. They then discuss five policy themes: the crisis of purpose in American education, the tie between education and economic growth, higher education's relationship to high schools, governance, and the setting of strategic priorities for attainment of quality education. They also consider implications for future research.

★388 National Commission on Higher Education Issues. *To Strengthen Quality in Higher Education: Summary Recommendations of the National Commission on Higher Education Issues.* Washington, D.C.: American Council on Education, 1982. 12 pages.

Recommendations for improving educational quality and strengthening public confidence in American higher education are offered, based on the deliberations of the National Commission on Higher Education. Areas of concern include setting priorities for the institution and strengthening administrative leadership, strengthening the relationship of institutional officers and faculties with state officials and the governing board, enhancing quality and strengthening finance, and assuring standards. The recommendations highlight the importance of the following: trustee support of priorities established for resource allocation, proper methods of recruiting and selecting top administrators, assurance that students attending college demonstrate mastery of basic skills, response to the mandate for professional continuing education and the needs of adult learners, faculty tenure as a means to protect academic freedom, and merit-based increases in faculty salaries.

389 Solmon, Lewis C. "A Multidimensional Approach to Quality." In Thomas Stauffer (ed.), *Quality—Higher Education's Principal Challenge*. Washington, D.C.: American Council on Education, 1981. Pages 6–14.

This paper analyzes how the notion of quality in higher education has been defined and measured in the past. Solmon points out the shortcomings of simplistic notions of quality used in the accrediting process. The uncritical acceptance of stated goals, that is, the failure to determine whether institutional or program objectives warrant support, is a major criticism. Solmon argues that as the function of postsecondary education changes to that of a vehicle for upward social mobility and expanded access for adults, women, and minorities, assessment of quality must be measured along multiple dimensions. He suggests a broader set of criteria for evaluation that accounts for the diversity of institutions and goals. Solmon concludes by pointing out that improved knowledge of opportunities and of quality is desirable if a diverse educational system is to work effectively— especially under retrenchment.

390 Stauffer, Thomas. "Quality in American Higher Education." In Thomas Stauffer (ed.), *Quality—Higher Education's Principal Challenge*. Washington, D.C.: American Council on Education, 1981. Pages 1–5.

This chapter introduces a book consisting of articles commissioned by the American Council on Education for its 1979 annual meeting on quality in higher education. The volume was intended to make a contribution to notions of academic quality, illuminating the problems in the field, setting practical solutions or directions, and providing leadership. The author discusses the inherent difficulty in the assessment of quality in higher education, both in the area of academics and in practices and procedures. For example, data on student development are often ignored in favor of resource data, which trustees and administrators feel they must emphasize for reporting and managerial purposes. He points out that even when definitions and methodology are designed with precision, controversy ensues. In addition, translating findings on educational quality, from whatever source, into operational policies is not easy. This volume presents model policies, exemplary programs, analyses, and suggestions to stimulate and aid campus leaders in confronting the problems they face.

16

Raymond F. Zammuto

Managing Declining Enrollments and Revenues

Declining enrollments and revenues are perennial problems for colleges and universities. For example, institutions of higher education experienced serious enrollment and revenue declines during the early 1800s (Burke, 1982), at the beginning of the twentieth century (Brubacher and Rudy, 1968), and again during the 1930s (Kauffman, 1982). But for today's institutional managers, many of whom cut their administrative teeth during the halcyon days of the 1960s, the enrollment and revenue problems of the past decade are a new and vexing experience.

The current period of concern with declining enrollments and revenues can be traced back to the downturn in the birthrate during the mid-1960s. Cartter (1965) was one of the first to discern the implications of the decreased birthrate in his projections of the downturn's effect on future demand for new teachers. But it was not until the early 1970s that serious and widespread attention was given to the potential effect of this demographic change on institutional enrollments and revenues. Projections and prognoses have varied widely. Some writers have foreseen the possibility of serious declines in aggregate enrollments nationwide (Dresch, 1975; Boulding, 1975; Crossland, 1980; Carnegie Council, no. 335). Others have projected little effect (Leslie and Miller, 1974; Frances, 1980; Bowen, 1984).

Today we are over half a decade into the decline of the traditional college-age cohort, and the full impact of that decline is still unclear. Zammuto (no. 413) shows that the incidence of

347

declining enrollments and revenues varied considerably between 1972 and 1983 and that there is only a weak relationship between declining revenues and declining enrollments. Zammuto (1983) also shows that some kinds of colleges and universities have been more affected by declining enrollments than others and that relationships among institutional control, type, and enrollment decline have varied considerably over time. Moreover, Birnbaum's (1983) and Zammuto's (1984a) analyses of institutional creations, failures, and transitions in response to the evolving higher education environment show that the process of institutional adaptation is very complex.

Given the past unpredictability of enrollments and revenues, future uncertainties, and the multitude of institutional responses available, one can reasonably ask how institutions are to prepare for the future and manage decline if it does occur. This chapter identifies resources available to institutional managers that may help them cope with these problems. The chapter is divided into three major sections. The first provides an overview of the literature on decline and retrenchment. The second outlines categories that are useful for organizing the literature and identifies important works within each category. The final section is an annotated bibliography of the most useful works. Information in this chapter should be of assistance to administrators and researchers who wish to learn more about the management of organizations with declining resources and about specific techniques that institutional managers can use to cope with declining enrollments and revenues.

Overview of the Literature

Prior to the mid-1970s, most writing about the management of decline focused on human behavior under crisis conditions (for example, Torrance, 1954; Hamblin, 1958a, b; Hermann, no. 402). The general topic of managing declining organizations received little attention. As Scott (1976) and Whetten (1980) noted, there were at least two reasons for this lack of interest. First, there has been a preoccupation with growth in the administrative and organization sciences that paralleled economic history following World War II. The majority of organizations in American society experienced growth, so declining organizations were seen as anomalies. Second, American society has a normative bias toward growth. Growth is equated with organizational success and effectiveness, which is more exciting to study than failure.

The increasing incidence of organizational decline in American society during the late 1960s and 1970s gave rise to a growing literature on the topic, however. The growth began in elementary and secondary education, which was one of the first areas to experience the effects of the declining birthrate. As the number of births in the United States decreased, so did enrollments in elementary and then secondary schools. By the mid-1970s a substantial literature on managing decline in elementary and secondary schools had emerged (see Butler, 1981, and Zerchykov, 1981, for bibliographies).

The 1974–75 recession also increased interest in decline and retrenchment. Reduced tax receipts forced many public organizations to undergo retrenchment, and researchers of the private sector began to examine the effects of the downturn on corporations. Higher education researchers began to study decline with the onset of serious enrollment and revenue problems in small private colleges during the early 1970s. The 1981–82 recession further heightened interest in the topic, turning research on decline into something of a growth industry. A bibliography by Zammuto (1984b) surveying the higher education, business, and public administration literatures provided clear evidence of this growth. Of the more than 400 articles, books, and chapters listed, over 75 percent had been published after 1977.

Framework for Organizing the Literature

As the literature has grown, so have the number of themes within it. This section uses three themes to categorize the literature: (1) causes of and strategies for responding to decline, (2) organizational dynamics associated with a period of decline, and (3) cutback management tactics.

Causes and Strategic Responses. The first category of literature focuses on causes of and strategies for responding to decline. Literature on the causes of decline reflects a growing sophistication of theory and research. Historically, decline was viewed as the result of inept management. But as the literature matured, it reflected a growing realization that decline was often caused by a complex interaction of changing environmental conditions and organizational strategies. This view of the cause of decline implied that the strategies needed to reverse organizations' fortunes had to fit the particular conditions causing decline. Levine—in one of the most cited articles on the management of decline (no. 393)—was the first to pay serious attention to the causes of decline, examining both internal and external causes, and to the different types of tactics that could reverse decline or adjust an organization to its new situation. Zammuto and Cameron (no. 397) took a different tack by focusing on how changing environmental conditions lead to different types of decline and on the different strategies that are required to ameliorate different types of decline.

Organizational Dynamics. A large part of the literature, particularly that on crises, has addressed the effects of decline on organizational dynamics. Broadly, the organizational effects of decline can be divided into two categories: (1) effects on areas such as communication and decision-making processes, and related effects on interpersonal dynamics, such as leadership and group cohesion, and (2) effects on individuals, such as physical and psychological withdrawal from the organization.

One of the earliest articles examining the effects of decline on organizations was that of Hermann (no. 402), which examined the effects of crises on organizational decision making and communication. This important article led to a significant amount of research on the structural effects of crisis and the effects of stress on individual decision-making behavior. Hermann argued that crisis situations lead to a centralization of decision-making authority in organizations, which results in a constriction of the organizational communication network. This constriction in turn reduces the likelihood that organizational decision makers will make decisions that succeed in reversing the organization's fortunes.

That centralization occurs during a period of decline is the strongest and most consistent finding from the empirical research on the topic. This is true regardless of whether the organization studied is in the public sector (Bozeman and Slusher, 1979; Levine, no. 393, 1979), is in the private sector (Hall and Mansfield, no. 401; Staw, Sandelands, and Dutton, no. 405; Billings, Milburn, and Schaalman, no. 399), or is a college or university (Bowen and Glenny, no. 391; Rubin, no. 403). Increased control is manifested in other ways as well. For example, Smart and Vertinsky (no. 404) report an increase in the use of standardized procedures in business organizations during periods of decline. Bozeman and Slusher (1979) argue that increased reliance on formal, written policies and procedures in public-sector organizations is common during decline. Whetten (no. 412) suggests that the overall effect of increased controls through centralization, standardization, and formalization is to reduce the innovativeness of an organization, which detrimentally affects its ability to create strategies for responding to decline.

Periods of decline also have a major effect on the interpersonal dynamics of organizations. Levine (no. 393), for example, noted that when resources available to satisfy conflicting interests in an organization are reduced, any latent conflicts that exist will be exacerbated. Organizational cohesion has been found to decrease (Hall and Mansfield, no. 401), and commitment to the organization also often decreases at a time that the organization most needs its members to pull together.

A period of decline also has a major impact on the leadership of an institution, often resulting in its replacement. Some of the early work on crises indicates that leaders have a window of opportunity to act (see Zammuto, no. 413, for a review), after which disillusionment arises due to their inability to resolve the organization's problems. If institutional leaders are unable to resolve a problem quickly, they usually are removed (Hamblin, 1958b). Their replacement can help the organization, because new leaders often bring new ideas about how to resolve the organization's problems (Starbuck, Greve, and Hedberg, no. 396; Jonsson and Lundin, 1977; Hamermesh, 1977). Chaffee (no. 173) also notes that leadership is extremely important in recovering from decline because effective leaders help various parties find a common definition of the situation, allowing them to pull together to revive the institution.

The primary initial effect of decline on individuals is an increase in the amount of experienced stress. Declining organizations are less appealing to work in than growing ones. Most people experience fears concerning the survival of the organization as a whole and of their own jobs in particular. The resultant stress affects their cognitive abilities. These fears and their outcomes cause three problems for an institution.

First, an institution usually has to reduce the number of persons it employs. A problem arises in that it needs to be selective about who leaves and who remains. A common dynamic in declining organizations is that the best leave first because they have the most options elsewhere (Levine, 1979). As a result, an institution can lose those individuals that it most needs to recover from decline, while retaining persons less critical to its future.

Second, those who remain in an organization often experience psychological withdrawal. Morale suffers, and commitment to the organization often decreases (Hermann, no. 402; Hall and Mansfield, no. 401). These conditions make it more difficult for organizational leaders to pull the organization together to respond to decline and place an organization at a serious competitive disadvantage (Whetten, no. 412). A major role of leadership during a period of decline is to counter this withdrawal.

Third, research on crisis behavior indicates that stress detrimentally affects the cognitive abilities of individuals. This can create problems for an institution, particularly with respect to the quality of decisions made by its leaders. Research shows that increased stress lessens the span of an individual's attention, increases cognitive rigidity, and shortens the individual's time perspective (Staw, Sandelands, and Dutton, no. 405). All of these factors reduce the ability of managers to develop and implement effective retrenchment strategies and tactics. Smart and Vertinsky (no. 404) offer a number of suggested techniques to combat these problems.

Cutback Management. The third broad category of literature on decline is concerned with the process of cutting back an institution's operations during a period of decline. Part of this literature describes the general process of cutback management (Levine, no. 393; Jick and Murray, no. 409; Hirschhorn, no. 407). Part is specific to higher education, focusing on issues such as faculty reductions and program cuts (Mingle, no. 410; Bowen and Glenny, no. 391; Hyatt, Shulman, and Santiago, no. 408). Generally, the literature warns of the dangers of using overly broad methods such as across-the-board cuts, hiring freezes, and voluntary attrition. Most authors argue that selective cuts, while harder to make, are more efficacious in turning around an institution during a period of decline. A number of the annotated entries identify specific cutback tactics that institutional managers may find useful.

Commentary on the Literature

As the number of articles on decline and retrenchment has increased, so has the field's sophistication in dealing with issues related to turnaround management. It has moved away from broad descriptions and prescriptions toward more theoretically based statements and studies, drawing the literature on management of decline into the mainstream of the literatures on administration and management. In spite of these improvements, much still needs to be done to increase our understanding of the processes for managing decline. For example, contingency models specify relationships in the form of "when x, do y," but the literature shows an imperfect correspondence between objective conditions leading to decline and subsequent organizational responses. Research is needed to increase our understanding of how decision makers' perceptions and attributions filter information about decline and affect their selection of retrenchment strategies and tactics. Two recent studies indicate that the literature is moving in that direction (Ford, 1985; Parker and Zammuto, 1986).

Moreover, while much has been written concerning the efficacy of different cutback methods, there is still no clear understanding of what works best in different situations. This suggests that it would be productive to conduct comparative research on the strategies and tactics employed by colleges and universities. The findings would be of great assistance to administrators in determining what actions have the greatest likelihood of being successful during a period of decline.

Finally, while the literature is still developing and incomplete in many respects, theory and research on the management of decline have developed to the point where there is a significant amount of useful information that can guide administrative action. This chapter's annotated entries identify many useful sources of information that can provide ideas on how to approach the problem of retrenchment as well as giving moral support to administrators by showing that institutions with declining enrollments and revenues can be managed successfully.

References

Birnbaum, R. *Maintaining Diversity in Higher Education.* San Francisco: Jossey-Bass, 1983.

Boulding, K. E. "The Management of Decline." *Change,* 1975, *7* (2), 8–9.

Bowen, H. R. "What's Ahead for Higher Education." *Change,* 1984, *16* (3), 8–13.

Bozeman, B., and Slusher, E. A. "Scarcity and Environmental Stress in Public Organizations: A Conjectural Essay." *Administration and Society,* 1979, *11,* 335–355.

Brubacher, J. S., and Rudy, W. *Higher Education in Transition: A History of American Colleges and Universities, 1636–1968.* (Rev. ed.) New York: Harper & Row, 1968.

Burke, C. B. *American Collegiate Populations: A Test of the Traditional View.* New York: New York University Press, 1982.

Butler, M. J. *Retrenchment in Education: Selected ERIC Resources.* Washington, D.C.: ERIC Clearinghouse for Teacher Education, 1981.

Cartter, A. "A New Look at the Supply of College Teachers." *Educational Record,* 1965, *46,* 267–277.

Crossland, F. E. "Learning to Cope with the Downward Slope." *Change,* 1980, *12* (5), 18, 20–25.

Dresch, S. P. "Educational Saturation: A Demographic-Economic Model." *AAUP Bulletin,* 1975, *61,* 239–247.

Ford, J. D. "The Effects of Causal Attributions on Decision Makers' Responses to Performance Downturns." *Academy of Management Review,* 1985, *10,* 770–786.

Frances, C. "Apocalyptic vs. Strategic Planning." *Change,* 1980, *12* (5), 18, 39–44.

Hamblin, R. L. "Group Integration During Crisis." *Human Relations,* 1958a, *11,* 67–76.

Hamblin, R. L. "Leadership and Crisis." *Sociometry,* 1958b, *21,* 322–335.

Hamermesh, R. G. "Responding to Divisional Profit Crises." *Harvard Business Review,* 1977, *55* (2), 124–130.

Jonsson, S. A., and Lundin, R. A. "Myths and Wishful Thinking as Management Tools." In P. C. Nystrom and W. H. Starbuck (eds.), *Prescriptive Models of Organizations.* New York: North Holland, 1977.

Kauffman, J. W. "Some Perspectives on Hard Times." *Review of Higher Education,* 1982, *6* (1), 69–78.

Leslie, L. L., and Miller, H. F. *Higher Education and the Steady State.* Washington, D.C.: American Association for Higher Education, 1974.

Levine, C. H. "More on Cutback Management: Hard Questions for Hard Times." *Public Administration Review,* 1979, *39,* 179–183.

Parker, B., and Zammuto, R. F. "Institutional Responses to Enrollment Decline: The Role of Perceptions." *Review of Higher Education,* 1986, *10* (1), 63–84.

Scott, W. A. "The Management of Decline." *Conference Board Record,* 1976, *13,* 56–59.

Torrance, E. P. "The Behavior of Small Groups Under the Stress Conditions of 'Survival.'" *American Sociological Review,* 1954, *19,* 751–755.

Whetten, D. A. "Organizational Decline: A Neglected Topic in Organizational Science." *Academy of Management Review,* 1980, *5,* 577–588.

Zammuto, R. F. "Growth, Stability, and Decline in American College and University Enrollments." *Educational Administration Quarterly,* 1983, *19* (1), 83–99.

Zammuto, R. F. "Are the Liberal Arts an Endangered Species?" *Journal of Higher Education,* 1984a, *55,* 184–211.

Zammuto, R. F. *Bibliography on Decline and Retrenchment.* Boulder, Colo.: National Center for Higher Education Management Systems, 1984b.

Zerchykov, R. *A Review of the Literature and an Annotated Bibliography on Managing Decline in School Systems.* Boston: Institute for Responsive Education, 1981.

Causes and Strategic Responses

391 Bowen, Frank M., and Glenny, Lyman A. *Uncertainty in Public Higher Education: Responses to Stress at Ten California Colleges and Universities.* Sacramento: California Postsecondary Education Committee, 1980. 65 pages.

This monograph examines the responses of ten California colleges and universities to financial uncertainties during the 1970s. The authors develop five categories to classify institutional responses: operational responses, programmatic responses, faculty reductions through attrition, faculty reductions based on program considerations, and procedural responses. Bowen and Glenny also examine the role of faculty participation and program review in making retrenchment decisions and the need for integrating the planning and budgeting functions. This monograph is very useful in providing an illustration and evaluation of the benefits and drawbacks of a number of common retrenchment strategies.

392 Kerchner, Charles T., and Schuster, Jack H. "The Uses of Crisis: Taking the Tide at the Flood." *Review of Higher Education,* 1982, *5* (3), 121–141.

This article examines the effects of slack resources and leadership credibility on institutional responses to crisis. The authors argue that crises are neither good nor bad; they simply present opportunities for redirecting an institution's energies. The mechanism through which such opportunities can be exploited is leadership's declaration of crisis. Depending on the level of resources available and leadership's credibility with institutional constituents, leaders can pursue a variety of strategies for redirecting an institution's energies. Six case studies illustrate the authors' model. A set of rules for crisis management is also presented. This article is useful for institutional managers in that it shows how the declaration of a crisis can have a major effect on their ability to subsequently manage the situation.

★393 Levine, Charles H. "Organizational Decline and Cutback Management." *Public Administration Review,* 1978, *38,* 316–325.

Levine identifies a number of organizational and environmental factors that can lead to a period of decline. He constructs a typology of decline and suggests a number of specific tactics that can be used either to reverse decline or to downsize an organization to fit new realities. The effectiveness of techniques such as hiring freezes, across-the-board cuts, and productivity criteria for cutting back is evaluated on the basis of relative efficiency and equity. This was the first article to examine different types of decline situations and to suggest that different types of tactics are required in each situation.

★**394** Mortimer, Kenneth P., and Tierney, Michael L. *The Three R's of the Eighties: Reduction, Reallocation, and Retrenchment.* AAHE-ERIC Higher Education Research Report no. 4. Washington, D.C.: American Association for Higher Education, 1979. 93 pages.

This monograph focuses on three areas that have caused increasing problems for colleges and universities: enrollments, revenues, and expenditures. Trends in all three areas are reviewed, indicating potential problems for many colleges and universities. The authors suggest a number of reduction, reallocation, and retrenchment strategies to cope with these problems. Specific ideas on expenditure control, internal resource reallocation, faculty and staff reduction, and program discontinuance are presented. This is a good source of information for managers whose institutions are experiencing or preparing for a period of decline.

395 Petrie, Hugh G., and Alpert, Daniel. "What Is the Problem of Retrenchment in Higher Education?" *Journal of Management Studies*, 1983, *20*, 97–119.

This article examines the problem of retrenchment in higher education within the context of organizational learning. The authors argue that basic assumptions about institutional life need to be questioned during retrenchment and that periods of decline present an opportunity to change institutional norms, behaviors, and structure. Departmental structure and federal research funding are discussed as factors that make it difficult to change a research-oriented university. The authors also address the difficulty of implementing many efficiency-oriented responses suggested in the literature, such as program termination, in large university settings. Their argument closes with a discussion of alternative strategies for responding to decline that focuses on setting priorities and attempting to reposition an institution within a changing environment. University administrators will find this article informative because it takes into consideration many university-specific factors not often discussed in the literature.

396 Starbuck, William H., Greve, Arent, and Hedberg, B.L.T. "Responding to Crisis." *Journal of Business Administration,* 1978, *9,* 111–137.

This paper presents an unorthodox view of the causes of, organizational dynamics associated with, and responses to crisis. The authors suggest that a primary cause of organizational crisis is past success. Success can decrease an organization's sensitivity to changing environmental demands and conditions, which in turn can lead to failure. They recommend responses that reject implicit assumptions about an organization and its environment and deter perceptual complacency. Institutional managers and researchers will find this article useful in providing a counterpoint to the more traditional literature on crisis. The article shows how successful organizations get themselves into trouble, and it provides a thoughtful analysis of ways to cope with the problems created by too much success.

★397 Zammuto, Raymond F., and Cameron, Kim S. "Environmental Decline and Organizational Response." In Barry M. Staw (ed.), *Research in Organizational Behavior.* Vol. 7. Greenwich, Conn.: JAI Press, 1984. Pages 223–262.

This article proposes a model of environmental changes that create different types of decline situations for industries and the organizations within them. The model is used to illustrate the different dynamics that occur in industries under each of four decline situations. It also explains why organizations in the same industry, such as individual colleges and universities within higher education, can face different types of decline. The authors suggest that different strategies for recovery are required in each type of decline situation. Short case histories from the baby food, automotive, higher education, and watch manufacturing industries are used to illustrate the model. The framework also proves useful in explaining differences in the prescriptions for managing decline apparent in the business, public administration, higher education, and other literatures.

Organizational Dynamics

398 Behn, Robert D. "Leadership for Cut-Back Management: The Use of Corporate Strategy." *Public Administration Review,* 1980, *40,* 613–620.

This article examines the roles of leaders in public-sector organizations during a period of retrenchment from the perspective of corporate strategy. Behn notes that leaders have three fundamental roles: establishing the inevitability of decline, dramatizing the opportunity costs of not cutting back, and creating an institutional strategy that matches new realities so as to make acceptance of retrenchment possible. The relationships among these roles, retrenchment tactics, and institutional morale are also examined. While written for a public administration audience, the article clearly highlights the roles that leaders in colleges and universities need to play during periods of declining enrollments and revenues. It illustrates how neglecting these roles can lead to institutional failure.

399 Billings, Robert S., Milburn, Thomas W., and Schaalman, Mary Lou. "A Model of Crisis Perception." *Administrative Science Quarterly,* 1980, *25,* 300–316.

This study modifies and evaluates Hermann's (no. 402) model of crisis behavior in organizations, using a sample of industrial and educational organizations. The results indicate that managerial perceptions of a situation moderate subsequent attributions and actions. The discussion suggests that contingency planning emotionally inoculates managers against the stressful effects of crisis, improving their ability to deal with crisis situations. This article is particularly helpful in explaining the role of contingency planning in increasing the likelihood that institutional managers will successfully respond to decreasing enrollments and revenues.

★400 Chaffee, Ellen E. "Successful Strategic Management in Small Private Colleges." *Journal of Higher Education,* 1984, *55* (2), 212–241.

For a full description of this article, please see entry no. 173.

401 Hall, Douglas T., and Mansfield, Roger. "Organizational and Individual Response to External Stress." *Administrative Science Quarterly,* 1971, *16,* 533–547.

This study examines organizational and individual responses to a decline situation in three research and development laboratories using questionnaire and interview data collected at points two years apart. The results show that in such a situation, organizations increase their emphasis on efficiency and short-term results, their internal climate becomes less potent, and turnover increases. Individuals reported decreased job satisfaction, reduced feeling of organizational cohesion, and increased needs for job security, but few changes in job involvement, performance, or effort. The authors' discussion focuses on how these individual responses can detract from an organization's ability to respond to decline and how increased participation in the retrenchment process may ameliorate this problem. This article presents one of the few empirical studies that describe the effects of decline on professional organizations and their employees.

402 Hermann, Charles F. "Some Consequences of Crisis That Limit the Viability of Organizations." *Administrative Science Quarterly,* 1963, *8,* 61–82.

This classic article presents a model of organizational crisis and its effects. Crisis situations are defined as having three characteristics: surprise, threat, and limited response time. The effects of these three characteristics on organizational integration, communication, goals, conflict, turnover, and decision making are explored in a series of propositions. This model has stimulated extensive research on crisis behavior over the past two decades, and most of its propositions have received considerable empirical support.

403 Rubin, Irene. "Universities in Stress: Decision Making Under Conditions of Reduced Resources." *Social Science Quarterly,* 1977, *58,* 242–254.

This study examines the effects of financial decline on five universities using a case study methodology. The study showed that decision making in universities moved from a unit to an institutional perspective and that more explicit resource allocation criteria were developed during decline. Overall, Rubin concludes, the decision-making process deteriorated. Criteria were subject to continual change as resources continued to decrease, which meant that the same decisions had to be made over and over again. Information was systematically distorted to protect certain types of expenditures, and the reluctance of institutional managers to commit resources in the face of uncertainty caused growing uncertainty down the hierarchy. The article is particularly useful in pointing out the effect of long-term resource reductions on institutional functioning.

★**404** Smart, Carolyne, and Vertinsky, Ilan. "Designs for Crisis Decision Units." *Administrative Science Quarterly,* 1977, *22,* 640–657.

This article describes techniques to avoid the decision pathologies caused by organizational crises. These techniques focus on preventing the perceptual biases common in crisis situations, increasing flexibility in the decision-making process, and increasing an organization's information-processing capacity. As important as the identification of specific techniques is the exploration of their potential drawbacks. Although written for an academic audience, the article provides a wealth of specific, usable information that can increase the likelihood of institutional managers' making good strategic choices in a crisis situation.

★**405** Staw, Barry M., Sandelands, Lance E., and Dutton, Jane E. "Threat-Rigidity Effects in Organizational Behavior." *Administrative Science Quarterly,* 1981, *26,* 501–524.

This paper summarizes and integrates the literature on crises. The authors present a general model of threat-rigidity effects and then apply it specifically to the individual, group, and organizational levels of analysis. They also discuss how threat-rigidity effects may aid organizational survival. The article is a very good overview of the literature on crisis. Researchers should find the integrated, cross-level model very useful in explaining crisis behavior in institutions of higher education and in explaining the interactions of effects across levels within an organization.

Cutback Management

406 Baldridge, J. Victor, Kemerer, Frank R., and Green, Kenneth C. *The Enrollment Crisis: Factors, Actors, and Impacts.* AAHE-ERIC Higher Education Research Report no. 3. Washington, D.C.: American Association for Higher Education, 1982. 79 pages.

This monograph presents a proactive view of how institutional managers can revitalize their schools and create dynamic responses to the ominous demographic and federal policy trends of the 1980s. A number of different points of institutional leverage in managing enrollments are discussed, with a primary focus on student recruiting and retention. Other topics include planning, governance, staffing policies, and program evaluation. Institutional administrators will find this a useful source of information because it provides a holistic overview of enrollment management. While it does not discuss specific techniques in great detail, the monograph does display all the pieces of the process in a systematic manner.

407 Hirschhorn, Larry, and Associates. *Cutting Back: Retrenchment and Redevelopment in Human and Community Services.* San Francisco: Jossey-Bass, 1983. 393 pages.

This volume offers a wealth of practical advice about tactics for coping with a period of decline. The book is divided into four major sections, respectively concerned with the psychology and politics of the retrenchment process, redesigning organizations, productivity planning, and a set of case studies. Individual chapters focus on topics such as managing rumors, consolidating functions within an organization, and sharing responsibility in the cutback process. Much of the material is applicable to colleges and universities, and much of the proffered advice also has direct application.

★408 Hyatt, James A., Shulman, Carol H., and Santiago, Aurora A. *Reallocation: Strategies for Effective Resource Management.* Washington, D.C.: National Association of College and University Business Officers, 1984. 86 pages.

This monograph examines how resource reallocation strategies may differ from institution to institution depending on factors such as the degree of management flexibility, duration of a fiscal crisis, and the extent to which institutional revenues are diversified. It also considers the role of faculty involvement and an institution's ability to reformulate its mission and maintain program quality. Five detailed case studies are used to illustrate the applicability of different reallocation and retrenchment strategies. The monograph presents a straightforward and thoughtful discussion of issues important to institutional decision makers faced with formulating retrenchment strategies.

409 Jick, Todd D., and Murray, Victor V. "The Management of Hard Times: Budget Cutbacks in Public Sector Organizations." *Organization Studies,* 1982, *3,* 141–169.

This article provides a synthesis of the cutback management literature. It presents a model that predicts whether managers will select "rational" or "political" strategies for responding to decline. Rational responses are viewed as likely when institutional managers feel that budget reductions are appropriate. On the other hand, political responses are more likely when institutional managers feel that cuts are inappropriate or that they have the power to resist them. Researchers will find the hypotheses presented in the article to be fertile ground for formulating research questions.

★410 Mingle, James R., and Associates. *Challenges of Retrenchment: Strategies for Consolidating Programs, Cutting Costs, and Reallocating Resources.* San Francisco: Jossey-Bass, 1981. 394 pages.

This book is a relatively comprehensive collection of information about the management of decline in higher education. Its nineteen chapters cover a variety of topics, including tactics for managing institutions with declining enrollments and revenues, faculty cutbacks, and the role of the state in managing retrenchment in public and private institutions. Most of the chapters are literature reviews or reports of case studies on different aspects of the retrenchment process. The book presents a wealth of ideas about specific retrenchment tactics that should be useful to institutional managers.

411 Mingle, James R., and Norris, Donald M. "Institutional Strategies for Responding to Decline." In James R. Mingle and Associates, *Challenges of Retrenchment: Strategies for Consolidating Programs, Cutting Costs, and Reallocating Resources.* San Francisco: Jossey-Bass, 1981. Pages 47–68.

This chapter presents the results from twenty case studies of the way colleges and universities responded to decline. The article calls attention to the importance of planning, both before and during a downturn, in formulating successful responses to decline. The case studies show that most institutions engaged in mixed strategies, where some actions were taken to resist decline (for example, finding new sources of enrollments and revenues) and others to adapt to decline (for example, cutting programs and faculty). The authors conclude that no single strategy should be relied upon for reducing operations and that boldness is required in taking action. The chapter presents a number of ideas useful to managers who are trying to prepare their institutions for an uncertain future. (For a description of the book as a whole, please see entry no. 410.)

412 Whetten, David A. "Organizational Responses to Scarcity: Exploring the Obstacles to Innovative Approaches to Retrenchment in Education." *Educational Administration Quarterly,* 1981, *17* (3), 80–97.

This article begins with the premise that innovation lies at the heart of adaptive organizational responses to decline. It notes, however, that the literature indicates little innovation on the

part of educational organizations responding to declining enrollments or revenues. Whetten reviews several factors that bias
institutional actions toward conservatism during periods of decline, including the effects of stress, the trained incapacity of
administrators, and innovation-resistant properties of institutional structures. The argument closes with a discussion of the
relative roles of actions to increase the efficiency and the effectiveness of institutional action. The article suggests that institutional managers need to see periods of decline as opportunities
for change.

★**413** Zammuto, Raymond F. "Managing Decline in Amer-
ican Higher Education." In John C. Smart (ed.), *Higher
Education: Handbook of Theory and Research*. Vol. 2. New
York: Agathon, 1986. Pages 43–84.

This chapter presents a review of the literature on managing
declining revenues and enrollments in higher education. It addresses two basic issues: what institutions should do before a
period of decline begins, and how they should manage the cutback process once decline has begun. The roles of mission and
program review, enrollment management, contingency planning, and environmental assessment in preparing for an uncertain future are discussed. Remaining in control once a period
of decline has begun is the theme of the section on managing
the cutback process. The chapter integrates a wide range of ideas
about the management of decline and examines a large array
of management tactics for preparing and responding to decline.

17

Richard C. Richardson, Jr.
Donald J. Vangsnes

Equity and
Affirmative Action

An Evolutionary Perspective

The concept of equity as currently defined in higher education is the product of court decisions, executive orders, legislation, and agency regulations covering little more than a quarter-century. For most of that time, the posture of higher education has been reactive. The implications for higher education of *Brown* v. *Board of Education* have been explored through litigation in many states into the 1980s. The desegregation plans of several ''Adams states'' have been accepted only within the past several years. And the important *Geier* v. *Alexander* stipulation became operational in Tennessee as recently as 1984.

The past quarter-century has been one of rapid change and substantial conflict. Student access issues emerged first following the legal requirement for the desegregation of public institutions. Typically, the attention of administrators focused initially on compliance with regulations rather than the broader concept of equal opportunity as reflected by comparable achievement. Desegregation issues quickly became intertwined with an entire panoply of related equity concerns, with the passage of new legislation that included denial of participation on athletic teams and other gender-related barriers among prohibited actions. The *Bakke* case changed the emerging rules for minority student access by limiting the scope of special admissions programs. A recent trend toward stricter admission standards in

366

four-year public institutions has contributed to a slowing down or reversal of previous gains in the proportions of some minority groups attending postsecondary institutions, while their proportions in the general population and among high school graduating classes have increased. Exacerbating the problem of underrepresentation has been the limited academic preparation available to many minority students and a decision by the federal government to limit the growth of financial aid programs.

Following close on the heels of student access and gender discrimination issues were a host of equity concerns involving faculty hiring and promotion and the granting of tenure. While the initial thrust of equity literature relating to employment issues was correction of past discrimination against minorities, gender-related issues soon became intertwined, just as they had with issues related to student access and participation. The problems with this approach are only now becoming apparent. The tendency in much of the equity literature has been to treat gender and race as somewhat interchangeable. In fact, however, problems related to the two are not the same, as has been recognized increasingly by the more thoughtful writers in the field.

Reverse discrimination became an important issue with the *Bakke* case, leading to a majority backlash that created a new set of ground rules following a reassessment by the courts of the extent to which protected classes can be given preferential treatment. More recently, the Supreme Court decision in *Wygant* v. *Jackson Board of Education* provided fuel for the effort by the Reagan administration to alter the legal basis for affirmative action. While the Supreme Court upheld preferential hiring where past discrimination could be proven, the ruling restrains the development and administration of special employment programs by requiring proof of specific instances of discrimination rather than permitting reliance on the general societal context as in earlier decisions.

Under these circumstances, it is not surprising that the literature on management of equity issues remains fragmented, with much of its emphasis remaining on advocacy or institutional response to legal requirements. No sooner did institutions begin to make sense of the myriad of state and federal regulations related to race and gender than they were confronted with additional regulations related to discrimination on the basis of age and handicaps. Gender-related issues became more complex with the introduction of such refinements as equal pay and comparable worth.

Equity issues became increasingly difficult to manage as the economic conditions of the 1980s produced new concerns for faculty, both minority and majority. Questions about fair treatment in employment practices gave way to issues of retrenchment as a growing number of institutions experienced financial difficulties brought on by losses in enrollment. Further, a continuing buyers' market for faculty members in most fields produced fewer favorable tenure and promotion decisions even in institutions where the traditional emphasis had been upon teaching rather than research. Since most departments numbered few, if any, tenured minorities or women among their membership, personnel decisions became increasingly suspect. Even in the absence of demonstrable bias, minorities and women were concerned about the expectations for them in terms of mentoring and committee service, activities that frequently left them little opportunity to do the research and publication upon which they were subsequently judged for promotion and tenure. Even tenured faculty, once seemingly secure in their educational niche, now found themselves with a stake in the issue of equity. For minorities and women, "last in, first out" became a threatening specter. The literature of the eighties is full of pieces on retrenchment, early retirement, and hiring freezes.

The number and range of issues raised but not yet resolved make it clear that affirmative action as a management concern is unlikely to go away. It is also evident that hiring a woman or minority person as an affirmative action officer to enforce the record-keeping requirements of state or federal bureaucracies does little to change the practices that produce the need for record keeping in the first place. If it is to move beyond monitoring institutional practices, progress requires commitment from all levels within an organization. Commitment, in turn, relies upon education and information. The problem of affirmative action is also a problem of supply and demand. Faculty search committees cannot recommend women or minorities who lack the qualifications established for a particular vacancy, and they will not recommend candidates who have little beyond their minority status or gender to submit by way of qualifications.

Part of the reason institutions have experienced frustration in dealing with equity issues can be traced to the difficulty in making progress in an area such as faculty hiring without first expanding the pool of minority doctorates. In turn, universities cannot produce more doctorates without addressing the extent to which minorities are underrepresented among baccalaureate degree recipients. Because none of these problems can be solved without addressing related issues, the temptation is to engage in token compliance. Fortunately, the dimensions of the problem have at least been identified and increasingly are receiving the benefit of coordinated efforts, as in the case of a current American Council on Education–Mellon funded project on minority doctorates that is being closely coordinated with two minority doctoral projects sponsored by the National Center for Postsecondary Governance and Finance and a third that focuses on baccalaureate production. Relatedly, major graduate institutions such as the University of California system have embarked upon special support programs designed to address the issue of minority hiring at its source.

Framework for Organizing the Literature

The concept of equity pervades virtually all aspects of higher education management. Affirmative action is arguably the centerpiece and the most readily identifiable part of this concept. The existence of affirmative action, the rationale for it, and the voluminous legislation and litigation that it has produced form the framework for organizing the literature described in this chapter.

The equity issue had its origins in questions of student access, but personnel policies and compensation issues have proven more sensitive to approach and more difficult and costly to resolve. Because compensation and job security are bread-

and-butter issues, faculty and staff have exercised all available remedies in contesting unfavorable decisions. In the process they have created the need for a host of new management and personnel procedures and a substantial body of literature.

Of course the "bottom line" for higher education institutions in evaluating the success of affirmative action legislation, court decisions, and personnel policies is student achievement. An increasingly important part of the equity literature focuses on student preparation, progress, degree achievement, and subsequent entry into a professional field. In many ways this is the most exciting and promising aspect of the movement toward equal opportunity. Data are getting better, at least at the state levels, and analysis is becoming more sophisticated. Correlational studies aimed at explaining student achievement in terms of institutionally collected data elements are being supplemented by naturalistic studies designed to improve understanding in terms of institutional context, including administrative policies.

The four categories constituting the framework for this review are defined as follows:

Affirmative Action. Affirmative action serves as the cornerstone of the equity issue and is the single most important and recognizable concept from a management perspective. While initially affirmative action provided great hope for providing more equitable inclusion of minorities throughout the various levels of higher education, its impact proved to be relatively limited because most institutions relied upon compliance with formal procedures rather than attempting to understand the underlying issues. Because of a rapidly changing external environment and slowly changing attitudes, affirmative action remains a controversial topic and a continuing target for critics.

Legislation and Litigation. Equity, as an aspect of educational systems, cannot be discussed without considering concurrently the accompanying regulatory and judicial context. Higher education in the United States has become accessible to underrepresented populations largely because of the legal remedies taken by those discriminated against in their educational pursuits. Concern about possible litigation resides under the surface of every decision administrators make. Similarly, past litigation governs the resolution of disputes related to the implementation of affirmative action procedures as well as the interpretation of current policies.

Personnel Policies and Compensation Issues. In recent years, this area has undergone rapid change because of financial problems that have affected the majority of higher education institutions, leading to program cuts, increases in part-time faculty, erosion of earning power, and the immobilization of a once institution-hopping faculty. As a result, younger faculty members, including many minorities and women, have experienced increasing difficulty in advancing through the rigid hierarchy of the academic world. The problems institutions experience in recruiting, tenuring, and promoting minorities and women in turn affect those institutions' ability to provide appropriate and relevant opportunities for an increasingly diverse student body.

Minority Status and Access. Personnel issues have their roots in the area of minority student access and achievement. Participation rates no longer serve as a satisfactory index of an institution's effort; increasingly there is concern about persistence and degree achievement. The effort to improve performance, as distinct from the simple achievement of numerical targets through increased recruiting efforts, is producing a rich and varied literature that will command increased attention from administrators and faculty concerned about equal educational opportunity.

Commentary on the Literature

A good case can be made for dating the useful literature on equity management from the mid-1970s. This review is based on that assumption. Because the field has changed so rapidly, the limited literature of the early 1970s offers little insight or guidance for managers in the 1980s. A review of outcomes indicates steady progress in improving representation in the years immediately following the enactment of need-based financial aid programs. Much of the improvement proves illusory upon closer examination, however. Minorities improved participation rates dramatically, but improved participation did not translate into better representation among graduating classes. Furthermore, even the illusory gains of the late 1970s had turned into a steady state or worse by the early 1980s.

Specific data are more available in today's literature, as has been noted. The data are also better focused and more widely disseminated because of a number of major efforts, including those of Astin (no. 438) and the Office of Minority Concerns of the American Council on Education (ACE). But there is also a negative side to the improved availability of data. Documenting the plight of underrepresented minorities remains a concern primarily of minority faculty members and administrators, as evidenced by the largely minority audience who attended the official release of the fifth annual status report on *Minorities in Higher Education* in October 1986 in San Francisco during the annual meeting of the ACE. Even among the minority professionals attending, sentiment was divided about the advantages of documenting annually in considerable detail the lack of substantial progress in reducing discrepancies between minority and majority participation and achievement.

Several changes differentiate the literature of the 1980s from that of the previous decade. While improving equity for underrepresented minorities and women remains a central concern, much of the recent literature suggests a dwindling interest in and support for equity issues. At the same time, recent writings are more sophisticated and more analytical. They also involve a broader spectrum of writers, leading to a less strident tone than that of the literature produced by the feminists and minority writers of an earlier period. At least one refereed journal, *Journal of Educational Equity and Leadership,* and the ACE annual report, *Minorities in Higher Education* (no. 436), have brought new levels of information and scholarly activity to bear on the topic.

Perhaps in part because of the more relaxed approach to affirmative action taken by the Reagan administration, a middle ground appears to be emerging where educational leaders, committed to continuing progress in affirmative action, engage in cooperative endeavors with those who once advocated a much swifter resolution of equity issues. Throughout the literature there appears a greater awareness of the problems facing educational administrators caught between the rising expectations of women and minorities, the limited pool of qualified minority applicants, and the continuing stagnation of employment opportunities in a wide range of fields resulting from declining enrollment in many parts of the country.

Affirmative Action

*414 Carnegie Council on Policy Studies in Higher Education. *Making Affirmative Action Work in Higher Education: An Analysis of Institutional and Federal Policies with Recommendations.* San Francisco: Jossey-Bass, 1975. 272 pages.

The first major work on affirmative action in higher education, this analysis of institutional and federal policies examines the status of minorities and women in the early 1970s. It is a comprehensive, in-depth look at early goals and expectations of affirmative action in higher education. A series of twenty-seven recommendations are interspersed throughout the report, each suggesting specific procedures or ideas. A useful discussion of the impact of affirmative action on academic policies deals mainly with personnel matters, including an outline of essential elements in a good affirmative action plan. A fairly extensive review of the legislation related to affirmative action is also included, along with suggestions and criticisms regarding its implementation, administration, and enforcement. While the data reported in this study are outdated, the ideas are not. The report's timeliness is an indication of the lack of progress in this area. This book is a benchmark in affirmative action literature and provides foundation information needed by any higher education personnel working in this area.

415 Exum, William H. "Climbing the Crystal Stair: Values, Affirmative Action, and Minority Faculty." *Social Problems,* 1983, *30* (4), 383–399.

This paper examines the continuing scarcity of minority faculty in predominantly white colleges and universities. The author discusses this problem at three related levels: social, institutional, and individual. He reviews the current status of minority faculty in terms of numbers and distribution, as well as the historical discriminatory practices that created it. He discusses affirmative action in the context of what has and has not been achieved and the reasons why. Exum singles out commitment and leadership as key factors in making equity programs work. He examines the values of typical institutions and identifies the traditional meritocratic and patronage system of selection and promotion as barriers to greater minority representation. He concludes that until reconciliation of competing interests and values is accomplished, minority faculty will remain scarce in predominantly white institutions. This is one of numerous pieces that emphasize the issues of commitment and leadership as important factors in the affirmative action process.

416 Hitt, Michael, and others. "Affirmative Action Effectiveness Criteria in Institutions of Higher Education." *Research in Higher Education,* 1983, *18* (2), 391–408.

This study surveys the policies of personnel and affirmative action officers in determining criteria for effective programs to eliminate discrimination. It is preceded by a review of the literature, on the basis of which the authors conclude that affirmative action has not effectively eliminated discrimination and that institutions are meeting only the minimum legal requirements in recruitment and hiring practices for minority and women faculty. The survey sample included fifty-five members of the Association for Affirmative Action in one southwestern state and resulted in thirty-one usable returns. Respondents were asked to rate the relative importance of thirteeen criteria in evaluating thirty simulated equity situations through the use of a regression model. Results indicate that attitudinal criteria may be most important for effective affirmative action programs. A commitment from higher administration and receptive attitude of key personnel were criteria singled out for particular attention. This survey approach could easily be replicated as a useful evaluation tool for concerned administrators and their institutions.

417 Hyer, Patricia B. "Affirmative Action for Women Faculty: Case Studies of Three Successful Institutions." *Journal of Higher Education*, 1985, *56* (3), 282–299.

This study addresses the failure of affirmative action policies to successfully create equity for women in higher education. It reviews the organizational change and implementation literature and focuses on the four recurring issues of leadership, government intervention, coalition group activity, and structural and/or environmental influences that affect affirmative action. The author compared 183 public and private doctorate-granting universities using NCES and HEGIS data in five areas related to changes in numbers and proportions of women faculty. Using a change index, she then selected the top three institutions for case studies. Her results indicate that leadership is a crucial factor throughout the process of adding women to the faculty, not just in the implementation phase. It also suggests that interest group activity is a variable of theoretical importance. This study provides current information on women faculty and the effects of policy decisions on their status.

418 *Journal of the College and University Personnel Association*, 1984, *35* (4). 52 pages.

This special issue is made up of articles dealing with affirmative action. While not all of them refer specifically to higher education, all do discuss basic tenets of affirmative action. Two of the articles deal with legislation and judicial action relative to Executive Order 11246 and its application, and the *Stotts* case, in which the use of quotas was banned by the Supreme Court. Equity for part-time employees is discussed through a review of affirmative action procedures at universities in the Southern Region of CUPA. Results indicate that searches for part-time positions are frequently handled quite differently from those for full-time work and are often inequitable. Two good articles, somewhat related, discuss the status of affirmative action, one through demographic representation and one through examination of institutional policies. This issue provides both general information and practical ideas for administrators in the area of personnel management.

419 Reed, Rodney J. "Affirmative Action in Higher Education: Is It Necessary?" *Journal of Negro Education,* 1983, *52* (3), 332–349.

The author reviews the success of affirmative action over the years by examining NCES and EEOC reports on the number and distribution of minority and women faculty in higher education. He notes that while there were slight gains in numbers, discrepancies still exist in tenure rates and salaries. A more important issue is the social and political climate of the 1980s, which finds dwindling support for and interest in equity issues. Such issues are clouded by the negative connotations of quotas, preferential treatment, and reverse discrimination. Reed concludes that affirmative action is indeed necessary. He makes a number of recommendations for improving its effectiveness, including stronger commitment from leaders, active campus committees, grants to assist research and publication for minority faculty, and perception of affirmative action programs as a set of interrelated, mutually reinforcing activities. This piece not only adequately reviews the status of affirmative action but also provides concrete ideas for the improvement of affirmative action programs.

420 Vanderwaert, Lois. *Affirmative Action in Higher Education: A Sourcebook.* New York: Garland, 1982. 259 pages.

This sourcebook provides a practical guide to affirmative action. It begins with a brief review of the concept and follows with a detailed account of developing and staffing an affirmative action office, including forms and data collection. The many appendixes include a glossary of common terms related to affirmative action, a topical and alphabetical index of key court cases, and an extensive bibliography of books, articles, resources, bibliographies, and addresses of publishers. Although it is slightly dated, this book offers a broad range of information in the area of affirmative action and can be of value to all higher education personnel, especially those with little background in equity issues.

Legislation and Litigation

421 Calvin, Allen. "Age Discrimination on Campus." *American Association for Higher Education Bulletin,* 1984, *37* (3), 8–12.

This article addresses the inequities of forced retirement by reviewing the changes in the Age Discrimination in Employment Act over the years. Opposition to forced retirement at any age is supported by refuting the arguments that the older professor becomes "deadwood" and that "new blood" is needed in the form of young professors. The suggestion of need for mandatory retirement to enable effective affirmative action programs is also refuted, as statistics do not support this supposition. The author points out that the age issue is a women's issue as well, since women historically have been paid lower salaries, resulting in lower pension payments. Calvin's position is consistent with recent congressional action terminating mandatory retirement as a function of age. Age discrimination is an important issue that has received limited attention.

422 Dreyfuss, Joel, and Lawrence, Charles, III. *The Bakke Case: The Politics of Inequality.* New York: Harcourt Brace Jovanovich, 1979. 278 pages.

This book reviews the case of Allen Bakke, who sued the University of California and charged reverse discrimination because of his failure to gain admission to medical school. Written in novel form, it offers an in-depth look at the personalities involved—including Bakke, minority medical students at the University of California at Davis, lawyers, and university personnel—as well as the legal issues related to the case. It also reviews the social conditions and legislative acts that led to the creation of minority admissions and comments on the publicity that surrounded the entire process. This engrossing account will be of special interest to administrators in the areas of admissions, legal offices, and affirmative action because it places a landmark case in the expanded context of the real world.

423 Fields, Cheryl M. "High Court Backs Affirmative Action in Certain Forms." *Chronicle of Higher Education,* 1986, *32* (13), 1, 15–18.

This article describes the recent action taken by the Supreme Court in *Wygant* v. *Jackson Board of Education,* in which the court upheld preferential treatment in hiring only in situations where past discrimination could be proven. The decision represents a more restrictive view of practices permissible in addressing affirmative action goals than the one guiding previous decisions. This change potentially affects many affirmative action programs. The article quotes opinions of the various justices.

424 Hendrickson, Robert M., and Lee, Barbara A. *Academic Employment and Retrenchment: Judicial Review and Administrative Action.* ASHE-ERIC Higher Education Research Report no. 8. Washington, D.C.: Association for the Study of Higher Education, 1983. 122 pages.

This monograph provides a review of equity issues related to programs and personnel in higher education. It examines litigation and judicial actions in discrimination cases involving the Civil Rights Act, the Equal Pay Act, Title IX, and the Age Discrimination in Employment Act. It addresses the scope of employment practices as they relate to retrenchment and financial exigency, as well as the major discrimination issues involving promotion and tenure, salaries, and retirement. It concludes with suggestions to help administrators deal with litigation and equity. These include general guidelines, such as efficient data collection and record keeping, uniform procedures, faculty participation, and accountability, as well as more area-specific suggestions. This monograph is a very useful reference for those looking for general information about equity issues.

*425 Kaplin, William A. *The Law of Higher Education: A Comprehensive Guide to Legal Implications of Administrative Decision Making.* (2nd ed.) San Francisco: Jossey-Bass, 1985. 621 pages.

For a full description of this work, please see entry no. 87.

426 Lindgren, J. Ralph, Ota, Patti, Zirkel, Perry A., and Van Gieson, Nan. *Sex Discrimination Law in Higher Education: The Lessons of the Past Decade.* ASHE-ERIC Higher Education Research Report no. 4. Washington, D.C.: Association for the Study of Higher Education, 1984. 75 pages.

This monograph is a comprehensive summary of legislation and resulting legal action related to sex discrimination in higher education. It aims to clarify the obligations of colleges and universities in this area through a review of specific laws such as Title VII of the Civil Rights Act, Title IX of the Education Amendments, and the Equal Pay Act, as well as discussion of major developments in the judicial process. The report has three sections. The first deals with sex discrimination against employees, the second deals with student issues, and the third consists of recommendations. The authors suggest that careful selection and training of personnel working in this area is a key factor and encourage specific policies, responsibilities, and a monitoring system. The monograph provides a good discussion of the basic issues related to sex discrimination.

427 Rosenthal, William, and Yancey, Bernard (eds.). *The Use of Data in Social Discrimination Cases.* New Directions for Institutional Research, no. 48. San Francisco: Jossey-Bass, 1985. 107 pages.

This book presents an overview of issues related to social action litigation in higher education and the role research plays in supporting an institution's social action policies through data bases and analytical models. Procedures for studying racism, sexism, and salary inequities through the use of planning, data collection, and methodology are discussed. The authors also pro-

vide a comprehensive review of topics specifically related to litigation, including models of proof, statutes, personnel involved,
and strategies for various stages of litigation. Finally, they discuss
the courts' gradual acceptance of the use of statistics in discrimination cases. This book is a useful tool for both institutional
researchers and administrators concerned with the analysis of
equity issues.

Personnel Policies and Compensation Issues

428 Bergmann, Barbara R. "'Comparable Worth' for Professors." *Academe*, 1985, *71* (4), 8–10.

This article suggests that nongender salary differentials are, in
part, a result of institutional policy stemming from a mistaken
notion that the market concept of employment provides equality.
The author refutes the argument that you cannot compare different fields by pointing out that faculty in all areas do the same
things: lecturing, teaching, and research. The problem is that
certain areas, especially in the humanities and liberal arts, are
not marketable in terms of supply and demand but nonetheless
constitute an integral part of any curriculum. Bergmann feels
that institutional policies concerning budget allocations and
salary schedules need to be revised to promote equity for both
gender and disciplinary affiliations. This article raises an important issue regarding the priorities of administrators and their
policy of rewarding mainly faculty in the "hot" market fields.

429 Fortunato, Ray T. "Affirmative Action and Personnel
Administrator Functions: A Case for Alliance." *Journal
of the College and University Personnel Association*, 1985, *36*
(1), 46–49.

This article discusses the relationship between affirmative action and personnel offices and efficiently addresses some key
issues of interest to administrators. The author briefly reviews
different organizational formats, focusing on reporting lines,
scope of charge, and degree of authority. One important issue
covered is the rank of the affirmative action officer relative to
that of the personnel director. The article's central emphasis

is on clearly delineated roles and responsibilities and on coordination, regardless of the organizational format.

430 Fortunato, Ray T., and Waddell, D. Geneva. *Personnel Administration in Higher Education: Handbook of Faculty and Staff Personnel Practices.* San Francisco: Jossey-Bass, 1981. 384 pages.

For a full description of this work, please see entry no. 285.

431 Koch, James V. "The Gunther Case, Comparable Worth, and Implications for Academe." *Educational Record,* 1983, *64* (2), 38–43.

This article reviews the *Gunther* case, through which the issue of comparable worth entered the public forum. It discusses the salary gender differential and its relationship to academic discipline as revealed by a National Research Council study that matched men and women Ph.D.s by education, experience, and type of employment. This study found women less likely to be employed than male counterparts and earning less when employed. Koch also warns of salary policies that exclude the market notion of worth and base compensation on "units of labor." Since the determination of salaries for faculty is a decentralized process, incorporating a comparable worth policy would probably mean committees of faculty and administrators making judgments about equity issues. The author emphasizes that institutions may encounter problems in initiating new programs or serving growing programs with the limitations that comparable worth may set. Koch offers a view of comparable worth quite different from Bergmann's (no. 428).

432 Menges, Robert J., and Exum, William H. "Barriers to the Progress of Women and Minority Faculty." *Journal of Higher Education,* 1983, *54* (2), 123–144.

This article examines the issue of tenure and promotion reviews as obstacles to women and minority faculty in higher education. The authors review the current underrepresentation through statistical examples and provide a brief discussion of problems impeding the advance of affirmative action. The first obstacle occurs because women and minority faculty are concentrated in the lower academic ranks. Their lack of seniority makes them vulnerable to layoffs. A second obstacle relates to the use of meritocratic criteria that emphasize research and scholarship. Minority and women faculty members frequently have heavier teaching loads, are asked more often to serve on committees, and may encounter expectations that they will serve as role models, a function that can impose heavy demands on available time. Such expectations leave little time to develop the skills that are rewarded in tenure and promotion decisions. The authors suggest that the lack of progress for women and minority faculty is due to the lack of commitment to ensure equity, a recurring theme in the equity literature.

433 Scott, Barbara A. *Crisis Management in American Higher Education.* New York: Praeger, 1983. 355 pages.

This book looks at changes in management policies of higher education that have been brought about by changing financial and political realities in the last decade. It draws heavily from the State University of New York's reaction to budgetary problems starting in the early 1970s. The second half of the book, Chapters Five–Ten, deals mainly with equity issues such as stratification of academic personnel, affirmative action, student issues, and meritocracy. Chapter Six, "The New Stratification of Academic Personnel," provides a good view of the inequities currently related to junior and part-time faculty, while Chapter Seven, "The Assault on Affirmative Action," offers a discussion of issues and the status of women and minorities in higher education. The authors apparently did not intend to offer practical recommendations, but they do a thorough job of describing the current state of affairs. This book will be of special interest to management personnel because of the contextual and historical information it provides.

434 Scott, Elizabeth L. *Higher Education Salary Evaluation Kit.* Washington, D.C.: American Association of University Professors, 1977. 55 pages.

This is a technical, "how-to" publication that focuses on the identification of salary inequities. It describes the necessary data format to be used with SPSS and how to interpret results. The "kit" includes a variety of methods for comparing salaries to reveal inequity, such as institutional differences or changes over time. Examples of computer procedures and output, as well as a bibliography of studies on the topic, are provided in the appendixes. Although its computer references may have to be updated, this book should be useful to information management specialists and institutional researchers.

435 Skaggs, Lionel C., and others. "Good Sense Management: The Economics of EEO/AA Training." *Journal of the College and University Personnel Association,* 1983, *34* (4), 1–10.

This article stresses the importance of a working knowledge of issues associated with affirmative action and equal opportunity legislation. Emphasizing the continuing changes caused by litigation and the large amounts of money being awarded in discrimination suits, the authors suggest that institutions must effectively train their personnel in nondiscriminatory management. They review a training model used at the University of Alabama in Birmingham, including its goals, cost, and effectiveness. They also provide a list of other EEO/AA training programs. This article offers a quick, practical look at a basic management issue.

Minority Status and Access

*436 American Council on Education. *Minorities in Higher Education.* Washington, D.C.: American Council on Education, 1986. 47 pages.

This is the fifth annual status report on minorities in higher education. It compares the four major ethnic minorities—black, Native American, Spanish-origin, and Asian-Pacific—with the white majority in terms of enrollments, retention, degree attainment, and concentration in subject fields. It relies on a variety of data sources, including the Census Bureau, the Office of Civil Rights, NCES, and the College Entrance Examination Board. A disturbing fact reported by ACE this year is the decreasing quality of the data available, due to cutbacks in record-collecting agencies and what is perceived as a lack of interest in collecting comprehensive data on the part of states and individual institutions. The conclusions reached in this report are not positive: the only minority group making notable gains is the Asian-Pacific–American population. Although Hispanics are increasing their presence in higher education, it is mainly at the two-year level. Black students and faculty are losing ground in most states as the lack of impact of court-ordered mandates in the Adams states becomes increasingly evident. This report is a valuable resource for all higher education personnel because it provides current minority data.

437 "American Indian Education." *Integrated Education,* 1981, *19* (1–2), 2–7.

This special issue includes articles covering a wide scope of issues on American Indian education, beginning with a brief historical review of its development and leading to current issues. The authors address the special needs and characteristics of Indian students relative to their lack of identity in a process that works toward assimilation. The finances, faculty, standards, and other resources of Indian community colleges, as well as their relationship with community needs, are also profiled. A final topic is the basic problems confronting American Indian students and programs in developing their cultural and educational goals within a structure that culturally and intellectually emphasizes a different set of values. The issue includes a bibliography of American Indian education. This is a valuable resource, since little has been written on the American Indian's involvement in higher education.

★438 Astin, Alexander W. *Minorities in American Higher Education: Recent Trends, Current Prospects, and Recommendations.* San Francisco: Jossey-Bass, 1982. 263 pages.

This study is a comprehensive review of minority groups in higher education, including both faculty and students, in the four largest racial groups: blacks, Mexican-Americans, Native Americans, and Puerto Ricans. Over 10,000 students, 600 minority faculty, and 487 institutions were included in the study. It presents a look at the education pipeline for minorities and minority distribution in various fields of study, then examines attitudes and factors that affect minority educational progress. The book also examines the role of state and federal programs and equal-opportunity legislation that affects minority education progress. The book's conclusion offers an extensive list of recommendations for various educational units to improve minority education. One of the major works in the assessment of the minority condition in higher education, this book is important to anyone working in the field.

439 College Entrance Examination Board. *Equality and Excellence: The Educational Status of Black Americans.* New York: College Entrance Examination Board, 1985. 52 pages.

This report is a comprehensive review of the status of black students at all educational levels. It includes extensive demographic data on black households, income, employment, and educational attainment, drawing on a variety of data sources, including government bureaus and educational organizations. Although legal barriers to their education have been removed, minority students are still placed in programs that are less likely to enhance the development of higher-order cognitive skills. The report examines high school curricula, "gifted and talented" programs, and remedial courses, as well as test scores, college enrollment, and retention. Policies that affect access and success are also reviewed, including financing, educational standards, and the teaching force. This report provides extensive and current data specifically on blacks.

440 Fleming, Jacqueline. *Blacks in College: A Comparative Study of Students' Success in Black and in White Institutions.* San Francisco: Jossey-Bass, 1984. 276 pages.

This cross-sectional study compares intellectual and social development of black students at predominantly black institutions with those at predominantly white institutions. The study includes 3,000 freshman and senior students at fifteen colleges in four states. Results indicate that black students encounter problems at white institutions but fare better at black institutions. The black college experience is promoted because of the supportive community and increased opportunities for participation that it provides. The author argues that black colleges do not promote segregation; rather, they prepare black students to function more effectively in society through more positive social and academic experiences. The study also reports that black colleges provide greater academic gains for black students, although the basis for this claim is not clear from the evidence reported. Not a status report on blacks in higher education, the book makes a case for the continuing support of black institutions.

441 Olivas, Michael A. (ed.). *Latino College Students.* New York: Teachers College Press, 1986. 360 pages.

Growing out of the Conference on Latino College Students, this is the newest and most comprehensive book dealing with Hispanic education. Olivas sets up a theoretical framework through a review of previous research on Hispanic students and uses it as a basis for dividing the book into three sections: the transition from high school to college, Hispanic student achievement, and economics and stratification. The first section looks at Hispanic family background and educational attainment, finding that generational differences, socioeconomic status, and high school curriculum are the most important factors. The second part consists of recent research findings relating to Hispanic students in the areas of stress, language, predictors of success, and the use of tests in selective admissions. The final section of the book includes a recent study on financial aid access, which reports a heavy reliance on Pell grants by Hispanic students.

The book concludes with a discussion of educational barriers and stratification. This book is a "must" for those doing research or policy work in areas dealing with the Hispanic population.

442 Orfield, Gary, and others. *The Chicago Study of Access and Choice in Higher Education.* Chicago: Committee on Public Policy Research Project, University of Chicago, 1984. 344 pages.

This study analyzes students' access and choice in higher education in the metropolitan Chicago area. It follows the progress of students through 229 high schools and into and out of almost sixty colleges, describing educational mobility and educational failure. Differences in backgrounds that affect choice of institution and persistence are documented. While income is an important factor, residential segregation also plays a role in shaping high school and community college experiences. Graduation rates, the channeling of students to schools based on their residence, and the resulting transfer problems for minority community college students are all treated. The study concludes that a comprehensive system of educational inequality exists in the Chicago area and inhibits the educational attainment of minority students. This controversial study covers a broad spectrum of educational issues that will be of interest not only to higher education personnel but also to public officials involved in education-related issues.

443 Pruitt, Anne S., and Isaac, Paul D. "Discrimination in Recruitment, Admission, and Retention of Minority Graduate Students." *Journal of Negro Education,* 1985, *54* (4), 526–536.

This article notes declining minority enrollments in graduate schools and identifies sources of discrimination from an internal labor market perspective. The authors claim that the admissions process for minorities is hampered by narrow sets of recruitment channels, objective admission standards, and subjective screening criteria. They suggest that recruitment and retention efforts need to be improved and should include financial support and mentoring. Students should also be selected from schools that have proven their ability to produce quality minority students, including historically black institutions, they say. This article addresses an important component of the equity issue, one especially relevant to administrators and faculty involved in graduate admissions decisions.

444 Richardson, Richard C., Jr., and Bender, Louis W. *Students in Urban Settings: Achieving the Baccalaureate Degree.* ASHE-ERIC Higher Education Research Report no. 6. Washington, D.C.: Association for the Study of Higher Education, 1985. 65 pages.

This report, part of a Ford Foundation project, examines the problems of articulation between two-year urban community colleges and their adjacent public universities. The status of minorities relative to educational quality, financial status, and aspirations is reviewed. The authors also provide an assessment of urban schools, focusing on the differences that may exist in mission, constituency, and access. Problems associated with transfer include institutional practices and relationships as well as performance factors related to lack of preparation and difficulty in coping with a new environment. The authors' suggestions for improvement include better coordination between institutions in the areas of academic and admissions standards, orientation practices, and academic programs. While the report focuses on policy and program decisions in urban schools, it also has implications for higher education institutions in general.

445 Zollinger, Richard A. "Impact of Financial Aid on Admissible College Choices: Equity for Blacks and Women." *Journal of Educational Equity and Leadership,* 1985, *5* (2), 145–168.

This study examines the influence of financial aid on equity of college choice by race and sex. The author suggests that financial aid has not created equity of choice for minorities and women, as they are more apt to attend low-cost two-year or four-year public colleges. The random stratified sample included over

2,500 Illinois aid recipients for 1979–80. The concept of academic choice set was used to represent the range of colleges a student could expect to attend, based on achievement as measured through the use of ACT composite scores. The author's comparisons included sex, race, college affordability, and achievement levels. While financial aid increased college choice, according to the author, a number of inequities were demonstrated for lower-achievement students dependent on aid. The results of the study warrant a closer look at the effectiveness of current financial aid policies.

18

David D. Dill
Patricia K. Fullagar

Leadership and
Administrative Style

The concept of leadership is an archetype, touching our most fundamental understandings of social organization. Theories of leadership have been debated throughout recorded history. It is likely that current theories of leadership and administrative style in higher education represent embellishments to these underlying themes rather than whole new symphonies.

Plutarch's Lives (Clough, 1910), the famous biographical sketches of the great men of Greece and Rome, provides today, as in the first century A.D., one characteristic view of leadership. Plutarch was concerned less with politics and changes of empires than with the personal character and individual actions of leaders. His classical conception was that the life of nations was contained in the lives of a few great men and that major social movements were determined by the actions of those for whom monuments remain: kings, ministers, generals, authors, and popes.

This conception of history and of leadership has been continuously challenged, most eloquently by Tolstoy (1958) in his second epilogue to *War and Peace*. While Napoleon was the most dominant leader of the nineteenth century, he was not in Tolstoy's view the cause of the turmoil in Europe. Rather, social movements were caused by deeper forces, and a leader's actions were determined by events: "The movement of nations is caused not by power, nor by intellectual activity, nor even by a combination of the two as historians have supposed, but

390

by the activity of *all* the people who participated in the events, and who always combine in such a way that those taking the largest direct share in the event take on the least responsibility and vice versa'' (p. 1335).

This classical debate on the role of leaders and leadership, on the influence of ''great men'' as compared to the inevitable tides of history in which leaders merely play the role of the most visible flotsam, has also shaped the literature concerning the leadership of organizations, including those of higher education. The history of American colleges and universities has traditionally been presented as providing substantial support for a ''great man'' hypothesis of history. Entrepreneurial giants such as Ezra White of Cornell, Charles Eliot of Harvard, Henry Tappan of Michigan, and Robert Maynard Hutchins of Chicago are held to have articulated the vision and constructed the unique reality of the American college and university.

This picture dimmed following World War II, when dominant personalities were less visible on the higher education landscape, and came under deeper question during the student disruptions of the 1960s and 1970s, when individual campus leadership seemed impotent in the face of powerful social and political forces. On the other hand, the Tolstoyan view of leadership received empirical and conceptual support from Michael Cohen and James March's influential study of the college presidency, *Leadership and Ambiguity* (no. 141). The models of higher education organization and decision making described by Cohen and March—''organized anarchy'' and ''the garbage-can model of decision making''—brought shocks of recognition and amusement from many experienced observers of higher education. The book's essential view of the college presidency was one of impotence, with larger social forces influencing the institution and college presidents playing largely ceremonial roles.

Today, the view of academic leadership and the college presidency is again undergoing change. ''Lives'' of entrepreneurial presidents are once more in vogue. Ironically, one of the influential current practitioners and writers on leadership in higher education, President Richard Cyert of Carnegie-Mellon, was a colleague and coauthor with James March of an early (1963) book on organizations. This essay reviews the classical and emerging trends in the literature of leadership and analyzes the particular research on leadership in higher education.

Overview of the Literature and Framework for Analysis

Traditionally, a review of the literature begins with a definition of the core concept. But in the field of leadership, definitions tend to vary depending upon the orientation or purpose of the author. Common to the majority of writings in the field are three assumptions: (1) leadership is a group phenomenon, involving the interaction of two or more persons; (2) the leader is a group member who can be distinguished from other group members (followers or subordinates); and (3) leadership is a process whereby intentional influence is exerted by leaders over followers (Yukl, 1981).

Five well-known models will be utilized as the defining framework for this review of theories of leadership and administrative style: (1) power-influence models of leadership; (2) trait models; (3) behavior models; (4) situational models; and (5) transformational models, a recent form that has aroused great interest.

Power-Influence Models. Within this body of literature the terms *influence, power,* and *authority* are used in particular ways (Yukl, 1981). *Influence* is the more generic term, defined as the effect of one party on the behavior of another party. *Power* is the potential of an agent to influence the behavior of a specified target person in the direction desired by the agent. *Authority* is the agent's right to exert influence; in organizations, authority most typically relates to the agent's position in the organizational hierarchy. But since position does not always equate with influence, what is the basis for power?

French and Raven's (no. 447) typology of power has been frequently cited. They define five bases of power: (1) reward power, in which the leader shapes and controls behavior through reward dispersal; (2) coercive power, in which control is accomplished through use of sanctions or punishments; (3) legitimate power, in which acquired position gives the leader the right to make requests of followers; (4) expert power, in which the leader has specialized knowledge and skills exceeding those of followers; and (5) referent power, in which the leader, by virtue of personal attributes, inspires followers to seek approval and emulate his or her behavior. A substantial number of studies utilizing French and Raven's model have been conducted in higher education as well as corporate settings (Bachman, no. 446; Kanter, no. 448; Pfeffer, no. 449; and Yukl, 1981).

A major weakness of the power-influence model is its attention to the personal or referent power of the leader. Consistent research evidence has suggested that influence based upon knowledge and expertise is the more critical base, particularly in higher education (Bachman, no. 446). However, the research on leadership has ignored the role of expertise until recently. Similarly, by focusing on the nature of influence, these studies have ignored the process by which influence is managed.

Trait Models. Early research on leadership in the United States focused on identifying physical characteristics, personality traits, and abilities of "natural leaders." It was misleading because it neglected situational determinants of leadership success (Yukl, 1981). More recent research, utilizing an "assessment center" approach, has suggested that certain patterns of traits and skills can be predictive of managerial advancement and success. These studies have reawakened interest in the trait approach. The effective administrator is said to display proficiency in human relations skills, conceptual skills, and technical skills (Katz, no. 450). It is worth noting that a carefully controlled study in the academically related environment of a research and development organization identified scientific or technical expertise as the best predictor of success in management (Rosen, Billings, and Turney, no. 453). Technical expertise, as Katz suggests, is particularly important in periods of rapid change, when strategic decisions become more critical.

Corporate-based research provides useful insights into leadership in higher education. For example, McClelland (no. 451) has suggested that managers with a dominant need for achievement attempt to do everything themselves, are reluctant to delegate, and fail to develop a sense of responsibility and commitment among subordinates. Furthermore, he makes a substantial and useful distinction between a need for "personalized" power, in which individual success may be the criterion, and need for "socialized" power, which translates into building up the organization as a whole. Those with a "socialized" power concern are more apt to sacrifice themselves for the welfare of the organization.

The trait and skill model of leadership has undergone a renaissance of interest because of attempts in the corporate sector to increase the reliability and validity of management selection and training processes. Within higher education institutions there have been few equivalent research studies and no application of these ideas to leadership selection. The use of trait-related research for the design of management development—for example, simulations for training academic administrative personnel—is worthy of more careful consideration.

Behavior Models. Beginning in the 1940s a substantial and influential body of research, known as the Ohio State Leadership Studies, focused on identifying those leadership behaviors instrumental for the attainment of group and organizational goals. Two positive patterns of behavior emerged from these studies: consideration or relationship-oriented (friendliness, consultation, and openness of communication with subordinates) and structure-initiating or task-oriented (directing and clarifying subordinates' roles, problem solving, criticizing poor work). Dill's (no. 455) review of research on the behavioral model of leadership found much support for the discoveries of the Ohio State Leadership Studies, with an interesting twist emerging in department-level studies: consideration behavior seems more critical in social science and humanities departments, where there is less agreement on the nature of the field, while task-oriented behavior seems more effective in disciplines with greater intellectual coherence, such as the physical and biological sciences.

More recently, behavioral studies have been substantially influenced by the integrative work of Henry Mintzberg (no. 458). Mintzberg sought to understand what managers actually do, and consequently he carried out his studies in the field employing observational techniques. A related national survey of college presidents by Cohen and March (no. 141) established how and with whom these CEOs interacted. Both studies found administrators leading lives at a busy pace, putting in long weeks (sixty or more hours), and functioning in a reactive fashion, utilizing primarily verbal skills. College presidents spend a majority of time with subordinates, while corporate executives interact most with persons outside the organization.

The power and trait models of leadership dominated the early tradition in American studies of leadership in the same way that biographies of great leaders dominated classical thought on leadership. The question that most interests contemporary authors, however, is not why leaders have influence, but how they accomplish results. The behavioral model of research has provided substantial insight into the process of managerial work and those behaviors that appear to be influential. However, the research has raised two critical questions: What is the process by which the activities *other* than relating to subordinates are carried out? and What are the situational constraints that influence the success of a leader's relationships with subordinates?

Situational Models. A number of leadership models address the aspects of a situation that determine the success of particular traits, skills, and behaviors. The models of Fiedler (no. 459) and Hersey and Blanchard (no. 461), like the trait and behavioral models that influenced them, equate leadership with the supervision and management of subordinates. The Vroom-Yetton (no. 465) model departs from this orientation and focuses on the decision-making component of leadership. All three of these models assume that the behavior selected by the leader is dependent upon situational circumstances detailed in the models.

While these representative situational models provide useful contingencies and better insights into the processes required for leadership, the complexity of the models raises additional issues. If, as Mintzberg and others argue, management is a hectic, fragmented, action-oriented activity, when will managers have the time or opportunity to reflect upon and decide when to apply these situational factors? Secondly, if relating to one's subordinates is only a part of the activity of managerial leadership, why do the situational models (with the exception of Vroom and Yetton's) so consistently focus on relationships with subordinates?

Transformational Models. While the transformational model of leadership incorporates issues of power, traits of leadership, and behavioral insights, it is most distinctive in its level of analysis. Rather than focusing on psychological or relational issues, it focuses on leadership as the reordering of values through collective action. The most striking thing about this view of leadership is its concentration on the power of ideas, the importance of language and meaning, and the role of symbolic activities.

The concept of transformational leadership has been attributed to Burns (no. 468), who distinguishes among administration, management, and leadership. Characteristics important to the concept are creation of a vision, mobilization of necessary commitment, and institutionalization of change. An earlier writer on leadership, Selznick (no. 473), also recognized the relationship between leadership and institution building. Selznick stressed the importance of investing a vision in the symbolic life of an organization—in its ceremonies, institutional events, and rituals—as a means of communicating the new values in a form that provides meaning and inspiration to subordinates. Bass (no. 466) has clarified the traits and behaviors of transformational leaders. They take a strongly developmental orientation toward their subordinates. They rely on charisma as a basis for power, particularly as shown through determination, self-confidence, and a strong sense of personal integrity. Finally, transformational leadership is intellectually stimulating in that the leader provides to followers a means of comprehending and understanding current problems and ways that they might be solved, thus empowering followers through the vision. Critical to this intellectual stimulation, in Bass's view, is technical expertise. As General George Patton once replied, on being accused of making snap decisions:

> I've been studying the art of war for forty-odd years. . . .
> [A] surgeon who decides in the course of an operation

to change its objective is not making a snap decision
but one based on knowledge, experience, and training.
So am I [Bass, p. 38].

The research on transformational leaders has thus re-
turned us to the earliest forms of leadership research: biographies
and analyses of great leaders. There are a number of effective
studies of transformational leaders in higher education, including
Clark's (no. 9) path-breaking study of distinctive liberal arts
colleges, which initiated the current interest in organizational
culture; Chaffee's (no. 173) valuable case studies of "interpretive
strategy"; and Cameron and Ulrich's (no. 469) synthesis of
management techniques appropriate to the role of transformational leadership.

The transformational model of leadership helps to expand the concept of leadership to better fit the variety of roles
performed by high-level managers. It also provides a basis for
comprehending the "irrational" aspects of organizational leadership, which can lead to outstanding performance. Unlike the
case with other models, substantive work on understanding the
"how" of this leadership model has already begun. The model,
however, raises serious questions as to whether leadership of
this power and quality is learned or simply discovered.

Commentary on the Literature

Given the classical and continuing debate between the
"great man" and contextual models of institutional change, what
can one conclude? Do leaders make a difference in higher education? The state of leadership research in higher education offers several insights.

While substantial attention has been given to situational
factors affecting a leader's influence on subordinates, there has
been little analysis of external environmental factors that may
affect the role of leaders. The United States, for example, is the
only developed country in the world that does not have govern-
mentally controlled higher education; in essence, higher education in the United States is a free market economy, with public

and private institutions competing with each other for students, faculty, resources, and prestige. From World War II until approximately 1977, demographic growth and economic support for higher education were at all-time high levels. Transformational leadership during such a period was irrelevant. For the rest of this century, however, the competition among institutions of higher education obviously will be keen, and those with creative, entrepreneurial leadership will have a definite advantage (Cameron and Ulrich, no. 469). Cohen and March (no. 141) had argued in a little-observed footnote that the seemingly irrational "garbage can" model of decision making would be modified to become more predictable as organizational slack (that is, excess resources) was reduced. In short, given the unique competitive structure of American higher education, the last twenty-five years have been the historical anomaly in institutional leadership; the future period is likely to be much more akin to past eras, when leadership was of significant importance.

Second, the vast majority of leadership studies have consciously or unconsciously adopted a psychological perspective, which equates interpersonal relationships between supervisors and subordinates with leadership. The work of Mintzberg, Clark, and Chaffee (nos. 458, 9, and 173) confirms the power of ceremonies, symbolism, and ideas to energize individuals to an uncommon commitment. How transformational leaders act—the processes by which they influence an institution—is still not well known and offers substantial opportunity for study.

Third, a striking and neglected discovery of the research on leadership is the consistent importance of technical expertise. Given that potential leaders in higher education are among the most highly trained individuals in the field, what is the exact relationship between technical expertise and leadership performance? How are expertise and conceptual ability brought to bear on strategic decisions? Does the importance of technical expertise differ in different institutions? These are questions of fundamental and unique importance to leadership selection and success in higher education; they deserve careful study.

Finally, what are the implications for practice? Much of the literature and research on leadership suggests that leadership "style" can be donned like a new set of clothes, dependent only upon the situation or fashion. But the recent emphasis on transformational leadership suggests that leaders who matter have significant integrity, deeply held values, and substantial experience and expertise. Their leadership is not style but substance. Leadership skill of this caliber is unlikely to be gained through special training. But certain critical skills, such as skill in interpersonal relations and knowledge of effective modes of participation in decision making, can be developed through training (see, for example, Vroom and Yetton, no. 465).

The most useful resource for practice would be the development of a specially designed assessment center or workshop for college administrators, modeled on those developed by AT&T and other corporations. The methods and processes for such simulations are well developed. Given the number of faculty members each year who take off unprepared on a solo flight of administration, the existence of a "preflight simulator" could save many a life and career.

References

Clough, A. H. (ed.). *Plutarch's Lives.* London: J. M. Dent, 1910.
Cyert, R. M., and March, J. G. *A Behavioral Theory of the Firm.* Englewood Cliffs, N J.: Prentice Hall, 1963.
Tolstoy, L. *War and Peace.* New York: Simon & Schuster, 1958.
Yukl, A. *Leadership in Organizations.* Englewood Cliffs, N.J.: Prentice-Hall, 1981.

Power-Influence Models

446 Bachman, Jerald G. "Faculty Satisfaction and the Dean's Influence: An Organizational Study of Twelve Liberal Arts Colleges." *Journal of Applied Psychology,* 1968, *52,* 55–61.

Based on French and Raven's model of five power bases, this study has important implications for any college or university leader. Use of expert and referent power by deans was found to be significantly and positively associated with job satisfaction but had no effect on faculty productivity. It is equally important to note that the three remaining power bases—reward, legitimate, and coercive—were significantly associated with job satisfaction as well, but in a negative direction.

★447 French, John R. P., Jr., and Raven, Bertram. "The Bases of Social Power." In Dorwin Cartwright and Alvin Zander (eds.), *Group Dynamics: Research and Theory.* (3rd ed.) New York: Harper & Row, 1968. Pages 607–623.

French and Raven have had the greatest impact on the study of power; virtually all research studies, articles, and books on this topic make reference to their work. It has been demonstrated that knowledge of the five power bases they cite is important because each has a variable effect: for example, referent power may result in a decrease in the need for direct contact as the subordinate becomes more like the leader, while coercive power may result in need for more contact as ever more stringent coercive methods become necessary. The leader who understands the distinctions among the five types may make the most effective use of power, guided by the relevant situation or set of circumstances.

448 Kanter, Rosabeth M. *The Change Masters: Innovation for Productivity in the American Corporation.* New York: Simon & Schuster, 1983. 393 pages.

It is paradoxical that Kanter has dealt solely with the corporate sector, as this book has a strong academic bent, and its findings and implications are as important for the public sector as for the private. Power should be used in order to effect change and innovation, Kanter states. Effective institutions have a person in the driver's seat. Support for that person has been gained through building and using teams. The driver's power has been derived from three primary sources: information, resources, and support. Kanter describes active listening as an essential skill, since she sees information as the most important tool of power.

449 Pfeffer, Jeffrey. *Power in Organizations*. Marshfield, Mass.: Pitman, 1981. 370 pages.

Pfeffer stresses that an understanding of power can enhance an individual's effectiveness. An important thesis of this book is that leaders of universities and other public/not-for-profit organizations have an even greater need for understanding the use of power than do leaders in the private sector because public organizations have more diverse and often conflicting goals. Power can be used to affect interdependence of units and people, achievement of heterogeneous goals, and the relative importance of issues or resources, especially when scarcity is present. Pfeffer points out gaps in the literature and in the understanding of power, with the hope of stimulating further research and analysis.

Trait Models

★450 Katz, Robert L. "Skills of an Effective Administrator." *Harvard Business Review*, 1974, *52*, 90–102.

Katz's typology of three managerial skills (technical, human, and conceptual) has provided an influential model within the trait approach. Technical skill refers to the professional expertise or skill the individual practices prior to becoming a manager. This kind of skill may be considered most important at lower levels. In a university setting, it would be represented by teaching and research in an academic discipline. Human relations skills, important at every level, are defined as interpersonal skills applied when a manager relates to superiors, peers, and subordinates. Conceptual skills, suggested as innate, are most important at upper levels. They are shown in the ability to think strategically through coordination and integration of the organization's diverse activities.

★451 McClelland, David C. *Power: The Inner Experience*. New York: Irvington, 1975. 412 pages.

McClelland's research on managerial motivation suggests that needs for achievement, power, and affiliation play a role in

leadership effectiveness. Effective use of power requires assertiveness and self-confidence. It may be most influential in large
organizations. In making his distinction between personalized
and social power, McClelland argues that those with socialized
power are more apt to sacrifice for the welfare of the organization. A high need for affiliation may decrease administrative
effectiveness, however. McClelland's work has been little applied
in higher education, but it raises important questions for that
sphere: If the need for achievement is dominant among professors, what is the effect of that need on commitment, satisfaction,
and productivity when a professor becomes an administrator?
Can a person dominated by that need learn to be a leader?

452 Ringle, Philip M., and Savickas, Mark L. "Administrative Leadership: Planning and Time Perspective."
Journal of Higher Education, 1983, *54* (6), 649–661.

The authors have developed a three-factor model conceptualizing individual and institutional "subjective time" (defined as
the personal experience of time, as opposed to the objective experience—as with clocks, calendars, histories, and so on), based
on a literature review and factor analysis of temporal experience.
They suggest that academic administrative leaders who subjec-
tively integrate past, present, and future create an atmosphere
of optimism, continuity, and accomplishment that facilitates pro-
activity. In contrast, the individual and institution focused in
the past are change resistant; those focused in the present are
crisis management oriented; and those focused in the future lack
purpose and stability. This paper makes a worthwhile contribution in recommending an objective assessment of priorities as
represented by the content of committee agendas, calendars,
and so forth.

453 Rosen, Ned, Billings, Robert, and Turney, John. "The
Emergence and Allocation of Leadership Resources over
Time in a Technical Organization." *Academy of Manage-
ment Journal,* 1976, *19,* 165–183.

In an empirical study conducted in a research and development
organization, the authors evaluated a group of research scien-

tists on demonstrated technical expertise and on human relations skills. In following the development of these scientists over time, they discovered that those with high levels of skill in both areas remained in management longer and received higher ratings on performance than those with lesser skills. Technical expertise was a stronger predictor of management effectiveness than human relations skills, but both were significantly influential. The close parallel between the environment in which this study was conducted and that of academe makes these results very significant for leadership in higher education.

Behavior Models

★454 Cohen, Michael D., and March, James G. *Leadership and Ambiguity.* (2nd ed.) Boston: Harvard Business School Press, 1986. 290 pages.

For a full description of this work, please see entry no. 141.

455 Dill, David D. "The Nature of Administrative Behavior in Higher Education." *Educational Administration Quarterly,* 1984, *20* (3), 69–99.

This article presents a ten-year (1973–1983) review of the literature on the behavioral model of leadership. Research during this period indicated that unlike other CEOs, college and university presidents spend their largest single block of time in contact with direct subordinates, such as members of the president's staff, and with academic and nonacademic administrators. Staffing problems and subordinate ineffectiveness appeared to be the major constraints on presidential productivity.

456 Glueck, William F., and Thorp, Cary D. "The Role of the Academic Administrator in Research Professors' Satisfaction and Productivity." *Educational Administration Quarterly,* 1974, *10,* 72–90.

In this empirical study conducted in research-oriented departments of a large state university, the authors found that a leadership style emphasizing ethical behavior, helpfulness in research projects, accurate and complete communication, frequency of communication, and a willingness to represent the interests of staff was positively associated with faculty satisfaction. There was some evidence that keeping track of research activities in progress through discussion rather than formal report was positively associated also. Attempts to restrict selection of projects by researchers were negatively associated with satisfaction. When given a choice of leadership roles, faculty members consistently preferred to have the leader be a "resource person/coordinator." They saw the ideal administrator as a facilitator, someone who smoothed out problems and sought to provide necessary resources.

457 Lewis, Darrell R., and Dahl, Tor. "Time Management in Higher Education Administration: A Case Study." *Higher Education,* 1976, *5,* 49–66.

This study deals predominantly with department heads rather than deans or presidents. It finds that the greatest source of stress in such people is fulfillment of administrative functions—but the best stress reducer is voluntarily spending more time on administration. This seemingly paradoxical situation occurs because department heads appear to resist allocating sufficient time to administrative demands, perhaps due to denial or lack of full comprehension of their obligations. Those who continue to engage in professional activities (teaching and research) for at least 50 percent of their time experience the greatest work enjoyment.

★458 Mintzberg, Henry. *The Nature of Managerial Work.* New York: Harper & Row, 1973. 298 pages.

Behavioral studies of leadership have been substantially influenced by the path-breaking work of Henry Mintzberg. By employing observational techniques, Mintzberg discovered certain constancies to managerial work and developed generic classifications for general management characteristics and roles. He found that managers engage at an unrelenting pace in work characterized as varied and fragmented; their work is verbal and active rather than reflective. Their varied roles include influencing subordinates, acting as a figurehead (symbolic and ceremonial activities), carrying out liaison activities (establishing and maintaining a network of relationships with individuals outside the organization), serving as a spokesperson (transmitting information and value statements to outsiders and subordinates), monitoring (seeking information and analyzing it for problems and opportunities), and performing entrepreneurial activities (designing and initiating controlled change within the organization). The patterns of behavior that appeared as a result of Mintzberg's codification of his observations are at variance with models of administrative behavior that emphasize the rational process of planning, organizing, and controlling.

Situational Models

★459 Fiedler, Fred E. *A Theory of Leadership Effectiveness*. New York: McGraw-Hill, 1976. 291 pages.

Fiedler's model and research suggest that leaders may be separated into those who value task success and those who value interpersonal success (compare the Ohio State Leadership Studies variables; see entry no. 461). The relative success of these leader values is contingent upon a complex variable termed "situational control," which is defined as the extent to which a situation provides the leader with influence over a subordinate's performance. Although this model has been subjected to many empirical tests, the results remain inconclusive. The model is dauntingly complex, at least from a managerial point of view.

460 Groner, Norman E. "Leadership Situations in Academic Departments: Relations Among Measures of Situational Favorableness and Control." *Research in Higher Education*, 1978, *8*, 125–145.

Groner used Fiedler's Group Atmosphere Scale to measure the quality of leader-member relations in community colleges and university settings. The quality of department head–faculty member relations was positively associated with feelings of control over the destiny of the department and with the extent to which the department reflected Fiedler's paradigm (high: physics; low: sociology). Groner found a strong negative relationship between the heterogeneity of faculty research interests and department head–faculty member relationships.

*461 Hersey, Paul, and Blanchard, Kenneth H. *Management of Organizational Behavior: Utilizing Human Resources.* Englewood Cliffs, N.J.: Prentice-Hall, 1982. 312 pages.

Hersey and Blanchard have developed a model directly dependent upon the key variables of the Ohio State Leadership Studies. It assumes that both relationship-oriented and task-oriented behaviors are relevant to supervising subordinates. The relevance and amount of each behavior are dependent upon the subordinate's "maturity"; immature subordinates receive more task-oriented behavior and less relationship-oriented behavior, while more mature subordinates receive the reverse. Subordinate maturity is defined with regard to the task that the subordinate is to perform. A "high-maturity" subordinate has the ability to do a particular task and a high level of self-confidence about performing it. A low-maturity subordinate lacks both. This model is relatively simple and is intuitively appealing, especially to those, like many faculty members, who are asked to assume supervisory positions with little prior experience. The situational aspects of the model have not been tested in higher education. Indeed, the model has received no direct study; it is based on reasoning rather than research or theory. It is used heavily in training and development activities, however. It has the virtues of simplicity, clarity, and consistency with the earlier research of the Ohio State Leadership Studies.

462 McCorkle, Chester O., Jr., and Archibald, Sandra Orr. *Management and Leadership in Higher Education: Applying Modern Techniques of Planning, Resource Management, and Evaluation.* San Francisco: Jossey-Bass, 1982. 229 pages.

McCorkle and Archibald discuss the role of the university in an evolving environment. Maintaining that institutions of higher education must serve the supporting society, they argue that no department, college, or university has a mandate to exist in the present or future. Planning, resource allocation, and evaluation—the primary and ultimate responsibilities of administrators—must involve all institutional segments, and this universal inclusion may necessitate changes in leadership attitude as well as style. Effective leaders in a changing world will emphasize creativity over constraint, continuity over crisis, initiative over conformity, and achievement over protocol. McCorkle and Archibald's book is based on actual occurrences in the University of California system. They also analyzed theory and applicability on ten campuses, public and private, outside California. They offer sound suggestions with broad applicability.

463 Taylor, Alton L. "Decision-Process Behaviors of Academic Managers." *Research in Higher Education,* 1982, *16,* 156–173.

In a study of decision making in higher education, based on the Vroom-Yetton model (no. 465), Taylor found that administrators in community colleges, four-year colleges, and a university tended to ignore situation-specific factors in deciding how to reach a decision. While they selected a participatory process the majority of the time, their rationale appeared largely ideological rather than aimed at increasing effectiveness. Similarly, autocratic styles were chosen without regard to obvious situational constraints.

464 Vroom, Victor H "Leaders and Leadership in Academe." *Review of Higher Education,* 1983, *6,* 367–386.

Vroom has systematically examined, in terms of relevance to higher education, theories such as those of Fiedler (no. 459), Hersey and Blanchard (no. 461), and Vroom and Yetton (no. 465). Each was found to lack applicability to this field, due to peculiarities of institutions of higher education: degree of freedom of upward communication and relative lack of downward control; extreme diversity of specialization, even within a department; and unprecedented individual freedom to control and

direct the type and amount of work performed. Vroom notes
that the external function—the role of mediator between the institution and the external environment—is an important part
of leadership that has been overlooked in the research literature.
He also urges leaders and students of leadership to examine more
closely the importance of transforming values as a sense of institutional purpose created by leaders.

★465 Vroom, Victor H., and Yetton, Philip. *Leadership and
Decision Making.* Pittsburgh, Pa.: University of Pittsburgh
Press, 1973. 220 pages.

The Vroom-Yetton model of leadership has received consistent
support in validation studies. This model analyzes the decision-
making component of leadership to identify the situational factors that determine the type of problem solving a leader should
employ. The critical factors appear to be "decision acceptance"
(the extent to which subordinate compliance with the decision
is critical to successful implementation) and "decision quality"
(the objective aspects of a decision that can affect group performance). Knowledge of this approach could be extremely valuable
to university administrators, since the culture of higher education has traditionally been one of collegiality and participation.

Transformational Models

466 Bass, Bernard M. "Leadership: Good, Better, Best."
Organizational Dynamics, 1985, *13,* 16–40.

Bass describes leadership traits and characteristics labeled transformational as emerging in response to a need for radical changes
in the values of individuals and organizations. Therefore, the
transformational leader motivates behavior beyond that expected, raises the consciousness level of followers to transcend
self-interest, sets high standards, and encourages autonomy and
self-development. These goals were accomplished by leaders who
exhibited charisma, individualized consideration, and intellectual stimulation. Charisma separates leaders from managers
through infusion of loyalty, respect, enthusiasm, and a unique

sense of determining priorities and mission. Individualized consideration involves delegating challenging work and increasing responsibility. Given the nature of change, intellectual stimulation may be the most crucial characteristic of high-performing systems. Innovative, creative, proactive thinking, at times paradoxical and Janusian, is the hallmark of the transformational leader.

467 Bennis, Warren. "Transformative Power and Leadership." In Thomas J. Sergiovanni and John E. Corbally (eds.), *Leadership and Organizational Culture: New Perspectives on Administrative Theory and Practice.* Urbana: University of Illinois Press, 1984. Pages 64–71.

A former university president (University of Cincinnati) and provost (SUNY/Buffalo), Bennis calls for leadership that reaches the souls of others by raising levels of consciousness, building meaning, and inspiring intent. The translation of intent into reality is defined as the basis of leadership. To achieve this translation, the leader must exhibit vision through the capacity to create and communicate and must exhibit persistence, consistency, and focus through molding the support of multiple constituencies. While Bennis's chapter does not specifically address higher education, he is regarded as a leader in the field, and his work could have wide application.

★468 Burns, James M. *Leadership.* New York: Harper & Row, 1978. 462 pages.

Because of this volume, Burns is the acknowledged father of the concept of transformational leadership. He cites examples of leadership throughout history, showing how such leaders as Lincoln, Churchill, Mao Zedong, and Gandhi engaged, mobilized, altered, and elevated the motives, aspirations, goals, and values of their followers. Burns's monumental work provides leaders and students of leadership with a major philosophical concept, defined through his masterful synthesis of the accomplishments of leaders who effected changes in history that transcended their own national boundaries and culture.

469 Cameron, Kim S., and Ulrich, David O. "Transformational Leadership in Colleges and Universities. In John C. Smart (ed.), *Higher Education: Handbook of Theory and Research.* Vol. 2. New York: Agathon, 1986. Pages 1–42.

Cameron and Ulrich argue that since universities are in the business of providing services to various constituencies, many of which are undergoing radical (transformational) change, universities themselves require a metamorphosis in order to survive. The authors dramatically highlight areas of American business and culture that are currently experiencing change in an effort to generate rethinking among leaders in higher education. They then propose a detailed five-step agenda for transformational leadership: create readiness, overcome resistance, articulate a vision, generate commitment, and institutionalize implementation. This agenda concretizes more theoretical works, such as those of Burns (no. 468) and Selznick (no. 473).

470 Chaffee, Ellen E. "Successful Strategic Management in Small Private Colleges." *Journal of Higher Education,* 1984, *55,* 212–241.

For a complete description of this work, please see entry no. 173.

★471 Clark, Burton R. *The Distinctive College: Antioch, Reed and Swarthmore.* Chicago: Aldine, 1970. 271 pages.

For a complete description of this work, please see entry no. 9.

472 Keller, George. *Academic Strategy: The Management Revolution in American Higher Education.* Baltimore, Md.: Johns Hopkins University Press, 1983. 177 pages.

For a full description of this work, please see entry no. 163.

473 Selznick, Philip. *Leadership in Administration: A Sociological Interpretation.* New York: Harper & Row, 1957. 162 pages.

Selznick's treatise should enjoy renewed attention in the literature and study of transformational leadership. He speaks of responsible creative leadership with concern for change and reconstruction exercised by strategic and tactical planning. Selznick defines leadership in terms of values and distinctive competencies: their building, developing, infusing, and protecting. The leader, he says, creates a social organism within an organization that is capable of fulfilling its values and competencies with a blend of commitment, understanding, and determination.

19

Charles F. Fisher

༺༺༺༺༺༺༺༺༺༺༺༺༺༺

Leadership Selection, Evaluation, and Development

Do presidential and other senior administrator search committees select a "leader" or a "manager"? Is there a difference? And where does the "administrator" come in? Are all three, or should they be, one and the same? Is it possible to find in one individual all of the qualifications desirable for leader, manager, *and* administrator? If so, how and where? In what ways do such people acquire their skills, abilities, and other attributes? And once in their posts, how effectively do they perform? How do we know? How do they maintain their effectiveness, keep informed, update their skills, sustain their motivation, and continue to grow, both professionally and personally?

Research, literature, and various organizations have begun to address these questions in recent years. This chapter will review some of the more relevant publications and briefly explore the major issues and deliberations. Administrator search and selection, performance evaluation, and professional development often are treated as discrete processes, but they are intrinsically related. All deal with the task and opportunity of finding, nourishing, and retaining the best executive talent—a task very crucial, as implied throughout this volume, to the effective governance, management, and leadership of the academy today. Underlying the overall concern, as Peterson and Mets point out in this book's introductory chapter, are the forces of

412

increasing diversity and complexity, growing in parallel with the cry for improved academic quality and the very finest leadership for American higher education.

Development of the Literature

In both practice and literature, education has lagged behind the corporate and military arenas in addressing the improvement of its leadership. Most of the relevant publications have appeared in the past two decades, reflecting the call for better management that paralleled the growth and increasing sophistication of postsecondary education during that time. The need for professional development was the first to be recognized, with programs that evolved substantially during the 1960s and 1970s and a literature that grew apace. Some major books and several dozen articles, many anecdotal, spoke to emerging needs and various approaches to in-service development through both internal and external programs and opportunities. The message was heard, and an abundance of such programs continues in the 1980s, even though the volume of literature has declined considerably.

Somewhat ironically, the interest in evaluating administrative performance arose several years after the professional development movement was well under way. The practice in any formal sense was rare and the literature sparse in this area until the mid to late 1970s. Prompted by the faculty evaluation movement and both internal and external pressures for improved management and greater accountability, however, the published works grew to over two dozen books and articles by the turn of the decade. Many presented the rationale and some offered guidelines for the formal evaluation of administrative leaders.

Curiously, higher education's attention to leadership search and selection has been an even more recent phenomenon, and literature on the subject thus has been relatively scarce. Most of that written during the 1970s focused on requirements for affirmative action and equal employment opportunity. While writings on "leadership" in general seemed to proliferate, and a few documents appeared on administrative search procedures, only in the 1980s did the literature begin articulating institutional leadership needs and discussing the means for finding the best and most appropriate candidates.

But if higher education has been a "Johnny-come-lately" in finding, assessing, and developing its leaders, it is barely at the threshold of addressing the need to sustain and renew those leaders. Most of the limited existing research and literature on this subject speaks to society in general, and among the paucity of publications looking at the academy, any focus on the career and personal revitalization of the college and university administrator is rare indeed.

Framework and Overview

Despite the historical evolution of interest in these topics, their interrelationships, and the occasional overlap of coverage in the literature, a logical review might proceed in sequence of actual application—that is, defining and finding leadership and then assessing, developing, and revitalizing leaders. This section will attempt to address some of the current thinking in the categories of leadership search and selection, evaluation, development, and renewal. Following will be a brief commentary on the state of the literature as an introduction to the annotated bibliography of principal publications in the field.

The Call for Leadership. Administrators, according to Kauffman (nos. 522 and 544), Kerr (no. 529), Nason (no. 524), Riesman and McLaughlin (no. 525), and others, have become one of the most significant investments academic institutions ever make. No longer simply scholars and part-time caretakers, today's administrators are full-time professionals overseeing sophisticated organizations that demand ever-greater management and leadership competencies. Many academic administrators do now come to their posts with better training and experience, but they still must be able to keep abreast of new developments, adapt to changing times, and hone their skills and abilities to provide the effective leadership that their institutions need.

It is fitting to try to understand what leadership is, or should be, so that we can identify potential leaders, help prepare them for major responsibility, and then assist them in sustaining their growth and that of their institutions. Bennis and Nanus (no. 475) report that there are more than 350 definitions of leadership, and descriptors abound in the literature—an art and a science, perspective, reason, intuition, vision, creativity, initiative, resourcefulness, charisma, and so on. Kerr (1984) defines a leader as someone who sets new goals or higher standards and then mobilizes efforts to achieve those goals, and Gardner (1986) suggests that a leader persuades by example in accord with shared purposes. *Management,* the literature suggests, is directing and supervising resources to reach organizational goals. While leaders thus are said to conceive and inspire and managers to follow through with implementation, the distinction often is blurred in both semantics and reality. The college administrator is certainly a blend of both.

But when is an administrator an *effective* leader and manager? Gilley, Fulmer, and Reithlingshoefer (no. 477) suggest that this occurs when a leader with a particular combination of experience, skills, and other attributes is matched with an institution that needs precisely those unique qualifications. Their findings tend to reinforce the "right person in the right place at the right time" theory and the importance of receptive and conducive environmental conditions. While our attempts to define and find leadership appear to focus on readily observed qualities and characteristics rather than on their often nebulous origins, most experts nonetheless agree that leadership must be cultivated, further developed from time to time, and continuously nourished.

Leadership Search and Selection. Higher education has no greater challenge—or opportunity—than the identification and selection of the most capable leaders for its institutions. As Kerr (no. 529), Nason (no. 523), and others admonish, the quality of the president that a board is able to attract and retain is at once its greatest responsibility and its ultimate test. Similarly, the measure of that president's leadership is largely in the quality and performance of his or her administrative team.

Most executive searches seek candidates with a whole litany of proven management skills, leadership abilities, and other desirable characteristics. However, as Kauffman (nos. 522 and 544) and other experts observe, institutions often launch top-level searches before determining what specific kind of leadership they really need at that point. And so frequently, as Riesman and McLaughlin (no. 525) caution, with the abundance of willing candidates these days, the process becomes one of elimination rather than of a genuine needs-based search to develop a pool of the best-qualified candidates. Indeed, the American Council on Education and the Association of Governing Boards (no. 474) suggest supplementing the traditional publicity and nomination letters with soliciting networks of professional colleagues for names of particularly suitable individuals who might not otherwise come to the search committee's attention.

Experts agree that letters of nomination or reference are less meaningful and helpful than telephone background checks on the serious candidates later in the process to verify their qualifications and suitability. The entire search process is obviously a delicate one because it deals with the lives of people and institutions. One of the most sensitive aspects is that of maintaining confidentiality, which is increasingly fragile during the final stages. Many authors emphasize this (mindful nonetheless of the "sunshine laws"), lest the total effort result, as Riesman and McLaughlin poignantly describe it, in a "search-and-destroy mission."

But a leak or other breach of security is only one of many risks, for any error in procedure or judgment could bring trouble. Horror stories abound about unsuccessful searches that have had to be reopened or even started over. Despite good intentions, many search committees find themselves hampered and frustrated by lack of experience, time, energy, and resources. Virtually all authors in the field are adamant that there be clear understanding and agreement on two essential considerations before any search is launched: (1) institutional needs and priorities as translated into candidate qualifications and selection criteria and (2) the process, procedures, steps, and time line of the search. Proper planning, execution, and support are as crucial as the outcome itself.

Evaluation of Administrators. Just as essential as finding the right leaders for higher education is helping to develop, motivate, and nourish them. This in turn requires some criteria-based means of assessing performance to identify developmental needs and interests. The desire for self-improvement is inherent in human nature, and while its development must often be encouraged, most people nonetheless monitor, appraise, and attempt to better their performance. Valid self-assessment seldom takes place without cues and clues from others, however—even for college administrators.

Indeed, those in such leadership positions often need constructive reinforcement the most. Unfortunately, academic executives usually receive feedback inversely proportional to the seniority of their positions, even though they continue to be tacitly judged. Since evaluation of administrators in some way is inevitable, many authors urge that it be given a more structured, productive approach so that both the individual and the institution can benefit. Whereas there are many alleged purposes for evaluating administrators, Farmer (no. 489), Genova, Madoff, Chin, and Thomas (no. 492), Miller (no. 240), Munitz (no. 494), Nason (no. 523), and others suggest that the *basic* rationale for the assessment of leaders is to reinforce positive behavior while identifying areas in which individual and institutional development could improve overall effectiveness. The implication is that administrator evaluation should be part of an ongoing review of the total organization. Thus the trend during the past dozen years has been toward a more pragmatic and institutionalized process, particularly in the public sector, where it is often part of a more formalized systemwide policy.

But even if its intentions are honorable, formal evaluation for senior administrators is not universally accepted. Reservations seem based not on objections to the primary purpose of improving performance, but rather on the delicacy and possible side effects of the process. Shaw (1985) observes the difficulty of keeping reviews confidential, noting that a breach can turn constructive motives into "disaster." Fisher (1986) believes that broad-based formal appraisals can threaten a president's ability to lead by further politicizing the role and inhibiting authority, charisma, and effectiveness. He suggests using periodic CEO reports, along with a modified MBO approach, as an alternative. Finally, some contend that when boards and supervisors are properly doing their job, there is no need for a more structured or formal review of their staff.

All the experts agree that administrator evaluation should never be arbitrary or ad hoc, and many question its use even for such personnel decisions as retention, promotion, or compensation. In fact, the collective wisdom emphasizes that assessment should be formative and developmental and must be well planned, with clear, mutually agreed upon goals. There should be representative constituency input along with self-appraisals, and all information should be treated in a confidential manner.

Professional and Leadership Development. Assessment assists in recognizing improvement needs, and development helps to meet those needs within the context of individual and institutional goals. Appraisal results help to fashion individual improvement plans, ranging from informal and formal learning activities to skills, management, and leadership enhancement and other opportunities for continuing professional growth.

The notion of professional development for college administrators predates the turn of the century. University research and degree programs in academic administration developed over the years to meet the expanding need for skilled administrators, reaching their peak in the 1960s and 1970s. But the traditional route for most deans and presidents continued to be up through the academic ranks, forcing them to learn administration "on the firing line." It was for this reason that the Institute for College and University Administrators was established in 1955 to offer intensive week-long orientation seminars for new presidents. As the 1960s progressed and administration grew more complex and specialized, it became apparent that *all* administrators, whatever their training or experience, needed professional updating and sharpening of management and leadership skills. Program offerings expanded, along with the literature, through the 1970s. Some efforts were sponsored by national associations, while others came from regional groups, universities, and commercial vendors.

The basic rationale for these seminars, workshops, and institutes was the realization that, fortunately for the preservation of the administrator's precious time, it was possible to telescope relevant learning about problems, issues, and opportunities into brief, intensive minicourses. Paralleling these short-term programs were two somewhat different but equally important approaches to improving management and leadership in higher education—the administrative internship and campus-wide management development. The internship, perhaps epitomized by the American Council on Education Fellows Program, has provided aspiring administrators with the opportunity to learn on the front line under the mentorship of senior administrators. The broader organizational development programs have focused more on ongoing needs-based improvement of management and leadership throughout the academic institution.

Though the literature on professional development has declined in the 1980s, its legacy remains in the numerous opportunities for administrators today, as evidenced by the *Chronicle of Higher Education's* listings each week. The feeling continues to be that even if "leadership" cannot be taught, possibly it can be nudged just a little bit.

Career and Personal Renewal. The professional and leadership development of administrators is not a one-time occurrence but a career-long process of cultivation, nourishment, and renewal—of life and meaning and motivation. In the final analysis it is the individuals of the academy, especially its leaders, who make possible its mission of cultivating the human resource potential of others.

There are at least six major factors today that contribute to the need for career and personal renewal, according to Hodgkinson (no. 514): (1) our increasingly complex world, with accelerating change in demands and life-styles—both inside and outside the academy—creating stress as people attempt to cope and adapt; (2) the declining mobility in higher education as enrollments, resources, and budgets become ever tighter; (3) the elusive rewards of administrators who, often without academic rank or tenure, summer "windows," or sabbaticals, must rely more on intrinsic satisfactions; (4) vanishing feedback and accolades as an administrator becomes more of a veteran and is taken increasingly for granted; (5) midlife transition, or "middlescence," arising from the gradual awareness that one is not going to live forever and that there are many things yet to accomplish; and (6) susceptibility, as members of the "helping professions," to career burnout—the consequences of the foregoing along with lack of challenge, creativity, and growth-oriented activities.

Certainly administrators pause occasionally to look in the mirror and take stock of themselves, their career, and their life's journey, just as others do. But often they fall short of assessing their real values, interests, aptitudes, and goals. Seldom do they receive or encourage feedback about ways they might more fully develop their potential and effectiveness, let alone translate their needs and desires into action plans and then follow through with a program of personal, career, and leadership renewal.

A few strategies and growth-oriented activities that administrators report as helpful in their own revitalization (see Brown, no. 548) include the following: (1) getting better organized and improving management practices and use of time; (2) developing sound health, recreation, and relaxation habits and hobbies, and *taking* holidays and vacations; (3) enriching cultural life beyond work and profession through library, museums, theater, community activities, and travel; (4) enhancing professional life through seminars, writing and lecturing, association networks, study visits, and sabbatical leaves; and (6) "standing back" occasionally to see where one has been, is heading, and wants to go.

In her 1987 volume, Green (no. 502) distinguishes between leadership "development" and leadership "enhancement" by defining the latter as "broadening one's perspectives, expanding one's vision beyond a particular position or institution, and integrating information and experience to help shape the course of institutions." Perhaps this captures the essence of what we are talking about—along with its implications for the renewal of the individual in the process. Revitalization restores motivation and happiness, which can become contagious in helping to shape institutions. And while responsibility for the initiative in revitalization may rest primarily with the individual, it behooves every college and university to facilitate the process and increase opportunities for it by providing policies and resources that encourage the fruition of the institution's human resources.

Commentary on the Literature

Most of the publications addressing management and leadership improvement in higher education focus on areas and issues that administrators should know to do their job effectively. The focus of this chapter, however, is on the process and methods of finding, developing, and sustaining those administrators in their management and leadership roles. Thus only a small part of the literature on higher education mangement and leadership improvement will be listed.

Leadership Search and Selection. The literature on "leadership" has important implications for higher education, but it seldom addresses search and selection as such. By way of introduction, Bennis and Nanus (no. 475) provide some thought-provoking perceptions, and Dressel (no. 476) offers some unique insights into the academy. Gilley, Fulmer, and Reithlingshoefer's recent study (no. 477) presents significant inferences on the appropriate "match" between institutions and their leaders. Kaplowitz (no. 478) was perhaps the first to provide a solid step-by-step handbook for the academic administrative search, and Kauffman (no. 522) offered a brief but thorough analysis of considerations and guidelines for selecting presidents. It was Nason's *Presidential Search* (no. 524), however, that finally gave higher education its most comprehensive and authoritative guidebook. Libby (no. 482) focuses on the community college search, Riesman and McLaughlin (no. 525) address the helpful and sometimes essential role of professional consultants, and the recent ACE/AGB monograph (no. 474) suggests ways to improve leadership searches. Both Kauffman (no. 544) and Kerr (no. 529) effectively describe the responsibilities of finding, supporting, and reviewing the academy's leaders. Marchese's handbook for administrative searches below the presidential level (no. 483) has been published recently.

Whereas most of the publications in this area, including a dozen or so articles, concentrate on the college president, they nonetheless offer helpful insights, guidelines, and caveats that can be applied to any administrative search. Still, there is a need for further research to improve the process, particularly in identifying the specific type of leader appropriate for the individual college or university in its time of need.

Evaluation of Administrators. Of the major literature on evaluating leadership performance, Nason again gives us the most comprehensive and authoritative guide with *Presidential Assessment* (no. 523). Munitz's contributions (nos. 494 and 495) likewise focus on the CEO evaluation process, identifying the important role of outside counsel. Other published works (nos. 486, 487, 488, 489, 490, 492, 493, and 503) address the appraisal of administrators in general. They provide helpful overviews of the process and the movement, many with case studies, and note their delicacy and primary developmental purpose. Sheikholeslami (1985), in the course of designing a presidential assessment instrument, has compiled the most extensive review of administrator evaluation to date. Anticipated soon is a welcome policy statement from the American Association of University Administrators on standards and guidelines for the evaluation of presidents and other senior administrators.

Most of these publications address, directly or indirectly, all of the major considerations essential in the assessment process: rationale, goals, criteria, methods, techniques, normative references, constituency involvement and qualifications, instruments, models, frequency, use of results, formality, problems, caveats, alternatives, and the experience of others. Although some central tendencies have emerged, the complexity and diversity of higher education, along with the challenge of defining and measuring management and leadership and agreeing upon appropriate approaches and criteria, have tended to preclude choice of any one method for evaluating administrators. Higher education needs further empirical research on the effectiveness of various approaches (both formal and informal) to assessing performance, particularly with regard to their validity in identifying areas of needed professional and leadership development.

Professional and Leadership Development. The relative surge of literature on in-service development in the late 1970s both reflected and spurred the movement. Fisher (no. 498), Nordvall (no. 503), Shtogren (no. 505), and Sprunger and Bergquist (no. 506) provide excellent overviews of leadership development efforts—formal and informal, on campus and off—aimed at improving the professional competencies of administrators. Gaff, Festa, and Gaff (no. 501); Schorr (no. 504); and Wasserman (no. 507) offer extensive summaries of the resources for professional development, while Fisher and Coll-Pardo (no. 499) describe the major national program offerings at the turn of the decade. A comprehensive treatment of human resource assessment and development is rendered in Craig's major handbook (no. 265) and their application in the academy is discussed by Fortunato and Keiser (no. 277). The volume by Green (no. 502) addresses strategies and resources for the identification and development of leaders for higher education as we approach the 1990s.

While substantial progress has been made in implementing professional and leadership development opportunities, empirical evidence of the effectiveness and value of the programs continues to elude researchers, primarily because those qualities are so difficult to assess. Indeed, research and writings about such programs, like the programs themselves, still tend to slight both a needs-based approach to planning and any empirical evaluation of outcomes. Nonetheless, impressionistic and anecdotal evaluations have suggested that these activities have been helpful in meeting at least some needs, have provided formative guidelines for subsequent programs, and have inspired many institutions to invest in their own staff development efforts. They also have revealed the increasing significance of career growth and personal revitalization for the college and university administrator.

Career and Personal Renewal. Regrettably, there is a dearth of literature addressing the career and personal renewal needs of administrators; indeed, this is perhaps the most neglected area of the literature that has an impact on higher education. Hodgkinson (no. 514) was the first to call attention to this, over a decade ago. Austin and Gamson (no. 508) provide some fascinating recent insights into the academic workplace and the need for response to its increasing demands and tensions. The only other works that really discuss academic career revitalization are those of Brown (no. 548) and Furniss (no. 511). Other publications speak about personal renewal in society in general. Among them, and certainly enlightening, are Levinson's (no. 515) and Sheehy's (no. 516) analyses of the life cycles and vicissitudes of adulthood. Bolles (no. 509) and Hagberg and Leider (no. 512) offer self-help guidelines for exploring life and career options, and Hall and Associates (no. 513) address career development in both public and private organizations.

Personal renewal obviously remains an area of needed exploration for academe—not only in the research and literature, but in the actual implementation of career and personal renewal programs. Such programs can be as vital to the welfare of the academy as they are essential to the revitalization of the individual administrator.

In summary, the literature on leadership search, selection, evaluation, and development in higher education has been mostly descriptive, and while some of its analyses and guidelines have been quite helpful, many topics need to be investigated further. We need more evidence about what has worked well and what has not—and why, and why not. We need more solid empirical research to help validate the anecdotal and shed additional light on where we go from here in our continuing quest to find, nourish, and retain the very best leadership possible for American higher education.

The annotated resources that follow include most of the significant and helpful books on these subjects that have been published during the past dozen or so years. Unfortunately, space precludes mention of other important contributions, including a number of articles. Books addressing more than one area are found under the category where they are deemed most pertinent and useful.

References

Fisher, J. L. "Presidential Assessment: A Better Way." *AGB Reports*, 1986, *28* (5), 16–21.

Gardner, J. W. *Leadership Papers*. Washington, D.C.: Independent Sector, 1986.

Kerr, C. *Impressions 1984: Higher Education Once Again in Transition*. Los Angeles: University of Southern California, 1984.

Shaw, K. "Presidential Assessment: Good Intentions Gone Wrong." *AGB Reports*, 1985, *27* (6), 20–23.

Sheikholeslami, R. "Development of a Process and Instrument for Assessment of Chief Executive Officers of Institutions of Higher Education." Unpublished doctoral dissertation, Graduate School of Education, University of Pennsylvania, 1985.

Leadership Search and Selection

474 American Council on Education and Association of Governing Boards of Universities and Colleges. *Deciding Who Shall Lead: Recommendations for Improving Presidential Searches*. Washington, D.C.: American Council on Education and Association of Governing Boards of Universities and Colleges, 1986. 15 pages.

"Tap the networks of informal professional contacts" is one of the principal messages of this recent monograph on finding the most qualified leaders for higher education. Prepared by ACE's Office of Women and Center for Leadership Development and the Association of Governing Boards, the monograph presents a succinct and very useful summary of the major considerations and steps for presidential/senior administrator search committees. Among other points, the authors stress the importance of enriching the pool of candidates by including women and minorities, the value of telephone checking over reference letters, and the use of candid discussions regarding social expectations. This brief volume is a most helpful reminder and should be required reading for all search committees.

475 Bennis, Warren, and Nanus, Burt. *Leaders: The Strategies for Taking Charge*. New York: Harper & Row, 1985. 244 pages.

A former university president and a futures researcher share their perceptions of effective leadership in this work. Based on in-depth analyses of ninety top corporate, government, academic, and other leaders, their book proffers a "transformative" model in which leaders shape and inspire the motivation and goals of their followers. The authors identify and interpret four key strategies: vision, communication, positioning, and self-deployment. They suggest that leaders develop most of their own skills and teach themselves the competencies of leadership. While written primarily for the would-be leader, this book could also be useful to an organization in selecting and/or helping to develop its leadership.

476 Dressel, Paul L. *Administrative Leadership: Effective and Responsive Decision Making in Higher Education*. San Francisco: Jossey-Bass, 1981. 243 pages.

This treatise is based on the author's more than fifty years of experience in higher education. Dressel's major premise is that postsecondary education must address its social role and obligations through more responsible and professional planning and institutional development. This theme carries through ten chapters that share insightful analyses and advice on the leadership role administrators should assume in dealing with both internal and external factors. The author advocates, among other things, more clear and open communications. He devotes a cogent chapter to evaluating administrative performance. The book also includes descriptions of key resources and a glossary of administrative/management terms. Dressel's admonitions speak to the entire academic community and are a helpful and welcome guide to improving administrative stewardship.

★477 Gilley, J. Wade, Fulmer, Kenneth, and Reithlingshoefer, Sally. *Searching for Academic Excellence: Twenty Colleges and Universities on the Move and Their Leaders*. New York: Macmillan, 1986. 192 pages.

A wide range of "flourishing" academic institutions are examined in this intriguing new casebook on excellence. The book focuses on institutions' responses to adverse conditions, their innovative and successful programs, and the styles and characteristics that their leaders have in common. The authors' findings support the importance of having the "right leader at the right time." They suggest that the most successful match occurs between those presidents who are "people oriented" and persistent and whose experience equips them with perspective, vision, and an enlightened conceptual plan, and those colleges and universities that are primed to accept and support such inspired leadership. This volume is enlightening to search committees and all who are concerned with identifying and facilitating more effective academic leadership.

478 Kaplowitz, Richard A. *Selecting Academic Administrators: The Search Committee*. Washington, D.C.: American Council on Education, 1973. 30 pages.

One of the seminal guides on the subject, this pamphlet is a most thorough yet succinct presentation of the essential considerations and procedures in administrative search and selection. The author, hoping to reduce the trial-and-error nature of so many searches, clearly and logically outlines and discusses each step and renders an extremely useful flow chart of the entire process. His guidelines are adaptable to special institutional needs and resources and are applicable to administrative and faculty searches alike. Kaplowitz's pamphlet remains a popular and helpful reference today.

479 Kauffman, Joseph F. *The Selection of College and University Presidents*. Washington, D.C.: Association of American Colleges, 1974. 82 pages.

For a complete description of this work, please see entry no. 522.

★**480** Kauffman, Joseph F. *At the Pleasure of the Board: The Service of the College and University President.* Washington, D.C.: American Council on Education, 1980. 122 pages.

For a complete description of this work, please see entry no. 544.

481 Kerr, Clark. *Presidents Make a Difference: Strengthening Leadership in Colleges and Universities.* Washington, D.C.: Association of Governing Boards of Universities and Colleges, 1984. 141 pages.

For a complete description of this work, please see entry no. 529.

482 Libby, Patricia A. *In Search of a Community College President.* Annandale, Va.: Association of Community College Trustees, 1983. 34 pages.

A monograph designed primarily for the two-year college, this booklet provides a useful guide for community college trustees and search committees. The author examines different procedures, outlines relevant problems and issues, identifies models, and develops a framework for the various phases of the search process. She discusses the pros and cons of using outside consultants and the conditions for optimum search and selection. This is a good practical overview of the topic.

483 Marchese, Theodore J. *Search Committee Handbook.* Washington, D.C.: American Association for Higher Education, 1987. 64 pages.

This guide focuses on administrative search and selection below the presidential level. Written in cooperation with TIAA/ CREF and with support from the Exxon Education Foundation, it is based on a survey of the research and literature, interviews with higher education practitioners and executive search firms, and the gleanings of the search experience in allied fields.

★**484** Nason, John W. *Presidential Search: A Guide to the Process of Selecting and Appointing College and University Presidents.* (Rev. ed.) Washington, D.C.: Association of Governing Boards of Universities and Colleges, 1984. 114 pages.

For a complete description of this work, please see entry no. 524.

485 Riesman, David, and McLaughlin, Judith. "A Primer on the Use of Consultants in Presidential Recruitment." *Change,* 1984, *16* (6), 12–23.

For a complete description of this work, please see entry no. 525.

Evaluation of Administrators

486 Anderson, G. Lester. *The Evaluation of Academic Administrators: Principles, Processes, and Outcomes.* University Park, Pa.: Center for the Study of Higher Education, Pennsylvania State University, 1975. 72 pages.

One of the major early contributions to the field of administrator evaluation, this volume is still frequently cited for its excellent command of the subject, clear perception of the issues, and logical presentation. The author's model for evaluation is applicable to all key administrators, makes use of the assessment portfolio technique, and is based on a set of specified criteria, with provisions for special circumstances and attributes. While primarily a "qualitative and judgmental" approach, Anderson's work remains a substantial and useful foundation for both practitioners and students of the evaluation process.

487 Carnes, Margaret L. *Evaluating Administrative Performance.* Arlington, Va.: Educational Research Service, 1985. 144 pages.

Written about and for elementary and secondary school educators, this book nonetheless is of interest to higher education because the movement in administrator evaluation at the pre-college level parallels that in colleges and universities. The author reviews literature and research, discusses purposes and methods, describes state mandates for evaluation in school districts, and provides examples of administrator assessment plans from various jurisdictions. This is essentially a report summarizing the results of a national survey of current practices. The survey showed that 86 percent of the responding school districts had formal procedures for evaluating their administrators.

488 Dressel, Paul L. *Handbook of Academic Evaluation: Assessing Institutional Effectiveness, Student Progress, and Professional Performance for Decision Making in Higher Education.* San Francisco: Jossey-Bass, 1976. 518 pages.

This is a complete overview of the evaluation process in higher education—from formulating objectives to determining needs, means, costs, politics, and decisions and then recommending and effecting changes. The handbook's major sections cover basic considerations, educational progress, and the evaluation of programs and personnel. The last section contains an excellent chapter on administrator evaluation, in which Dressel shares discerning insights on the problems, criteria, factors, and approaches involved in what he believes is a critical component in assessing the effectiveness of the academy.

★489 Farmer, Charles H. *Administrator Evaluation: Concepts, Methods, Cases in Higher Education.* Richmond, Va.: Higher Education Leadership and Management Society, 1979. 217 pages.

This is a very helpful "how to do it" guide, based on the experience of the author and five other authorities who contribute chapters. The book presents a well-organized overview of the field of administrator assessment, addressing questions like these: Why evaluate? Who should be evaluated? What should be evaluated? How? The authors discuss issues, perspectives, approaches, and such methods as rating scales, growth contracts, ad hoc committees, and management by objectives. They share case studies and offer advice "from the trenches." Farmer emphasizes that administrator evaluation and development are integral parts of the same process. The book includes a very useful annotated bibliography. This volume is relevant to all involved or interested in the assessment of administrative performance.

490 Fisher, Charles F. *The Evaluation and Development of College and University Administrators.* ERIC/Higher Education Research Currents. Washington, D.C.: American Association for Higher Education, March and June 1977. 5 pages.

In this often-referenced two-part article the author surveys the literature and presents a succinct picture of the state of administrator evaluation and development. Perhaps for the first time, these subjects are treated as integral parts of an overall, ongoing process of institutional improvement; Fisher stresses that they are "two sides of the same coin." He summarizes the rationale, goals, criteria, approaches, and opportunities involved, admonishing that "institutions must assume the initiative in developing their own human resources and in shaping their own destinies." Emerging interest in the topic resulted in unprecedented additional printings and reproductions of this article.

491 Fortunato, Ray T., and Waddell, D. Geneva. *Personnel Administration in Higher Education: Handbook of Faculty and Staff Personnel Practices.* San Francisco: Jossey-Bass, 1981. 384 pages.

For a complete description of this work, please see entry no. 285.

492 Genova, William J., Madoff, Marjorie K., Chin, Robert, and Thomas, George B. *Mutual Benefit Evaluation of Faculty and Administrators in Higher Education.* Cambridge, Mass.: Ballinger, 1976. 222 pages.

As the title suggests, the authors strongly believe that evaluation can be a mutually positive experience. Their book is a practical guide for developing programs of faculty and administrator evaluation with an emphasis on performance improvement as the goal. They describe operating principles, summarize research, display example practices, and reproduce twenty-nine rating scales. Their eight recommended steps for presidential evaluation help to assess effectiveness in goal formation and attainment, resource acquisition, and constituency satisfaction. They discuss appropriateness in terms of institutional factors and describe how the process can be adapted for other administrators. This guide blends the principles of organization development with tested measurement techniques, providing a helpful addition to the research and literature on personnel assessment.

493 Miller, Richard I. *The Assessment of College Performance: A Handbook of Techniques and Measures for Institutional Self-Evaluation.* San Francisco: Jossey-Bass, 1979. 374 pages.

For a complete description of this work, please see entry no. 240.

494 Munitz, Barry. *Leadership in Colleges and Universities: Assessment and Search.* Oak Brook, Ill.: Johnson Associates, 1977. 53 pages.

Probably the first nationally published guidebook on presidential assessment, this step-by-step workbook is a concise "hands-on" document for chief executive officers and governing boards. The author discusses the premises, objectives, conditions, procedures, and caveats of evaluating a president and also suggests the considerable benefits to both CEO and board. He stresses the usefulness of having a qualified outside consultant serve in the crucial role of adviser and facilitator/catalyst throughout the process. Although the title also mentions "search" (and there certainly are parallel considerations), this volume actually addresses only presidential evaluation. Munitz's guidelines have contributed directly to a number of CEO assessment programs and to research and writings related to many others.

495 Munitz, Barry. "Reviewing Presidential Leadership." In Richard T. Ingram and Associates, *Handbook of College and University Trusteeship: A Practical Guide for Trustees, Chief Executives, and Other Leaders Responsible for Developing Effective Governing Boards.* San Francisco: Jossey-Bass, 1980. Pages 377–404.

Munitz summarizes and updates his and other earlier writings in this sourcebook of the Association of Governing Boards. He comments upon both the fragile nature and the advantages of the review process, presents a range of assessment models along with recent refinements, and shares some "lessons learned" and general caveats. He again advocates the use of external advisers, particularly in establishing the initial framework and plan. This chapter offers a succinct and helpful overview of leadership evaluation in higher education. (For a description of the handbook as a whole, please see entry no. 114.)

★496 Nason, John W. *Presidential Assessment: A Guide to the Periodic Review of the Performance of Chief Executives.* Washington, D.C.: Association of Governing Boards of Universities and Colleges, 1984. 109 pages.

For a complete description of this work, please see entry no. 523.

Professional and Leadership Development

497 Craig, Robert L. (ed.). *Training and Development Handbook: A Guide to Human Resource Development.* (2nd ed.) New York: McGraw-Hill, 1976. 866 pages.

For a complete description of this work, please see entry no. 265.

★498 Fisher, Charles (ed.). *Developing and Evaluating Administrative Leadership.* New Directions for Higher Education, no. 22. San Francisco: Jossey-Bass, 1978. 120 pages.

Twelve national authorities share their insights in this helpful collection of articles. Chapters cover performance appraisal through goal setting, advantages and caveats of presidential evaluation, a value-based method of assessing deans, the faculty's role, needs-based administrative development, improving departmental leadership, development through internships, accessing the pool of talented women, and administrative development in the stream of adult life tasks. The underlying theme of this volume is that administrator evaluation and development are intrinsic facets of an ongoing process intended to enhance professional and personal growth, administrative performance, and institutional effectiveness. These articles are still germane, and several have been adapted by their authors for subsequent published works.

499 Fisher, Charles F., and Coll-Pardo, Isabel (eds.). *Guide to Leadership Development Opportunities for College and University Administrators.* Washington, D.C.: American Council on Education, 1979. 197 pages.

Once a principal reference, this turned out to be the final edition of a decade-long service to higher education. The *Guide* advocated professional development and encouraged further in-service opportunities. Ironically, the very proliferation of such programs in the late 1970s, along with the increased staff load and rising publishing costs, curtailed its production. This edition offers a compact overview of professional development at the turn of the decade, including its rationale, dimensions, considerations, and program offerings. Descriptions of some 600 national, regional, and institutional seminars, institutes, workshops, internships, and conferences cover virtually every aspect of administrative concern and development, all of which remain of interest today.

500 Fortunato, Ray T., and Keiser, Dennis W. *Human Resource Development in Higher Education Institutions.* Washington, D.C.: College and University Personnel Association, 1985. 80 pages.

For a complete description of this work, please see entry no. 277.

501 Gaff, Sally S., Festa, Conrad, and Gaff, Jerry G. *Professional Development: A Guide to Resources.* New Rochelle, N.Y.: Change Magazine Press, 1978. 110 pages.

Following a chapter on major resources, this guide presents a summary of the need for professional development in ten major academic function areas—teaching, curriculum development, advising, and others—and provides both annotated and general bibliographies for each. One chapter deals with administrator development, noting that "what higher education needs more than money is good management." This document has been very useful in identifying resources for professional development in the academy. Were a similar guide available today, it would be most welcome.

502 Green, Madeleine F. (ed.). *Leaders for a New Era: Strategies for Higher Education.* New York: Macmillan, 1987. 192 pages.

Nine contributors address the identification and development of leaders for the academy. Chapters focus on the department chair, preparing presidents, developing women and minority leaders, team leadership in an information society, career development, selecting leaders, and programs and resources.

503 Nordvall, Robert C. *Evaluation and Development of College Administrators: Theories and Practices.* AAHE-ERIC Higher Education Research Report no. 6. Washington, D.C.: American Association for Higher Education, 1979. 60 pages.

Nordvall's thorough and cogent summary of this topic additionally reinforces the important relationship between administrator evaluation and development. As a lawyer and practicing administrator, he shares keen insights from an extensive review of the literature and his own observations. His treatment is equally balanced between evaluation and development, covering rationale, types and models of programs, and considerations essential in selecting and implementing them. One chapter focuses on the "Evaluation and Development of College Presidents." A significant contribution, this little volume offers a clear overview of the state of the movement.

504 Schorr, Marilyn S. (ed.). *Directory of Higher Education Programs and Faculty.* Washington, D.C.: Association for the Study of Higher Education and ERIC Clearinghouse on Higher Education, 1987. 47 pages.

This biennial sourcebook lists the ninety or so U.S. institutions that have graduate degree programs and/or centers in the study of higher education, including their directors, faculty members, and areas of teaching and research. Although the directory does not describe them, a number of these universities also offer professional continuing development programs, including seminars and workshops, that would be of interest to college and university administrators.

★505 Shtogren, John A. (ed.). *Administrative Development in Higher Education: The State of the Art.* Richmond, Va.: Higher Education Leadership and Management Society, 1978. 205 pages.

Sixteen knowledgeable authors contribute to this enlightening volume dealing with "upgrading the level of leadership of those who are running higher education." They report on administrative and organizational development programs at campuses across the country and suggest various considerations, techniques, and strategies for improving administrative performance. The book's final chapter synthesizes their writings, presents seventeen "maxims" and practical tips, and offers an integrative model guided by individual growth plans in the context of both program and overall institutional development. This book is of interest to all who are concerned with the continuing growth of their campus leaders.

506 Sprunger, Benjamin E., and Bergquist, William H. *Handbook for College Administration.* Washington, D.C.: Council for the Advancement of Small Colleges, 1978. 340 pages.

Covering virtually every aspect of college administration, this comprehensive handbook is organized around six traditional management functions—planning, organizing, staffing, leading, evaluating, and developing. Each comprises a major chapter. Subsumed sections skillfully address personnel selection, leadership theories and development, administrator evaluation, and professional, personal, and organizational development. A unique feature is the documents section of each chapter, which contains numerous examples, helpful forms, and skill-development exercises. This guide is an immensely practical and relevant document whose usefulness is not limited to the smaller institution. Its detailed table of contents and chapter references are most helpful but, regrettably, are in lieu of an index and general bibliography, which could have enhanced it even more.

507 Wasserman, Paul (ed.). *Training and Development Organizations Directory.* (3rd ed.) Detroit, Mich.: Gale Research Co., 1983. 1,198 pages.

This major reference describes almost 2,000 organizations, firms, institutions, and other agencies and the training, professional, and personal development programs they offer for business, industry, government, and the professions. Every conceivable subject and delivery method is covered, including executive development programs. The volume is cross-indexed by subject area, organization name, location, and principal individuals. The most comprehensive directory of its kind, this publication contains a wealth of opportunities for the continuing education of all, with many programs that could appeal to educational administrators.

Career and Personal Renewal

★508 Austin, Ann E., and Gamson, Zelda F. *Academic Workplace: New Demands, Heightened Tensions.* ASHE-ERIC Higher Education Research Report no. 10. Washington, D.C.: Association for the Study of Higher Education, 1983. 122 pages.

Addressing a much-neglected concern in higher education, the authors look at the increasing pressures and declining rewards and mobility in the academic workplace and explore the situation's implications for job satisfaction and commitment and the prospects for revitalization. They examine the social structure and culture of colleges and universities and identify intrinsic and extrinsic factors affecting both faculty members and administrators. They suggest that business and industry HRD programs could provide ideas for higher education and recommend early attention to instituting "persuasive programs of career planning and development" for all academy staff members. This timely contribution deserves most serious attention.

509 Bolles, Richard N. *What Color Is Your Parachute?* Berkeley, Calif.: Ten Speed Press, 1986. 397 pages.

A best-seller since its first edition in 1972, this "practical manual for job hunters and career-changers" is updated annually. With a refreshing and stimulating style, Bolles covers every aspect of career and self-assessment (interests, aptitudes, skills), exploring new life options, and developing a strategy for change. Included are useful questionnaires and exercises, information about the world of work, job-searching techniques, extensive resources, and an abundance of practical advice. The metaphorical theme is that individuals can better discover themselves and the "color of their parachute" so that they can take steps to help it open to its fullest. The book contains many ideas that could be helpful to anyone, including administrators, interested in career and personal renewal.

510 Brown, David G. *Leadership Vitality: A Workbook for Academic Administrators.* Washington, D.C.: American Council on Education, 1979. 108 pages.

For a complete description of this work, please see entry no. 548.

511 Furniss, W. Todd. *The Self-Reliant Academic.* Washington, D.C.: American Council on Education, 1984. 80 pages.

While focusing on the career assessment and enhancement of faculty members, this fascinating little book contains a message and ideas that also could be helpful to administrator renewal. The author, building on the theme of his earlier volume, *Reshaping Faculty Careers* (1981), suggests that individuals look beyond the traditional career paths in their institution and profession to explore other interests and opportunities that might enrich their lives. "The way to a continuing satisfactory career," Furniss states, "is to invest in oneself," and the objective is to develop "self-reliance." He discusses "broadening options," self-help organizations, collaborative approaches, entrepreneurial venturing, and both psychic and financial factors. His intriguing notion has the potential for considerable interest among academic administrators.

512 Hagberg, Janet O., and Leider, Richard. *The Inventurers: Excursions in Life and Career Renewal.* Reading, Mass.: Addison-Wesley, 1978. 179 pages.

The basic ingredient in life and career renewal, say the authors, is "the choice of taking responsibility for yourself." This book is a personal step-by-step guide to a renewal process called "inventuring"—looking inward to mind, body, and spirit to determine untapped potential and life and career priorities, and then taking positive action in expanding and exploring the options. With numerous case examples of such "risk-takers," practical guidelines and exercises, and an "excursion map" that threads the themes together, Hagberg and Leider offer a systematic and adventurous approach, not unlike that of Bolles (no. 509), to developing a plan for life and career revitalization.

513 Hall, Douglas T., and Associates. *Career Development in Organizations.* San Francisco: Jossey-Bass, 1986. 370 pages.

Sponsored by the Society for Industrial and Organizational Psychology, this volume covers the cultural and organizational contexts of careers, individual career development processes, and career management programs. Of particular interest are chapters discussing life career roles and motivation; midcareer needs, choice, and identity development; and innovative career building based on cumulative experience. Drawing upon examples from both public and private sectors, the authors share insights and recommendations that are as relevant to the academy as to other organizations.

★514 Hodgkinson, Harold L. "Adult Development: Implications for Faculty and Administrators." *Educational Record,* 1974, *55* (4), 263–274.

In this fascinating and penetrating article the author applies the studies on adulthood done by Levinson (no. 515) and others to the academy. Administrators and faculty members, like all mature human beings, continue to grow psychologically. Hodgkinson discusses their adulthood in several stages of development, explores their particular problems and adjustments at each level,

and interprets the emotional and mental state of academics in
the context of their job demands and pressures. Of special interest are his observations on personal and professional dynamics
during and following "middlescence," when the need for career
renewal is typically the greatest.

★515 Levinson, Daniel J. *The Seasons of a Man's Life.* New
York: Knopf, 1978. 363 pages.

This frequently referenced volume presents the author's theory
of adult development, which he bases on a ten-year study of
adult life cycles. Levinson describes the characteristics, vicissitudes, and influences of the various stages of growth and development in the evolution of adult life, including early adulthood,
the settling-down period, midlife transition, and middle adulthood. The developmental tasks necessary in each, he suggests,
involve "building, reappraising, modifying, and rebuilding for
the future." The basic theme is that adults must work toward
constructive change in their lives, particularly at these crucial
stages. Levinson's work is a valuable contribution to appreciat-
ing the needs and dynamics of life and career growth.

516 Sheehy, Gail. *Passages: Predictable Crises of Adult Life.* New
York: Dutton, 1976. 393 pages.

Very humane and coherent, this popular and well-documented
book deals with the pattern of adult developmental stages. The
author summarizes her findings from three years of research
and 115 in-depth interviews and presents a fascinating narrative
of personal, life, sex, family, and career development. She relates
short case studies to adult development theories, describes potential crises and personality changes during the life cycle, and compares the developmental rhythms of men and women. Sheehy's
message is that "passages," particularly during middle age, are
as predictable as they are opportune—for redefining attitudes,
for personal growth, and for life renewal. Her treatise is readable, enlightening, and helpful, as many have discovered.

20

Joseph F. Kauffman

The College and University Presidency

There is a vast literature on the subject of leadership, reflecting a fascination with the concept. Certainly our political system is dependent on the willingness of citizens to assume positions of leadership in our government. Studies of political leaders have always been of general interest. In more recent years, there has been an interest in the leadership of our social and economic institutions as well, including not only successful business and corporate leaders but also the leaders of our educational institutions.

This chapter reviews the literature pertaining to the college and university presidency. One assumes that the president will play a central role in the management and governance of an institution of higher education—but what role? The conflict and controversy that frequently surround a college presidency often arise from differing perceptions by various constituencies of the proper leadership role of the president. Studying the presidency and governing board–president relationship is one way of understanding the dynamics of our colleges and universities.

This chapter provides a brief overview of the evolution of the college presidency, followed by a description of the framework utilized in organizing the literature resources. It also offers a brief commentary on that literature, including the identification of gaps that need to be addressed in the future.

Note: Kathryn A. Verage's assistance in the preparation of this bibliography is gratefully acknowledged.

441

Evolution of the College Presidency

One image many of us still retain, especially with respect
to the small liberal arts college, is that of the college as the
"lengthening shadow" of its president. The old-time college
president as head of the faculty, teacher of a senior course in
ethics and moral philosophy, and chapel preacher contrasts
sharply with the contemporary metaphors of crisis manager or
entrepreneur.

Considering the relatively small number of individuals
involved, there is a considerable amount of writing about the
college and university presidency. We tend to think of the 1960s
as the watershed period for higher education and the study of
presidents. Yet an annotated bibliography issued by the U.S.
Department of Health, Education and Welfare (no. 517) describes
700 articles, books, and monographs from 1900 to 1960, solely
on the subject of the college president. The annotations give
a broad sense of what was written in the first half of this century
about this unique role and person. The titles of articles include
familiar subjects and have a contemporary ring: "The Vacant
Presidencies" (1920), "What Professors Want in a President"
(1959), "Women as College Presidents" (1902), or "The Burden of the College Presidency" (1905).

The history of American higher education reveals the
unique character of the American college and university presidency. Although our colonial colleges were patterned after their
English and European counterparts, they had no academic guild.
The absence of a strong national government authority resulted
in the creation of lay governing bodies. The president, therefore, became the central figure, both academically and adminis-
tratively, and traditionally received a great deal of delegated
authority from the board. Since the president served "at the
pleasure of the board," however, all delegated authority could
be quickly withdrawn.

The emergence of the American university began with
strong presidents supported by builders of great fortunes. The
names of successful businessmen such as Rockefeller, Clark,
Hopkins, Cornell, and Stanford become linked with "builder"

university presidents like Harper, Hall, Gilman, White, and Jordan. Laurence Veysey (1965) tells of Leland Stanford's selection of David Starr Jordan as the first president of Stanford, founded as a memorial to Stanford's son: Stanford selected Jordan because he admired firm-minded executive ability and wanted someone who could manage things "like the president of a railroad."

Social critics and faculty leaders engaged in criticism and attacks on these "empire-builder" presidents as the academic profession gained strength in the late nineteenth century. Thorstein Veblen (1954) railed against university presidents as "merchandisers" of good will and "captains of erudition," all too closely linked with the captains of industry. Robert Maynard Hutchins (1956), a believer in strong presidential leadership, bitterly observed in 1956, "the faculty prefer anarchy to any form of government."

Any examination of the literature on the college presidency during the post–World War II expansion period will reveal how different and contradictory the expectations for the president's role were. Successful alumni often remembered fondly the personal attention of grand old "prexy" and decried the new president's launching of a major expansion drive that was sure to change their alma mater for the worse. Others criticized the "old-fashioned" president for continuing in the ways of the past while new-style leadership was expanding and altering the image of competitor colleges.

The 1960s began with much optimism concerning higher education. It was a "growth industry," and one seldom heard a negative word about its potency or its future. Colleges and universities were credited with accommodating the "tidal wave" of students seeking admission, which was expected to quadruple enrollments during the decade. It was in this context that Clark Kerr delivered the Godkin Lectures at Harvard University in 1963, analyzing the forces that had brought about what he termed the "multiversity," with all of its diversity. Kerr, then president of the University of California, attempted to portray the ideal multiversity president, providing a marvelous recapitulation of all the role expectations that have ever existed for

American college presidents. Perhaps the most often quoted section of these lectures, published in *The Uses of the University* (no. 518), begins with "expected to be a friend of the students, a colleague of the faculty, a good fellow with the alumni" (p. 29) and goes on and on through the countless contradictions and absurdities that have marked people's definitions of the effective president (pp. 29–41).

By the end of the decade, campuses were places of strife and protest. Difficult questions were raised, both on and off campus, and presidents were besieged. Now we had metaphors of crisis manager, mediator, and "cool under fire" to describe new expectations of presidents. The public image of the college president became one of a harried, if energetic, executive type rushing through revolving-door positions.

For the past decade, the main challenge of presidents has been seen as coping with retrenchment or steady-state conditions, coupled with growing constraints on administrative authority. Governors and legislatures have had little hesitation in extending their oversight roles to cover academic standards and testing. Faculty collective bargaining, compliance and reporting requirements, and the like have added new staff in legal services and personnel. The lack of flexibility, the new constraints on authority, and the dim fiscal outlook cause many observers to see the higher education presidency as less attractive than before, as the current literature shows.

Framework for Organizing the Literature

Unlike the literature on some subjects in higher education, writing about the college and university presidency does not delineate its topic in a clear and rational manner. Still, it is possible to categorize the published works, and a careful reading of the annotations that follow should enable the reader to select material of interest.

The framework chosen for the organization of the chapter's annotations consists of seven categories. This division is primarily descriptive, and the categories are not mutually exclusive.

1. *Portraits of the American College President.* Beginning with an extensive bibliography covering the period 1900–1960 (no. 517), this section identifies writing on the various images of presidents.
2. *The Selection and Assessment of Presidents.* The citations here include material useful in understanding the process of selecting presidents and conducting performance reviews. Much of this writing is in the form of guidebooks, although the principles involved often stem from research.
3. *Conceptions of Presidential Leadership.* This section presents some of the more substantial works based in part on ethnographic or field studies.
4. *Differing Role Expectations.* This is a series of journal articles focusing on expectations of the presidency.
5. *Unique Aspects of the Small College Presidency.* These publications typify the recent attempt to differentiate the special characteristics required for success in the presidency of small colleges.
6. *Governing Board–President Relationships.* Presidents are employed as the executive officers of governing boards. These publications deal with the relationship between presidents and their boards, including the conflicting expectations that exist.
7. *What Presidents Actually Do and How They Feel About It.* These works attempt to portray the personal side of the presidency, including its pressures on spouse and family.

Commentary on the Literature

A great deal of the literature is in the form of autobiography or memoir, written by former presidents. While some of it is excellent (for example, Harold W. Stoke's *The American College President,* 1959), much of it is trivial and self-serving. Actual research literature on the higher education presidency is sparse.

One problem in the literature flows from the enormous diversity of our colleges and universities. The presidency is different in the private and the public sector. It is different in two-year and four-year institutions. Even within sectors, the history, ethos, and culture of one institution are different from those of another, and this makes for a different presidency. Ethnographic approaches seem to capture best what presidents actually do and experience, but there are not many social scientists like David Riesman (nos. 525 and 535). More typical broad-brush portrayals, often reflecting survey data, are interesting but have been treated skeptically by individual presidents.

Another gap in the literature comes about because one aspect of the presidency is to be an advocate for one's institution, expressing confidence in its quality, worth, and future prospects. Presidents thus do not feel free to share their complaints with strangers and often must put the best face on their actions. If there are problems, they feel it is the president's responsibility to solve these problems. One example of this reticence concerns the president–governing board relationship. Although this relationship is often the most difficult and painful memory of a presidency, almost nothing in the research literature reveals its problems. Board members and presidents simply do not want to talk about such matters to researchers. Yet this is one of the most important, if not the most important, relationship a president has. His or her success and satisfaction often depend on the quality of the relationship with the members of the governing board.

Research is also needed to define the special nature of multicampus institutions and systems of institutions. The model of governance we utilize presupposes a governing board that is a defender and champion of the institution and the chief executive officer for that institution. When campus heads report to a system head, we need to adjust the model. When a governing board attempts to behave as an impartial arbitrator among campuses, we need to adjust the model. Conflict between heads of systems and campus heads, especially the head of the flagship campus, requires new understandings.

There are other gaps in the research literature, such as the lack of exploration of faculty collective bargaining's impact on the conduct of the presidency. The special challenge of the Catholic college presidency, including the challenge presented to the layperson president of a religious institution, is seldom portrayed in the literature. Perhaps most important of all, where is the research literature on the unique presidencies of black colleges and universities?

Finally, although the heroic president may not be gone, we need new studies of leadership that involve the behavior of more than one individual, because campus leadership today involves more than a president. It involves a governing board, senior officers of administration, faculty and student leaders, and a structure and process of governance that encourage satisfaction and productive effort. The relationships among all these factors need to be carefully explored.

References

Hutchins, R. M. *Freedom, Education and the Fund: Essays and Addresses, 1946 1956.* New York: Meridian Books, 1956.
Stoke, H. W. *The American College President.* New York: Harper & Row, 1959.
Veblen, T. *The Higher Learning in America.* Stanford, Calif.: Academic Reprints, 1954.
Veysey, L. R. *The Emergence of the American University.* Chicago: University of Chicago Press, 1965.

Portraits of the American College President

★517 Eells, Walter C., and Hollis, Ernest V. *The College Presidency 1900–1960: An Annotated Bibliography.* Washington, D.C.: U.S. Department of Health, Education and Welfare, 1961. 143 pages.

This is a precious resource for anyone studying the American college presidency in the twentieth century. Covering the years 1900 through 1960, this annotated bibliography contains over 700 books, monographs, and periodical articles about the college presidency. Many deal with the qualifications and selection of a president. Almost half deal with the duties and responsibilities of the president. The annotations are useful and usually contain brief quotations from the works. In addition, the index is most helpful. The book gives each author's position and institutional affiliation. This work is a great aid for anyone interested in the subject of higher education generally and the college presidency specifically.

★518 Kerr, Clark. *The Uses of the University.* (3rd ed.) Cambridge, Mass.: Harvard University Press, 1982. 224 pages.

Originally delivered as the Godkin Lectures at Harvard University in 1963, these three essays described recent developments in American higher education. The focus was on the major research university, which Kerr termed the "multiversity." This classic work has been issued three times, with "postscripts" added in 1972 and 1982. Although the work as a whole is not on the subject of the presidency, Kerr did devote a section of his first essay to a portrayal of the university president, capturing the myriad competing and contradictory expectations for the role. Kerr chose the term *mediator* to describe the realities of the position—a choice he came to regret because of subsequent criticism. Every student of higher education should be familiar with this brilliant work.

519 Kramer, John. "College and University Presidents in Fiction." *Journal of Higher Education*, 1981, *52* (1), 81–95.

Kramer examines the portrayal of presidents in American "academic novels" by citing examples from some thirty-five works. He shows that these fictional presidents are vain, pompous, ambitious, and devoid of leadership qualities and administrative skills. Noting that the novels in which the president is most harshly treated were written by faculty members, Kramer suggests that the negative depiction of presidents serves as an "allegorical attack" on the administrative authority that presidents represent. Presidents who read this article may feel relieved that their situation does not "imitate art." On the other hand, those whose situations do resemble the fictional portrayals may wish to follow the example of one fictional president. Annually the subject of a scurrilous novel, he considers enrollment problems and then distributes each novel widely because "kids like coming here after reading those books."

520 Sharp, Paul F. "American College Presidents Since World War II." *Educational Record,* 1984, *65* (2), 11–16.

Sharp recounts some major post–World War II societal changes and considers how these diverse forces affected the college and university presidency. He notes that not all presidents during the past forty years demonstrated "transforming leadership," but all successful presidents "exhibited a leadership that perceived what should be done, demonstrated an ability to influence others to achieve results, and revealed a sensitivity about the human and organizational costs" (p. 16). Despite the changes in presidential styles and management skills during these years, Sharp suggests that the uses of power, the ethical dimensions of the presidential role, and the highly individualized art form the presidency embodies remain the critical aspects of leadership. The article gives hope that despite profound societal change, strong leadership is a constant that will enable colleges and universities not only to survive but to flourish.

The Selection and Assessment of Presidents

521 Gilley, J. Wade. "The Past Is Prologue: A Perspective on Leadership." *Educational Record,* 1985, *66* (3), 24–29.

In studying twenty effective colleges and universities, including community colleges, small private colleges, land-grant universities, private institutions, and regional state universities, Gilley observed that the perspective a college or university president brings to the position may determine his or her ability to provide institutional leadership. Gilley found that successful presidents possessed a quality he calls the "parallel perspective"— the ability to apply to a new presidency the leadership approach that had been used successfully in a prior presidency. The major components of this perspective are an ability to regard an issue with objectivity and skill in conceiving a unique and innovative approach to issues and problems. Selection committees may find this article useful when considering traits to seek in a new president.

★522 Kauffman, Joseph F. *The Selection of College and University Presidents*. Washington, D.C.: Association of American Colleges, 1974. 82 pages.

This handbook for trustees and presidential search committees was prepared by the author with the advice and counsel of an AAC Task Force on Presidential Selection and Career Development. Based on a study of the best practices in the search process, the book guides readers through all the necessary steps in the selection of a new president. It includes sections on screening candidates, conducting interviews, and making the appointment. Attention is also given to the president's spouse, relationships with the board, and criteria for performance evaluation. The underlying premise is that the potential effectiveness of a president is, at least in part, a function of the process by which he or she is selected. As Frederick deW. Bolman's volume, *How College Presidents Are Chosen* (1965), was useful to search committees for almost a decade, so Kauffman's guidebook was the standard until the AGB handbook by John W. Nason (no. 524) was published in 1980.

523 Nason, John W. *Presidential Assessment: A Guide to the Periodic Review of the Performance of Chief Executives*. Washington, D.C.: Association of Governing Boards of Universities and Colleges, 1984. 109 pages.

This handbook, addressed to governing board members, is a companion publication to *Presidential Search*, also by John W. Nason (no. 524). It recognizes the increasing pressures on boards to assess presidential performance and at the same time is mindful of the clumsy and often destructive ways in which such reviews may be conducted. It orients trustees to the peculiar nature of a president's responsibilities and reminds boards of their own roles and responsibilities. It considers the pros and cons of informal as compared to formal evaluations and presents examples of good practices. Its appendixes are a rich storehouse of case materials, including a spectrum of presidential evaluations (with identities masked) and various rating scales and questionnaires. This is now a standard guide on performance reviews of presidents.

524 Nason, John W. *Presidential Search: A Guide to the Process of Selecting and Appointing College and University Presidents.* (Rev. ed.) Washington, D.C.: Association of Governing Boards of Universities and Colleges, 1984. 114 pages.

This volume is the standard guide for presidential selection committees and governing boards. It is based on a reconstruction of dozens of successful searches (this reviewer conducted some of that research) and thus contains a great deal of advice based upon actual cases. The book takes the reader through the nine essential steps in a presidential search, beginning with establishing the machinery of the search and selection process and concluding with easing the transition. Throughout, the book offers checklists, reminders, and helpful aids to keep a committee on schedule. There are also twenty-three pages of exhibits, ranging from a typical search committee budget to model letters for candidates who do not survive the screening. This work is valuable for those who want to understand the search and selection process, including presidential aspirants. The normative data concerning present practices are helpful to governing boards, especially to those that will conduct their own searches rather than relying on outside consultants.

525 Riesman, David, and McLaughlin, Judith. "A Primer on the Use of Consultants in Presidential Recruitment." *Change,* 1984, *16* (6), 12–23.

This article contributes to an understanding of the growing use of consultants to aid governing boards and search committees in the recruitment and selection of new presidents. The authors have been studying the presidential search process for several years and know a great deal about some specific cases, especially in private colleges. The conventional attitude of suspicion and skepticism about external consultants is changing, and the authors explain the various reasons why consultants can provide invaluable assistance. They are especially helpful in recruiting candidates who otherwise would not "apply" and in obtaining background information not otherwise available to a screening committee. Equally important, they are of value in maintaining confidentiality, which frequently becomes a major problem. The potential hazards of using outside consultants are also described in this informative article.

Conceptions of Presidential Leadership

526 Benezet, Louis T., Katz, Joseph, and Magnusson, Frances W. *Style and Substance: Leadership and the College Presidency*. Washington, D.C.: American Council on Education, 1981. 121 pages.

This book is based on interview data collected between 1976 and 1979. A total of 250 persons were interviewed, including presidents, senior academic administrators, faculty, and students of twenty-five colleges and universities. The aim of the interviews was to explore the "human dynamics" of the college presidency. As a context for reporting their results, the authors provide a chapter synthesizing other writers' observations on presidential leadership. The heart of the book is the analysis of presidential styles, as presidents explain how they execute the responsibilities of office. The authors develop six characterizations to describe the different presidential styles observed: the take-charge president, the standard-bearer president, the organization president, the moderator president, the explorer president, and the founding president. The style or leadership metaphors are interesting, but one wonders if they were created by the authors in advance rather than flowing from the research data.

*527 Cohen, Michael D., and March, James G. *Leadership and Ambiguity: The American College President.* (2nd ed.) Boston: Harvard Business School Press, 1986. 290 pages.

For a complete description of this work, please see entry no. 141.

528 Fisher, James L. *Power of the Presidency.* New York: Macmillan, 1983. 240 pages.

This book, produced by the American Council on Education, is addressed to college and university presidents and those who want to be presidents rather than to scholars. It is a provocative work that attempts to apply research findings about power to the college presidency. Fisher, a former university president, is a psychologist by training and is familiar with the concepts and theories of leadership and power. He describes five types of power that the president can exercise, ranging from the least to the most effective: (1) coercive power, (2) reward power, (3) legitimate power, (4) expert power, and (5) charismatic power. Research on each of these forms of power is discussed, giving special attention to implications for the college presidency. Fisher believes that charismatic power is the single most effective form of influence, and he illustrates this with a variety of maxims for presidents. This is a controversial work, but it is a significant one for anyone who wants to be familiar with the full range of writing on the presidency.

529 Kerr, Clark. *Presidents Make a Difference: Strengthening Leadership in Colleges and Universities.* Washington, D.C.: Association of Governing Boards of Universities and Colleges, 1984. 141 pages.

A report by the Commission on Strengthening Presidential Leadership, headed by Clark Kerr, this volume is the culmination of a two-year effort involving some 800 interviews with presidents throughout the United States. Its premise is that the American college presidency is in trouble, and it cites as evidence a variety of factors, such as inability to attract and retain high-quality presidents, erosion of presidential authority, and increasing constraints caused by power sharing with more and more

groups on and off campus. The report deals with presidential
selection and evaluation, and the day-to-day workings of the
college presidency, placing special emphasis on the relationship
between the president and the board. It concludes with recommendations and suggestions for strengthening presidential leadership, addressed to governing boards. Some would criticize the
commission's emphasis on the negative aspects of the presidential
experience, but its observations and recommendations are useful
for those concerned with strengthening the presidency.

Differing Role Expectations

530 Enarson, Harold L. "The Ethical Imperative of the College Presidency." *Educational Record,* 1984, *65* (2), 24–26.

Ethical issues in business, industry, and government have sur-
faced regularly over the years, yet educational publications reveal
little, if any, writing on the ethics of the college presidency. Instead, one finds much information relating to the college or
university president as a manager skilled in the corporate world
of finance, personnel, communication, and public relations.
Enarson suggests that we return to a belief held by early college presidents that education and ethics are a "seamless web,"
not separate dimensions. Enarson proposes that today's college
presidents have an "ethical imperative" to reflect in their administrative decisions the true values and missions of their institutions. The article is a timely reminder of the true nature
of educational institutions in an era that emphasizes strategic
planning and corporate skills.

531 Kauffman, Joseph F. "Profile of the Presidency in the
Next Decade." *Educational Record,* 1984, *65* (2), 6–10.

Kauffman reviews characteristics of the future internal and external environments of colleges and universities that will com-
plicate the presidential leadership role. To deal effectively with
pressures such as changing demographics, diminishing financial support, complex governance arrangements, and low faculty
morale, not only will higher education require outstanding

leadership, it will also need to adopt a new way of thinking about leadership. Kauffman sees the necessity for a "visible and transforming" leadership that understands and communicates the "essence" of the college or university, a leadership that restores to educational institutions their original purpose of bettering humankind, and a leadership that promotes the release of people's capacity for renewal. For presidents struggling in the quagmire of their daily grind, Kauffman's article provides a reminder that the presidency is a "calling" with its own spiritual dimension.

532 Laney, James T. "The Moral Authority of the College or University President." *Educational Record*, 1984, *65* (2), 17–19.

In this article, adapted from a speech at the 1983 Southern University Conference, Laney presents three factors upon which rests "a president's ability to provide a sense of moral direction for an institution." Laney suggests that restraint (respect for the rights of others), an appreciation of reality (the ability to deal honestly with the hard truth), and the notion that education is a privilege are what allow the president to provide moral direction and leadership. Laney believes that this moral authority of the president and the moral dimension of the university are one and the same and that moral direction is achieved through the person of the president as well as in the set of circumstances inherent in the institution. The article reminds us that at the heart of the decision-making process there should be a concern for values—the "moral dimension."

533 Ryan, John W. "The Mosaic of the College and University Presidency." *Educational Record*, 1984, *65* (2), 20–22.

Ryan examines the presidential role by using the metaphor of a mosaic that contains "chips" varying in size, color, and intensity. Despite these variations, the outlines of the chips are always clear. Ryan suggests additional "chips" to be included in the mosaic, such as working with public officials, fostering international relations, and serving on corporate boards. Since there is no one pattern or prototype of the college president, Ryan challenges presidents to construct their own mosaic. In doing so, they should consider leadership of higher education and of public policy and not merely service as the "captain" of their institution. Ryan's premise that there is no standard formula for leadership style will reassure presidents that they are free to create their own pattern.

Unique Aspects of the Small College Presidency

534 Peck, Robert D. "The Entrepreneurial College Presidency." *Educational Record,* 1983, *64* (1), 18–25.

Peck interviewed presidents, chief academic officers, and financial aid officers at nineteen successful small colleges to identify the administrative characteristics of these colleges and determine whether any common factors contribute to their success. Underlying his study were two assumptions: (1) that success is not accidental, and (2) that the key to success may be found in administrative practices. His findings show that intuitive decision making, "future-focused planning," innovative response to topical problems, risk taking, and the development of an efficient intelligence-gathering network are among the more important characteristics that successful small college presidents have in common. Peck's findings are valuable in "legitimizing" the entrepreneurial-style presidency, and his investigation provides an important jumping-off point for further exploration of administrative methods and practices in small colleges.

535 Riesman, David, and Fuller, Sharon Elliott. "Leaders: Presidents Who Make a Difference." In Arthur Levine, Janice Green, and Associates, *Opportunity in Adversity: How Colleges Succeed in Hard Times.* San Francisco: Jossey-Bass, 1985. Pages 62–104.

This chapter shows one application of the ethnographic approach of David Riesman to the study of colleges and universities. Riesman admonishes all observers of higher education to "disaggregate" in order to illuminate reality. This essay is a part of a study of several private liberal arts colleges, focusing on the challenges of leadership. The chapter discusses two colleges, Mary Baldwin and Carleton, and their presidents, Virginia Lester and Robert Edwards. The authors believe that presidents can play a crucial role in leadership and document that belief in their account of these two colleges. They make clear that their focus is on very small "manageable" institutions, where the president can know all the faculty and staff. This is an excellent example of writing up brief case studies in a manner that is both interesting and insightful.

536 Tuckman, Howard, and Arcady, Pat. "Myths About Size and Performance: Managing the Small College." *Educational Record*, 1985, *66* (3), 16–30.

Tuckman and Arcady believe that administrators of small liberal arts colleges face unique challenges and difficulties because their colleges are not microcosms of larger schools. For example, some concentrate on providing "quality" instruction to a small group of students with high aspirations, while others offer a "non-distinct" education to students otherwise unqualified for college, and still others emphasize remedial, religious, or other highly specialized programs. Whatever its size and mission, the survival of the individual small college in perilous economic times is largely dependent on development and maintenance of a management style appropriate to that institution. Tuckman and Arcady recommend and discuss several survival strategies, including "differentiation" of product and "creative" financing. Their article contains valuable suggestions for small college presidents and administrators whose institutions are caught in the double bind of spiraling costs and declining enrollments.

Governing Board–President Relationships

537 Cleary, Robert E. "Trustee-President Authority Relations." *Educational Record*, 1979, *60* (2), 146–158.

The purpose of Cleary's study was to clarify the responsibilities of trustees and presidents by examining trustee and presidential opinions regarding their authority relationship. A sixteen-item questionnaire covering such matters as academic program change, long-range planning, budgeting, tenure limits, and collective bargaining was sent to 213 board chairpersons and presidents in a six-state Middle Atlantic area. Responses were received from sixty presidents and sixty-one governing board chairpersons. Cleary found general agreement between trustees and presidents on half of the survey questions, particularly those concerning policy and administration. However, significant opinion differences were evident regarding the social and moral issues he raised. This article is useful to governing board members and presidents for its delineation of significant disagreement regarding responsibilities of the two groups in certain controversial matters.

538 Cote, Lawrence S. "The Relative Importance of Presidential Roles." *The Journal of Higher Education,* 1985, *56* (6), 664–676.

Cote surveyed 129 Pennsylvania colleges and universities to determine how closely university presidents and governing board chairpersons agreed on the relative importance of twenty selected presidential roles. Using a "presidential roles profile" constructed from Mintzberg's concepts of managerial work, Cote collected data from 243 presidents and governing board chairpersons. He found that board chairpersons and presidents closely agreed about the relative importance of the twenty presidential roles. For example, both presidents and governing board chairpersons ranked as number one the presidential role of "visionary," or articulator of the vision of what the institution could or should be. Useful at the basic level of defining a myriad of presidential roles, Cote's findings could also help governing board members and presidents as they strive for consensus regarding presidential expectations.

539 Jones, W. T. "From Guardians to Agents: The Changing Role of Trustees." *Educational Record,* 1985, *66* (2), 10–15.

Jones reminds us that American society is not only democratized but also politicized, as various publics seek to extract gain from legislators and other decision making groups. Noting that some boards of trustees have divested their South African holdings because of political pressure from their student public, Jones then develops the larger issues. Are trustees shifting from the "responsible for" attitude to one that is "responsible to"? In divesting, are they abrogating their power to act for the good of the institution in favor of a view that they are merely conduits along which public demands flow? Jones cautions that the end result of "responsive to" decision making may be to politicize educational institutions, with trustees serving as "foreign policy" lobbyists. Jones's article challenges college and university trustees to define their decision-making role as they struggle with increasingly sophisticated and complex institutional problems.

540 Wood, Miriam M. "Crosscurrents and Undercurrents in the Trustee-President Relationship." *Educational Record,* 1984, *65* (1), 38–42.

Drawing on interviews with ten presidents and forty trustees from ten private, nonsectarian liberal arts colleges, Wood addresses the problem of tension between trustees and presidents. She concludes that tension is caused by the perception of both trustees and presidents that college presidents are politicians who must keep their constituents satisfied; by the perception of trustees that the formal relationship of trustees and presidents is based on the assumption that a college is a rational hierarchy; and by the president's perception of the trustee committee system as "devaluing" his or her contribution to the institution. The article raises serious questions about the trustee-president relationship and suggests that because of the tensions underlying this relationship, the problems of collegiate leadership and educational innovation are being ignored.

What Presidents Actually Do and How They Feel About It

541 Berendzen, Richard. *Is My Armor Straight? A Year in the Life of a University President.* Bethesda, Md.: Adler & Adler, 1986. 351 pages.

This book is not a "scholarly treatise," as its author makes clear at the outset. It is, instead, a personal account of Richard Berendzen's life as president of American University during the 1983–84 academic year. During that year he kept a journal and dictated each night his recollections of each full day's activities. The result is a fascinating chronicle that casts considerable light on both the professional and the personal life of a private university president. Berendzen actually does own a suit of armor, but as David Riesman points out in a Foreword, Berendzen uses the metaphor to refer to "his own protection against not only the mild hurts of ungenerosity but also the great stress of threats and physical abuse" (p. viii). Despite some aspects of public relations implicit in such a work, this volume enlightens readers about the personal side of the presidency, especially its effects on the president's spouse, children, and family life.

542 Clodius, Joan E., and Magrath, Diane Skomars (eds.). *The President's Spouse: Volunteer or Volunteered?* Washington, D.C.: National Association of State Universities and Land-Grant Colleges, 1984. 178 pages.

The subject of the college president's spouse is a relatively new area for study, but it represents a growing area of concern. This volume consists of an introductory chapter reporting the results of a survey of the spouses of presidents and chancellors of the 144 NASULGC member institutions, followed by thirteen essays describing personal points of view and experiences. The essays reveal how difficult it is to portray the needs and expectations of the president's spouse in aggregate terms. There surely will be more research on this topic, but until then this volume, along with Marguerite Corbally's book (no. 543), will be a standard reference.

543 Corbally, Marguerite W. *The Partners: Sharing the Life of a College President.* Danville, Ill.: Interstate, 1977. 164 pages.

Written by the "partner" of former University of Illinois president John Corbally, this book reports the results of a survey of presidents' wives in 1975. Although a memoir had been published by Muriel Beadle (*Where Has All the Ivy Gone?* 1972), wife of a former president of the University of Chicago, Corbally's book represents the first study of presidents' spouses. As such, it is considered a significant contribution to this area of study. The survey covers many factual areas, including financial support for entertaining, and applies a "frustration" scale to forty items in the experience of a president's wife. The study provides the reader with a good idea of the job of a president's wife and the personal experiences of a wife in a "two-person career." Hopefully, there have been improvements and a new sensitivity by governing boards and others since 1977. Newer studies will reveal the extent to which there has been progress.

544 Kauffman, Joseph F. *At the Pleasure of the Board: The Service of the College and University President.* Washington, D.C.: American Council on Education, 1980. 122 pages.

This book attempts to describe the college and university presidency, especially the way the presidency is experienced by the men and women who occupy such positions. It is based partly on field research involving over forty institutions and partly on the personal experiences of the author. Following a brief history of the position, chapters deal with presidential selection, the new college president, relations with the governing board, the special nature of multicampus systems, the personal side of the presidency, and assessing presidential effectiveness. The book concludes with a chapter on the president's responsibility for educational leadership. The explicit premise of the work is that the concept of "service" is an important legacy of the presidency and that we must restore this concept as an incentive for good women and men to assume such roles. This work is widely cited and is useful to governing boards, presidents, and presidential aspirants as well as students of the presidency.

545 Kerr, Clark, and Gade, Marian L. *The Many Lives of Academic Presidents: Time, Place and Character*. Washington, D.C.: Association of Governing Boards of Universities and Colleges, 1986. 260 pages.

This report is described as a sequel to Kerr's *Presidents Make a Difference* (no. 529). Utilizing some of the material from the same 800 interviews, the authors supplement it with a wide variety of related studies and data. The book is clearly an analysis of the academic presidency in all of its dimensions and diversity. Although presidents function as leaders of many constituencies, they serve in a specific context, and that context must be understood. With many illustrations, Kerr and Gade take the reader through the experiences of new presidents, the impact of the external and internal environments on the presidency, the variety of forms of governance, and the responsibilities of governing boards to make the presidency effective. The volume is enriched by tables of data and appendixes, including a superb annotated bibliography on governance of higher education. All presidents, trustees, and students of the presidency will find this a useful work for reading and reference.

546 Vaughan, George B. *The Community College Presidency*. New York: Macmillan, 1986. 224 pages.

This work, produced by the American Council on Education, includes extensive survey data, material gathered in intensive personal interviews, and the fruits of Vaughan's own rich experience in fourteen years as a community college president. Over 500 two-year public college presidents participated in the survey. Respondents also identified presidents they considered outstanding, and seventy-five such leaders were research subjects, as were thirty-eight spouses of presidents. The author does make some comparisons of community college presidents with presidents of four-year institutions, although that was not the purpose of his study. Chapters cover background data on current presidents, paths to the presidency, descriptions of what presidents actually do, and a variety of governance issues.

There is interesting material on the personal aspects and stress of the presidency, including the perspectives of spouses. The final chapter deals with leadership concepts and styles. Readers will find this a comprehensive and contemporary look at a subject that has needed more illumination.

David G. Brown
Robert A. Scott
Linda C. Winner

21

Academic and Administrative Officers

The purpose of this chapter is to review the relevant literature on academic and administrative officers below the level of president. Chief academic officers (CAO), chief business officers (CBO), chief student affairs officers (CSAO), development officers (DO), and department chairs control budgets, assign and train support personnel, select the students who will attend the institution, and negotiate matters with state and federal offices. They manage academic and administrative units and often have assistants reporting to them. These are the campus officials who develop and transmit the information that creates the public image of the college or university, and they help to attract gifts that allow the faculty to have increased freedom to pursue their academic interests.

     The literature on these positions is uneven in quality and scattered throughout several fields. There are reminiscences by college presidents, studies of the deanship, observations and descriptions by administrators and faculty in higher education, policy studies, theoretical works in psychology and sociology, compensation studies and training manuals, and studies in educational administration—but only a few good studies have contributed to a basic understanding of the roles and functions of these administrative officers. (For a review of these works, see no. 550.)

     While the complexity of these positions varies with the scale and scope of the institution, they all fulfill three basic organizational functions: serving as liaison with external suppliers of resources, whether financial, human, or material; implementing procedures for internal allocation of resources and control of activities, especially in matters of campus coordination and compliance with external requirements; and working with student activities and curricular responsibilities to help students become oriented to college requirements, standards, and opportunities. Their responsibilities cause these officers to constantly face a tension between providing service to faculty and students and providing controls on the use of resources as part of their accountability to more senior officers and the board of trustees.

The Field and Its Literature

The positions under review have been found in colleges and universities for years. In England, the precursors of today's academic registrars, chief academic officers, and bursars were appointed during the Middle Ages. In the United States before the Civil War, most colleges employed a president, a treasurer, and a part-time librarian in addition to the faculty. After the war, college administration began to grow and splinter because of enrollment increases and demands for new services. First, a secretary of the faculty was appointed, then a registrar, and then in succession a vice-president, a dean, a dean of women, a chief business officer, an assistant dean, a dean of men, a director of admissions, and in time a corps of administrative assistants to the president who were in charge of anything and everything—(alumni and) public relations, church relations, civic relations, student relations, and faculty relations (see Scott, no. 550).

In time, of course, these "assistant to" positions became autonomous offices. The literature on academic and administrative officers parallels the development of these positions. Individual officers, often as part of emerging professional associations, wrote histories of their positions and undertook rudimentary surveys of peers in order to compare job responsibilities, working conditions, and compensation. There have been expositions on the worth of such positions and the importance of their contributions. There have been descriptive essays by practitioners as well as theoretical pieces by scholars trying to develop and test models of academic and administrative management. Milestone publications in this literature are cited by Rudolph (1962) and Scott (no. 550). These works include *Administrators in Higher Education* by Burns (1962) and *The Academic Deanship* by Gould (1964). Biographies of persons who have held a diversity of leadership positions within higher education, such as *Being Lucky* by Herman Wells (1980), also allow readers to use one of the oldest, most traditional means of learning leadership—observation and example.

Framework for Organizing the Literature

The literature on academic and administrative positions can be organized into two distinct categories. The first category concerns academic administration or management in higher education in and of itself. Works in this category review internal and external forces on decision making, strategic planning, organizational program and individual performance assessment, and so on, at the campus and system level as well as in associations. Also included here are works devoted to topics of training and "how to." Authors report the demographic shifts in higher education and their effects on enrollments, as well as changes in the labor market, intensifying public control of campuses, increasing interest by students in their own academic environment, new electronic technologies and their effects on teaching and learning, the increasing number of alternatives to higher education, and the growth of a society oriented toward lifelong learning and human capability development. Other topics of such books and articles include the career paths of administrators and their background and training, mobility and organizational commitments, administrators' rights and grievance procedures, women and minorities in collegiate administration, communication channels on campus, liability of administrators, satisfactions and incentives for increased competence and performance, and professional associations. Much of this literature, although useful to administrators in all positions, is annotated in earlier chapters. The second category of literature, by contrast, provides job-specific information pertinent to a variety of positions in higher education administration.

The literature annotated in this chapter focuses on academic and major administrative officers below the president. As higher education management and leadership grow more complex, key administrative functions become more distinct and specialized. So too does the related literature, which is scattered through a wide array of practitioner journals, books, and other publications. Much of this literature is based on questionnaire surveys, case studies, and individual observations. The following categories serve as a useful framework around which to organize such diffuse literature:

1. Leadership and management in general
2. Chief academic officers
3. Department chairs
4. Business and development officers
5. Student affairs officers

Commentary on the Literature

The literature on academic and administrative positions evolves constantly as the pressures and demands on American higher education change. New positions emerge in some institutions; new responsibilities for existing officers emerge at others. In recent years the amount of attention given to theoretical works has increased, and new models of policies and decision making are receiving greater attention. The newest literature appears to be oriented to function and policy questions that have arisen in response to the changing demographic environment, to new tax laws, and to the increasingly frequent tendency to borrow models from industry. New issues that affect the management practices and responsibilities of these positions include changes in tuition policy, changes in admissions policy, new positions such as enrollment management, new trustee responsibilities that affect the role of institutional officers, and changing interests of state and federal government with regard to higher education. Mention is now being made of incentive programs for college administrators, and increasingly sophisticated analysis is being given to the effects of external forces on internal organization and the role of particular positions.

Immense opportunities still exist for writing and research in this area. The literature relating to chief academic officers is diffuse and largely unhelpful; indeed, the entire profession of chief academic officer is rather loosely defined. The literature relating to chief business officers is sparse and inadequate, while that relating to chief student affairs officers is voluminous and shallow. Although the literature relating to chief development officers is well catalogued, it too is sparse. Only the literature relating to department chairpersons is both diverse and practical.

Six particularly productive areas for additional research come to mind. First, a statement of the common set of intellectual beliefs that underpin each profession is extremely important. We need to articulate the premises that are shared by all chief academic officers—the boundaries that define the profession of the chief academic officer. Further, we need to define common concepts and intellectual common ground for each of these positions.

Second, research and analysis need to identify and define the skills and talents needed for each of the jobs. Antecedent experience and activities currently pursued by prospective recruits give some idea of these talents but do not fully represent them.

Third, more workshops and sessions of annual meetings should be structured around biography. Case studies and show-and-tell sessions on programs have proven to be extremely popular and useful. Biographies are in fact case studies that focus upon the leaders themselves, and they seem to offer substantial potential as useful sources of information. We need to focus on whole people, not just on isolated skills.

Fourth, as is the case with many practitioners, the most helpful literature is often anecdotal. We need to encourage administrators in comparable positions to visit one another at home, and research needs to be conducted on the effectiveness of these visits as developmental techniques.

Fifth, we need to develop mechanisms for trading literature and policy statements that are relevant to each particular position. We also need research that documents the effectiveness of such trades in stimulating the imagination.

Finally, we need better indexes and catalogues of the occasional as well as the journal literature in the field of leadership as it relates to particular positions. Much of the best information is exchanged in regional and disciplinary meetings and never reaches print. Although sessions for department chairs in the larger disciplines such as literature, history, and chemistry are common elements in the annual meetings of professional associations, and although many presentations in these sessions are based upon written scripts, it is rare for them to be published. One of our many centers for the study of higher education could undertake to collect and catalogue this occasional literature along with the research journal literature that is already available.

References

Burns, G. P. *Administrators in Higher Education: Their Functions and Coordination.* New York: Harper & Row, 1962.
Gould, J. W. *The Academic Deanship.* New York: Teachers College, 1964.
Rudolph, F. *The American College and University: A History.* New York: Knopf, 1962.
Wells, H. B. *Being Lucky: Reminiscences and Reflections.* Bloomington: Indiana University, 1980.

Leadership and Management in General

547 Astin, Alexander W., and Scherrei, Rita A. *Maximizing Leadership Effectiveness: Impact of Administrative Style on Faculty and Students.* San Francisco: Jossey-Bass, 1980. 238 pages.

Appendix F of this well-researched volume provides "detailed profiles of chief administrators," including academic officers, fiscal officers, development officers, student affairs officers, registrars, admissions officers, and financial aid officers. The age and experience characteristics of each of these officers are identified. This volume provides a well-researched comparison of the various administrative positions and is especially useful as a general introduction to middle-level management positions for students of higher education governance.

*548 Brown, David G. *Leadership Vitality: A Workbook for Academic Administrators.* Washington, D.C.: American Council on Education, 1979. 108 pages.

This workbook and the Leadership Vitality Conference it describes are based on the premise that professional vitality is best promoted by sharing information with colleagues in professional groups. Over fifty college and university presidents and chief academic officers participated in a project sponsored by the Carnegie Corporation of New York and the American Council on Education. Drawing upon their remarks, David Brown has compiled a compendium of quotations, ideas, recommendations, and helpful hints. Rather than merely describing good leadership, Brown shows readers how to develop it. Exercises at the end of each chapter and a questionnaire provide a useful means for improving skills in leadership and decision making for all college and university executives who seek new ideas concerning institutional renewal, self-improvement, and revitalization.

*549 Eble, Kenneth E. *The Art of Administration: A Guide for Academic Administrators.* San Francisco: Jossey-Bass, 1978. 160 pages.

Drawing on his personal experience as a department chairperson and observer of administrators, Eble has written a handbook for academic leaders. It is particularly useful for those entering administration for the first time. The author makes no claim to explore the aims of higher education, the current state of academic governance, or the like. Rather, he focuses on the administrative skills, attitudes, and qualities that can contribute to attainment of institutional goals. He stresses leadership as a quality to be sought in all administrative tasks. Twelve chapters dealing with such topics as communicating, planning, and exercising authority use frank and perceptive discussion to relay imaginative ideas for dealing with the leadership needs of administrators. Eble conceives of administration as an art and contends that all administrators should develop the skill and sensitivity to fulfill their visions through working with other people. As the book's jacket suggests, it should be of value to department heads, chairpersons, deans, divisional administrators, and faculty members. An extensive bibliography is provided.

★550 Scott, Robert A. *Lords, Squires, and Yeomen: Collegiate Middle Managers and Their Organizations.* AAHE-ERIC Higher Education Research Report no. 7. Washington, D.C.: American Association for Higher Education, 1978. 83 pages.

This study of collegiate middle managers should be useful to a wide range of readers. It presents an overview of the effects of federal compliance requirements on collegiate administrators; the causes of growth, elaboration, and differentiation in middle-level collegiate administration; the functions, status, roles, and values of midlevel administrators; and the role of national occupational associations in providing professional standing. The study's data were gathered through well-designed surveys, interviews, and a literature survey. The study focuses on the deans and directors of support services and excludes presidents, provosts, academic deans, department chairpersons, and librarians. Topics addressed include the background and training of administrators; career paths, mobility, and organizational commitment; administrators' rights and grievance procedures; women and minorities in middle management; communication on campus; liability of administrators; satisfactions and incentives for increased competence and performance; training and development; role conflicts among collegiate middle managers; and professional associations. Recommendations and a bibliography are also included.

551 Scott, Robert A. "Uncertain Loyalists: A Brief Look at Role Conflicts Among Collegiate Middle-Managers." *Review of Higher Education,* 1979, *2* (3), 21–28.

Collegiate middle managers (deans and directors of support services) are described as working in a complex setting that is part bureaucratic, part collegial, and part political. They are loyalists to begin with, and many strive to maintain allegiance to their institution. However, the pressures and attractions of professional work, together with the general lack of regard for administrators by faculty, encourage middle managers to question their loyalty and commitment. Other strains on their loyalty include the strict hierarchical ranking of status levels on campus, limited career mobility and advancement potential, and limited rewards of other kinds. Finally, their loyalty becomes uncertain. This is a useful and thoughtful account of an important aspect of morale and commitment. It should be read especially by college presidents and policymakers.

Chief Academic Officers

552 Brown, David G. (ed.). *Leadership Roles of Chief Academic Officers.* New Directions for Higher Education, no. 47. San Francisco: Jossey-Bass, 1984. 104 pages.

This book includes ten essays that present examples of effective action to help academic leaders—CAOs and deans—anticipate the future with wisdom. The volume begins with thirty-six aphorisms and ends with an example of courageous and comprehensive planning, the recommendations of Notre Dame's Committee on Priorities and Commitments for Excellence. A highlight is Maurice Glicksman's projections of new academic structures that encourage change and growth.

★553 Jedamus, Paul, Peterson, Marvin W., and Associates. *Improving Academic Management: A Handbook of Planning and Institutional Research.* San Francisco: Jossey-Bass, 1980. 679 pages.

Written for "everyone concerned with the effective management and efficient operation of institutions of higher education," the thirty-one chapters in this collection of essays provide overviews of such topics as planning, program review, resource allocations, faculty evaluation, governance structures, needs and environmental assessment, and future trends. Each chapter concludes with a bibliographical essay. Authored mostly by highly respected researcher-practitioners, these essays are excellent pathways to the literature covering a broad range of concerns specific to chief academic officers.

554 McCarty, Donald J., and Reyes, Pedro. "Models of Institutional Governance: Academic Deans' Decision-Making Patterns as Evidenced by Chairpersons." Paper presented at annual meeting of the Association for the Study of Higher Education, Chicago, March 1985.

The perceptions of department chairpersons concerning the leadership roles of academic deans in several colleges of a major research university were identified, based on interviews with fifty-five chairpersons. The typical chairperson was male, from the College of Letters and Science, had served for about four and a half years, was a full professor, was about fifty years old, and had served at the institution for about eighteen years. Of the fifty-five chairpersons, forty-nine were not interested in being a dean, citing such reasons as commitment to teaching and research and the unpleasantness of administrative work. Some respondents offered reasons why other individuals might like to be dean even though they themselves would not, including the opportunity to have influence in shaping the direction of the college. Chairpersons did not conceive of the dean as a powerful and bureaucratic administrative figure; however, over 80 percent of the interview protocols pictured the deans as responding primarily to departmental initiatives. Deans were perceived to govern in a variety of ways. While bureaucratic position enabled the dean to follow a rational decision-making model, the traditional doctrine of freedom in teaching and research supported a collegiality model of academic governance. Also relevant was the political governance model, which recognizes that conflicts inevitably arise. This work provides an in-depth view of leadership at the deanship level and should be useful to students and practitioners.

★555 Moore, Kathryn, and Sagaria, Mary Ann D. "Differential Job Change and Stability Among Academic Administrators." *Journal of Higher Education,* 1982, *53,* 501–513.

The lead author, Kathryn Moore of the Pennsylvania State University, has recently completed the most comprehensive study of mobility of academic administrators that has ever been undertaken. This article is a precursor of a larger work and represents a study of 646 academic administrators in 80 Pennsylvania four-year colleges and universities. The study demonstrates that job change propensities differ by gender and position type as well as by age, marital status, and academic credentials. Researchers and those interested in academic mobility will find this article, as well as Moore's subsequent work, most interesting. Also available through Dr. Moore at the Pennsylvania State University's Center for the Study of Higher Education are research monographs entitled *Today's Academic Leaders: A National Study of Administrators in Community and Junior Colleges* (1985), *The Top Line: A Report on Presidents', Provosts' and Deans' Careers* (1983), and *Women and Minorities: A Leaders in Transition Report* (1982).

556 Scott, Robert A. "The 'Amateur Dean' in a Complex University: An Essay on Role Ambiguity." *Liberal Education,* 1979, *65,* 445–452.

Academic deans, especially in liberal arts colleges, have been called "amateurs" because they have not been schooled for the position and have not had previous experience in the dean's office. A study of the official logbooks of three deans and the author's own experience are used to document the elements of the role of a dean. Those who teach in higher education programs and those who contemplate moving to a deanship should read this account of what deans actually do.

Department Chairs

557 Bennett, John B. *Managing the Academic Department: Cases and Notes.* New York: American Council on Education, 1983. 182 pages.

This volume represents a comprehensive introduction to the role of department chairperson. Although it is neither original in research nor comprehensive in coverage, the case studies it includes provide valuable insights into the dilemmas faced by people in this position. Its concluding chapter discusses the varied roles of the department chairperson as entrepreneur, creative custodian of standards, and politician in terms of the satisfactions of the position. Perhaps one of the most valuable portions of this work is its identification of the forces faced by a faculty member on first becoming a chairperson. This same topic is covered by Bennett's article "Ambiguity and Abrupt Transitions in the Department Chairperson's Role" (*Educational Record*, 1982, *63*, 53–56). This book would be useful to those contemplating moving into a deanship as well as practicing deans and teachers in higher education programs.

558 Knight, W. Hal, and Holen, Michael C. "Leadership and the Perceived Effectiveness of Department Chairpersons." *Journal of Higher Education*, 1985, *56*, 677–690.

Surveys of faculty perceptions of the effectiveness of department heads indicate that leadership styles affect such perceptions. Two elements of leadership style, "initiating structure" and "consideration," relate strongly to faculty evaluations, which have implications for the recruitment, selection, and professional development of department heads. Those who serve on selection and faculty development committees will benefit from a better understanding of leadership style as it relates to department heads.

★**559** Tucker, Alan. *Chairing the Academic Department: Leadership Among Peers.* Washington, D.C.: American Council on Education, 1981. 307 pages.

Originally funded by a W. K. Kellogg Foundation Grant, Allen Tucker conducted, first in Florida and then throughout the country, a series of seminars and workshops for chairpersons. This book, which includes many case studies of common departmental problems as well as extensive analysis of the department chairship, is a compilation and extension of the materials used in these training sessions. Topics covered include leadership styles, delegation, decision making, faculty development and evaluation, goal setting, budgeting, faculty activity reports, and many more. This well-referenced work is the most detailed and fullest analysis of the department chairship to date. Although some portions are laborious reading, it is a "must" for both practitioners and researchers.

560 Waltzer, Herbert. *The Job of Academic Department Chairmen: Experience and Recommendations from Miami University.* Washington, D.C.: American Council on Education, 1975. 35 pages.

Published as an occasional paper, this monograph explores the job definition of the department chair, including the position's satisfactions and dissatisfactions, as perceived by chairpersons from several institutions. Specific issues such as summer stipends, easing paperwork flows, developing form letters, and thinking through salary recommendations are discussed. The author also considers the formal role of the chairship, especially as described in university policy manuals. This monograph is probably most valuable for department chairpersons who have been in the job for a year or two.

★561 Whitson, Linda J., and Hubert, Frank W. R. "Interest Groups and the Department Chairperson: The Exertion of Influence in the Large Public University." *Journal of Higher Education,* 1982, *53,* 163–176.

This article is valuable reading for practitioners. It reports the results of a survey of department chairpersons in fifty-eight large public universities. The survey reveals that, although there are certain differences by field of study, geographical region, size of institution, collective bargaining status, and size of department, department chairpersons feel relatively free from the constraining influence both of groups external to the university and of the board of regents. On the other hand, they do feel constrained by many of the interest groups internal to the university. In those tasks related most directly to faculty, such as curriculum development and hiring decisions, department chairpersons have substantial freedom. This article is valuable for its identification of the managerial tasks of department chairpersons as well as for the research itself.

Business and Development Officers

★562 Fisher, James L. (ed.). *Presidential Leadership in Advancement Activities.* New Directions for Institutional Advancement, no. 8. San Francisco: Jossey-Bass, 1980. 98 pages.

Following a keynote chapter by Theodore Hesburgh, nine chapter authors educate presidents and chief development officers concerning their individual responsibilities in the many-faceted area of university development. Advancement, public relations, alumni affairs, fund-raising, and governmental relations are among the topics covered. Denton Beal provides a final bibliographical chapter on resources and information for presidents and professionals. This monograph is meaningful reading not only for presidents and chief development officers but also for researchers in the area of university development.

563 Heemann, Warren. *Criteria for Evaluating Advancement Programs*. Washington, D.C.: Council for Advancement and Support of Education, 1985. 25 pages.

Developed by leading professionals in the field, this booklet provides accepted guidelines for program evaluations that can be used for internal or external audits. It includes lists of questions for evaluating the areas of alumni relations, fund-raising, government relations, institutional relations, periodicals, publications, and management. Development officers should find the booklet invaluable.

564 Pray, Francis C. (ed.). *Handbook for Educational Fund Raising: A Guide to Successful Principles and Practices for Colleges, Universities, and Schools*. San Francisco: Jossey-Bass, 1981. 442 pages.

For a full description of this work, please see entry no. 228.

★565 Rowland, A. Westley (ed.). *Handbook of Institutional Advancement: A Modern Guide to Executive Management, Institutional Relations, Fund Raising, Alumni Administration, Government Relations, Publications, Periodicals, and Enrollment Management*. (2nd ed.) San Francisco: Jossey-Bass, 1986. 796 pages.

Many of this book's authors are chief advancement officers. The book includes the best current thinking on a wide variety of topics. Of particular interest is Steven Muller's prologue on "The Definition and Philosophy of Institutional Advancement." If a vice-president of development, university relations, or advancement could read only one book, this should be it.

★566 Welzenbach, Lanora F. (ed.). *College and University Business Administration*. (4th ed.) Washington, D.C.: National Association of College and University Business Officers, 1982. 527 pages.

A basic manual, this comprehensive reference has been developed by nearly 100 volunteer chief business officers. Most of the volume is devoted to technical explanations of details in administrative management, business management, fiscal management, and financial accounting and reporting. The first chapter focuses on the role of the chief business officer in the academic hierarchy and on the leadership skills needed by the effective CBO. An extensive bibliography, arranged by category, is included. This volume is a must for the reference shelf of every chief business officer.

Student Affairs Officers

567 Cox, David W., and Ivy, William A. "Staff Development Needs of Student Affairs Professionals." *NASPA Journal*, 1984, *22*, 26–33.

This article reports the results of a survey in which 142 student affairs professionals assess their specific needs for professional development. The taxonomy of skills used here—goal setting, assessment, instruction, consultation, management value, and evaluation—can provide a valuable framework for planners of their own professional development. This survey identifies the highest developmental needs as the needs to "communicate program goals to the larger academic community," "be able to gain commitment from top decision makers," and "engage in collaborative efforts with other faculty and staff." Of least importance were needs to "maintain student confidentiality" and "demonstrate a sense of empathy for students' needs." The research itself is solid. Its main application is not in its findings, however, but in its comprehensive statements of skills and development needs. These should be useful to student affairs personnel in self-appraisal and career development and to those who provide support for such activities.

★568 Delworth, Ursula, Hanson, Gary R., and Associates. *Student Services: A Handbook for the Profession*. San Francisco: Jossey-Bass, 1980. 503 pages.

A compendium of individual essays on the multiple aspects of the student affairs responsibility, this reference volume is targeted for professional practitioners. In addition to describing the responsibilities of student services, this book touches on learning theory and provides a rich analysis of the theoretical underpinnings of the student affairs profession. Uneven in quality, this compendium is nevertheless a valuable resource.

569 Kirby, Alan F., and Woodard, Dudley (eds.). *Career Perspectives in Student Affairs*. NASPA Monograph Series, no. 1. Columbus, Ohio: National Association of Student Personnel Administrators, 1984. 76 pages.

Seven chief student affairs officers offer essays on the complexities of making choices regarding personal careers and professional development. They reflect upon the advice they wished they had received from, or would like to give to, others in the field. This monograph also includes an excellent bibliography on student affairs as a profession. The authors start with a historical perspective of the student affairs profession, then propose changes in doctoral training programs, trace career paths, characterize life as a manager, and speculate on the future environment likely to be faced by student personnel officers. For those practitioners who learn from experiential essays, this volume could be valuable.

570 *NASPA Journal*, 1982, *20* (2). 61 pages.

This entire issue by the National Association of Student Personnel Administrators is devoted to careers in student affairs. Article titles are "Career Development for the Experienced Student Affairs Professional" (K. Arnold), "Who Leaves the Student Affairs Field?" (Martha A. Burns), "Burnout Is Not Necessary: Prevention and Recovery" (T. Thorne Wiggers and others), "Enhancement and Advancement: Professional Development for Student Affairs Staff" (M. Anne Lawing and others), "Exploring Career Patterns in Student Affairs: Problems of Conception and Methodology" (David R. Holmes), "Turnover at the Top: A Study of the Chief Student Affairs Officer" (Scott T. Rickard), "Women and Minority Professional Staff and Student Personnel" (Carol C. Harter and others), and "Professional Preparation Programs in Student Personnel Services in Higher Education: A National Assessment by Chief Student Affairs Officers" (Arthur Sandeen). Most articles include good bibliographies. The articles should be of interest to a wide audience, including students, practitioners, administrators, and policymakers.

571 Rickard, Scott. "Career Pathways of Chief Student Affairs Officers: Making Room at the Top for Females and Minorities." *NASPA Journal*, 1985, *22*, 52–59.

The reader can gain perspective regarding career paths and opportunities in student personnel from this article. Based upon a survey response by 162 newly appointed CSAOs, this study notes that, among those who reach the top, females are younger, have less full-time experience in student personnel work, and have less formal training. There were no significant differences between minorities and nonminorities on any of the variables. In addition to treating a rather specific topic, this article includes valuable references to recent literature. It should be useful to students and researchers as well as practitioners.

Appendix A. Higher Education Journals, Periodicals, and Monograph Series

Journals and Periodicals

AAHE Bulletin, the monthly bulletin (except July and August) of the American Association for Higher Education (Washington, D.C.), features articles on current issues in higher education.

AGB Reports, the bimonthly journal of the Association of Governing Boards of Universities and Colleges (Washington, D.C.), contains articles designed to provide trustees and chief executives with comprehensive and timely perspectives on their basic roles and responsibilities and their working relationships with their constituencies.

Black Issues in Higher Education, a newsletter published twice monthly by Cox, Matthews and Associates, Inc. (4002 University Drive, Fairfax, Va. 22030), includes higher education information of importance to those interested in the education of blacks.

Business Officer, published monthly by the National Association of College and University Business Officers (Washington, D.C.), provides reports on national events affecting higher education business officers.

Change, a bimonthly journal of the American Association for Higher Education, published by Heldref Publications (Washington, D.C.), is a well-researched volume with topical articles that cover all aspects of higher education. Contributors include academics and political leaders as well as essayists and journalists.

Chronicle of Higher Education (Washington, D.C.) is a weekly newspaper (forty-six issues annually) devoted to the field of higher education.

Community and Junior College Journal, published quarterly by the American Association of Community and Junior Colleges (Washington, D.C.), focuses on program, teaching, curriculum, and planning and management issues in two-year colleges.

Economics of Education Review, published quarterly by Pergamon Press (Elmsford, N.Y.), features articles on financial and economic issues in education.

Educational Record, published quarterly by the American Council on Education (Washington, D.C.), contains articles on higher education topics, particularly administrative concerns.

Higher Education, published bimonthly (Amsterdam, the Netherlands: Elsevier Science), is the international journal of higher education and education planning. It considers all aspects of higher education. Its articles are contributed by academics from featured countries.

Higher Education and National Affairs, published by the American Council on Education (Washington, D.C.), is a biweekly review of national policy related to higher education.

Journal for Higher Education Management, a biannual journal of the American Association of University Administrators published by College Press Service (Denver, Colo.), features articles on management issues in higher education.

Journal of College and University Law, published quarterly by the National Association of College and University Attorneys

(Washington, D.C.), contains articles and commentaries on recent court cases and legislative and administrative developments.

Journal of the College and University Personnel Association, published quarterly by the College and University Personnel Association (Washington, D.C.), features articles primarily of interest to personnel administrators.

Journal of Higher Education, a bimonthly publication of the Ohio State University Press (Columbus) and the American Association for Higher Education, presents research and theory on organizational and other topics in higher education.

Journal of Student Financial Aid, the journal of the National Association of Student Financial Aid Administrators (Washington, D.C.), is published three times annually and reports on a wide range of topics relevant to student financial aid.

NACUBO Professional File, published monthly by the National Association for College and University Business Officers (Washington, D.C.), contains articles that focus on business management issues in higher education.

Research in Higher Education, the journal of the Association for Institutional Research, is published in eight issues annually by Agathon Press (Albany, N.Y.). It publishes organizational and other topical research relating to higher education and frequently uses quantitative research methods.

Review of Higher Education, the journal of the Association for the Study of Higher Education (Washington, D.C.), has three issues annually and publishes theoretical, empirical, and review articles on organizational and other topics in higher education.

Monograph Series

Administrator's Update, a monograph published quarterly by the American Association of University Administrators and the ERIC Clearinghouse on Higher Education (Washington, D.C.), contains feature articles on current issues in higher education.

ASHE-ERIC Higher Education Research Reports, published by the Educational Resources Information Center of the Association for the Study of Higher Education (Washington, D.C.), are an annual series of eight monographs that analyze key issues in academe based on research and institutional experiences. The primary purpose of the series is to help administrators, faculty, and others stay abreast of current key literature, including institutional research practices.

New Directions for Community Colleges, quarterly sourcebooks published by Jossey-Bass (San Francisco), focus on a broad range of issues related to community or two-year colleges.

New Directions for Higher Education, quarterly sourcebooks published by Jossey-Bass (San Francisco), cover a variety of higher education topics, including statewide planning, budgeting, and designing of academic program reviews.

New Directions for Institutional Research, quarterly sourcebooks published by Jossey-Bass (San Francisco), cover higher education topics with the institutional researcher in mind.

New Directions for Program Evaluation, quarterly sourcebooks published by Jossey-Bass (San Francisco), cover program evaluation issues ranging from value judgments made during evaluation to ways to analyze data.

New Directions for Student Services, quarterly sourcebooks published by Jossey-Bass (San Francisco), focus on issues and topics of interest to student service administrators.

Appendix B. Other Related Publications

Federal and State Government

American Education, a monthly publication of the Department of Education (Washington, D.C.), provides information on federal policies that affect education.

Federal Funds for Research and Development, an annual publication of the National Science Foundation (Washington, D.C.), provides information on and obligations for federally funded research and development projects.

State Government, published quarterly by the Council of State Governments (Lexington, Ky.), focuses on major aspects of state programs, problems, and proposed solutions. It emphasizes pragmatic rather than theoretical considerations.

State Government News, published monthly by the Council of State Governments (Lexington, Ky.), is considered to be the prime source of information about current activities in all branches of state government.

Human Resource Development and Training

Performance and Instruction Journal, published monthly (ten issues annually) by the National Society for Performance and Instruction (Washington, D.C.), features articles on human resource management.

Personnel Administrator, published monthly by the American Society for Personnel Administration (Alexandria, Va.), features articles on personnel management.

Training, published monthly by Lakewood Publications (Minneapolis, Minn.), is devoted to human resource development.

Training and Development Journal, published monthly by the American Society for Training and Development (Alexandria, Va.), contains articles on human resource development.

Legal

Journal of Law and Education, published quarterly by the Jefferson Law Book Co. (Cincinnati, Ohio), features commentaries on cases affecting education.

NOLPE Yearbook of School Law, published by the National Organization on Legal Problems in Education (Topeka, Kans.), is an annual summary of significant cases in elementary/secondary education law and higher education law. From 1977 to 1981, a separate *Yearbook of Higher Education Law* was published; since 1981, a section in the *Yearbook* has been devoted to higher education issues.

Specialty Law Digest, published monthly by Clayton R. Smalley (Blaine, Minn.), includes digests of court opinions that address education law issues, as well as reprints of law journal articles on education law topics.

Legal Deskbook for Administrators of Independent Colleges and Universities (Atlanta/Macon, Ga.: Center for Constitutional Studies, Mercer University), edited by Kent M. Weeks, was originally published in 1983 and is supplemented annually. This reference work presents brief discussions of important legal issues faced by administrators of independent colleges and universities. Topics include governance, employment, students, physical facilities, liability, taxation, and church-related institutions. A selected bibliography and a list of cases end each chapter.

Appendix C. Higher Education Associations

American Association for Higher Education
One Dupont Circle, N.W., Suite 600
Washington, D.C. 20036

American Association of Collegiate
Registrars and Admissions Officers
One Dupont Circle, N.W., Suite 330
Washington, D.C. 20036

American Association of Community and
Junior Colleges
One Dupont Circle, N.W., Suite 410
Washington, D.C. 20036

American Association of Presidents of
Independent Colleges and Universities
Grove City College
Grove City, Pa. 16127

American Association of State Colleges
and Universities
One Dupont Circle, N.W., Suite 700
Washington, D.C. 20036

American Association of University
Administrators
Box 6221
Tuscaloosa, Ala. 35487–6221

American Association of University
Professors
One Dupont Circle, N.W., Suite 500
Washington, D.C. 20036

American Conference of Academic
Deans
1818 R Street, N.W.
Washington, D.C. 20009

American Council on Education
One Dupont Circle, N.W., Suite 800
Washington, D.C. 20036

American Society for Training and Development
1630 Duke Street
Box 1443
Alexandria, Va. 22313

Association for Institutional Research
314 Stone Building
Florida State University
Tallahassee, Fla. 32306

Association for the Study of Higher Education
One Dupont Circle, N.W., Suite 630
Washington, D.C. 20036

Association of American Colleges
1818 R Street, N.W.
Washington, D.C. 20009

Association of American Universities
One Dupont Circle, N.W., Suite 730
Washington, D.C. 20036

Association of Community College
Trustees
6928 Little River Turnpike, Suite A
Annandale, Va. 22003

Association of Governing Boards
of Universities and Colleges
One Dupont Circle, N.W., Suite 400
Washington, D.C. 20036

Association of Independent Colleges
and Schools
One Dupont Circle, N.W., Suite 350
Washington, D.C. 20036

CAUSE (Information Technology Association)
737 29th Street
Boulder, Colo. 80303

College and University Personnel Association
Eleven Dupont Circle, N.W., Suite 120
Washington, D.C. 20036

Council for Advancement and Support of Education
Eleven Dupont Circle, N.W., Suite 400
Washington, D.C. 20036

Council of Independent Colleges
One Dupont Circle, N.W., Suite 320
Washington, D.C. 20036

Education Commission of the States
1860 Lincoln Street, Suite 300
Denver, Colo. 80295

National Association of College
and University Attorneys
One Dupont Circle, N.W., Suite 650
Washington, D.C. 20036

National Association of College
and University Business Officers
One Dupont Circle, N.W., Suite 500
Washington, D.C. 20036

National Association of Independent
Colleges and Universities
122 C Street, N.W., Suite 750
Washington, D.C. 20001

National Association of State
Universities and Land-Grant Colleges
One Dupont Circle, N.W., Suite 710
Washington, D.C. 20036

National Association of Student
Financial Aid Administrators
1776 Massachusetts Ave., N.W., Suite 100
Washington, D.C. 20036

National Association of Student
Personnel Administrators
160 Rightmire Hall
1060 Carmack Road
Columbus, Ohio 43210

National Center for the Study
of Collective Bargaining in Higher
Education and the Professions
Baruch College
City University of New York
New York, N.Y. 10010

Organizational Development Institute
6501 Wilson Mills Road, Suite K
Cleveland, Ohio 44143

Organizational Development Resources, Inc.
2900 Chamblee-Tucker Road
Building 16
Atlanta, Ga. 30341

Professional and Organizational
Development Network in Higher Education
c/o Betty Lesere Erickson
Instructional Development Program
201 Chafee
University of Rhode Island
Kingston, R.I. 02881

Society for College and University Planning
The University of Michigan
2026M School of Education Building
Ann Arbor, Mich. 48109

Special Interest Group on Education Law
American Educational Research Association
1126 Sixteenth Street, N.W.
Washington, D.C. 20036

State Higher Education Executive
Officers Association
1860 Lincoln Street, Suite 310
Denver, Colo. 80295

Name Index

A

Ackoff, R. L., 288
Adams, C. R., 275
Adams, J., 283
Adelman, C., 226
Allen, R. H., 198, 210, 211–212
Alm, K., 226–227
Alpert, D. P., 146, 151–152, 357
Altbach, P. G., 102
Andersen, C., 132
Anderson, D., 332
Anderson, G. L., 429
Anderson, R. E., 198, 209
Arcady, P., 457
Archibald, S. O., 406–407
Armijo, F., 223
Arnett, T., 195, 202
Arnold, K., 480
Arns, R. G., 231
Astin, A. W., 6, 339, 372, 385, 469–470
Atwell, R. H., 135–136
Austin, A. E., 424, 437

B

Babbidge, H. D., 70, 76
Bachman, J. G., 393, 399–400
Bailey, S. K., 75, 78, 287, 289
Bakke, A., 377
Balderston, F. E., 7, 168, 175, 297
Baldridge, J. V., 6, 13, 30, 35, 105, 144, 146, 147, 152, 158–159, 180, 306, 312–313, 317–318, 362

Baldwin, R. G., 252
Bantel, K., 322n
Barak, R. J., 42, 57, 59, 218, 228, 230, 234
Bardach, E., 168, 175
Bare, A. C., 330
Barnard, C. I., 17, 19
Bass, B. M., 396–397, 408–409
Bauer, R. A., 287, 289–290
Beadle, M., 461
Beal, D., 477
Beck, H., 5
Becker, W. E., Jr., 208
Behn, R. D., 359
Bender, L. W., 68, 69, 76, 388
Benezet, L. T., 452
Bennett, J. B., 475
Bennis, W. G., 318–319, 409, 415, 421, 426
Berdahl, R. O., 6, 13, 19, 40, 42, 45, 48, 59, 102, 135–136, 230
Berendzen, R., 460
Bergmann, B. R., 380, 381
Bergquist, W. H., 223, 225, 423, 436
Bernstein, M. H., 206
Bess, J. L., 144, 162
Beyer, J. M., 341–342
Billings, R. S., 351, 359, 393, 402–403
Birnbaum, R., 147, 148, 348, 354
Blackburn, R. T., 343–343
Blanchard, K. H., 395, 406, 407
Blischke, W. R., 42, 49
Bogue, E. G., 227
Bolles, R. N., 424, 438, 439
Bolman, F., 450

Bouchard, R. A., 242–243, 256
Boucher, W. I., 190
Boulding, K. E., 23, 24, 27, 39, 178, 287, 290–291, 347, 354
Bowen, F. M., 13, 146, 156–157, 351, 353, 355–356
Bowen, H. R., 42, 199, 203–204, 287, 297–298, 347, 354
Bowen, Z. P., 241, 250
Bozeman, B., 351, 354
Braskamp, L. A., 229
Braybrooke, D., 291
Breneman, D. W., 7, 42, 79, 198, 204–205
Brewer, G. D., 187
Brewster, K., Jr., 1, 19
Brinkerhoff, D., 333
Brinkman, P. T., 198, 210, 211–212
Brint, S., 236
Brody, A., 41, 48
Brooks, G. E., 12, 20, 168, 175
Brown, D. G., 420, 424, 438, 464, 470, 472
Brown, K. C., 278
Brubacher, J. S., 2, 19, 347, 354
Budig, G. A., 43, 48
Burke, C. B., 347, 354
Burns, G. P., 466, 469
Burns, J. M., 295–296, 396, 409, 410
Burns, M. A., 480
Butler, M. J., 349, 354

C

Cage, B. N., 208
Caldren, S. L., 69, 77
Calkins, D., 260
Callan, P. M., 54
Calvin, A., 377
Cameron, K. S., 7, 30–31, 38, 147, 148, 322, 331, 332, 334, 350, 358, 397, 398, 410
Campbell, D. F., 200, 214
Campbell, J., 335
Carlson, E. D., 277
Carnes, M. L., 429–430
Carnevale, A. P., 255
Carter, E. E., 209
Cartter, A., 341–342, 347, 354

Cartwright, D., 400
Caruthers, J. K., 55, 215
Cattell, J. M., 322, 341
Centra, J. A., 241, 252–253
Chaffee, E. E., 17, 19–20, 21, 23, 27, 28, 181, 351, 359, 397, 398, 410
Chait, R. P., 125, 240, 253
Chambers, C., 227
Chambers, M. M., 42, 48, 95, 101
Chew, R. L., 271
Chickering, A. W., 225
Chin, R., 417, 431–432
Chittipeddi, K., 189–190
Chronister, J., 42, 48
Churchill, W., 25, 409
Churchman, 265
Clague, M. W., 105–106
Clark, B. R., 6, 11, 17, 20, 32, 141, 144, 146, 148, 153, 168, 397, 398, 410
Clark, J. G., 442
Clark, M. J., 231
Cleary, R. E., 457–458
Cleveland, H., 134
Clodius, J. E., 460
Clough, A. H., 390, 399
Cochran, T. R., 234–235
Cohen, M. D., 15, 143, 144, 146, 153, 159–160, 168, 391, 395, 398, 403, 453
Coldren, S. L., 215–216
Coleman, J. S., 287, 292
Coll-Pardo, I., 241, 254, 423, 434
Conant, J. B., 44, 48
Conrad, C. F., 224, 232, 310, 314–315, 342–343
Coons, C. A., 135
Cope, R. G., 34, 181–182
Corbally, J. E., 144, 150, 461
Corbally, M. W., 460, 461
Corcoran, M., 302
Cornell, E., 442
Corrozzini, A. J., 71, 76
Corson, J. J., 3, 10, 20, 116–117, 122, 144, 148
Cote, L. S., 458
Cowley, W. H., 6
Cox, D. W., 479
Craft, R., 53

Craig, R. L., 239, 250, 423, 433
Craven, E., 227
Cross, K. P., 239, 253
Crossland, F. E., 347, 354
Crosson, P. H., 47, 50
Curtis, D. V., 146, 147, 152
Cyert, R. L., 264, 271, 391-392, 399

D

Daft, R. L., 39
Dahl, T., 404
Dahrendorf, R., 143, 149
Dalglish, T. K., 43, 142, 146, 154
Darwin, C., 52
Davidson, E. E., 217
Davis, C. K., 235
Davis, G. B., 272-273
Deal, T., 30
Delworth, U., 479-480
Demerath, N. J., 144, 149
Dexter, L. D., 290
Dill, D. D., 13, 20, 22, 32, 313, 390, 394, 403
Dodds, H. W., 12, 20
Dougherty, E. A., 235
Dresch, S. P., 84, 347, 354
Dressel, P. L., 50-51, 225-226, 229, 421, 426, 430
Drew, D. E., 343
Dreyfuss, J., 377-378
Dror, Y., 188
Dugan, D. J., 71, 76
Dunnette, M. D., 37
Duryea, E. D., 140, 149
Dutton, J. E., 351, 352, 361-362
Dyer, L. D., 258

E

Eble, K. E., 470-471
Ecker, G. P., 146, 147, 152
Edwards, H. T., 101-102, 111, 113
Edwards, R., 457
Eells, W. C., 447-448
Eisenhower, D. D., 11, 81
Eliot, C., 5, 391
Elliott, E. C., 95, 101
Elliott, J. M., 261

Elmore, R. F., 188
Enarson, H. L., 454
Etzioni, A., 143, 146, 148, 149, 154, 292-293
Eulau, H., 43, 48
Ewell, P. T., 62
Exum, W. H., 374, 381-382

F

Falender, A. J., 200, 216
Farmer, C. H., 417, 430-431
Feasley, C. E., 57
Feller, D. E., 19
Fenske, R. H., 71, 76
Ferry, D., 333-334
Festa, C., 423, 434
Fiedler, F. E., 395, 405-406, 407
Fields, C. M., 378
Fincher, C., 282, 293
Finkin, M. W., 19
Finn, C. E., Jr., 42, 75, 79, 80-81, 198, 199, 204, 206
Firnberg, J. W., 299-300
Fisher, C. F., 241, 254, 412, 423, 431, 433-434
Fisher, J. L., 417-418, 425, 453, 477
Fleming, J., 386
Flexner, A., 5
Floyd, C., 55
Folger, J. K., 44, 51, 52, 59-60, 62-63
Ford, J. D., 353, 354
Forester, J., 182
Fortunato, R. T., 238, 241, 243, 246, 254, 257-258, 261, 380-381, 423, 431, 434
Fossum, J. A., 258
Frances, C., 300, 347, 354
Franchak, S. J., 235
Franke, W. B., 195, 202
Franklin, H. B., 144, 149
Frantzreb, A. C., 125-126
Freeman, J., 335
French, J. R. P., Jr., 392-393, 399, 400
Friedland, E. I., 143, 149
Friedman, C. P., 313
Friedmann, J., 175-176
Froomkin, J., 83-84

Fuhrman, S., 53
Fullagar, P. K., 390
Fuller, S. E., 456–457
Fulmer, K., 415, 421, 427
Furash, 289
Furniss, W. T., 424, 438

G

Gade, M. L., 462
Gaff, J. G., 423, 434
Gaff, S. S., 423, 434
Gaffney, E. M., Jr., 111–112
Gamso, G., 212
Gamson, Z. F., 17, 20, 424, 437
Gandhi, M., 409
Garbarino, J. W., 19
Garcia, H., 194n
Gardner, J. W., 135–136, 415, 425
Genova, W. J., 417, 431–432
Gentile, A. C., 232
George, M. D., 229
Georgiou, P., 143, 149
Gergen, K. J., 289
Gerrity, T. P., 269, 271
Gerth, H. H., 143, 149
Ghorpade, J., 332–333
Gilley, J. W., 415, 421, 427, 449–450
Gilman, D. C., 443
Gladieux, L. E., 75, 79, 80, 83, 84
Glenny, L. A., 6, 42, 43, 45, 47, 49,
      51–52, 142, 146, 154, 210, 351, 353,
      355–356
Glicksman, M., 472
Glover, R. H., 278
Gluck, F. W., 182–183
Glueck, W. F., 258, 403–404
Goheen, R. F., 144, 149
Goldstein, H., 255
Gonyea, M. A., 212–213
Goodall, L. E., 43, 49
Goodman, P., 11, 20
Goodman, P. S., 334–335
Gordon, R. A., 236
Gould, J. W., 466, 469
Gould, R. A., 223
Gouldner, H., 102
Gove, S. K., 63
Grabowski, H. G., 71, 76

Grambsch, P. V., 144, 149
Gray, W. S., 67, 76
Green, K. C., 57–58, 340, 362
Green, M. F., 420, 423, 435
Greenberg, E. M., 223
Greenberg, J. A., 238
Greenwood, A. G., 276
Greer, D., 53
Greve, A., 351, 358
Groner, N. E., 405–406
Gross, E., 144, 149
Guba, E. G., 48, 49
Gueths, J., 240, 253
Gulick, L., 142, 149
Gusfield, J., 17, 20

H

Hagberg, J. O., 424, 439
Hall, D. T., 351, 352, 360, 424, 439
Hall, G. S., 443
Halliburton, D., 225
Halstead, D. K., 42, 44, 45, 49
Hamblin, R. L., 348, 351, 354
Hamermesh, R. G., 351, 355
Hammond, L. W., 279
Hannan, M., 335
Hansen, L., 83
Hanson, G. R., 479–480
Harcleroad, F. F., 55, 210, 227
Hardy, C., 35
Harper, W. R., 195, 202, 443
Harter, C. C., 480
Hartman, R. W., 71, 76, 79
Hartmark, L. S., 63–64
Havelock, R. G., 168, 314, 319
Hearn, J. C., 189
Hedberg, B. L. T., 35–36, 351, 358
Heemann, W., 478
Helsabeck, R. E., 144, 146, 155
Henderson, A., 5, 6, 7
Henderson, L. E., 114
Hendrickson, R. M., 378
Heneman, H. G., 258
Hengstler, D. D., 234–235
Henry, D. D., 141, 149
Hermann, C. F., 348, 350, 352, 359,
      360
Hersey, P., 395, 406, 407

Herzlinger, R., 260
Hesburgh, T., 477
Heydinger, R. B., 189, 224, 233
Hiltz, S. R., 280
Hines, E. R., 63-64
Hipps, G. M., 319-320
Hirschhorn, L., 353, 362
Hitch, C. J., 265, 271
Hitt, M., 374-375
Hobbs, W. C., 88, 102-103, 112
Hodgkinson, H. L., 115, 117, 122, 144, 146, 149, 158, 236, 419-420, 424, 439-440
Hodgkinson, V. A., 88-89
Hofer, C. W., 168, 185-186
Holen, M. C., 475
Hollander, E., 53
Hollis, E. V., 447-448
Holmes, D. R., 480
Hopkins, D. S. P., 145, 168, 198, 216, 273, 276
Hopkins, J., 442
Hoskins, J. C., 281
House, E. R., 229
Howard, J. A., 144, 149
Hoy, C. J., 206
Hoyt, K. B., 229
Huber, G. P., 271
Hubert, F. W. R., 477
Hudson, B., 175-176
Huff, R. P., 71, 76
Hughes, 341
Hungate, T. L., 195, 202
Hunt, P., 160
Hurst, J., 129, 236
Hurwitz, E., Jr., 43, 49
Hussain, K. M., 265, 271
Hutchins, R. M., 5, 391, 443, 447
Hyatt, H. J., 55
Hyatt, J. A., 353, 363
Hyer, P. B., 375

I

Ihlanfeldt, W., 206
Ingram, R. T., 114, 126
Isaac, P. D., 387-388
Ivancevich, J., 258
Ivy, W. A., 479

J

Jackson, G. A., 71, 76
James, B. G., 179
Jamieson, D. M., 281
Janis, I. L., 294
Jedamus, P., 224, 268, 271, 300, 473
Jefferson, T., 5
Jennings, D. M., 271
Jick, T. D., 353, 363
Johnson, E. A., 136
Johnson, J. R., 64
Johnson, L. B., 11, 68, 81
Johnson, L. G., 192-193
Jones, W. T., 459
Jonsen, R. W., 54
Jonsson, S. A., 351, 355
Jordan, D. S., 443
Josephs, D. C., 11
Judy, R. W., 265, 271

K

Kahn, R. L., 13, 20, 143, 149
Kaiser, H. H., 127
Kanter, R. M., 333, 393, 400
Kaplin, W. A., 7, 103-104, 379
Kaplowitz, R. A., 421, 427
Karlesky, J. J., 91
Karpf, R., 343
Katz, D., 13, 20, 143, 149
Katz, J., 452
Katz, R. L., 393, 401
Kauffman, J. F., 147, 149, 414, 416, 421, 427-428, 441, 450, 454-455, 461
Kauffman, J. W., 347, 355
Kaufman, M., 44, 49
Kaufman, S. P., 182-183
Kean, T., 61
Kearsley, G., 243, 250-251
Keeley, M., 335
Keen, P. G. W., 264, 273-274
Keiser, D. W., 241, 243, 254, 423, 434
Keller, G., 168, 176, 410
Kelly, F. J., 41, 49
Kemerer, F. R., 105, 146, 158-159, 362
Kennedy, J. F., 11, 81, 199

Kerchner, C. T., 36, 356
Kerr, C., 9, 41, 414, 415, 421, 425,
    428, 443, 448, 453–454, 462
Kerr, J. C., 81
Kirby, A. F., 480
Kirkpatrick, D. L., 243, 251, 320
Klein, D., 320–321
Knight, W. H., 475
Knowles, A. G., 300
Knowles, M. S., 239, 255–256
Koch, J. V., 381
Kotler, P., 183
Kramer, J., 448–449
Kramer, M., 83
Kuh, G. D., 233, 339–340
Kuhns, E., 316

L

LaMorte, M. W., 108
Laney, J. T., 455
Langley, A., 35
La Noue, G. R., 106–107
Lasher, W. F., 299–300
Lawrence, C., III, 377–378
Lawrence, G. B., 14, 20, 168, 175
Lawrence, J. K., 340
Lawring, M. A., 480
Lee, B. A., 93, 106, 107, 378
Lee, E. C., 13, 146, 156–157
Lee, J. B., 65
Lehmann, T., 42, 49
Leider, R., 424, 439
Leslie, L. L., 55, 194, 198, 200, 207,
    210, 347, 355
Lester, V., 457
Levin, H. M., 213
Levine, A., 315
Levine, C. H., 350, 351, 352, 353, 355,
    356
Levine, H., 236
Levine, J. B., 265, 271
Levinson, D. J., 424, 439, 440
Lewin, K., 321
Lewis, D. R., 404
Libby, P. A., 421, 428
Licata, C. M., 240, 253–254
Licklider, J. C. R., 264, 271
Lincoln, A., 409
Lincoln, Y. S., 48, 49

Lindblom, C. E., 160, 287, 291, 294–
    295
Lindgren, J. R., 379
Lindquist, J., 225, 306, 310–311, 313–
    314
Lohmann, R. A., 211
Long, J. P., 236
Lovell, J. B., 92
Lozier, G. G., 189–190
Luconi, F. L., 269, 271
Lundin, R. A., 351, 355

M

McCartt, A. T., 279
McCarty, D. J., 473–474
McClelland, D. C., 393–394, 401–402
McConnell, T. R., 5, 6, 15, 20, 142,
    144, 146, 149, 159
McCorkle, C. O., Jr., 406–407
McCredie, J. W., 274
McGrath, E., 5, 6
McGrath, M., 332
MacKay, K. H., 281
McKeachie, W. J., 241, 250
McKean, R. N., 265, 271, 272
McLagan, P. A., 239, 251
McLaughlin, J., 414, 416, 421, 429, 451
McMurrin, S. M., 201, 202
McNamara, R., 265
McNeely, J. H., 41, 49
McNurlin, B. C., 268, 272
Madoff, M. K., 417, 431–432
Magnusson, F. W., 452
Magrath, D. S., 460
Malone, T. W., 269, 271
Mandelbaum, S. J., 179
Mann, L., 294
Manning, T. E., 300–301
Mansfield, R., 351, 352, 360
Manski, C. F., 85, 200, 207
Mao Zedong, 409
March, J. G., 7, 15, 28–29, 143, 144,
    145, 146, 150–151, 153, 159–160,
    168, 264, 271, 391–392, 395, 398,
    399, 403, 453
Marchese, T. J., 422, 428
Marcus, L. R., 53, 64
Marshall, A., 199, 202
Martin, J., 268, 272

Martinez, N., 194n
Martorana, S. V., 316
Masland, A. T., 17, 20
Mason, R. O., 265, 272
Mason, T. R., 274
Massy, W. F., 145, 168, 198, 216, 276
Matthews, J. B., 193
May, E. R., 295
Mayhew, L. B., 70, 76, 225
Mayo, E., 142, 149
Meadows, R. B., 108
Meeth, L. R., 144, 149
Meisinger, 42
Melchiori, G. A., 236–237
Menges, R. J., 381–382
Merson, J. C., 200, 216
Mets, L. A., 1, 412
Meyer, G. J., 248, 250, 261
Meyer, J. W., 29, 33
Meyer, M. W., 33
Michael, D. N., 176
Miko, M-B., 226–227
Milburn, T. W., 351, 359
Millard, R. M., 52
Miller, H. F., 347, 355
Miller, L. S., 71, 77
Miller, R. I., 227, 230, 417, 432
Millett, J. D., 4, 11, 13, 20, 43, 45, 49, 52–53, 144, 146, 149, 155–156
Millington, W. G., 108–109
Mills, C. W., 143, 149
Minar, D. W., 43, 49
Mincer, J., 199, 202
Mingle, J. R., 29, 60, 110, 142, 353, 363–364
Mintzberg, H., 29, 35, 183–184, 394, 395, 398, 404–405, 458
Minugh, C. J., 236
Mitchell, B. I., 344
Mitroff, I. I., 39
Moon, R., 70, 76–77
Mooney, R. L., 141, 149
Moore, K., 474
Moore, L. J., 276
Moos, M., 42, 49
Moots, P. R., 111–112
Morgan, A. W., 42, 129, 210, 344
Morrison, J. L., 171, 190
Mortimer, K. P., 6, 15, 16, 20, 142, 146, 149, 159, 210, 357

Mueller, R. K., 127–128
Muller, S., 478
Munitz, B., 227, 417, 422, 432–433
Murphy, P. E., 183
Murray, V. V., 353, 363
Myran, G. A., 184

N

Nadler, L., 239, 251–252, 256
Nanus, B., 415, 421, 426
Napoleon, 390
Nason, J. W., 128, 414, 415, 417, 421, 422, 429, 433, 450–451
Nelson, S. C., 198, 204–205
Neustadt, R. E., 295
Newman, F., 61, 70–71, 75, 77, 85–86, 137
Nordin, V. D., 101–102, 109
Nordvall, R. C., 303, 311, 423, 435
Norgaard, R., 193
Norris, D. M., 29, 163, 177, 364
Nystrom, P. C., 35–36

O

Oberst, D. J., 271, 272
Odell, M., 53
Ohmae, K., 191
Okimi, P. H., 180
Olivas, M. A., 386–387
Olsen, J. P., 143, 159–160
Olson, M. H., 272–273
Olswang, S. G., 107, 110
O'Neil, R. M., 104, 111, 112–113
Orfield, G., 387
Orlans, H., 7
Orwig, M. D., 55, 73, 77, 215
Ostrom, V., 143, 148, 149
Ota, P., 379
Otto, H. L., 55

P

Pace, C. R., 338
Palola, E., 42, 49
Paltridge, J. G., 122, 129
Parker, B., 353, 355
Parsons, T., 142, 150

Patton, G., 396-397
Peck, R. D., 456
Peltason, J. W., 295-296
Pennings, J. M., 160-161, 334-335
Perkins, J. A., 12, 20, 144, 149
Persavich, J. J., 229
Peters, T. J., 17, 20
Peterson, M. W., 1, 5, 20, 23, 59, 144, 145, 149, 151, 162, 177-178, 224, 300, 302, 412, 473
Petrie, H. G., 229, 357
Pettigrew, A. M., 38
Petty, G. F., 130-131
Pezzoni, J. V., 261
Pfeffer, J., 23, 27, 31, 330-331, 335-336, 393, 401
Platt, G. M., 142, 150
Plutarch, 390
Poland, W., 231
Pondy, L. R., 39
Pool, I. S., 290
Porter, M. E., 191-192
Poulton, N. L., 163, 277
Pray, F. C., 129, 217, 478
Preer, J. L., 110-111
Price, E., 194n
Pruitt, A. S., 387-388
Purves, 42

Q

Quarterman, J. S., 281
Quinley, H., 43, 48
Quinn, J. B., 36, 185
Quinn, R. E., 331-332

R

Rabineau, L., 44, 49
Radner, R., 71, 77
Rainsford, G. N., 81-82
Ramey, G. W., 198, 200, 207
Ransdell, G. A., 233
Raven, B., 392-393, 399, 400
Reagan, R., 69, 75, 82, 90, 367, 372
Redford, E. S., 147, 150
Reed, R. J., 376
Reeves, F. W., 5, 195, 203
Reithlingshoefer, S., 415, 421, 427
Renfro, W. L., 190

Reyes, P., 473-474
Richardson, R. C., Jr., 366, 388
Rickard, S. T., 480, 481
Riesman, D., 7, 17, 20, 144, 150, 414, 416, 421, 429, 446, 451, 456-457, 460
Riley, G. L., 146, 147, 152
Ringle, P. M., 402
Rivlin, A. M., 70, 86-87
Rockart, J. F., 269, 271
Rockefeller, J. W., 442
Rogers, E. M., 314
Rohrbaugh, J., 279, 331-332
Rose, J., 35
Rosen, N., 393, 402-403
Rosenthal, A., 53
Rosenthal, W., 379-380
Rosenzweig, R. M., 70, 76, 89
Ross, R. D., 310, 316-317
Rourke, F. E., 12, 20, 42, 49, 168, 175
Rowan, B., 29, 33
Rowland, A. W., 478
Rowse, G. L., 192
Rubin, I., 37, 351, 360-361
Rudolph, F., 1, 20, 466, 469
Rudy, W., 2, 19, 347, 354
Russell, J. D., 5, 195, 203
Ryan, J. W., 455-456

S

Sagaria, M. A. D., 474
Salancik, G. R., 31, 330-331, 335-336
Sandeen, A., 481
Sandelands, L. E., 351, 352, 361-362
Sanford, T., 44
Santiago, A. A., 353, 363
Saunders, C., 84
Savickas, M. L., 402
Scaggs, S., 321
Schaalman, M. L., 351, 359
Schaefer, 289
Schein, E. H., 33
Schendel, D. E., 168, 185-186
Scheps, C., 217
Scherrei, R. A., 469-470
Schlesinger, L. E., 317
Schmidtlein, F. A., 42, 47, 51-52, 139, 143, 150, 161
Schorr, M. S., 423, 435-436

Schrodt, P. A., 262
Schroeder, R. G., 273
Schultz, T. W., 199, 203
Schuster, J. H., 36, 356
Schwab, D. P., 258
Schwartz, J., 260
Scott, B. A., 382
Scott, E. L., 383
Scott, R. A., 464, 465, 466, 471–472, 474–475
Scott, W. A., 348, 355
Scott, W. R., 335
Scott Morton, M. S., 264, 269, 271, 272, 273–274
Seabury, P., 68, 89–90
Seashore, C. N., 317
Selznick, P., 396, 410, 411
Sergiovanni, T. J., 144, 150
Service, A. L., 14, 20, 168, 175
Sharp, P. F., 449
Shaw, K., 417, 425
Sheehan, B. S., 263, 269, 272, 275
Sheehy, G., 424, 440
Sheikholeslami, R., 422, 425
Shirley, R. C., 34, 186, 237
Sholtys, P. A., 269, 272
Shtogren, J. A., 423, 436
Shulman, C. H., 68, 77, 353, 363
Sikes, W. W., 317
Simon, H. A., 28, 142, 143, 150, 168, 175, 264, 272
Simpson, W. A., 233–234
Skaggs, L. C., 383
Slusher, E. A., 351, 354
Smalley, C. R., 487
Smart, C., 351, 352, 361
Smart, J. C., 105, 342, 365
Smith, A., 199, 203
Smith, B. L. R., 91
Smith, D., 227
Smith, K., 226–227
Smith, S. B., 271, 272
Smock, H. R., 229
Snipper, R., 341–342
Solmon, L. C., 339, 345
Sparks, D. S., 234
Sprague, R. H., Jr., 268, 272, 277
Sprunger, B. E., 423, 436
Stampen, J., 56–57
Stanford, L., 442, 443

Starbuck, W. H., 35–36, 37, 351, 358
Stark, J. S., 109
Stauffer, T., 345–346
Staw, B. M., 38, 39, 351, 352, 358, 361–362
Steers, R. M., 336–337
Stephens, R. W., 144, 149
Stevenson, M., 269, 272
Stoke, H. W., 12, 20, 445, 447
Stroup, H., 11, 20
Studd, S. M., 40n
Sunly, E. M., Jr., 79
Swanson, E. B., 265, 272

T

Tappan, H., 391
Taylor, A. L., 407
Taylor, B., 210
Taylor, R. R., 144, 149
Tetlow, W. L., 280
Thelin, J., 53
Thomas, G. B., 417, 431–432
Thompson, M., 332
Thorp, C. D., 403–404
Tierney, M. L., 16, 357
Tolbert, P. S., 147, 150
Tolstoy, L., 390–391, 399
Torrance, E. P., 348, 355
Truman, H. S., 81
Tucker, A., 476
Tuckman, H. P., 199, 208, 457
Turlington, B., 89
Turney, J., 393, 402–403
Turoff, M., 280

U

Ulrich, D. O., 38, 397, 398, 410
Updegrove, D. A., 266, 272
Urwick, L., 142, 149
Usdan, M. D., 43, 49

V

Van Alstyne, C., 69, 77
Vanderwaert, L., 91, 376–377
Van de Ven, A., 333–334
Van Gieson, N., 379
Vangsnes, D. J., 366

Van Maanen, J., 33
Vaughan, G. B., 462–463
Veblen, T., 443, 447
Verage, K. A., 441n
Vertinsky, I., 351, 352, 361
Veysey, L. R., 141, 150, 443, 447
Volkwein, J. F., 61, 237
Vroom, V. H., 395, 396, 399, 407–408

W

Waddell, D. G., 238, 246, 257–258,
    381, 431
Walker, D. E., 144, 146, 156
Walleck, A. S., 182–183
Walleri, R. D., 269, 272
Wallhaus, R. A., 229
Waltzer, H., 476
Warmbrod, C., 229
Wasserman, P., 423, 437
Waterman, R. H., Jr., 17, 20
Waters, J. A., 183–184
Wattenbarger, J. L., 208, 321
Weathersby, G. B., 297
Weber, M., 11, 20, 143
Webster, D. S., 340–341
Weeks, K. M., 136, 137–138, 487
Weick, K. E., 15, 31–32, 37, 39, 143,
    144, 162, 335
Wells, H. B., 466, 469
Welzenbach, L. F., 478–479
Whalen, E., 199, 207–208
Whetten, D. A., 7, 30–31, 34–35, 334,
    348, 351, 352, 355, 364–365
White, A. D., 443
White, E., 391
Whitehead, A. N., 1, 20
Whitson, L. J., 477
Whorton, J., 332
Wiggers, T. T., 480

Wiggs, G. D., 239, 252
Wildavsky, A., 7, 168, 175, 180, 203,
    287, 296
Willey, M. M., 67, 77
Wilson, J. T., 82
Wilson, R., 87
Wilson, R. A., 55
Wilson, R. F., 58–59, 229–230, 232
Wilson, W., 142, 150
Wing, P., 192
Winner, L. C., 464
Winstead, P., 319
Wise, D. A., 85, 200, 207
Wolanin, T. R., 75, 79, 80, 84
Wolk, R., 73, 77
Wood, M. M., 131, 459
Woodard, D., 480
Wortman, M. S., Jr., 186–187
Wright, D., 227
Wright, T. H., 107–108
Wriston, H. M., 12, 20

Y

Yancey, B., 379–380
Yetton, P., 395, 396, 399, 407, 408
Young, K., 227
Yukl, A., 392, 393, 399

Z

Zammuto, R. F., 38, 337–338, 347, 348,
    349, 350, 351, 353, 355, 358, 365
Zander, A., 400
Zeckhauser, 289
Zentner, R. D., 190–191
Zerchykov, R., 349, 355
Zirkel, P. A., 99, 101, 379
Zollinger, R. A., 388–389
Zwingle, J. L., 115, 122, 129–130

Subject Index

A

Academic Press, 334

Academy for Educational Development, 52, 122–123

Accountability, and states, 46, 59–61

Ad Hoc Committee on Government-University Relationships in Support of Science, 88

Adams case, 110, 366

Addison-Wesley, 256, 273, 280

Administration: analysis of leadership by, 464–481; background on, 464–465; by business and development officers, 477–479; by chief academic officers, 472–475; commentary on, 467–469; by department chairs, 475–477; development of, 465–466; evaluation of, 417–418, 422–423, 429–433; framework for, 466–467; general works on, 469–472; and human resource development, 241–242, 254–255; research needed on, 468–469; by student affairs officers, 479–481. *See also* Presidents

Administrative style: analysis of, 390–411; background on, 390–392; behavior models of, 394–395, 403–405; commentary on, 397–399; framework for, 392–397; power-influence models of, 392–393, 399–401; situational models of, 395–396, 405–408; trait models of, 393–394, 401–403; transformational models of, 396–397, 408–411

Advisory Commission on Intergovernmental Relations, 77–78

Affirmative action: and equity, 370, 373–377; evolution of, 368–369

Age Discrimination in Employment Act, 377, 378

Alabama at Birmingham, University of, and affirmative action, 383

Aldine-Atherton, 290

American Association for Higher Education (AAHE), 6, 9, 61, 181, 190, 215, 236, 340, 357, 471, 482, 483, 484, 490

American Association of Collegiate Registrars and Admissions Officers, 490

American Association of Community and Junior Colleges, 483, 490

American Association of Presidents of Independent Colleges and Universities, 490

American Association of State Colleges and Universities (AASCU), 218, 226, 259, 490

American Association of University Administrators, 278, 422, 483, 484, 491

American Association of University Professors (AAUP), 11, 146, 148, 157–158, 209, 491; Committee T on College and University Government of, 144

American Conference of Academic Deans, 491

American Council on Education (ACE), 9, 11, 78, 87, 103, 157, 195, 202,

241, 289, 343, 344, 345, 369, 372,
383–384, 416, 419, 421, 425, 453,
462, 470, 476, 483, 491
American Political Science Association,
488; Woodrow Wilson Award from,
290
American Society for Personnel Administration, 487
American Society for Public Administrators, 489
American Society for Training and Development, 239, 250, 251, 487,
491
American University, president's experiences at, 460
Antioch College, organizational study
of, 32
Arizona, University of: Annual Conference on Financing Higher Education at, 45, 55–56; Center for the
Study of Higher Education at, 56;
Higher Education Finance class at,
194*n*
Arizona State University, in consor-
tium, 8
Aspen Institute of Humanistic Studies,
87
Association for Affirmative Action, 374
Association for Institutional Research
(AIR), 9, 220, 234, 276, 302, 484,
491
Association for the Study of Higher
Education (ASHE), 6, 9, 19, 162,
220, 232, 253, 437, 484, 485, 491
Association of American Colleges, 75,
76, 450, 491
Association of American Universities,
89, 492
Association of Community College
Trustees, 492
Association of Governing Boards (AGB)
of Universities and Colleges, 11,
117, 123–125, 128, 132–134, 157,
416, 421, 425, 432, 482, 492
Association of Independent Colleges
and Schools, 492
Association Press, 255
Associations: in higher education, 490–
494; as literature sources, 8–9,
482–485

B

Bakke case, 366, 367, 377–378
Ballinger, 112
Basic Educational Opportunity Grant
(Pell Grant), 70, 85
Behavior models, of administrative
style, 394–395, 403–405
Bladen Commission, 265
Boards. *See* Governing boards
Boston University, administrative in-
tern program at, 242
Brookings Institution, 80, 86, 204
Brown v. *Board of Education,* 366
Budgeting and financing, by states,
45–46, 55–57
Business officers, 477–479
Business Publications, 258

C

California: autonomy in, 154; financial
uncertainties in, 355–356; Master
Plan of 1960 in, 11
California, Berkeley, University of:
Center for Research and Develop-
ment in Higher Education at, 7, 42,
129; literature from, 5, 6, 9
California, Davis, University of: and
Bakke case, 377; *Law Review* from, 104
California, Los Angeles, University of:
Center for Evaluation at, 8; ERIC
Clearinghouse at, 8; Higher Educa-
tion Research Institute at, 7
California, University of: administra-
tive style at, 407; affirmative action
at, 369; literature from, 153; and
presidency, 443; research program
at, 145
California State University System,
computing in, 274
CAMPUS, 265
Canada, computer models in, 265
Carleton College, and presidential
leadership, 457
Carnegie Commission on Higher Edu-
cation, 9, 42, 48, 70, 73, 76, 144,
148, 201, 202, 298–299
Carnegie Commission on the Future of
Higher Education, 72, 76

Carnegie Corporation of New York, 106, 470
Carnegie Council on Policy Studies in Higher Education, 9, 13, 19, 72, 91–92, 199–200, 205, 218, 299, 347, 373
Carnegie Foundation for the Advancement of Teaching, 6, 42, 48, 49–50, 75, 85
Carnegie Institute of Technology, decision making at, 264
Carnegie-Mellon University: and administrative style, 391; and competitive advantage, 171; computing at, 274
CAUSE, 269, 492
Centers for the Study of Higher Education, 6, 198
Change. See Planned change
Chicago, access in, 387
Chicago, University of: administrative style at, 391; president and wife at, 461; publication from, 195
Chief academic officers, 472–475
Cincinnati, University of, and administrative style, 409
City University of New York, open admissions at, 208
Civil Rights Act of 1964, 378; Title VII of, 104–105, 379
College and University Personnel Association (CUPA), 245, 246, 254, 256, 257, 259–260, 375, 484, 492
College Entrance Examination Board, 384, 385
Colorado: autonomy in, 154; state role in, 60
Columbia University: in consortium, 8; literature from, 6
Commission on Strengthening Presidential Leadership, 453
Commission on the Financing of Higher Education, 265
Committee for Economic Development, 201
Committee on Education Beyond High School, 11
Communications, and decision support systems, 269–270, 280–281
Compensation, equity of, 371, 380–383

Competitive advantage, and planning, strategy, and policy formulation, 171, 191–192
Computers. See Decision support systems
Conference on Latino College Students, 386
Congressional Research Service, 83
Connecticut, governance legislation in, 2
Consolidated Omnibus Budget Reconciliation Act, 245
Cornell University: administrative style at, 391; Johnson Graduate School of Management at, 488
Council for Advancement and Support of Education, 492
Council for the Advancement of Small Colleges, 225
Council of Independent Colleges, 492
Council of State Governments, 486
Cox, Matthews and Associates, 482

D

Dartmouth College, computing at, 274
Decision making: administrative structures and processes for, 139–162; campus structures for, 146, 151–156; commentary on, 147–148; concepts in, 140, 142–143; development of, 144–145; evolution of, 140–142; faculty structures for, 146, 157–159; framework for, 145–147; institutional processes of, 146–147, 159–162; literature reviews on, 145, 150–151; multicampus structures for, 146, 156–157; overview of, 139–140; readings on, 147, 162
Decision support systems (DSS): analysis of, 263–281; commentary on, 270–271; and communications, 269–270, 280–281; development of, 263–266; and end user computing, 267–269, 278–280; foundation readings on, 266–267, 272–275; framework for, 266–270; and management information system, 267, 272, 273, 275–278
Denison University, costing at, 214

Departments: chairpersons of, 475–477; quality and effectiveness of, 330–331, 341–343

Development: framework for, 221; for leadership, 418–419, 423, 433–437; literature on, 220, 225–226; officers for, 477–479

Drake University, costing at, 214

E

Education amendments. *See* Higher Education Amendments; Title IX

Education Commission of the State (ECS), 42, 44, 48, 56, 59, 61, 62, 130, 198, 230, 492

EDUCOM, 274

Effectiveness. *See* Quality and effectiveness

Elsevier Science Publishing, 483, 489

Employee Retirement Income Security Act, 245

End user computing, and decision support systems, 267–269, 278–280

Enrollments and revenues: analysis of declining, 347–365; background on, 347–348; causes of and responses to, 350, 355–358; commentary on, 353–354; and cutback management, 353, 362–365; framework of, 349–353; and organizational dynamics, 350–352, 359–362; overview of, 348–349

Equal Employment Opportunity Commission (EEOC), 376

Equal Pay Act, 378, 379

Equity and affirmative action: analysis of, 366–389; commentary on, 371–373; evolution of, 366–369; and federal government, 69–72, 86–87; framework of, 369–371; legislation and litigation for, 370–371, 377–380; and minority status and access, 371, 383–389; and personnel and compensation issues, 371, 380–383. *See also* Law

ERIC Clearinghouse for Junior Colleges, 8, 214

ERIC Clearinghouse on Counseling and Personnel Services, 8

ERIC Clearinghouse on Higher Education, 8, 86, 117, 181, 190, 215, 232, 236, 253, 340, 357, 437, 471, 484, 485

Evaluation: of administrators, 417–418, 422–423, 429–433; framework for, 221; general works on, 226–227; and institutional review, 231–234; literature on, 220, 226–237; and program review, 228–230, 234–237

Ewing case, 108

Executive Order 11246, 375

Exxon Education Foundation, 428

F

Faculty: decision-making structures of, 146, 157–159; employment of, and law, 96–97, 104–108; and human resource development, 240–241, 252–254

Fair Labor Standards Act, 245

Federal Bureau of Apprenticeships and Training, 243

Federal government: analysis of influences by, 65–92; background on, 65–67; commentary on, 74–76; framework for, 68–74; future issues of, 75–76; general works on, 77–86; history of role of, 67–68; and institutional diversity, 73–74; and manpower development, 72–73, 88–90; and professional education, 91–92; publications by, 486; regulation by, 68–69, 90–91; regulation by, and institutional mission, 98, 111–113; and social equity, 69–72, 86–87

Financial management: analysis of, 194–217; background on, 194–195; commentary on, 200–202; and costing and resource allocation, 200, 211–214; development of, 195–197; framework of, 197–200; functions in, 200, 214–217; internal, 200, 209–217; and resource allocation policy, 199–200; 203–208; strategies and issues in, 200, 208–211

Florida: chairpersons in, 476; sunshine laws in, 134

Ford Foundation, 9, 388

Ford Research Program for Research in University Administration, 145
Free Press, 191, 289, 294
Fund for the Improvement of Post-secondary Education, 73
Furman University, planned change at, 319–320
Futures research, and planning, strategy, and policy formation, 171, 189–191

G

Geier v. Alexander, 366
George Washington University, ERIC Clearinghouse at, 8
Georgetown University, financial management at, 209
Governance: analysis of, 21–193; concept of, 3–4; in constraint era, 15; and decision making, 139–162; in disruption era, 13; and federal influences, 65–92; and governing boards, 114–138; in growth era, 11; and judiciary, 93–113; organizational studies of, 21–39; and planning, strategy, and policy formulation, 163–193; in reduction era, 17; state involvement in, 40–64
Governing boards: analysis of, 114–138; background on, 114–115; commentary on, 119–122; development of, 115–117; framework for, 117–119; functions and responsibilities of, 118, 122–130; issues for, 119, 120–121, 135–138; membership of, 118, 132–133; organization of, 119, 133–135; and presidents, 115, 457–459; types of, 118, 130–132
Government. *See* Federal government; Law; States
Group Atmosphere Scale, 405
Guaranteed Student Loan Program, 86
Gunther case, 381

H

Harper & Row, 335, 409
Hartford, University of, decision support systems at, 278

Harvard University: administrative style at, 391; Godkin Lectures at, 443, 448; governance of, 2; Institute for College and University Administrators at, 242; publications from, 153, 160, 260, 401, 488
Hawaii, autonomy in, 154
Health Maintenance Organization Act, 245
Heldref Publications, 9, 483
Higher education: analysis of evolution of, 1–20; background on, 1–3; conceptual framework for, 3–5; conclusion on, 19; constraint and consolidation in, 14–16; contributors to literature of, 6–10; current and future development of, 18; development of literature on, 5–6; disruption and revolution of, 12–14; evolution of field of, 10–18; growth, expansion, and optimism in, 10–12; journals and periodicals in, 482–484; monographs on, 484–485; reduction and redirection in, 16–18
Higher Education Act of 1965, 82, 83, 84, 86, 283
Higher Education Act Reauthorization of 1972, 70–71
Higher Education Amendments of 1965, 70
Higher Education Amendments of 1972, 13, 71, 74, 79, 84, 283, 301
Higher Education Amendments of 1986, 86
Higher Education General Information Survey (HEGIS), 375
Higher Education Leadership and Management Society, 430, 436
Horowitz case, 108
Human resource development (HRD): and administrators, 241–242, 254–255; commentary on, 243–245; contextual overview of, 239; and faculty, 240–241, 252–254; framework for, 239–243; general works on, 250–252; issues and trends in, 244–245; journals on, 486–487; literature on, 250–256; for support staff, 242–243, 255–256

Human resource management (HRM): commentary on, 248–249; contextual overview of, 245; framework for, 246–248; general works on, 256–258; issues and trends in, 249; literature on, 256–262; of people, 246–247, 260; of positions, 246, 259–260; of processes, 247–248, 261–262

I

Illinois: autonomy in, 154; equity in, 389; public and private sectors in, 136
Illinois, University of: Policy Studies Organization at, 489; president and wife at, 461
Indiana, state role in, 51
Information technology. See Decision support systems
Innovation. See Planned change
Inservice Education Program State Leadership Seminars, 44
Institute for College and University Administrators, 418
Institute for Government and Policy Studies, 331
Institute of Medicine, costing model of, 212–213
Institutional Functioning Inventory (IFI), 158, 209
Institutional research. See Policy analysis and institutional research
Institutions: decision-making processes of, 146–147, 159–162; diversity of, and federal government, 73–74; and evaluation, 231–234; federal regulation, and mission of, 98, 111–113; quality and effectiveness of, 331–332, 338–346
Iowa, sunshine laws in, 134
Irvington, 401

J

JAI Press, 488
Japan, corporate planning in, 187
Jefferson Law Book Co., 487

Johns Hopkins University Press, 131, 176
Jossey-Bass, 9–10, 103, 126, 159, 203, 210, 223, 252, 253, 255, 280, 298, 299, 302, 334, 338, 363, 373, 385, 433, 470, 473, 477, 478, 479, 485
Journals: on administration, 474, 477, 480; on decision making, 151; on decision support systems, 281; on equity, 372, 375–376, 384; on enrollment and revenue declines, 356, 361; on evaluation, 228, 231, 235, 237; on financial management, 195–196, 197; on higher education, 482–484; on human resources, 241, 246, 247, 251, 252, 253, 486–487; on law of higher education, 104–105, 487–488; as literature sources, 9–10, 482–489; on organizational behavior and management, 488; on personnel issues, 419, 439; on planned change, 313, 314, 316; on planning, 185, 188; on public policy, 488–489; on quality and effectiveness, 330, 331, 332, 333, 336, 340, 341; on state role, 53, 61
Judiciary. See Law

K

Keller Plan of Personalized Instruction, 304
Kellogg Foundation, 476
Kentucky, state role in, 60
Keppel Task Force, 71
Knopf, 440

L

Lakewood Publications, 487
Law: analysis of, 93–113; background on, 93–94; commentary on, 98–101; development of, 94–96; and equity and affirmative action, 370–371, 377–380; and faculty employment, 96–97, 104–108; framework for, 96–98; general background on, 96, 101–104; and institutional mission, 98, 111–113; journals on, 487–488; and resource allocation, 97, 110–

111; and student academic and disciplinary rights, 97, 108–109. *See also* Equity and affirmative action

Leadership: by academic and administrative officers, 464–481; and administrative style, 390–411; analysis of, 390–481; background on, 412–413; call for, 414–415; career and personal renewal for, 419–421, 423–424, 437–440; commentary on, 421–424; concepts of, 4, 445, 452–454; in constraint era, 15; development of literature on, 413–414; in disruption era, 13–14; evaluation of, 417–418, 422–423, 429–433; framework of, 414–421; in growth era, 12; personnel issues for, 412–440; by presidents, 441–463; professional development for, 418–419, 423, 433–437; in reduction era, 17; search and selection for, 415–416, 421–422, 425–429

Leadership Vitality Conference, 470

Lilly Endowment, 210

Little, Brown, 185, 296

Lorain County Community College, program planning at, 223

M

McGraw-Hill, 156, 272, 405

Macmillan, 9, 427

Management: and academic quality and effectiveness, 322–346; analysis of, 194–389; concept of, 4; in constraint era, 15–16; and decision support systems, 263–281; of declining enrollments and revenues, 347–365; in disruption era, 14; for equity and affirmative action, 366–389; financial, 194–217; in growth era, 12; of human resources, 238–262; and planned change, 303–321; and policy analysis and institutional research, 282–302; program, 218–237; in reduction era, 18

Management information system (MIS), for decision support systems, 267, 272, 273, 275–278

Manpower development, and federal government, 72–73, 88–90, 91–92

Mary Baldwin College, and presidential leadership, 457

Maryland: autonomy in, 154; public and private sectors in, 42, 136; state role in, 60, 64

Maryland, University of, in consortium, 8

Massachusetts, governance legislation in, 2

Massachusetts Institute of Technology, Project MAC at, 264

Mellon funding, 369

Michigan, autonomy in, 154

Michigan, University of: administrative style at, 391; Center for the Study of Higher and Postsecondary Education at, 6, 7; ERIC Clearinghouse at, 8; literature from, 5, 6; National Center for Research to Improve Postsecondary Teaching and Learning at, 8; program review at, 235

Minnesota: autonomy in, 154; computing at, 274; state role in, 42; sunshine laws in, 134

Minnesota, University of, Experimental Team for Environmental Assessment (ETEA) at, 189

Minority status, and equity, 371, 383–389

MLR Publishing Company, 488

Montana, sunshine laws in, 134

Morrill Act of 1862, 67, 82

Morrill Act of 1867, 82

Morrill Act of 1890, 110

N

National Association of College and University Attorneys, 95, 483–484, 493

National Association of College and University Business Officers (NACUBO), 56, 195, 196, 197, 213–214, 256, 363, 478, 482, 484, 493

National Association of Independent Colleges and Universities, 493

National Association of State Universities and Land-Grant Colleges, 460, 493

National Association of Student Financial Aid Administrators, 484, 493

National Association of Student Personnel Administrators, 480, 493

National Center for Education Statistics (NCES), 375, 376, 384

National Center for Higher Education Management Systems (NCHEMS), 7, 14, 56, 58, 145, 193, 198, 211, 212, 228

National Center for Postsecondary Governance and Finance, 8, 369

National Center for Research in Vocational Education, 229, 235, 236

National Center for Research to Improve Postsecondary Teaching and Learning, 8

National Center for the Study of Collective Bargaining in Higher Education and the Professions, 493

National Commission on Higher Education Issues, 344–345

National Commission on Student Financial Assistance, 83, 86

National Commission on the Financing of Postsecondary Education, 72, 301–302

National Conference on Higher Education Finance, 209

National Conference of State Legislatures, 43

National Council of Economic Advisors, 289

National Defense Education Act (NDEA) of 1958, 67, 81, 283

National Endowment for the Humanities, 75, 77

National Institute of Education, 75, 77

National Organization of Legal Problems in Education, 487

National Research Council, 381

National Science Foundation (NSF), 73, 82, 91, 324, 486

National Society for Performance and Instruction, 486

National Task Force on Student Aid Problems, 71

National Training Laboratory, 317

New England Board of Higher Education, 44, 206

New Jersey, state role in, 61

New York: drawing power in, 192; public and private sectors in, 42, 136; state role in, 64

New York University, planned change at, 312

Newman Reports, 70–71

North Carolina: public and private sectors in, 136; state role in, 44

Northwest Ordinance of 1787, 300

Notre Dame, University of, Committee on Priorities and Commitments for Excellence at, 472

O

Office of Civil Rights, 384

Office of Naval Research, 160

Ohio, state role in, 51

Ohio Board of Regents, 228–229

Ohio State University: institutional review at, 231; Leadership Studies at, 394, 405, 406

Ohio University, program planning at, 223

Organizational Development Institute, 494

Organizational Development Resources, 494

Organizational studies: adaptive, 25–26, 30–32, 35–38; analysis of, 21–39; background on, 21–22; commentary on, 26–27; development of, 22–25; and enrollment and revenue declines, 350–352, 359–362; framework for, 25–26; interpretive, 26, 32–33, 38–39; journals on, 488; linear, 25, 26, 28–29, 34–35; organization/environment focus of, 26, 34–39; organization focus of, 25–26, 28–33; of quality and effectiveness, 330–338

P

Pell grants, 70, 386

Pennsylvania: administrators in, 474; governing board and presidential roles in, 458; public and private sectors in, 136; state role in, 50; sunshine laws in, 134

Pennsylvania State University: Center for the Study of Higher Education at, 7, 474; issues management at, 189

People, and human resource management, 246–247, 260

Pergamon Press, 483

Personnel administration, equity in, 371, 380–383. *See also* Human resource management

Planned change: analysis of, 303–321; background on, 303–304; case studies of, 307, 314–317; commentary on, 307–310; framework for, 306–307; literature review for, 307, 310–311; models of, 304–306, 307, 309–310, 312–314; strategies for, 307, 317–321

Planning: framework for, 221–222; literature on, 219–220, 223–225; by states, 45, 54–55

Planning, strategy, and policy formulation: analysis of, 163–193; commentary on, 170–174; and competitive advantage, 171, 191–192; criticisms of, 169–170, 178–180; development of, 164–167; and external relationships, 174, 192–193; framework for, 169–170; future of, 170, 189–193; and futures research, 171, 189–191; history of, 169, 175–178; literature and research in, 165, 168–169; policy formulation, 170, 187–188; strategic, 170, 180–187

PLATO system, 304–305

Policy analysis and institutional research: analysis of, 282–302; background on, 282–283; commentary on, 287–288; framework for, 283–287; journals on, 488–489; methods of, 284; and policy-related research, 285–287, 297–302; and public policy, 283–285, 288–296

Policy formulation. *See* Planning, strategy, and policy formulation

Politics, and state roles, 46, 63–64

Positions, and human resource management, 246, 259–260

Power-influence models, of administrative style, 392–393, 399–401

Praeger, 207

Prentice-Hall, 277, 406

Presidents: analysis of leadership by, 441–463; commentary on, 445–447; conceptions of leadership by, 445, 452–454; evolution of, 442–444; framework for, 444–445; and governing boards, 445, 457–459; personal side of, 445, 460–463; portraits of, 445, 447–449; role expectations for, 445, 454–456; selection and assessment of, 445, 449–452; of small colleges, 445, 456–457. *See also* Administrative style

President's Commission on Government and Higher Education, 67–68, 77

President's Commission on Higher Education, 10–11, 20, 69

Processes, and human resource management, 247–248, 261–262

Professional and Organizational Development Network in Higher Education, 494

Professional education, and federal government, 91–92

Program for Developing Institutions, 73

Programs: analysis of management of, 218–237; background on, 218; commentary on, 222; development of, 220, 221, 225–226; evaluation of, 220, 221, 226–237; framework for, 221–222; literature on field of, 219–220; planning of, 219–220, 221–222, 223–225; review of, 46, 57–59, 228–230, 234–237

Public policy, and policy analysis, 283–285, 288–296

Publications, as literature sources, 9–10. *See also* Journals

Q

Quality and effectiveness: academic, 322–346; background on, 322–323; commentary on, 328–329; definitions of, 324–326; framework for,

326–328; in graduate programs, 341–343; of higher education system, 344–346; importance of, 323–324; methodological issues in, 332–334; models of, 334–338; organizational, 330–338; and states, 46, 61–63; in undergraduate institutions, 338–341

R

Rand Corporation, 265
Reciprocal Trade Act of 1953, 290
Reed College, organizational study of, 32
Regulation, by federal government, 68–69, 90–91, 98, 111–113
Reserve Officers Training Corps, 72
Resource allocation: and costing, 200, 211–214; and law, 97, 110–111; policy on, 199–200, 203–208. *See also* Financial management
Resource Allocation and Management Program, 317–318
Retrenchment: and law, 110; and states, 60. *See also* Enrollments and revenues
Revenues. *See* Enrollments and revenues
Richard D. Irwin, 258
Rosenberg Commission, 64

S

Santa Fe Community College, costing at, 214
Senate Committee on Labor and Human Resources, 83
Servicemen's Readjustment Act of 1944, 283
Situational models, and administrative style, 395–396, 405–408
Sloan Commission on Government and Higher Education, 68, 90, 199, 207
Society for College and University Planning, 494
Society for Industrial and Organizational Psychology, 439
Southern Political Science Association, 489

Southern Regional Education Board, 44
Southern University Conference, 455
Special Interest Group on Education Law, 494
Staff, support, and human resource development, 242–243, 255–256
Stanford University: computing at, 274; literature from, 6; organizational study of, 28; planning models at, 168, 266, 276; Project on Academic Governance at, 105
State Higher Education Executive Officers Association, 56, 198, 494
State University of New York, and affirmative action, 382
State University of New York, Buffalo: and administrative style, 409; planned change at, 315, 318
States: and accountability, 46, 59–61; analysis of involvement of, 40–64; background on, 40–41; budgeting and financing by, 45–46, 55–57; commentary on, 46–48; development of role of, 41–44; and flexibility, 60; framework for, 44–46; general works on, 45, 49–53; issues in, 46, 59–64; planning by, 45, 54–55; and politics, 46, 63–64; and program reviews, 46, 57–59, 230; publications for, 486; and quality, 46, 61–63; and retrenchment, 60
Stotts case, 375
Strategies for Change and Knowledge Utilization, 313
Strategy. *See* Planning, strategy, and policy formulation
Student academic and disciplinary rights, and law, 97, 108–109
Student affairs officers, 479–481
Swarthmore College, organizational study of, 32

T

Tennessee: equity in, 366; state role in, 61
Tennessee, University of, literature from, 81
Texas, sunshine laws in, 134

TIAA-CREF, 428
Title VII of Civil Rights Act, 104–105, 379
Title IX of Education Amendments, 112, 378, 379
Trade Expansion Act of 1962, 290
Trait models, of administrative style, 393–394, 401–403
Transformation strategies. *See* Planned change.
Transformational models, of administrative style, 396–397, 408–411
Truman Commission, 10–11, 20, 69
Trustees. *See* Governing boards

U

United Kingdom, administrative structures in, 141, 465
U.S. Bureau of the Census, 384
U.S. Department of Education, 7, 8, 75, 80, 486
U.S. Department of Health, Education, and Welfare, 111, 442, 447
U.S. Department of the Interior, 67
U.S. Office of Education, 7, 70

V

Vermont, University of, institutional review at, 231

W

Wassell Commission, 64
West Publishing Co., 108, 488
Western Interstate Commission for Higher Education, 44, 58
Westview, 224
Wichita State University, financial management at, 209
Wiley, 251
Wiley-Interscience, 333
Willamette University, program planning at, 223
William and Mary College, governance of, 2
Wisconsin: autonomy in, 154; state role in, 51, 60
Wisconsin, Madison, University of, in consortium, 8
Wisconsin, University of, costing at, 214
Wygant v. *Jackson Board of Education*, 367, 378

Y

Yale University, governance of, 2

Z

Zook Commission, 205